MEDIATING MENTAL HEALTH

Michael Birch offers an extensive, academically robust and thought provoking analysis of mental health mediation. Historically and contextually situated, it is an excellent critical inquiry into the nature of these powerful and often negative discursive practices. The text would be a valuable resource to many readers, particularly for those interested in mental health, media studies, discourse analysis and policy development.

James Trueman, Anglia Ruskin University, UK

Michael Birch's compelling work questions the mental health of a society, rather than that of those it defines as unhealthy. He demonstrates that modes of representation of mental health in Britain in particular, offer insights into the conventions underlying cultural practices and institutions. Drawing upon examples of ethnographic experiments derived from applied television and theatre practices, Birch shows masterfully that it is within representations as locations of power that 'disability' is imagined, enforced, and contested.

Awam Amkpa, New York University, USA and
author of *Theatre and Postcolonial Desires*

Michael Birch has accomplished one of the most qualitatively rigorous studies of media representations of mental health that has ever been attempted. It embraces the perspectives of all major stake-holders, and yields profound and practical insights into mediated constructions of stigma.

Oliver Boyd-Barrett, Bowling Green State University, USA

For my sister, Carrie,
Michele and Mark

Mediating Mental Health
Contexts, Debates and Analysis

MICHAEL BIRCH
Massachusetts College of Liberal Arts, USA

ASHGATE

Published by
Ashgate Publishing Limited
Wey Court East
Union Road
Farnham
Surrey, GU9 7PT
England

Ashgate Publishing Company
Suite 420
101 Cherry Street
Burlington
VT 05401-4405
USA

www.ashgate.com

British Library Cataloguing in Publication Data
Birch, Michael.
Mediating mental health : contexts, debates and analysis.
1. Mental illness in mass media. 2. Mental health--Press coverage.
I. Title
362.2-dc22

Library of Congress Cataloging-in-Publication Data
Birch, Michael.
Mediating mental health : contexts, debates and analysis / by Michael Birch.
p. cm.
Includes bibliographical references and index.
ISBN 978-0-7546-7474-0 (hardback) -- ISBN 978-1-4094-2501-4 (ebook)
1. Mental illness in mass media. I. Title.
P96.M45B57 2011
362.2--dc23

2011027180

ISBN 9780754674740 (hbk)
ISBN 9781409425014 (ebk)

MIX
Paper from responsible sources
FSC® C018575
www.fsc.org

Printed and bound in Great Britain by the MPG Books Group, UK.

Contents

List of Figures

List of Tables

Foreword

Part One

Forewords to academic works conventionally carry out the task of providing a few preliminary pages in which a volume of research and of commentary can be placed in a perspective and a framework of judgement complementary to that subsequently offered by the author or authors. In that sense, they act as a comment from outside before the book gets started and before the author situates the principal themes within an introductory chapter. They might, for instance, indicate some of the special circumstances surrounding the production of the volume; they might relate it to specific professional contexts or locate its ideas and approach within the setting of previous and concurrent inquiries of a related kind. It is the last of these options that provides the focus here.

There is no doubting the centrality and importance of this book's chosen theme. Mental health and ideas about its loss and the consequences both for those 'losing' it and for the society within which they live have long been a key dimension of the fluctuating borderlines between individuality and sociality, between the personal and the public, between the ordinary and the disturbing. It is therefore not at all surprising that they have also been a regular theme for cultural expression in many different art forms, including more recently the popular arts. However, Michael Birch can quickly establish his own good grounds for choosing to explore an aspect of this topic. Here, I want to give some focus to the issues of mediation which this study takes as the principal set of practices and processes it wishes to investigate and which therefore make it primarily a study in media and culture research. My contribution can be indicated by two categories relating to the study of media, that of the cross-generic and that of audiences. Under both of these headings, it seems to me that Michael Birch has made important connections and significant progress in his pursuit of his theme.

Within most conceptual and analytic work on media form, the notion of 'genre', the order to which something belongs, has become an important descriptive category, one carrying normative implications. Genre defines, even if only provisionally, different kinds of mediated artefact and although it also relates to questions of 'content' it is primarily a categorization of form. Deciding what 'kind' of thing a given item of mediation belongs to clearly informs a sense of what kind of formal 'rules' it might follow in its construction, what kinds of satisfaction and modes of knowledge it might give and what kind of criteria might be most appropriate to judgements regarding its quality. Cross-generic analysis, examining comparative genre by taking a theme (as here) or even a specific story and tracking its various articulation across and within media formats, holds out possibilities for international media research which are still under-recognized. Too often, research has made one generic form the primary or even exclusive focus for study (news, say, or drama, or documentary), sometimes making claims for what is going on which are ignorant of parallels and contrasts elsewhere in the pattern of output. Academic sub-specialization has contributed to this tendency. Cross generic study corrects this. It provides a broader sense of aesthetic and discursive co-ordinates to complement other kinds of analysis. It allows comparative investigation of the changing uses of types of narrative within different media and thereby takes inquiry further into the complex strands of storytelling now at work within the culture more generally. In particular, as in this study, it raises questions about the differences between the 'factual' and the 'fictional' and about the tendencies both towards the fictionalization of facts and the factualization of fiction which can be seen at work across a number of different media formats. By doing so, it also poses issues concerning the different ways in the media supply what we 'know' and the different kinds of knowing (including emotional knowing) which they encourage in us. No study of how the media contribute to our understanding of, for instance, politics, economics, health, education, war, crime, or even who we are, can afford to ignore these differences and the way in which media productions not self-consciously in the 'knowledge business' (like popular drama series) can impact upon public consciousness more than those which are self-declared to be 'informative' (like the news).

This question of the generic aspect of the media links directly with audiences and audience research. Since the 'turn to the audience' within the television studies of the 1980s, the possibility of different kinds of work on audiences providing something of a 'solution' to lines of media inquiry unable to proceed further without a stronger unravelling of at least some of the mysteries of consumption has been regularly re-stated. Audience studies have combined qualitative and quantitative approaches and moved out to provide a broad anthropological engagement with how people use the media. Notwithstanding this, the amount of significant empirical work seems surprisingly low given the theoretical emphasis that was placed. Moreover, one important early strand of inquiry, into the local interplay between specific texts and specific interpretations, has not had the development that it deserves. There are a number of reasons for this, including aversion to the methodological hazards of pursuing detailed reception analysis in contexts which, quite quickly, incline towards the 'experimental' rather than the 'natural' in their character, whatever the debate that can be had about this kind of terminology.

To some critical researchers in media studies, audience-based projects were viewed as something of a 'blind alley', what might have seemed their evidential promise turning into a largely repetitive and too often banal descriptive citation of respondent accounts. However, many (perhaps most) strands of inquiry into media output are forced into unacceptably high levels of speculation if some level of systematic knowledge about audiences is not included in their design. It is not that this knowledge ends all speculation. The data emerging from audience research will continue to present further challenges and uncertainties about mediation, as is the case with the studies contained in this book. But direct connection with the practices of attending to media items as an 'ordinary' reader and viewer and of converting them into meanings and values is a necessary not simply desirable dimension of serious attention to matters of power, form and subjectivity (the spaces of self-identity and self-consciousness). Michael Birch has strengthened his approach here not only by including in his study discussions with people who are amongst the group portrayed, the categories of person around which the analysed depictions are constructed, but also a selection of those involved in the portraying, the media workers whose own frameworks of value and routines of practice lie at the centre of any realistic attempts to change the ways in which issues of mental health are mediated to us as pictures, sounds and words.

I have given primary attention to two areas of media research. It is appropriate to mention a third one too – history. Many studies in media scholarship have worked with an unhelpfully foreshortened view of their topic, one in which the contemporary situation looms so large as to block out a clear sense of continuities and contrasts with the past. Here again, the author's research design has been a suggestive one, placing current mediations of mental health not only against earlier media productions but also against previous, and often very different, accounts of the mentally 'normal' and the mentally 'ill' and against the cultural anxieties and fears, as well as social and legal sanctions, that have, in different periods, surrounded the precarious relationship between the two.

As I noted earlier, the main substantive aims and approaches of the book can be left for the author himself to state and defend. The point deserving of recognition here is the wider resonance which his inquiries have for our more general understanding of media structures and processes.

John Corner, Visiting Professor in
Communication Studies, University of Leeds

Part Two

Theatre for Development is closely related to forms and practices included under descriptions such as Community Drama and Applied Theatre. It implies engagement and intervention in real worlds, using the aesthetic potential of fictional worlds. Against the mass didactic effects of global media output, TfD creates spaces for challenge, with a view to their becoming spaces for change. In the Freirean sense, TfD is a form of critical pedagogy, contesting coercive corporate monologues and nurturing dialogue and democratic engagement. The peerless Edward Said asserts a core truth of human history in the phrase, 'silenced voices inevitably emerge'.[1] TfD practices are a powerful midwife to the otherwise

1 Said, E. 2003. Afterword: reflections on Ireland and postcolonialism, in *Ireland and Postcolonial Theory*, edited by C. Carroll and P. King. Cork University Press, 182.

slow gestation of historical inevitability, and they contain within them inspiring histories of dialogue between the academy and the marginalized, from Canada to Nigeria, Bangladesh, Kenya, the Philippines and beyond. In the fieldwork detailed here – conducted in one of the world's most advanced societies – Michael Birch extends and deepens our sense of the enabling potential of both interventionist and dialogical features of TfD. His work does two important things: it presents a body of evidence of institutional prejudice which cannot be credibly dismissed; it demonstrates the progressive contribution of cultural interventions by academic researchers who are prepared not only to record the existence of inequity, but to address it. Drawing on empirical data, Birch and his collaborators harness the creative power of structured reflection on lived experience of stigma, and of critical dramaturgies. In doing so, they produce not only impact statements, but statements with impact.

Tim Prentki argues that 'thinking about the poetics of applied theatre necessitates critical analysis of the relationships *between* all aspects of the creative process: the theatre form, its application and its reception'.[2] Michael Birch's transformative projects, clearly indebted to TfD practices, are rightly understood as examples of critical poetics, a creative praxis with applications beyond his exemplar studies here. Mediation is the primary nexus of power in our time, with control of public narratives the contemporary manifestation of what Volosinov called 'the struggle for the sign'.[3] In crafting coercive public narratives, corporate interests produce a vociferous 'realism', of the sort that – in the insightful words of Michael D. Higgins – 'ignores so much reality'.[4] Stigmatized groups are well used to the disabling effects of being located at one end of a discursive spectrum organized around binaries including norm/transgression, legitimate/fugitive, enabling/coercive and vocal/silenced. Michael Birch's field work exposes the reality that for too long, such people have been mediated as if they were a 'threat population', disruptive of decency and civility, inconvenient, unsightly, requiring to be curbed, disciplined and even expelled. It also exposes, at the level of lived experience, the systematic denigration and abuse of others which is a direct consequence of such mediations, for actual people. Faced with such evidence, Michael Birch intervenes, but critical cultural intervention has a perennial difficulty: what means to use? As Audré Lorde warns us, 'the master's tools will never dismantle the master's house. They may allow us temporarily to beat him at his own game, but they will never enable us to bring about genuine change'.[5]

Michael Birch has used his impressive interdisciplinary understanding of live and recorded representations to considerable effect in forging tools adequate to

2 Prentki, T. 2009. Introduction to poetics of representation, in *The Applied Theatre Reader*, edited by T. Prentki and S. Preston. London and New York: Routledge, 19.

3 Volosinov, V.N. 1973. *Marxism and thc Philosophy of Language.* New York: Seminar Press, 23.

4 Address to National Conference of the Irish Labour Party, 1996.

5 Lorde, A. 1984. *Sister Outsider.* Berkeley, CA: Crossing Press, 100.

the task. His understanding of the facts of oppression is a Freirean understanding; oppression is not a dead end, but the site of a turn to liberation. His use of one of Freire's great interpreters, Augusto Boal, is rigorous, nuanced and original – something that is not always true of applications of Boal's *Theatre of the Oppressed*. In the work theorized and described in Chapter 8, Michael Birch struggles with his collaborators to achieve outcomes of considerable significance, both for themselves and for the out-group to which they have been reduced in popular discourse. His background in TfD shows through here, with his commitment, not to technique, but to practices grounded in ethical and practical principles. Crucially, he struggles to structure conditions in which the stigmatized group produces not only culture – crafted counterblasts to harmful representations – but also critique. And this is a project of the greatest importance, for 'a culture has not found its own voice until it has expressed itself in a body of critical as well as creative work'.[6] So Michael Birch's rigorous ethical commitment not only to the production of imagery and narratives by people living under stigma, but to their reflexive critique of that work within and beyond their local groups, produces a brave and progressive example of dialogical TfD practice.

Across the Anglo-American sphere, the state is withdrawing from historical obligations to govern in the long-term interests of the majority in favour of advancing the short-term projects of plutocratic elites. People who are differentiated from dominant social groups by birth, race, gender, health or economic status are aggressively targeted, as frugal resources once reluctantly shared are greedily re-appropriated by those who have no material need of them. Michael Birch's rigorous ethical interventions are worthy of close attention in and of themselves. Even more significantly, perhaps, their deployment of values and processes developed by TfD practitioners models a principled reassertion of television, and the academy, as forces for public good, and enablers of more equitable and affirming options for collective living in a troubled world.

Victor Merriman
Liverpool Hope University

6 Gibbons, L. 1998. Alternative enlightenments, in *1798: 200 Years of Resonance*, edited by M. Cullen. Irish Reporter Publications, 119.

Preface

Prior to taking up an academic career, I was professionally involved in caring for people with a range of disabilities. My first job was working as a community service volunteer (CSV) with people then termed 'physically and mentally handicapped'. Next, I dedicated nine-and-a-half years to social work with children with special needs and people who, again, experienced a range of disabilities. Integral to this profession was teamwork with educational psychologists, psychiatrists, psychiatric social workers, and educators, supporting client groups that included boys labelled as 'maladjusted' and who would be later termed 'emotionally and behaviourally disordered'. I also spent several years working with 'profoundly hearing impaired children with additional handicaps', and later, I was employed by *Mencap*, an organization providing services for people with learning disabilities and their families. After I totalled 13 years of work in this field, a return to education beckoned beginning with a BA (Hons) Drama (Theatre and Television), which introduced me to the use of drama as a transformative process for developing important community issues.

Central to this qualification were the ideas of Augusto Boal and Paulo Freire, with language, a special focus. Further training led to an MA in Cultural Studies facilitated by an ESRC Studentship at the Department of Sociology in 1994 at Lancaster University. An idea for a dissertation topic emerged one Sunday morning during a television political interview programme. The genre's opening moments focused on a government policy called 'Care in the Community' with its introduction containing the phrase '*killings by mentally ill people*'. The programme's language caught my attention as problematic not just because of gross generalizations made about a special group of people with whom I had worked, but equally because of their misrepresentation. Language about this group's identity and the possibility of change to the problem of mental health mediation opened up a research project that evolved into a PhD using drama practices from *Theatre and Media for Development*, which would then evolve into this book. Since then, the issue of improved mental health mediation has emerged as one with global significance. Subsequently, as I learned about this topic, students have been at the forefront of my target audience and I hope they will find clarity in their reading about this important issue.

Michael Birch
Massachusetts College of Liberal Arts, USA

Acknowledgements

My first acknowledgement goes to John Corner. His supervision of doctoral work at the University of Liverpool and subsequent support helped shape this book. Also, his long-term criticisms deserve recognition; I owe him a noteworthy debt of gratitude and a full degree of authorial thanks. I am also indebted to Dr Kay Richardson for her critical input. A very special debt of gratitude is also owed to Dr Awam Amkpa from the Tisch School of Arts at New York University; his input at several stages of this work proved highly important.

This project was made possible through an Economic and Social Research Council Studentship. This enabled me to pursue a new career and I am grateful to the ESRC for the opportunity to study at Lancaster University. There I received encouragement from Dr Celia Lury, Professor Norman Fairclough and Dr Mick Dillon. I extend a heartfelt thanks to them and to Dr Oliver Boyd-Barrett for reviewing several chapters in their final stages. Dr Vic Merriman must also be recognized for his helpfulness in contributing expertise about *Theatre for Development* which proved central to this study.

A very special thanks go to the managers, day centre staff and users of the Bird in Hand Day Centre and Park Club in Winchester, and Bedford House in Southampton; the Crown Street Centre, Mary Seacole House and the 115 Centre in Liverpool; and the Old Rectory Day Centre, Stepping Stones, and MIND at Newquay, Cornwall. I am sincerely grateful to have been invited into each centre to undertake my work. I am also deeply indebted to the journalists and mental healthcare professionals who participated in the Reception Study to provide valuable information.

Numerous people have provided invaluable help to this work. I am grateful to Dr Vian Bakir, Prof. Robert Bishoff, Dr Monica Joslin, Knut-Eric Joslin, Prof. Jill Gilbreth, Prof. Ben Jacques, Dr David Langston, Dr Susan Edgerton, Dr Juna Snow, Dr Paul Nnodim, Dr Rita Nnodim, Nick Raby, Dr Anne Goodwin, Dr Tim Jay, Dr Harris Elder, Glenn Lawson, Linda Kaufmann, Kyle Frazier, David Bassett, Mark Kinver, Chuck Forsman, Melissa and Amy Mendes, Tony, Joanne and David Hood, Ed Grosso, Bill Arzt, Peter Gentile and also Jon Parkes. My class in *Film Mediations of Mental Health* has proved central to moving thoughts forward particularly during the long, cold New England winters; a big thank you to my students. Thanks also go to John Richards, David Bassett, Mark Winsor, Kelly Kelleher, Patricia Liverod, Paula Roy, Dr Colin A. Holmes, Richard Bayly, Dr Roger Bown, Prof. Tim Prentki, Jeremy Tridgell, Hannah Balcam, Rebecca Ball, Carrie Jones, Des Gaynor, Jean Porter, Sharon Lowenna, Dr Steven Tee at the University of Southampton, Brad Higgins and Gareth Allen, then at Carlton Westcountry Television. I also must acknowledge the support of Dr R.J. Marshall, Teresa Bergin O.B.E., Dr Denis Gartside, Guy Pannell; Brendan Byrne formerly of The College of St Mark and St John in Plymouth; Andy Jago at Bodmin Hospital and Alan Miles at the Institute for Health Studies in Pool, Redruth, Cornwall; all were very helpful. Beth White, Peter Felstead and Alan Barnes MBE offered assistance for which I am appreciative in television studios as did Roger Jelbert, formerly at King Alfred's College. Mark Ledbury, Jay Clark and Sarah Hammond at the Clark Art Institute in Williamstown, Massachusetts were also instrumental in the field of art history, I am grateful to them as I am to Neil Jordan and Caroline Spender at Ashgate Publishing for their assistance in the process toward publication. While many have contributed their support, the book's work, its strengths and limitations, errors or judgements remain mine.

The task of writing any book such as this would not be possible without the helpful space of international conferences sponsored by the Clifford Beers Foundation. Here, ideas were developed which proved useful to setting out empirical research which always carries with it burdens of logistics and planning; these opportunities proved indispensable. Also, the energy and drive required for this isolated task is a special one and the example of one person was significant. I cannot say enough how much Bill Shankly (Manager of Liverpool F.C. 1959–74) made a difference to my life and even though he is gone some years now, he still figures daily in my thoughts. If you're looking in on things Bill – thanks. Finally, I am especially grateful for support from Carrie Birch and also Michele Ridgeway for their unstinting, critical feedback and relentless dedication to reading chapters and rewrites.

Michael Birch
Massachusetts College of Liberal Arts, USA

A Note about Language and Mental Health

A number of authors in discussions about mental health raise warnings about terminology; the work contained in this book is no different. A pilot study recognized that some words alienate people with unwell mental health and across the mental health field, terms and their usage are fraught with politically charged meaning for identity. 'Mental illness' are two words belonging to the dominant discourse of psychiatry, government, and the public that are representative of this and were identified as negative. Also, having a mental health 'problem' was met with objection. Aware that language is an important component, this book generally employs the term 'people who experience a condition' except where circumstances demand other usage. In addition, the book, by way of its intellectual journey, seeks to expose further the problems of language in this field. Therefore, this book employs the title 'mental health' as the broad paradigm within which other terms can be located and which it is the purpose of this book to highlight as complex. This is particularly so where mediations might have implication for the identity of people living with a mental health condition.

The undertaking of any work involving mental health mediations and people with conditions carries ethical implications. Participation was a major hurdle and overcome by maintaining individual anonymity and confidentiality across the project. Yet, participants proved extremely motivated and far from shy in addressing mediations, seized the opportunity to contribute their ideas. Indeed, as the reader will discover across the work, change is possible but advances could only occur under confidentiality constraints set up from the project's beginning. Across this project, participants' wishes and a safe environment were the first regard. At the core of this environment were fundamental qualities of dialogue, sensitivity and mutual respect, dedicated toward development but only in so far as each person felt comfortable and agreeable.

Introduction

A Problem

Mediations[1] of mental health are a problem. When referenced in media, depictions are usually awry. A study by Philo (1996) demonstrated that two-thirds of media references to mental health in the United Kingdom relate to violence, with these often receiving more headline treatment and encouraging vague concepts about madness. In the United States of America, Wahl (1995) records similar findings. With themes of dangerousness triumphing over clear ideas about mental health in both countries, this book questions mediations, asking: What 'mental health' meanings are being made? Central concerns in the above studies are the misrepresentation of cultural identity in mediations and; how *stigma* impacts upon a person's sense of self. Wahl (1995, 1999) and Philo (1996) point to strong concerns about stigma, how potential patients resist seeking healthcare and fear disclosure of the mental health aspect of their identity. Full participation in society is denied as negative media messages further generate stigma. The problem is also worrisome because of the type of knowledge communicated to the public about mental health: What do they understand from mediations about it? In the Philo (1996) study, members of the public could draw easily on cultural memory to reproduce stories in form and content with mental health referencing violence. All of this research points to another concern: that public knowledge about mental health is not improving the situations of the unwell, those who will become unwell or indeed, those who will remain well but come to know people who are not. This book also poses the question: how can improvement be made to media meanings about mental health?

According to projections in Murray and Lopez (1996a: 375–81), unipolar major depression will be the second most popular disease across the globe by the year 2020, up from fourth place in 1990. Studies compiled in Lopez et al. (2006) accord with these findings, and indicate that other conditions such as anxiety disorders and schizophrenia will increase in frequency. As individuals in societies, we have identities that are the subject of significantly mediated experiences; addressing who we could be like, what fashion trend we should follow, what we should do, etc. Our increasing susceptibility to unwell mental health rightfully concerns public health policy makers. Lessening stigma and finding new ways to educate citizens not just about people with unwell mental health but also the

1 A mediation is any form of communication including a newspaper, magazine, e-zine, web page, theatre play, television or radio programme, book, poster etc.

conditions can help individuals to understand, prevent and/or work through mental health issues; this should be one element of a sensible policy. One in four of the UK population (approximately 15 million people) 'will experience some kind of mental health problem in the course of a year' (Bird 1999: 5). This experience affects all sections of the community irrespective of class, race, age, gender, sexuality or health. These statistics accord with figures from the National Institute for Mental Health (NIMH), which state that in the United States one in four individuals suffers from a diagnosable disorder in one year, a total of 77 million people, in 2010.[2] In the UK, approximately four million people will resist seeking professional therapeutic advice, the stigma of stereotyped dangerousness contributing a 'tremendous power in creating and perpetuating discriminatory attitudes towards mental health service-users' (Dunn 1999: 43).

If, in these two countries, approximately one quarter of each population will experience a mental health problem, and such conditions are increasing, then we must ask how mental health knowledge could be better mediated. In this book, contexts and debates informing the question of mediation are examined in analyses that point to ways forward in mediation improvement. This is accomplished by using a creative approach to the study of mediated mental health identity and audience, with a special emphasis given to genre forms.

The Study in the Context of Media and Cultural Studies Research

The agenda for this inquiry is particularly mindful of points proposed by Gauntlett (2007), focusing upon reception and identity. This study adopts a creative new approach to the study of identity through its focus on audiences in the reception and community theatre sections. Here, methodology is critically important in a research tradition where the effects model has had a long, complex and debate-filled history. Gauntlett re-examines the effects models in several of his publications (1998, 2001 and 2007) and questions researcher expectations for project outcomes in terms of what involved participants offer; he decides to give his study participants more time in his project. He also questions the effects research tradition stating that it is not exactly something 'you'd want to buy into' (2007: 5) and cites many things wrong with it. Due to scepticism regarding aspects of effects research this study attempts to improve knowledge and understanding about an important topic in the community, by focusing upon this real social problem and by exploring questions and ideas about power in terms of influences and effect through creative methodologies: Through a critical approach, this study examines mental health meaning-making in mediations. Since meanings are base units of knowledge (i.e., epistemes), they are integral elements of power in the relationship between a context, a producer and

2 The figure of 77 million is drawn from one quarter of the total 308 million people estimated by the US Population Census Bureau for 2010.

audience. Accordingly, the work is sensitive throughout to the connection between 'meaning' and 'power'.

Rather than simply revealing that mental distress is negatively portrayed in mediations, this book presents new knowledge from people with experience of a mental health condition by enlisting their advice for better understanding of their situation. The study describes the ways in which the subjectivities of people with mental health conditions are guided by interpretation and also how these subjectivities are in part constituted in mediations. With a change in future mediations clearly needed, the approach taken employs a two phase programme of study to address this. In the first phase, media meaning-making is analysed across a range of genre forms portraying mental health, madness and distress. The second phase includes a Media Reception-Production Study – incorporating new forms of media meaning-making by people with experience of a mental health condition.

Analysing and Improving Mediations: A Two-Phase Study

The aim of Phase One is to study representation focusing on meaning-making about the 'unwell subject' and cultural knowledge about mental health across a range of genre forms. Looking at the interactions between the media's generic forms and the cultural power of people with experience of mental health conditions, the social practice of making mediation meanings is critically questioned. Currently, meanings are made in the context of an environment where media institutions, public service or commercial broadcasters vie aggressively for audience share. Producers shape genre to secure not only audience attention but also quantity. However, as the old formal division between information and entertainment has become blurred, so too have knowledge properties. The division between genres is now more complicated requiring critical attention as producers create new hybrid genres. This means, as John Corner (1991) advises, we should be sensitive to differences between the 'public knowledge' in non-fictional forms and 'popular culture' projects in those fictional, thus allowing for the development of understanding about social knowledge across all forms. The latter project is concerned with patterns of taste and pleasure focusing upon a range of genres like soap operas and dramas, but mainly those associated with entertainment. The former focuses upon the dissemination of information into the public sphere and is concerned about what people know and how they came to know it. Whatever the meaning or topic of a mediation today, properties in communicative forms are often embellished. This complicates knowledge content and in the case of mental health, the knowledge produced is widely inaccurate.

Another distinctive characteristic of today's mediations is the multitude of ways in which 'drama' features in fictional and non-fictional forms. Any aspect of 'the dramatic' can be applied, elaborating events or actions and the ways in which they may be seen, heard or read. For example, in the non-fictional form of news, few days (sometimes hours) might pass without the phrase

'Breaking News' occurring. There was a time when 'Breaking News' happened occasionally. Today, on CNN or the BBC or any other major broadcast news institution, this generic element occurs so frequently it begs the question: is the News broken? With new communications technologies enabling institutions to show more information about faraway places more regularly, there are immense pressures on corporations to keep an audience's attention. With these pressures come needs to arrange the rhythms of visual, aural, musical and linguistic experience for the audience in ways dramatic. In fictional forms, this dramatic mode is a 'creative' tool for making meaning; this influences the editing of imagery or sound, and actors' facial expressions. In a recent trailer for the TV show *Torchwood*, the editing cuts between images of fear-filled people and a vicious-looking monster diving toward the screen gave the impression of hunting not only characters but also the viewer; the dramatic nature of the trailer was realized because of the speed in editing cuts. In the context of mental health and the genres used to communicate about it, it is useful to question: how do forms impact upon the social life of people with conditions, making meanings that serve to support or deny social agency? How are image, language, sound and music selected and organized to construct meanings about identity, stereotypes, stigma, realisms and myths in narrative systems, in various dramatic modes and performance cultures? The first phase therefore examines: a) how media forms construct a mental health space; b) how related realities and identities are portrayed; c) how language organizes meaning about mental health; d) how drama plays a significant role in media communications; e) how media forms, non-fictional and fictional, address audience regarding a range of health and mental health issues.

Media Reception-Production Study

Phase Two incorporates the audience and the community as key factors in the study. The phase seeks to develop further understanding about mental health and move toward the development of new images and so employs a media reception-production study. The reception study aims to determine new knowledge about stigma in portrayals from people with experience of a mental health condition. In particular, it seeks to discover the ways in which the subjectivities of people with mental health concerns are guided by interpretation and also, how these subjectivities are in part constituted by expositional and aesthetic discourses of mediations. This part of the study also includes mental healthcare workers and media personnel; all three constituencies were represented in three different communities. In this portion of the study, cultural knowledge about mental health and the identities of people with related conditions was sought and further explored the role of *drama* in constructing meaning in mediations. A production study involving individuals with experience of a mental health condition developed new images of mental health in a community theatre-based project, leading to new indicators to improve future mental health portrayals in media.

Methodology

This book also raises the thorny issue of methodology, identifying strengths and limitations. A strong point of Heatherton et al. (2000) is that they recognize methodological shortcomings in the approaches they take, something which Gauntlett (2007) also illuminates about reception studies (see above). No method is perfect in the extrapolation of data and all have shortfalls, a point this book explores in registering how methods inform data in research outcomes. Thus, the methodology for the textual analysis integrates a strong critical focus on genre form sensitive to differences in meaning-making across non-fictional and fictional texts and hybrid forms (this first phase answering a set of key questions). The analysis of linguistic elements is undertaken along with a focus upon dramatic communicative components as well as those developing from image, sound and music.

Book Outline

Chapter 1 explores the problem of mis-mediating mental health and problems of recognition that go with this for people who have experience of a condition. It addresses what is known about how people with mental health conditions relate to dominant forms of media representation. It also introduces how the study of mental health representation connects with recent developments in the study of identity politics and concepts/theories which are used in the book. Chapter 2 explores some of the contexts that inform the problem as well as many methods that have addressed mis-mediation without providing adequate solutions to the problem. In this chapter the social, media, mental health, and media research contexts are examined. Through taking an historical view, Chapter 3 addresses how cultural meanings about madness, with their deficits and distortions, have evolved in society and media, and become popularized in a range of genre forms. Chapter 4 marks the beginning of the first of two study phases, both of which provide indicators useful for the development of alternative images and practices. The first phase involves mediation analyses, taking a broad look at representations in film, television and radio. Chapter 5 analyses non-fictional forms looking at news mediations and a documentary. Chapter 6 explores broadcast drama forms, from television, including an award-winning portrayal. Chapter 7 marks the beginning of the second phase in the reception study which reveals new knowledge about the circulation of meanings about mental health and cultural identity in selected mediations from three particular groups. Chapter 8 explores new cultural representations made by people who have a mental health condition and the concluding chapter provides directions for development in future mental health mediations.

Chapter 1
Mediating Mental Health

Most mediation about mental health, including mediations about madness, is problematic because of the potential that exists for stigma production. Examining this problem, Greg Philo wisely points out not just the pertinence of history but also how pervasive stigma is:

> The stigmatisation of those who are mentally distressed has a long history in our culture and obviously predates our contemporary media. It must also be said that the portrayal of mental illness in films, on television and in the press is not the only source of public information and understanding in this area. Nonetheless, media coverage does have an important influence. Our study in this volume of the content of press and television showed that two-thirds of media references to mental health related to violence and that these negative images tended to receive 'headline' treatment while more positive items were largely 'back page' in their profile, such as problem pages, letters or health columns. (Philo 1996: 112)

Stigma, as quoted above, has an extensive past but it is not only the mentally distressed that are affected by problematic mediations. bell hooks (1994) identifies how contemporary media usually show negative stereotypes of African-American women, seen as lazy and/or dishonest. In her work with students, she learnt what it meant to be poor in America. hooks notes that, 'If to be poor in this society is everywhere represented in the language we use to talk about the poor, in the mass media, as synonymous with being nothing, then it is understandable that the poor learn to be nihilistic' (1994: 169). For people to learn to be nihilistic, as hooks puts it, is to 'drown in the image that a life is valueless' (1994: 169), and a devaluation of self-identity. How others might see that identity is one thing, but how a person views their own self-identity is another; problems of identity formation are numerous for a range of minority groups.

David Morrison (1992) addresses identity formation issues about homosexuality in British broadcasts; the homosexual *wants* to be recognized by broadcasters rather than through the hostile definitions by which s/he usually is recognized. Morrison reports from empirical work within UK contemporary culture that the homosexual struggles to 'define their own sexuality as legitimate in the face of hostile definitions of sexuality' (1992: 91). Examples of this are cited by Susan Benson (1997) in her explorations of how representations of Aids/HIV have come to stigmatize the homosexual body when the heterosexual has in fact been more affected. The ensuing mobilization of moral panic over the fear of infection during the 1980s, following from health prevention advertisements the UK government thought necessary, only served to alienate the homosexual community. What was wished for by this community was to be able to 'establish for themselves a sense of identity not infected by the imposition of ideas from the heterosexual world that distorted who or what they were' (Morrison 1992: 91). The representations of race and sexuality have produced a range of problems for each cultural group. Mental health representations produce equally if not more serious issues for identity because, as this book proposes, obscure ideas about madness prevail.

Guiding Ideas and Areas

In the examination of variant ideas about mental health, key concepts include: stigma, reflexivity, identity and the politics of identity, myths and stereotypes generated by media representations and the issues of genre. All of these areas raise questions about representational differences and similarities with the identity politics found in new social movements around gender, race and sexuality. Furthermore, the ways in which drama as an ingredient in meaning making has intervened in contemporary mediations is another important point.

Identity Formation, Recognition and Stigma in Theory

Calhoun (1994) notes that the problem of identity formation operates in relation to recognition, both recognition by others and self-recognition. 'Problems involving recognition – or nonrecognition – by others are integrally related to issues in personal self-recognition' (1994: 20). Necessarily, problems of recognition and the politics of identity play a key role for people with a mental health condition, who may be portrayed through stigmatizing stereotypes. Trends in mediations show inaccurate portrayals of minority groups and also a tendency to stigmatize in a way which generates a 'fear of shame-based humiliation' (hooks 1994: 169). This stigmatizing-by-shame begs two questions about the problem of representing madness: What is stigma in theory? With stereotypes developing in concert with stigma, how may stigma impact people who have a condition?

Among the scholars who examine stigma theory, Erving Goffman's famous study *Stigma* (1963) is notably complemented by two works: *Social Stigma: The Psychology of Marked Relationships* by Jones et al. (1984), and *The Social Psychology of Stigma* by Heatherton et al. (2000). All three begin by addressing the notion of a person being 'marked', of being devalued and 'different' in some way and all illuminate ideas about a person's identity being spoiled. Goffman presents three categories of stigma: a) abominations or deformities of the body; b) blemishes of individual character and; c) tribal stigma of race, nation, religion which Goffman (1963: 4–5) extends to low class, especially in Britain. For Jones et al. there are six dimensions:

1. *Concealability*. Is the condition hidden or obvious? To what extent is its visibility controllable?

2. *Course*. What pattern of change over time is usually shown by the condition? What is the ultimate outcome?

3. *Disruptiveness*. Does it block or hamper interaction and communication?

4. *Aesthetic qualities*. To what extent does the mark make the possessor repellent, ugly, or upsetting?

5. *Origin*. Under what circumstances did the condition originate? Was anyone responsible for it and what was he or she trying to do?

6. *Peril*. What kind of danger is posed by the mark and how imminent and serious is it?

(Jones et al. 1984: 24)

Heatherton et al. (2000) critically explore Goffman, Jones et al. and a range of scholars but propose new ways of understanding and thinking about stigma, not just as a list of elements of functions but as a process. In view of this, their work is given more space for exploration as well as drawing from the other scholars across this and remaining chapters.

In Heatherton et al. (2000), Dividio, Major and Crocker confirm that stigma contests a person's identity, challenging it as a deviant to an expected norm in a society. However, while the concept can be understood as negative, it can sometimes be seen in a positive light; the statement, 's/he's filthy rich' could serve as one example. But as stigma is closely connected to prejudice, the stigmatized person is usually subject to a practice with the consequence of negative intent, an attitude aimed at marginalizing identity. As Heatherton et al.'s introduction says; 'Thus, the major negative impact of stigmatization normally resides not in the physical consequences of the mark, but rather in its social and psychological consequences' (2000: 5). Such consequences implicate not just those stigmatized, termed as *targets*, but those who are the stigmatizers, *perceivers*. In any examination of stigma, both groups must be taken into consideration as well as, where possible, *interactions* which occur between them.

Examining Crocker et al.'s (1998) view, Dovidio et al. note 'that "visibility" and "controllability" are the most important dimensions of stigma for the experience of both the stigmatizer and the stigmatized person' (2000: 6). If a stigma is visible, it may provide the basic schema through which everything about an identity or group is known. The visibility of the stigma and reactions to the stigmatized are indicators as to how stigma can impact a person's situation. It may determine how conscious a person is of the stigma but in the case of people with conditions that are invisible, concerns occur: how do people with conditions that are not outwardly apparent respond to stigma as a result of negative mediations? Keeping a condition invisible means a spoiled identity is being 'managed' in ways that consume time and energy in denying exposure of identity and avoidance of self-expression. Controllability of stigma is important for this group. While some groups such as people with obesity may be seen as 'in control', they will be disliked because they are seen as having responsibility for 'maintaining or eliminating the mark' (Heatherton et al. 2000: 7). In the situation of people with mental health conditions, where the perceived ability to control a condition might be questioned by people in the outside world, this may lead to serious consideration as to whether or not divulgence of their identity or condition is appropriate.

Stigma as a Process: Perceivers, Targets and Mental Health Identity

Heatherton et al. (2000) develop a conceptual framework around three fundamental dimensions which inform about stigma as processes. The dimensions are: '(1) "perceiver-target", (2) "personal-group-based identity", and (3) "affective-cognitive-behavioural response"' (2000: 9) and show how mental health identity may be impacted. Conceding that their framework is not comprehensive, they identify its usefulness in a perspective, locating stigma as part of larger context of general social psychological perspectives; a context complementary to this study's purpose of unveiling the nature of stigma for people with mental health conditions and other groups.

The perceiver-target dimension results in consequences for both groups: those who perceive stigma and those who are targeted by it. Each group has similar characteristics. While the division is not clear cut, perceivers are those deemed 'normal' or 'non-stigmatized', as those who exacerbate stigma. This said, a perceiver can be stigmatized. The English may stigmatize the French and vice-versa. As a dimension, it usefully differentiates the points of view of each group and also illuminates the stigmatizing situation of people with conditions. Each group has different 'needs, goals, and motivations which can further shape how they perceive and interpret information in different ways' which Heatherton et al. (2000: 11) confirm in accord with Deaux and Major (1987), and Swann (1987).

The second dimension concerns personal and group-based (social) identity. Personal and social identity can be that of the perceiver or target but in making distinctions between these two identity sets, we can understand how people make impressions about others. Fiske and Neuberg propose that, perceiver impressions of targets will be formed 'through a variety of processes that lie on a continuum reflecting the extent to which the perceiver utilizes a target's particular attributes' (1990: 2). Perceivers do this by category-based responses in which category membership determines a target's attributes with little attention given to individual attributes (Heatherton et al. 2000: 12). While this occurs at one end of the continuum, at the other end individuating responses play a significant role in which individual characteristics are attributed. For people with mental health conditions (the targets), self-categorization theory also lies along a continuum where individuals determine their own responses. Here, the distinction between personal and social identity is more critical. Following the trajectory offered by Tajfel and Turner (1979), Dovidio, Major and Crocker propose that:

> when personal identity is salient, an individual's needs, standards, beliefs, and motives primarily determine behaviour. In contrast, when people's social identity is activated, 'people come to perceive themselves more as interchangeable exemplars of a social category than as unique personalities defined by their individual differences from others' (Turner et al. 1987: 50). Under these conditions, collective needs, goals, and standards are primary (Verkuyten and Hagendoorn 1998). (2000: 13)

Thus, the salience of personal or collective identity matters in shaping how the person 'perceives, interprets, evaluates, and responds to situations and to others' (2000: 13) and this makes identity a more complex project to understand, as the changeability of social identity makes it more fluid than unique.

The final dimension of 'affective-cognitive-behavioral response' to stigma shows that any of these three items can occur in any sequence with effects that are not necessarily independent. The affective system dominates reactions to stigma in a fast, primitive or fundamental way, while the cognitive system is a slower, goal-directed and deliberated reaction. Behavioural reactions may occur before or after affective and cognitive processes or may even result from the simultaneous effects of both. Affective reactions can be characterized as those that are negative responses to significant physical deformities; causing a quick emotive reaction culminating in a behavioural aversion to people with disfigurement. Yet, cognitive processes may teach specific people to react in more understanding or what Katz (1981) terms 'ambivalent' ways (for discussion about this see Jones et al. 1984), like nurses or doctors dealing with patients who have diseases associated with stigma. However, affective reactions may be secondary in some instances. This is the situation in the Philo study, when respondents draw on cultural memory to rewrite news stories about people with mental health conditions in the news and then reject the individual as 'crazed'. Dovidio et al. suggest that collective responses to stigmas rather than individual ones may be more cognitive or cooler as these are 'often associated with well-learned consensual stereotypes'. Connected to deeply entrenched schemas, they are spontaneously ready for response and according to Fiske and Taylor (1991: 122) will be cued to affect how we interpret what we see, hear and read. However, stigma is a damaging part of the complex problem mediations cause for the person with unwell mental health.

The Person with Unwell Mental Health and Stigma in Practice

Research about people living with a mental health condition evidences cultural marginalization through the requirement to negotiate stigma and raises concerns about the development of subjectivity. A phenomenological study by Barham and Hayward (1991) examined the subjective meanings that users of mental healthcare services gave to their experiences in the social world. They identified the following themes in people who had been patients: a) feelings of being excluded from participation in social life; b) burdened by a cultural freight they felt obliged to carry; and c) needing reorientation toward 'coping' with their vulnerabilities (see Pilgrim and Rogers 1993: 171–2). These qualities of stigma contributed to feelings of marginalization, making them feel reluctant to enter, or re-enter patienthood.

Dunn (1999) seeks solutions to stigma and the social exclusion of people with mental health conditions. After the collapse of mental institutions and the walls that were once its physical barriers, more evidence about the continuous exclusion of people with mental health problems reveals economic and social obstructions, hindering inclusion within the community. The key impediments to living a normal life include employment, economics and media. Two studies cited in Dunn (1999), when coupled, provide strong grounds for the fear people with a mental health condition recognize when seeking employment. Link et al. (1997) determined that 75% of people with a mental health condition considered that they would not tell a prospective employer about their health condition. Glozier (1998) found that employers were less likely to employ a prospective candidate with a mental health condition than someone with another disability such as diabetes. Insurance, both for health and other types (auto and/or travel etc.) in other parts of the world also become significant issues. People with mental health conditions are seen as a financial liability rather than as people who are in need of support.

If cultural practices and discourses marginalize people with mental health conditions, then issues of trust surface in prominent ways. In Philo's (1996) study and a pilot study for this book (Birch 1996), and in Wahl (1999), evidence shows how mediated stigma can impact subjectivity nurturing distrust not just by people in general but also by medical professionals. In the Wahl study, participants discussed how they would not reveal the condition, keeping it secret and only revealing it to their closest friends, if they did at all. 'I never reveal' was the most common remark, offering credence to Goffman's notion of 'covering' the identity spoiled by stigma. Wahl further says that the notion that the person practicing honesty sometimes becomes, against their will, dishonest as a result of stigma. The Link study reinforces this point about distrust as well as the resulting change in behaviour and the ways in which they bring feelings of social isolation into play.

In examining personal and media narratives of unwell mental health, Birch (1995) showed how participants operated careful social management in their everyday life. These narratives further illuminated issues of distrust and isolation. Examining a tabloid depiction about schizophrenia, one participant related: 'I am not a person who inspires fear in others. I am well-liked by a number of elderly neighbours, though I have always been careful not to let them know of my diagnosis of schizophrenia'.

In the Wahl study, a woman experiencing a severe case of post-natal depression said that she felt terrified about revealing she had been in hospital. Another was alarmed at divulging she had been hospitalized, particularly as she worked in the field of psychology. One participant indicated that she felt both fear and anger. Considerable energy was employed in her dealings with work colleagues: 'The people where I work and a lot of people I socialize with don't know that I've had these problems. And I live in fear of them finding out because I know they will treat me differently' (1999: 135).

Language and history often play a significant part in the ways in which stigma is generated. One respondent described where he had first encountered stigmatic knowledge about his condition.

> When I was told I was schizophrenic, I was very intimidated by it – I thought I was some sort of monster. I didn't actually feel like a monster, but when they said I was schizophrenic, I just couldn't believe it. … It's just such a hell of a word, you know and it's got a hell of a stigma. … My window cleaner asked me 'would you not hit me over the head with the hammer?' – I had to reassure him that 'look mate, I'm not violent' and he was telling the neighbours. It rots you, it just rots you. … Jane Eyre was my mother's favourite programme and I think I got it from her. We watched it faithfully everyday Saturday night. She [a character in the story] was insane and she ran around screaming and shouting and burnt the house down – that instilled real fear in me. … They'll burn the house down, they'll stab you, they'll kill you – that's what I thought myself until I realised I had a problem myself. (User of Services, Glasgow) (Philo 1996: 111)

The quotation at the beginning of chapter resonates with these users, the problem of cultural marginalization perpetuated in mediations through stigmatizing themes of dangerousness. If, as this evidence indicates, meanings of stigma produced in cultural and media discourses are deeply embedded in the lived experiences of people with admitted health conditions, then further questions are raised about how its pejorative power influences other people in the forming of their sense of self and identity; particularly people who suffer from anxiety (approximately 2.8 million in the UK) (Bird 1993: 11) or people with depressive conditions who account for one in six of the population (Bird 1999: 6). Also, anorexia nervosa, identified as the third most 'chronic illness' in teenage girls, is more likely to affect women rather than men by a factor of 12:1 and bulimia nervosa will affect 1–2% of women in the UK (Bird 1999: 6–8). These figures constitute major sections of the community. If concerns are raised about how these significant numbers of people with mental health conditions perceive their own identity in pejorative mediations, then, the need arises to seek out what these people make of mediations and to determine alternative ways in which mental health can be portrayed. Consequently, part of the purpose in undertaking a Media Reception-Production Study is to focus upon identity and the struggle by people with mental health conditions around it. It seeks out those discourses impacting the subject in his/her struggle to define individual identity and in the production process, look innovatively for new portrayals offering indicators about ways forward in mediating mental health.

Revealing that stigma is everywhere, and resident in nearly every society, Dovidio et al. (2000) say it produces existential anxiety in people. From this anxiety, perceptions of difference and deviance give rise to increased awareness about a person's (i.e., a target's) own vulnerability and exposure in society. Revelation of an identity as a perceived threat mobilizes people to reinforce their world view of difference about a social group and support notions about stigma as having a number of functions. Those who under the perceived influence of a sense of threat, stigmatize others do so because it restores their sense of a social status quo. On the one hand it allows the illusion of self-control to be maintained. On the other, it pushes down the identity of the outcast person, the target, simultaneously elevating that of stigmatizer. In doing so the stigmatizer ascribes to a particular social group qualities of deviance whether due or not. Stigmatizing is not only a process of marking but often is accompanied by stereotyping. History also plays a part in the upholding of stigma. For example, the Jewish religion as well as people with mental health conditions have endured stigma in Europe; both were the focus of marking out by Nazis before and during World War II and both were subject to the horrors of concentration camps. Certainly, the marking of a person or social group involves a complex range of processes, contexts and social relations but, in a new era in which we now live, these require careful examination.

The Context of Late Modernity, Reflexivity, Subjectivity and Identity

Stigma and its relationship to cultural identity is a multifaceted phenomenon in the context of late modernity. In a period in which globalization and technology increasingly pervade society, cultural and economic shifts, often propelled by media systems, can significantly impact people's lives. Calhoun (1994) and Giddens (1991) respectively identify that we understand subjectivity and identity as ongoing projects in this period. Discussing how subjectivity informs identity, Calhoun notes that it is the site of an individual's consciousness in thinking about 'the self'. In being able to think, we are able to separate self from other, to partition subject from object, and distinguish reality from thought. Subjectivity is, on the one hand, where the very idea of it as a representation of self is positioned, and on the other, where a person's idea of their subjectivity can be *othered* and/or objectified. However, implications arise when subjectivities are contradicted in a sentient way and when notions of the subject as a citizen are challenged. Mediations characterizing the mentally unwell person's practice as dangerous or violent present complex problems for subjectivity and identity, particularly when the unwell person has to reflect about such stigma in mediations.

Giddens argues that all social activity is reflected upon and analysed at all levels of society. He also asserts that self-identity against the backdrop of new mediated experiences 'becomes a reflexively organised behaviour' (Giddens 1991: 5); we reflect upon what we do before we do it, analysing it, which then often influences how we do it. 'The reflexivity of the self, in conjunction with the influence of abstract systems, pervasively affects the body as well as psychic processes' (Giddens 1991: 7). Mediated experiences, as part of these systems, influence our everyday conduct as well as other dominant social discourses. For instance, TV advertisements indicate what is 'okay' to be like, as well as whom not to be like; the notion of what is 'normal' is often alluded to. In the United States, pharmaceutical companies propose medication as the way forward to 'normal' mental health. This is all set within a dynamic of how media *can* contribute to change and development around any issue. We all think about our identity in the period in which we live and clearly, mental health is becoming an increasingly significant issue. The statistic that one in four of us will, across our lifetime, experience a mental health condition raises the question: what occurs reflexively in the self-identity of someone who was at first mentally healthy and then, becomes unwell? How does mediated stigma reflexively figure in this process?

Identity and the Politics of Recognition

Calhoun further argues that 'Identity turns on the interrelated problems of self-recognition and recognition by others' (1994: 20). 'Recognition', he says, 'is vital to any reflexivity … to look at oneself, to choose one's actions and see their consequences, and to hope make oneself something more or better than one is'. In modernity, recognition is singularly the most important component linked to identity in that social changes prove influential in producing ever new problems for identity itself. Calhoun also notes Cascardi's view (1992: 3) that, 'the modern subject is defined by its insertion into a series of separate value-spheres, each one of which tends to exclude or attempts to assert its priority over the rest' (from Calhoun 1994: 12). For the person with a mental health condition, whether it is depression or schizophrenia, a mediated experience defines her/him through a number of value spheres that negatively demarcate and marginalize identity. Reflexivity then comes into play, questioning that identity's worthiness of belonging to society; or rather recognizing preferred exclusion. If any mental health identity is excluded or not recognized, then ideas of trust, security, risk and existential anxiety are important components in our understanding of its development, as are the notions of shame and by-passed shame. What transpires is another complication for identity recognition in the form of a newly required political project of having to manage a new ontological insecurity. Giddens defines ontological security as 'a sense of continuity and order in events, including those not directly within the perceptual environment of the individual' (1991: 243). Subsequently, a spoiled identity means having to modify self-identity to acquire a new, more secure one. Giddens notes that individuals reflexively monitor action carried out by all human agents and these inform an individual's actions; they also become motivated by social and media experiences to shape behaviours. When self-identity is subjected to media discourses about madness, existential anxiety about the adequacy of a narrative and its coherence in the social world mobilize feelings of shame. Citing work by Helen Lewis, Giddens identifies the correlative theme of 'by-passed' shame as a significant aspect for unwell identity.

> By-passed shame is the correlate of unacknowledged guilt: it is shame that comes from unconsciously experienced anxieties about the inadequacies of self. As described by Lewis, bypassed shame links directly to feelings of ontological insecurity: it consists of repressed fears that the narrative of self-identity cannot withstand engulfing pressures on its coherence or social acceptability. (Giddens 1991: 65)

In the subjectivity and identity of the mentally unwell identity, shame and trust are tightly connected and to own these feelings is, at an unconscious level, to feel anxiety and thus, ontological insecurity. Relationships with people in society become complicated by shame motivating what Goffman (1963) termed 'cover' in an identity shielding not just a hidden vulnerable identity but wherever possible any behaviour that might add to self-exclusion. Thus, begin problems for identity formation as and when 'mad' stereotypes emerge in representations.

Stereotypes and Myths

Research about mental health mediations reveals the generation of stereotypical themes about dangerous identities as people with conditions are often presented with a range of qualities associated with violence. These stereotypical meanings derogate and discriminate, offering essentialist notions about identity, fixed in negativity. Broadly, these meanings mobilize knowledge content about people with conditions as potential killers, or as part of an outlaw culture. As studies show, these stereotypes lead to the occlusion of actual identity. The first person cited (see above) sees the need to implement the management or as Goffman terms it, 'cover' (1963: 125) of identity from public view, maintaining a hold on disclosure about an important side of his identity. Language is identified as the key element in media, naming the health group from which this person's experiences are medically typed but which are labelled in a way which is abusive and demeaning. The respondent in my pilot study said about a tabloid depiction:

> Terms such as 'nuts', 'nutters' and 'psychos' are in their ignorance and prejudice equivalent to racist terms such as 'wogs'. The media use of the latter would

> rightly lead to an outcry and public bodies would take action against such racism and yet, where the mentally ill are concerned ... (Birch 1996)

Drawing parallels with racism of what is a healthism, he points out how necessary regulation is in the case of tabloid media: How do unwell people, many of whom are quite passive, when depicted as violent killers to others, respond to such stereotypes? If these stereotypes are offensive, how does this community of people read them? How are they constituted by them?

The very dimensions of these stereotypes of dangerousness are extreme. Parameters constituting the nature of mental illness/health are detailed and maintain a propensity for gore and horror, particularly in tabloid news. These pejorative mediations work to mobilize moral panics in the audience by giving the public set characteristics about mental health which originate in myth. Their temporality has such magnitude that the stereotype itself has, across history, become an ossified complex of meanings difficult to disentangle. This is in part due to the regularity with which they have been communicated, helping to evolve mental illness myths through equivalencies of it with the nebulous concept of 'madness'. In such communications, the development of myth has aided the promotion of stigma, *othering* individuals through stereotypical qualities, serving only to maintain meanings that are the antithesis of mental well-being.

The respondent in the Philo study, when he knew he was schizophrenic, said, 'it's got a hell of a stigma'. The issue of stigma is significant in relation to social identity; in that it exacerbates the stereotype by reinforcing the initial boundary between an 'in' and an 'out' crowd – creating a politics for, and of, identity. Goffman (1963) discusses how disqualification from full social acceptance leads to stigma; but, in contrast to the case of many physical examples, the manifestations of mental illness are usually invisible to the eye. That a person who has a condition is made into a stranger through cultural and media discourses is significant in that for many, the ability to cover unwell mental health is a remarkably easy action to undertake. This ability to cover does, however, raise a number of problems.

A person with a condition subject to discriminatory discourses is probably unlikely to reveal those qualities which a perceiver might devalue. As Giddens points out, 'the individual's biographical narrative is of vital importance for feelings of ontological security' (1991: 58); discredit and social exclusion in relationships is naturally to be avoided. Such personal practice leads to an imposed behavioural pattern which the stigmatized person must address, to be part of the world seen as normal. To be seen as outside that norm is to be seen as inferior and incomplete in identity, thus leading to the *management* of self-image. From this process, problems occur in the development of a subjectivity that might be formed in a completely different way, had it not been subject to such discriminatory discourses. It leads to a politically difficult situation for the individual to manage on daily basis; it leads to a politics of identity, a fear of being recognized and rejected from what is perceived as the normal part of society and also, of not being able to be recognized as an integral part of the world. As in feminist studies, where the 'personal is political', people face problems of recognition only 'because socially sustained discourses about who it is possible or appropriate or valuable to be inevitably shape the way we look at and constitute ourselves, with varying degrees of agonism and tension' (Calhoun 1994: 20–21). Ultimately, negative mediations organize problems of belonging or, to paraphrase Pickering (2001) in two of his chapters about stereotyping, a politics of belonging and a politics of *not* belonging; again, a politics for and about identity.

Calhoun (1994) accepts that there have always been differences between people as well as tensions; identity is at the very core of discovering who we are. However, facing the new world in which we live has brought what appears to be 'qualitatively' new 'problems of both individual and collective identity and the problems of relating to each other across lines of difference in the modern world' (1994: 1); all this in a period when plurality is a key element of tolerant, multicultural western societies. Modern individualism has placed new demands upon collective identity in the context of global capitalism. Calhoun shows that whilst ethnicity and ethnic antagonism are very ancient, genocide like that which has been initiated by forms of nationalism in the former Yugoslavia is distinctively modern. He identifies democratic structures and processes as key elements which have changed the relationships between citizens, evolving notions about identity as a 'product of self-construction, [which] was open to free choice' (1994: 2). The Protestant Reformation, in its thinking, developed individual identity giving it 'new moral and social weight' (1994: 2). Foucault's disciplines of power are further identified as key in joining 'problems of individual and collective identity' (1994: 2) because public discourses shaped policy and modified power over people, qualifying what sort of person could participate in society; who it was okay and not okay to be.

In Calhoun's expositions, modern social theory is also critiqued as the need to develop it is identified as key to the further understanding of identity. He argues for the challenge of 'moving beyond a constraining, either/or opposition of essentialism to constructionism' (1994: 4), and also for examining why cultural diversity is harder to deal with the modern discourse of identity than the commonplace relativists' rhetorics would imply: Calhoun proposes a rethinking of the politics of identity with a special focus on 'struggle'. Whilst the way forward lies in awareness concerning approaches to identity historically, Calhoun proposes the inclusion of essentialist reason and notes that by the adding of:

> constructionism and to this dualism we add the possibilities of *both* deconstructing and claiming identities. Moreover, we can see that essentialism itself need not be essentialized, that there are a plethora of claims to 'basic' or 'root' or essential identities that stand on different grounds, that cohabit with different political bedfellows, that open (or foreclose) different insights or coalitions or conflicts. … This means paying attention to the agnostic, fractured, problematic aspects of identity. (Calhoun 1994: 19)

As Calhoun indicates: 'The politics of identity – politics either starting from or aiming at claimed identities of their protagonists – have to be taken seriously' (1994: 19–20). A central focus of this project is the struggle for identity by people with experience of a mental health condition. Therefore, in developing social theory where ideas about identity begin, the study commences its inquiry by placing, a special emphasis on its formation into coherent subjectivity and the attainment of a healthy *self*-recognition.

Studying Mediations across Genres

When mental health is (mis-)mediated, then the question is raised in the current era: How do we go about analysing representations when communications are complicated by hybridization of forms? Recognizing this analytical problem, this book focuses upon the critical inspection of genre as part of a methodology, aimed at teasing out meanings. Focusing on genre, the analytical approach is sensitive to differences in meaning-making across non-fictional and fictional forms. Exploring the division between these forms and the knowledge properties that stem from each is a useful way of critically determining mental health meaning. Corner (1991) examines the problematics of 'public knowledge' in new audience studies, advising that critical attention be focused on the difference between fictional/non-fictional forms; so sensitivity to differences between the 'public knowledge' and 'popular culture' projects can allow for the development of understanding about social knowledge across forms. While the latter project is concerned with patterns of taste and pleasure focusing upon a range of genres like soap operas and dramas, they are mainly those associated with entertainment. The former focuses upon the dissemination of information into the public sphere and is concerned about what people know and how they came to know it. Corner warns that the distinction between the two projects should not be understood as clear cut. If the distinction is followed:

> too emphatically, to mutual exclusion, it undoubtedly has the effect of reducing the richness and intellectual reach of analysis; but some allowance for divergent concerns may be a necessary prerequisite for achieving optimum linkage. (Corner 1996: 284)

This is a helpful way forward, as are his discussions concerning certain principles (or variations) of television grammar, here extended to all media covered in this book:

> the level of referentiality, modes of address, forms of propositional or more associative, symbolic discourse and the presence or otherwise of television's own representatives (e.g. presenter, host, reporter) serve to mark the two areas out into distinctive communicative realms. (Corner 1991: 276)

Thus, understanding about the patterns of pleasure meanings in fictional and non-fictional are helpful ways of comprehending meaning making in a generic system.

Grounded in a balance of description with critical analysis of meaning-making as a social practice, this book employs the Barthesian couplet of denotation and connotation. These are used in conjunction with myth, which is very much at work in many mental health mediations. In a production process ultimately social in its practices, various personnel help in making decisions not only about what these meanings are but also, how they are communicated. 'How' meanings we see/hear/read play a part in what is known through them lead us into understanding about the consequences of representations and the ways in which they can locate and specify cultural identity and mental health realities. The suggestive work of Stuart Hall (1997) is employed also across this textual analysis in studying the social character of representations.

Representation and Drama

A range of representations facilitate insight into the different ways in which meanings about mental health and madness are portrayed; thus, representation and drama in mediations are key concepts. Dramatic aspects are an important element for both the textual analysis and later, the reception-production study.

Stuart Hall notes that 'representation is the process by which members of a culture use language (broadly defined as any system which deploys signs, any signifying system) to produce meaning' (1997: 61). In this study, this includes the sign systems of language, image, music, sound and sound effects. Using a constructionist approach linked to that of Calhoun, the book broadly examines the making of mediated meanings forged between three different points: 'what we might broadly call the world of things, people, events and experiences; the conceptual world – the mental concepts we carry around in our heads; and the signs, arranged into languages, which "stand for" or communicate these concepts' (1997: 61). Hall re-employs his notion of codes from 1980 in his essay about the *encoding* of meanings/signs at the production stage and their *decoding* at the reception stage. Consequently, at the encoding stage, meaning-making about mental health potentially includes numerous media personnel interpreting and helping reinforcing meaning too; many of these borrowed from perceptions about mental health taken from culture and society. Again, how meanings are communicated play a major part in what is known through them; forms provide major bearings on how they may be interpreted. As O'Sullivan et al. point out, the term representation also refers 'both to the process and the product of making signs stand for their meanings' (1994: 265). Therefore, representation is about the ways in which significations are organized through signifying practices and the symbolic systems which supply ideas about who and what we are, and who and what we can become, and how we can be positioned as subject. Representation, as Woodward notes, through its cultural processes can also suggest answers to questions of collective or individual identity such as: 'who am I?; what could I be?; who do I want to be?' 'Discourses and systems of representation construct places from which individuals can position themselves and from which they can speak' (1997: 14) and it is with these latter points in mind that this book is concerned about how people will interpret meanings made in mediations or, as Hall has put it, *decode* them. Representations of mental health or madness are taken from knowledge resident in our society and processed, next they are organized into signs standing for concepts we have about them. Knowledge produced in media forms has implications for audiences. The relationships between mental concepts (i.e., signifieds) and signifiers about mental health, distress and madness, lie at the heart of 'representing' in this book. It is when these two systems are linked that they constitute representations.

Consequently, we must have two systems to be able to make sense of a sign: A conceptual map in which correlations can be made with a topic such as mental health and a representational system into which portrayals of mental health issues can be fitted. In making sense of meanings through signs, the relationship between referent and sign requires a degree of clarity or, as Hall puts it, if, 'the relationship between the sign and its referent becomes less clear-cut, the meaning begins to slip and slide away from us into uncertainty' (1997: 20). It also follows that for Hall, making-meaning depends on codes which we all recognize but which, because they are always in a state of flux, change and move within a culture. If in the context of mental health issues there are significant uncertainties as well as difficulties when the referent has quite small relationships with things actually to do with mental health, it is further complicated by codes which reference myth, another significant factor in representations.

If, according to Barthes (1972), a denotative signifier is the first order of signification and refers to the relationship with its referent, there is no deeper value associated with it; it is quite simply what it is. However, in the second order of signification where connotation and myth reside a connotation occurs when a denotative signifier contains a level of evaluative meaning. It generates and integrates new value, this, only meaningful to people in the cultural system who know the value system in which it is placed. With regard to myth, Barthes notes that it is a meta-language:

> It can be seen that in myth there are two semiological systems, one of which is staggered in relation to the other: a linguistic system, the language (or modes of representation which are assimilated to it), which I shall call the *language-object*, because it is the language which myth gets hold of in order to build its own system; and myth itself, which I shall call *metalanguage*, because it is a second language, *in which* one speaks about the first. When he reflects on a metalanguage, the semiologist no longer needs to ask himself questions about the composition of the language-object, he no longer has to take into account the details of the linguistic schema; he will only need to know

> its total term, or global sign, and only inasmuch as this term lends itself to myth. (Barthes 1972: 114–15)

Thus, when a meaning about mental health/madness is communicated, a chain of mythical concepts are mobilized in a culture. A meaning will be recognized and accepted in relationship and the concept of mental illness today connects with commonly taken-for-granted idea of dangerousness. Notions of dangerousness also trigger myths which include a range of meanings which, in actuality, are far from accurate. This book also contends that a dramatization culture in contemporary media assists the development of myth at the expense of knowing mental health.

Ideas about dramatizing meaning stem from a range of writers including Raymond Williams (1975). His ideas about drama develop through themes including 'dramatic culture' in a 'media dramatized world'. Alan O'Connor (in the introduction to the Williams 1989) tells how Williams argued about Strindberg's desire for the moving image in a time when theatre was unable to deliver such a technology but that then (writing in 1974), television, following film, extended drama to millions of people in their homes. Williams further argued that what we had in television was 'drama' as a habitual experience, so much so it was a basic need. His argument may now be widened not only with the further inclusion of radio, film, the Internet and print media but also, with a review of 'drama' itself as a new notion, an evolved concept with a currency gaining greater diversity and value today. Discussing the contribution made by Williams' two themes of naturalistic drama and the extension of drama to a majority popular form, O'Connor notes that:

> the conventions and forms of television drama, [are] now raised to an everyday need, the continual dramatic flow that attempts to link viewers-and sometimes does-also involves the dramatisation of state power, the advertising of commodities, and, most critically, the dramatisation of political representation, as in political speakers 'who speak for Britain'. It is against this dramatisation of consciousness that Williams speaks out. (Williams 1989: xv)

In the contemporary moment, drama has become a more sophisticated tool in media forms and this, in my view, is what Williams is proposing, not just in fictional genres but also non-fictional. Today, media dramatizing cultures produce a range of genres. In this *media dramatized world* the 'flow' of cultural forms communicating about a *knowable world* has increased. With this increase has come an increase, too, in the complexities of social boundaries about 'managed' versions of what Williams raised questions about what the world is like, including those versions that serve the interests of political groups. This is what Williams wants to question and identify as social risk. Consequently, media culture and how its dramatized forms attempt to reflect everyday life is another focus; this, in a world where the space between the media institution(s) and its audience has become a frenetic battle to capture vast, and by vast it is also meant valuable, audience numbers.

Thus, at a general level, the work questions drama's usage in media culture (both commercial and public service broadcasting) as a process of representing mental health is explored. Williams noted that 'Drama is a special kind of use of quite general processes of presentation, representation, signification' (1989: 7) and can therefore, be a tool – essentially of *enactment* – employed to communicate to people in their everyday lives, in the form of the everyday language through the codes and conventions of a form accessible to the cultural norms at a given time. It can even be employed via the form a narrative takes which is what Williams called the dramatization of consciousness itself (1989: 9). These representations include codes and conventions of dramatizations, and embody considerable significance since they are 'our ways of seeing and knowing' *our everyday world* in forms which change only when our relationships with them alter. Thus, this book proposes that we experience different aspects of drama across a range of genres as a fundamental part of social knowing and in its study, seeks to illuminate these while making an appraisal on what these are. In the Media Reception-Production Study, another use of drama is an integral part of a community based project.

Finally, it is important to conclude this chapter by saying what this book is not about and does not make claims to be. The book is not intended as a comprehensive examination of *all* mental health mediations but makes critical points about both problematic and useful texts, identifying points of interest. It cannot 'solve' the problem of mental health mediations but certainly attempts to search for ways forward. Large populations of people with mental health conditions in many western countries, especially in the UK and USA, are affected by stigma when they need not be. By concentrating on this group among the larger population, the book aims to indicate how mental health mediations may be improved. And in doing so, stigma is a major factor and focus.

Chapter 2
Critical Contexts

This chapter critically examines four framing contexts that inform the project: a transforming social context, a new media world, mental health and media research contexts. The intent is to look at the contemporary moment, examining the changing nature of the social world in particular and its implications for mental well-being in culture and society. Questions are raised about media portrayals of mental illness in light of developing media industries, a changing broadcasting service, and public sphere. How will media meaning-making access a range of voices about mental health issues and make them known in a new media world? This question is important not only for its implications for mental well-being but also concerning the issue of exclusion. Seeking a conception of improved community contexts, the Mind inquiry (Dunn 1999) and *A Future Vision for Mental Health* (Future Vision Coalition 2009) are scrutinized as a way to consider how media might contribute to inclusivity against a background of prior media research studies on mental health. Finally, the work of Seedhouse (1998, 2002) is examined to explore how work in promoting mental health provides useful ways of understanding the meaning-systems at work in the development of identity.

Social Contexts: The Contemporary Situation and Mental Well-being

As shown in Chapter 1, recent years have seen considerable change in the relationships of power in our societies and cultures (Philo and Miller 2001). Technological as well as economic influences, indeed, the mutual relationship of each with the other, have evolved a new form of capitalism. Global in its reach, many countries have been affected, national and local communities changing in ways never previously imagined. Mental well-being in the late modern period is confronted by significant challenges, brought about by swift and uncompromising economic change.

Lash and Urry (1987) propose that 'organized capitalism', which was the hallmark of western democracies from near the end of the last century, has changed. Whereas capital was concentrated in banks within commercialized centres, new technologies now facilitate the continuous flow of money across the globe 24 hours a day. Whereas the state once had some control over the economic management of a country, now capital flows across its borders with little governmental control. The company that once limited its development to one country is now a corporation with global concerns. Indeed, these new organizations have changed their spheres of production with two major factors assisting the shift.

In the first instance, large companies, once composed of an organizational form of production and management that mass-produced major products on a long production line, have transformed. A centralized management generating an economy located in the factory no longer produces its main product. Instead, economies previously based on heavy industry crucial to a country's wealth, have been replaced by 'information' technologies. Hence the mode of production has come to be known as the *mode of information* as Mark Poster (1990) terms it, where information production is an economy's main force. With old information systems once necessary for company efficiency upgraded, new technological means facilitate faster and more effective information communication from a corporation's base anywhere on the globe. The speedier transference of information has helped production located in another country. Now, information is constituted by knowledge in planning and production, and this has led to the second aspect: technologies now configure and provide meaning to the flows of information necessary to administer organization and clear increases in productivity. Confidence in the form of capital investment to support a corporate project is informed by technology, facilitating the global and speedy circulation of money. This confidence in capital investment has implications for a considerable number of people working for corporations, particularly with the outsourcing of jobs and the steady demise of manufacturing in places like the USA and Europe.

Across this period of change a major new class structure has developed and many of the 'information' tasks are now supported by a new service class servicing the needs of new corporations. Castells argues:

> Service activities mix information processing with the support of production and distribution, the satisfaction of consumer demands, and the management of organisations and institutions of society. Behind the expansion of the service sector, directly in terms of its effects on output, lies the development of the information economy. (Castells 1989: 136)

The development of a 'service class' sector has meant the disintegration of working and upper classes and the development of the new wider middle grouping; new class fractions have emerged, with the new service class directly dependent upon market forces for employment in the information economy. Naturally, the cultural space and lives of people have been transformed in real and substantial ways, these structural transformations having significant implications for identity at local, national and global levels. Whichever way this period is termed, be it post-modern, late modern or new modernity, the implications for human subjects and their conditions are significant. With the social world in a state of flux, so too, is social identity and subjectivity; as these conjoined elements are never fixed but always in a constant project to secure their localized aims, be they economic and/or political. And with these social transformations taking place, it has never been more difficult to ensure the security of identity projects in a turbulent world. For instance, new service class workers will, at the very moment of a serious downturn in the global informational economy, lose their jobs. In 2001, Marconi, Rolls Royce and Nortel were but a few of a wide range of major corporations affected by global economic downturns. Other information based concerns such as Ericsson and British Telecom have also become overwhelmed, laying off thousands of workers at a moment's notice. Ford and General Motors in the USA continually announce job losses in the thousands and as of 2009 are entering into major structural transformation. Indeed, with the global downturn beginning in 2008, nearly a half million Americans were losing jobs every month across the summer of 2009, making the security of self and family a major issue.

With this job insecurity, many people are more likely to be affected by mental illness. Murray and Lopez (1996a) anticipate that unipolar major depression[1] will be the second most popular disease across the world in terms of 'years lived with a disability' by the year 2020. The recent increase in suicide by young men (Mental Health Foundation 1999) and men in general (Dunn 1999), is related to multiple pressures, with rises in unemployment a significant factor. Increased suicides in the UK farming community were reported in 2000 but again, the global downturn of the economy in 2008–9 saw further intensification of unemployment increases with countries like the UK finding nearly 250,000 increases in the three months up to June 2009 (Office for National Statistics, UK). In the USA figures for the month of June 2010 record 467,000 people out of work. With an unemployment rate of 9.5% for July registered, down just 0.1% from the previous month, these are just some of the macro social structures affecting contemporary society – and transforming social life. If social contexts are problematized by major economic and technological transformations in a new capitalist order, what are the consequences at the micro level? What is happening to those whose identity and subjectivity may become susceptible to mental health pressures? When media portray two thirds of meanings about mental health as relating to 'dangerousness' (Philo 1996) in the current social context, there is a significant need for research seeking new ways of mediating about mental health.

Media Contexts and Future Mental Health Mediations

With social changes taking place because of economics and technology, these factors have also influenced media by contributing to significant changes in the media production of cultural forms. Eric Louw (2001) focuses upon concerns

---

1 According to Davies and Craig (1998: 25), unipolar depression can be mixed anxiety and depressive disorder (with prominent anxiety); depressive episode (single episode); recurrent depressive disorder (recurrent episodes) and dysthymia (persistent and mild 'depressive personality').

about future struggles over meaning and raises questions about precisely where we are going in our new globalized communications network. With culture industries continuing their consolidations of corporate capital through mergers, their output of popular forms increasingly burgeoning, the future for meaning-making about mental health across a pattern of rapid commercialization and globalization remains deeply uncertain.

> Certainly all individuals play a role in making, re-making and circulating meaning. But some individuals or groups have more power than others within the communicative process. People are positioned differently by the power relationships into which they are embedded, and these positions impact the access individuals have to media production and circulation systems. (Louw 2001: 3)

In the contemporary moment, meanings are seemingly made for audiences as consumers, rather than as citizens who are targeted for their ability to spend on commodities. One example is Wahl's (1999) book focusing upon people as 'consumers'. For Louw, these groups become 'identity' constituencies in which global network capitalism mobilizes 'lifestyle groups' for niche products to satisfy their formation of self-identity. Attaining the symbols of global capitalism, identities collect their iPods, iPads, Kindles, Xbox 360s or Nike sport shoes in order to create their difference with other societal groups; difference being the key to making contrasts. In fact, this difference is the difference with the mass cultural identity associated in modernity.

> The processes of 'identity formation' via the consumption of commodified cultural forms within global network capitalism overlaps with the commodified cultural production/consumption of managerial-capitalism as described by Adorno and Horkheimer (1979). The only difference is that under managerial-capitalism, 'mass' media generated a 'mass' affirmative culture (i.e. a 'mass' identity), whereas under global network capitalism, niche media generate a mosaic of mini 'niche' affirmative cultures ('niche' identities). (Louw 2001: 151)

It would seem that new media meaning-making mainly recognizes those whose identity and formation needs are identifiable as a potentially marketable target, but overlooks constituencies who cannot be qualified in this way: what will happen for people positioned with less power and access to media meaning-making systems in future?

Louw (2001) also presents the concept of the public sphere as facing a new and complex dilemma in a period of globalization. Exposing how new global media and the world wide web are in the process of shaping a new global sphere or even, several public spheres, the current concept is made more perplexing: What the nature and shape of the public sphere(s) will look like is open to debate. Public service broadcasting is also examined in relation to commercialization. This critique gloomily suggests that governments in contemporary Western societies usually operate in alternations between political parties, and that 'Governments are unlikely to select board members who do not conform to the dominant discourses of their society, and "appropriately" selected board members will, in turn, select "appropriate" managers' (2001: 46). Louw states that commercialization will continue to affect institutions like the BBC, which must acclimatize to market conditions in the independent sector. Paddy Scannell explores public service broadcasting (Buscombe 2000) and reflects upon impending implications for the UK. Re-examining the Peacock Report of 1986, Scannell notes how it 'has redefined broadcasting as a private commodity rather than a public good' (Buscombe 2000: 59). More seriously, he goes on to say about the audience, as individual consumers, that:

> in the media universe of the next century as envisaged by Peacock, [consumers] will choose what they want and pay for what they get. But consumers are not equal in their purchasing power. The privatization of informational and cultural resources may well create a two-tiered society of those who are rich and poor in such resources. Such a development would undercut the fundamentally democratic principles upon which public service broadcasting rests. … In the political climate of today public service broadcasting may seem a concept that has outlived its relevance. (Buscombe 2000: 59)

Whatever crises are occurring in modern day media, it is evident that communications about mental health are problematic and that dangerous stereotypes will endure, if not increase. Whilst lack of knowledge may well have been the reason for the finding of two thirds of media portrayals referencing themes of violence, as discovered in the Philo study, new media institutions should, nevertheless, reflect more adequately the complexity of society and the needs of its cultures. Therefore, this research, as part of its action purpose regarding future mediation meaning-making, includes people who have experience of a mental health condition in production processes or people who would not normally get access to media production systems. This reception study community therefore includes people who have experienced a condition, as well as media professionals and mental healthcare workers, in the examination of media meaning making regarding mental health.

Mental Health Contexts: Social Exclusion and Community

The studies cited in the first chapter (Pilgrim and Rogers 1991; Dunn 1999) highlight the need for social *inclusion* of people with mental health concerns; so that these individuals can seek therapeutic assistance free of stigmatizing influences. Across the Mind inquiry (Dunn 1999) and *A Future Vision for Mental Health* (2009) contribution to a Department of Health consultation document

New Horizons, social inclusion and community are central themes. People with mental health concerns need their identity to be recognized as members of the community.

By way of seeking a clearer vision about how 'inclusion' might be achieved, the Mind inquiry employs four versions of community proposed by Miller and King (1999) in order to identify which one would better facilitate inclusion. The models include a) exclusive diversity, b) inclusive diversity, c) required inclusion and d) voluntary inclusion. The first model is composed of a 'diverse range of social exclusive groups' in society. The second exemplar similarly views society as constituted of diversity rather than being homogeneous. Whereas the first example sees social groups like people with mental health concerns developing their own positive self-image and self-help groups, the second model sees people fostering 'interdependence between people and diverse groups' (1999: 49). In particular, the second model recognizes that:

> some members of the community will be able to pursue their preferred lifestyles, but that others may lack the resources to do so and need help, both from other groups and from the state. It also recognises that diversity can lead one group to discriminate against another, and that the state needs to intervene both to foster diversity and to arbitrate over conflicts. (Miller and King 1999: 49)

The third model of required inclusion is one in which the state produces opportunities for inclusion and determines the moral code of community. In a very state-organized and state 'values' oriented approach, this model also 'promotes policies that limit the impact of the excluded upon the included' (1999: 49). The last model of voluntary inclusion accepts the homogeneity of a society to which everyone should want to belong. In becoming separated from society because of their own lack or skills deficits, this model sees the excluded group mobilizing their own inclusion.

In completing the quest for information, the consensus of data in the Mind inquiry points toward the idea of inclusive diversity and, to quote from Miller and King, a model of society which recognized the relatedness of society's parts as:

> more real, and diversity a feature of all parts of all communities rather than that of specific groups. It views inclusion as the interdependence of people and wishes to exploit the potential to be gained by people working together. However, it does not assume that this will always occur naturally but believes it must be continually fostered. (1999: 64)

Across the entire range of data taken, the need to recognize in identity the 'absolute and equal value of every individual' (1999: 50) was discerned because inquiry participants felt that, once labelled by the term 'mental illness', they were 'implicitly and explicitly' devalued. Clearly, inclusion in the community through diversity was important but recognizing individuals as equal and valued was a key and integral element.

A Future Vision for Mental Health (2009) states that 'mental health and well-being is everybody's business' (2009: 3) and presents several ways forward for developing a better understanding of mental health for the community. One is the development of piloting and building community engagement approaches to commission new relationships between carers and users of services. Another new and innovative way toward change is the promotion of mental health within school settings which the consultative document *New Horizons* recommends. In future, a multifaceted approach towards inclusivity in the community which includes media will help change take place. As Jenny Kitzinger notes:

> Cultural representations and media power matter. … Media representations can literally serve as a life-line in the face of suicidal despair, or constitute a powerful barrier to seeking help. Cultural debate and intervention must include engaging with the production, content and reception of such messages. (Kitzinger, cited in Philo 1999: 17)

A review of media research contexts, with the above themes kept to the fore, combined with the purpose of questioning how previous studies might contribute to a media that recognizes value and equality in people with mental health concerns raises the question: *how might communications facilitate a more inclusive community?*

Media Research Contexts

The study is mindful of concerns relative to media and cultural studies research: it is sensitive to ideas about media audiences, influence and power in representations and seeks interventions in portrayals for community development. With a number of research studies about media and mental health accomplished across the last 45 years, a general review of studies is first offered. After which a selection of previous research studies indicating positive elements in portrayals are examined with a view to identifying how these studies might usefully inform this research as well as to tease out potential problems in theory and method by way of developing new mediations.

Table 2.1 Research review; methods examining mental illness

Study	Location	Sample	Aims	Method	Miscellaneous
MacLean (1969)	Edinburgh	500 people	To examine beliefs and attitudes.	Respondents requested to indicate the extent of their agreement or disagreement about beliefs and attitudes in statements.	–
MORI (1979)	National study	2,000 people	To determine issues of relevance to employers and others who might make charitable donations to mental health causes.	Based mainly on a structured questionnaire with one or two open questions.	–
Dept. of Health (1993)	National study	2,000 people	To examine beliefs and attitudes.	Used statements which asked respondents to indicate their agreement or disagreement about beliefs and attitudes.	Developed from American CAMI or Community Attitudes to Mental Illness.
Brockington et al. (1993)	Worcestershire	2,000 people	To appraise the impact of community care by comparing beliefs and attitudes in areas where community-based mental health services have been developed.	The researchers used statements which asked respondents to indicate the extent of their agreement or disagreement about beliefs and attitudes.	–

Hall et al. (1993)	Worcestershire	2,000 people	–	Researchers employed case vignettes in combination with fixed response or open-ended questions. These were adapted for the American study.	Used vignettes in which the investigator gave the respondent a written description of behaviour associated with mental illness. Respondents were then asked questions about the person whose behaviour had been described.
Huxley (1993)	North of England	154 people	To assess the impact of community care by comparing beliefs and attitudes in areas where community-based mental health services had developed.	Researchers used case vignettes in combination with fixed response or open-ended questions which Huxley constructed from his own materials.	Used vignettes in which the investigator gave the respondent a written description of behaviour associated with mental illness. Respondents were then asked questions about the person whose behaviour had been described.

Source: Based on data from Philo 1996 and original research.

Table 2.2 Methods examining media content and its impact on beliefs and attitudes

Study	Aims/Description	Method	Outcomes	General comments
Day and Page (1986) Canada	Two researchers rated 103 reports from eight major newspapers, about people described as mentally ill examining them for 'tone and ideology'.	Content Analysis: Rated newspaper reports in tone and ideology about people termed as 'mentally ill' and compared with articles in two non-popular mental health publications.	Depictions contain mainly negative stereotypes and assumptions. Implicit is the portrayal of the unwell as a homogenous, parasitic group devoid of social identity. Pessimism indicated toward mental health treatment in tone and ideology.	Studied media content in relation to mental health issues.
Signorielli (1989) USA	Week-long samples of prime time networked drama were compiled annually for a period of 16 years.	Critical analysis.	Characters who were portrayed as mentally ill were likely to be depicted as violent and as victims, more than any other character type. Portrayals leaned toward *bad* rather than *good*. Dramatic plots represented half the mentally ill characters as failures. Those considered normal were rated as one-fifth of the cast. This was closely related to a perceived inability to obtain or hold down a job.	Studied media content in relation to mental health issues.

Wober (1991) UK	Information collected from 2,385 respondents examining what they notice as mental-ill health in various genres. Also explored possible relationships between perceptions.	Respondents answered questions in a diary for the week ending 20 January 1991 about three 'realms' informing mental ill-health. a) Knowledge of what is on TV about it; b) respondent views about the nature of mental ill-health; and c) if they know a person with an illness.	Wober determined UK television representation was largely positive. Documentaries, one-off plays and dramas dealt with mental illness 'sympathetically'. Veracity was seen as high in these texts and the news but low in sitcoms and action genres. TV drama could inform about the topic; mental ill-health was influenced by environment and respondents who knew a person with ill-health would notice TV depictions about it.	Studied media content in relation to mental ill-health.
Steadman and Cocozza (1977) USA	Examined public perceptions of 'the criminally insane' as a 'sub-group of the mentally ill' and explored how these perceptions might be related to media coverage.	Random sample of 413 households in the Albany area of NY State asked to identify 14 items in a series of statements applied to 'most people', 'mental patients' and the 'criminally insane' on a seven-point scale; this included good–bad, safe–dangerous, etc.	Underlying concepts distinguishing between 'mental patients' and 'most people' were dangerousness and unpredictability. These concepts fused concerning the 'criminally insane' with unpredictability becoming a component about the posed danger concepts. Those identified as criminally insane in reports were mass murderers, assassins of presidents and notorious public figures.	When asked to name an individual they remembered seeing or hearing from media, most named actual or alleged murderers of US Presidents. Generally, the study determined that strong media criticism could be justified in line with previous research.

Table 2.2 Continued

Domino (1983) USA	Examined impact of *One Flew Over the Cuckoo's Nest* on college students.	Researcher administered 108 attitude questionnaires across five areas of interest before the film's release. Accessed attitudes among a sample of 146 students. Questionnaire re-administered three months after the release of the film between those students who later saw it and those who did not.	There were no differences in attitude prior to the film between those who saw it and those who did not. After the release of the film, the attitudes of the students who had seen it were significantly less positive than the attitudes of those who had not.	Designed to assess the impact of media coverage on beliefs and attitudes.
Wahl and Lefkowits (1989) USA	Examined possible impact on college students of prime time television film based on a real incident involving a mentally ill man committed to a mental hospital and who murdered his wife while on a day pass.	Researchers showed the film to 86 psychology students. Simultaneously a control group of 19 students viewed a different film featuring murder but not mental illness. After seeing the films, students were asked to complete a standardized questionnaire based on the Community Attitudes toward Mentally Ill inventory.	Findings confirm concerns that depictions add to stigma about mental illness and presenting corrective information may not be enough to halt the impact of stigma in mass media portrayals.	Designed to assess the impact of media coverage on beliefs and attitudes.

Appleby and Wessely (1988) UK	Examined responses of the reporting of the Hungerford massacre by Michael Ryan, who took the lives of 15 people before then taking his own life. Three months before the massacre Appleby and Wessely performed a survey looking into public attitudes to mental illness.	A sample of 965 people were requested to indicate the extent to which they agreed or disagreed with the following three statements: 'mentally ill people are likely to be violent'; 'people who commit horrific crimes are likely to be mentally ill'; 'people suffering from mental illness should be encouraged to live in the community'. In the 2nd week after the Hungerford massacre, public attitudes were surveyed again with another sample (1,000 people approx.). A further six months on the same survey was repeated.	Outcome 1: fewer respondents agreed with the first statement than disagreed. Responses to the second were more similarly divided: 47% agreed, 43% disagreed. Despite this, 57% agreed that the mentally ill people should be encouraged to live in the community, 21% disagreed. Outcome 2: a marginal difference in responses to the first and third statements but the second about the link between mental illness and the perpetrators of horrific crimes increased critically to 54%. Accepting inconclusively the exact part played by media in the evident shift in attitudes, the researchers suggest this almost certainly played a large part. Outcome 3: no significant differences between any of the statements obtained prior to the massacre.	Designed to assess the impact of media coverage on beliefs. Efforts should be made to encourage more positively contextualized media coverage and attitudes.

Source: Based on data from Philo 1996 and original research.

Secker and Platt's Review

Secker and Platt (in Philo et al. 1996), offer a critical review of a range of projects. In their chapter 'Why media images matter', two sections of research are explored: The first examines how British mass media portray mental illness and investigates media image content and its impact on beliefs and attitudes; these include the Day and Page study (1986, in Canada), which rated tone and ideology in newspaper reports; Appleby and Wessely's (1988) research, which examined responses to reporting after the Hungerford tragedy in which a man took 15 lives; the long term project by Signorielli (1989) which examined prime-time drama across 16 years; Wober's study (1991, discussed below), which looked into a national sample extracting perceptions of the extent and quality of mental illness coverage; the Steadman and Cocozza project (1977, in the USA), which was designed to assess the impact of media coverage on beliefs and attitudes; Domino's study (1983, in the USA), which assessed students' beliefs and attitudes after examination of the film, *One Flew Over The Cuckoo's Nest*; and Wahl and Lefkowitz (1989, in the USA), whose aim was examine the impact of a television film based on a real incident. The second section of research reviews previous studies into the impact of media images on public attitudes and beliefs: MacLean's (1969) study of beliefs and attitudes; MORI's (1979) examination of issues of relevance to employers; the Department of Health's (1993) study of beliefs and attitudes; Brockington et al.'s (1993) attempt to assess the impact of community care by comparing beliefs and attitudes in areas where community-based mental health services have been developed; Hall et al.'s (1993) vignettes revealing respondents' thoughts about the behaviour of a person associated with mental illness; and Huxley's (1993) attempt to assess the impact of community care by comparing beliefs and attitudes in areas where community-based mental health services have been developed. These studies show how little is known about the part the media play in shaping public beliefs as there is a scarcity of research assessing the impact of media images, either positive or negative, on beliefs and attitudes. With a purpose to supply some contextualizing data to determine the significance of the research, their aims were to 'provide a systematic analysis of the way in which British mass media portray mental health issues' and 'to develop research methods which would allow us to explore the complex processes involved in the interpretation of media messages' (Philo et al. 1996: 17). Focusing mainly on the formulation of public beliefs and attitudes about mental health, most, if not all of the studies centre on the understanding of negative issues; of questions linked to dangerousness, crime and risk, whilst few provide more positive data or perspectives (Tables 2.1–2.2). In addition to Secker and Platt's review, Wahl's (1999) study and a government study (TNS 2009) complete the assessment. However, providing little in the way of positive data, these projects do not reveal media coverage holding the potential for acting as positive indicators. Few studies proactively seek information to facilitate change around a social-mediation problem. Consequently, the following analysis explores selected studies which have suggested media could be positive in impact and, following Kitzinger's proposition, examines representation in studies with a view to intervention in production, content and reception. Commencing with two reception studies are examined from Secker and Platt's review: One is by Belson (1967), the other by Wober (1989). Also, two approaches by Philo (1996), while addressing mainly negative issues about media mental health coverage, are examined as they uncover useful data.

The Belson and Wober Studies

Belson (1967) examined the impact of one television documentary series screened in 1956 for the BBC, entitled *The Hurt Mind*, on viewers' ideas and attitudes about mental health issues. Six programmes covered a range of perspectives connected with mental illness, particularly perceptible causes and different methods of attending to them. Wober (1989) examined the effects of a Channel 4 mental health 'campaign' between 1 October and 21 November 1986, in which 12 programmes were broadcast including three entitled *Living With Schizophrenia*. The main study intention was to 'discover something about the attitudes of viewers towards people with mental health problems or disturbance, and to see what kinds of attitudes relate with viewing more, or less of the set of programmes' (1989: 3).

Each method took account of demographic variables of age, gender and class but utilized different approaches to extracting data. In Belson's method, after respondents had viewed the second, third, fourth and/or fifth programme, special recruiting procedures[2] drew together large groups (45 people) in one large room for questioning by a single interviewer.

Viewers and non-viewers of the series were invited without foreknowledge of study content and asked to write down answers to questions without discussion. Questions aided three purposes: first, 'whether or not it was necessary to spend program time in correcting images and in softening attitudes' (Belson 1967: 76); second, that 'they should identify the kinds of information that (most lacked with respect to type, causes and treatment of mental illness) so that the effort to inform them might be most efficiently focused' (1967: 76); and finally that 'they should help the producer to avoid showing things especially upsetting to the viewer' (1967: 76).

Wober's methodology involved respondents from a Broadcasters' Audience Research Board panel of viewers based on a nationally representative sample. Keeping a diary, respondents recorded answers to a list of questions in a booklet along with other questions about television. Statements supplemented by questions worded in a positive and negative sense to balance for 'leading' opinion were presented. The first statement was about 'attitudes towards mental ill health; the

2 Belson's recruiting procedures are lengthy and detailed. For a more specific account, see Belson (1967: 13–26, 76–7).

mentally ill'; the second, 'attitudes towards mental ill health: social closeness'; the third about, 'attitudes towards mental ill health programmes; identification and effects'. Measurements were applied and calibrations linking the variables informed further critical findings.

Table 2.3 Media content and its impact on beliefs and attitudes cont'd

Study	Aims/ Description	Method	Outcomes
Belson (1967) UK	To examine impact of documentary series about mental health issues on viewers' attitudes.	Sample of 800 people participated, including some who had seen at least one of the documentaries and a sample who had not. Invited to attend a meeting to complete a series of tests. Controls on pre-existing differences within groups were addressed.	People who watched the programmes were broadly more knowledgeable about mental illness and confident about treatment effectiveness. An expressed willingness to associate with former or current patients was recorded but this did not extend to offering employment. Mental illness was also judged as something not to keep quiet about and people expressed feelings of sympathy for this social group. Belson concludes that despite small group differences the series had a mainly positive impact.
Wober (1989) UK	Examined impact of positive campaign coverage for the IBA. The study drew on information obtained from an audience appreciation survey during October and November 1986 from 14 programmes, 12 from Channel 4, designed to be educational and informative.	Viewers maintained diaries to answer questions about mental health. At the end of 1986, viewers revealed responses to Broadcaster's Audience Research Board via questions designed with some 'negative' questions, some positive to address impact of the series.	Wober reports that viewing of the programmes was associated with a greater score on social closeness, i.e., personal aquaintance with people who had been unwell or other perceptions and attitudes. Wober acknowledges these findings do not prove a programme viewing effect as no information was available about respondents attitudes before the Channel 4 campaign. However, he concludes that the campaign had a positive effect.

Source: Based on data from Philo 1996 and original research.

The studies by Wober and Belson produce useful lessons in methodology about 'social context' and 'genre'. However, their procedures seem unaware of formal properties in fictional and non-fictional texts and the knowledge properties that stem from each. This study is also aware of the critical approaches in 'situating' acts of viewing. Toward methodological development, Corner raises awareness about the *social relations* of viewing. Researchers must ask 'what are the social relations of viewing?' and be aware of these factors in the research design; going beyond demographic variables in order to understand the 'complex structures and processes which might bear on the *sociality* of interpretative action' (1991: 278). Accordingly, the study is aware of different venues and their potential impact because in developing social relations, Corner identifies 'variations in disposition and "cultural competence" which occur *within* as well as between the conventional sociological categorizations' (1991: 278). Types or experience categories of occupational groups such as mental healthcare workers and media professionals who are a part of this study are therefore afforded careful attention.

Philo et al.'s (1996) Study

Both users and non-users of mental healthcare services were included in two separate inquiries. The main aim of the non-user study was to inquire into people's expectations about what they would see via media as well as their understanding and memory of particular styles of output. Philo also examined the interpretative processes by which beliefs and attitudes develop. In an exercise of 'writing the news' for two printed news media around one positive 'achievement' story (a former patient achieving status as one of the top five learners in Scotland) and one associated with dangerousness (later disclaimed by the newspaper used as the source), non service-users were asked to develop their own story from a given newspaper headline. Another process of 'writing the dialogue' for a fictional programme in *Coronation Street* drew out members' own ideas, creatively calling upon a range of responses relative to dialogue, character and plot structure. Given only photographs, members had to reproduce dialogue around a mentally ill character called Carmel. Six focus groups (of approximately 10 people), broadly representative of earning levels, job and housing class or type for the area of the west of Scotland, were randomly chosen. Each group's sessions were divided into three specific phases. First, a group was divided into smaller units of two or three people, and given exercise work in writing either a news report or the dialogue for the fictional programme. The exercises were identified as having an important function, facilitating a collective activity in which people could begin to express their own ideas in a relatively informal way; an attempt to produce 'natural' responses in people. Second, a series of answers to questions that focused on belief about mental illness and the sources of such beliefs were sought. Third, individuals were later interviewed in depth about their own answers. Two questions were constructed for these exercises but there were also other questions designed as indicators of sources of beliefs about mental illness. One question looked at what new kinds of media content might look like with three others inquiring as to how content might relate to the development of belief.

The second part of Philo's research was a nation-wide service-user interview study at drop-in centres, with carers sitting in on discussions. In small groups, sensitively approached discussion opened out issues exploring media images and their stigmatizing nature. Highly structured and open-ended questions inquired about change in user belief and attitudes *before* and *after* diagnosis of unwell mental health; the focus was 'public attitudes to mental illness and the sources of information which underpinned people's beliefs and emotional responses' (1996: 106). Inquiries also sought reaction to their condition as well as reflection about new personal beliefs.

Table 2.4 Based on data at Philo et al., first part: content analysis of media coverage of mental illness in news reports

Study	Aims/Description	Method	Outcomes	General Comments
Philo et al. (1996: 45–81) UK	To show dominant messages which are communicated about mental illness across a variety of fictional and non-fictional media. Non-fictional: Looked at the use of news stories, use of headlines, at how central characters and their actions are portrayed. Fictional: story lines examined structure of plots and looked at how they operate in relation to dramatic action. Explored relationships between characters; who are victims or villains.	Content analysis of both fictional and non-fictional stories about mental illness in which reference to people with mental health problems are reported or shown. Three dimensions constitute the content analysis: 1) The identification of explanatory or interpretative themes. 2) The examination of the manner in which the theme is developed in a specific context. 3) The assessment of the frequency with which different themes appear.	Grouped categories: 1) 'Comic' images. 2) Violence/harm to others. 3) Violence to the self. 4) Prescriptions for treatment/advice/recovery. 5) Criticisms of accepted definitions of mental illness.	Language is a problem in that a wide range of material is found in everyday discourse.

Table 2.5 Based on data at Philo et al., second part

Study	Aims/ Description	Method	Outcomes	General Comments
Philo et al. (1996: 82–104) UK	The main aim/ purpose is to test people's expectations of what they will see in the media as well as their understanding and memory of particular styles of media output. The function of socio-economic groupings (see General Comments) was to examine the processes by which beliefs and attitudes develop in different social contexts.	Focus groups were structured, broadly representative of income levels, occupation and housing type of this area. They were divided into three specific phases. 1) A group is divided into smaller units of two or three people. These work on exercises which consist of writing a news report or the dialogue for a fictional programme (i.e., a soap opera). The exercises have an important function of facilitating a collective activity in which people can begin to express their own ideas in a relatively informal way. Philo's study attempted to produce in people 'natural' responses. 2) Each group answers a series of questions which focus on beliefs about mental illness and the sources of such beliefs. 3) Each person is interviewed in depth about his or her own answers. The texts include a soap opera (*Coronation Street*) and two printed news media, one positive story, one negative. The sample was randomly chosen.	For more detailed examination of material see Philo (1996: 82–104). People can be greatly influenced by media messages. The Philo study explores this quite clearly at a number of different levels. Media are important sources of information and can generate strong emotional responses in viewers and readers of texts. Media reinforce key elements of social cultures which they themselves create. Personal experience was a much stronger influence on belief than media content.	The first two elements of the methodological techniques generate a great deal of data, but it is also positive that some group members may not wish to divulge sensitive information in a group context.

Confidentiality, the most important qualifier in undertaking this study, was maintained in terms of name, date and place of interview. Such an interview study is crucial to understanding service-user interpretative processes about both *what* 'meanings' they read in media messages about mental health/illness and *why*. Central to Philo's findings were identity and difference (1996: 108–11). Although this study did not directly engage with these concepts, this project seeks clarification about them, facilitating clearer recognition of user 'life-worlds'.

The work by the Glasgow Media Group is both creative and useful but its outcomes largely suggest reinforcement of previous findings and concerns, fears that the social impact of media representations on service-users *are* a worry, worthy of yet more consideration. Therefore, in seeking new understanding and development around the development of media portrayals, this project recognizes there are contradictions between media research methods and people with mental health conditions. To paraphrase Maria Mies, in her work there is a '*contradiction between the prevalent theories of social science*, media *and methodology and the political aims of those in* the mental health movement' (Mies 1993: 66, my non-italicized words), particularly those who want to be free of the shackles of stigmatization. Accordingly, the shape and structure of this study's design takes note of the limitations covered above. These themes are addressed in Chapter 7 in more detail.

Table 2.6 Based on data at Wahl et al. (1999) – Telling is a risky business

Study	Aims/Description	Method	General Comments
Wahl et al. (1999) Focused on USA but includes other North American, European and Australian countries	Several goals: **1** Widespread sample. **2** Sought specific experiences of stigma, not general perceptions about public attitudes and reactions. **3** Wanted to include experiences of consumers not touched upon in previous research. **4** Securing qualitative as well as quantitative information so frequency of stigma experiences gets recorded as well as consumer experiences. **5** Study sought to go beyond experiences and look at consumer reactions to stigma experiences.	**1** Survey questionnaire – option of anonymity for participants. Four different approaches: a) NAMI published questionnaire in June 1996 *Advocate* newsletter. b) NAMI Consumer Council across US distributed 25 survey questionnaires to programmes in home state. c) Questionnaire placed on NAMI website. d) Miscellaneous sources: interested organizations and individuals offered to distribute photocopied surveys to various groups. **2** Pilot study led to a 3 main section, qualitative questionnaire survey: a) Stigma: focused upon a treatment by others, negativity in media and fears relating to disclosure of consumer status. Five-point experience rating scale for consumers to measure the extent of occurrence of stigma. b) Discrimination: 12 items to explore discrimination; apartment renting, getting a job, volunteering, driver's licence and connected legal and law enforcement contexts/ avoidance of disclosure of consumer status. 5 point rating scale used again. Distinction requested from respondents between unsuccessfulness and discrimination. c) Elaboration: respondents offered opportunity to elaborate on their ratings info. d) Demographic information sought, as was consent.	People from as far away as Ireland, Wales, Australia and Canada as well as across the USA participated. Minority populations not well served but diverse mental health experience constituency – 25% had bipolar condition, 19% schizophrenia, 15% major depression and 14% with multiple conditions (e.g., post traumatic stress with depression). Anxiety and obsessive compulsive conditions were seldom reported. 1,388 responses between 1 June 1996 and 1 January 1998. Average age 42 (stretching from 12 to 94) but youth identified as absent – NAMI primarily a parental membership. Respondents 40% male, 56% female. When contacted for follow-up interviews, some respondents changed their minds.

Table 2.6 Continued

Outcomes
61% of respondents reported being shunned or rejected by others (26% indicated this occurred frequently). Avoidant behaviours with negative looks, gestures and short conversations accorded with opinion poll findings. Fear of behaviours in public attitudes to people with conditions led to them being and feeling distanced from the public. **a)** Stigma Stigma and discrimination produced strong emotions; feelings of anger, sometimes furiousness and enragement at portrayals. A resultant feeling of 'hurt' followed these emotional responses with other feelings of discouragement, disappointment and frustration at public attitudes that mainly presented obstacles to acceptance. 95% indicated stigma had a lasting impact, changing the ways they viewed and interacted with others, with more than a quarter becoming *distrustful*. Trust became a significant issue with respondents finding relationships undermined by the impact of stigma. Risk of revealing a condition led to respondents hiding it and usually honest people would, in respect of their health condition and in contradiction to their integrity, become dishonest about it; the fear of marginalization or loss of employment was significant. Relationships became marred by a secret that could not be shared, often, even with their closest partner, fear of rejection large in the mind of the person with a condition. Notions that because of a condition, they were somehow lacking of competence produced a sense of diminishing the self-worth of the individual; this, according to many had 'powerful and devastating effects', these, significant impediments to recovery. However, other responses included becoming; toughened up to deal with society; a more empathetic person; and a more determined person. **b)** Discrimination and the Americans with Disabilities Act: 'exclusion of qualified individuals based on disability – including mental disability – is also discrimination and therefore illegal' (Wahl 1999: 79). Discrimination in terms of employment, (applying for work and within the work place), accommodations, volunteers, housing, education, driving licences, health insurance (mental healthcare), and life insurance, automobile insurance, law were cited as connected items. 1) 38% identified they had withheld information about a condition on the grounds they feared information would be used against them; 18% said they never withheld information. 2) 31% indicated employment was turned down when they revealed their mental health status, these results according with other studies that reveal employment discrimination as a long standing tradition. Informing employers about medication often resulted in dismissal. Furthermore, when a concealed condition became known, you were either asked to resign or encouraged to quit. In other cases, promotion would probably be lost.

3) At the work place, revelation about a condition would be met with a lack of acceptance within the working community. 'Reasonable accommodations' is a term in the Act that permits people with a disability to continue employment but the word 'reasonable' is open to such interpretation that accommodation often does not occur.

4) Even in the volunteer sector of the mental health field, when the health status was revealed, a position would be lost.

5) In general, outside the mental health field, employers were unwilling to be accommodating: 26% recorded being turned away from a voluntary position. In some instances employers were very good, just focusing on qualifications, but others exploited the worker with ridiculously low wages.

6) Denial of housing was another aspect of discrimination with refusal of accommodation the result of being honest in divulging a condition.

7) 15% reported denial of educational opportunities. Though such discrimination is difficult to establish, incoming students might be barred in terms of 'one's ability to function successfully within an academic environment' (1999: 93) because of possible 'lower grades, conflict with instructors' (ibid.).

8) Obtaining a driver's licence could be a problem if a psychiatric history was available, despite a clean driving history.

9) Insurance in terms of health became more complicated. 29% indicated US insurers would not offer health insurance for someone with a pre-existing condition. 31% reported that 'they had sometimes, often, or very often been denied mental health treatment because of insufficiencies of health insurance coverage' (1999: 95). If you did have insurance and the company allowed for 45 days, going over that period meant you lost out. If the coverage ran out and you could not pay then you were, according to one respondent, discharged from the facility. The division between how insurance companies addressed physical and mental health was significant.

10) Life insurance could be refused if a condition was admitted – the provider might avoid identifying the condition and the patient's overall health.

11) Similarly, automobile insurance was denied on the grounds that medication was being taken (in one instance for depression and manic depression, despite an 18-year spotless driving record; in another case, the premium was significantly increased).

12) The law had significant impact on a person with a condition, their mental health history could be used against them in a court concerning divorce and child custody. In a general sense, the cases cited in the Wahl study show a knowledge problem about mental health in the court system. The rigid nature of the legal structure allowed for only an insanity plea to be heard rather than any variation of it, thus constraining full exposition of a condition.

Table 2.7 Based on data at Department of Health: TNS – attitudes to mental illness 2009 report

Study	Aims/Description	Method	Outcomes	Summary of Findings
TNS 2009 England	1,741 adults interviewed by TNS in January 2009, with the main aim of monitoring public attitudes to mental illness. The study examines: a) attitudes to mental illness; b) ways of describing people who are mentally ill; c) attitudes to people with mental health problems; d) personal experience of mental illness.	Questions were asked every year from 2007; from 1993 to 2007, questions were asked every three years, calibrated by a tracking mechanism. Questions were presented face-to-face in homes. 156 trained interviewers used CAPI (Computer-Assisted Personal Interviewing) to collect data. Attitude statements were grouped in four themes: a) fear and exclusion of mental illness; b) understanding and tolerance; c) integration of people into the community; d) causes of mental illness. Data weighted to be representative of target population in age, gender and work status. Respondents offered a range of statements about mental illness covering attitudes towards perceptions of people with a mental illness and opinions on services provided for people with conditions. Five-point Likert scale employed to indicate dis/agreement with statements. Questions originated from studies in Toronto and the West Midlands and remained consistent. Other questions have been added since, including personal experience with mental illness, descriptions of the mentally ill and new questions were added to connect with *Time to Change* anti-discrimination campaign.	Attitudes to mental illness Since 1994 the proportion of people saying they would not want to live next door to someone who has been mentally ill have increased from 8% to 11%. Acceptance of someone with mental illness taking public office and taking responsibility has 'grown' but exclusion from taking public office decreased from 29% to 22% from 1994 to 2009. That people with mental illness should not be given any responsibility decreased from 17% to 13%. However, agreement about negative statements toward people with conditions have changed little overall since 2000. Differences in age, sex and social grade reveal the following:	Findings also include some developments from the 2008 study and contrasts from 1994. Attitudes towards people with mental illness in England Some changes occurred toward greater tolerance – provision of best possible care for people with conditions increased from 89% to 92%. Agreement that anyone can become mentally ill increased from 89% to 91% but this was the same as in 1994. Services should be community-based facilities increased 72% to 79%. Opinions moved toward integration of people with mental illness into the community.

Outcomes	Summary of Findings – General contrasts with 1994 data
Those aged 55+ hold the most negative attitudes toward people with conditions. They would believe a) a mental health facility downgrades their area; b) a woman marrying a person with a mental illness is foolish; c) a person with a condition should be excluded from office. 35–54 years were less likely to agree that as soon as a person shows signs of a condition, they should be hospitalized. Gender differences were significant: women were generally less negative toward people with conditions. Social grades C2 and DE were more negative toward people with mental illness than AB and C1. C2 and DE groups were more likely than ABs to agree it was frightening to think of people with mental health conditions living in the neighbourhoods and that they should be excluded from office, and also that persons with conditions should be hospitalized. DEs also thought this group should not be given responsibility. ABs also viewed this group as downgrading an area. <u>Understanding and tolerance of mental illness</u> From a range of statements, levels of understanding and tolerance were generally high though since 1994, the proportion of respondents voicing more tolerant views on some of the following statement has decreased. The proportions of respondents with 'understanding attitudes' ranged from 76% around the statements that 'people with mental illness have for too long been the subject of ridicule' with 92% charted for 'We have a responsibility to provide the best possible care'. Since 1994, the following statements decreased concerning more tolerant opinions: 'We have a responsibility to provide the best possible care' decreased from 95% to 92% in 2009. Increased spending on mental health services is a waste of money' went down from 89% to 83% (in the same year) and 'People with mental illness don't deserve our sympathy', down from 92% to 86% in 2009.	People with mental illness are far less of a danger than most suppose, increased 57% to 61% (back to 1994 levels). The best therapy for many with mental illness is to be part of a normal community, increased 70% to 78% (on a par with 1994). People with conditions should have the same rights to jobs as anyone else, increased from 66% to 73%. Mental illness is an illness like any other increased from 74% to 77%. No-one has the right to exclude people with mental illness from their neighbourhood, increased in agreement from 74% to 79%. Mental hospitals are an outdated means of treating people with conditions, increased from 31% to 37% (down from 42% in 1994). Opinions on the causes of mental illness and the need for special services became less favourable. Those who thought sufficient services exist increased from 20% to 24%. Those who believed people with a mental health condition are easy to tell from normal people increased from 17% to 21% though this was down from 29% in 1994. The idea that lack of self-discipline was one of the main causes of mental illness increased from 14% to 18%. A lower proportion of respondents selected the following descriptions to indicate which they felt usually describes someone mentally unwell: someone who has a split personality (from 59% to 54%); someone who cannot be held responsible for his or her own actions (from 49% to 45%); someone who is incapable of making simple decisions about his or her own life (from 37% to 32%).

Table 2.7 Continued

Outcomes	Summary of Findings – General contrasts with 1994 data
'We need to adopt a more tolerant attitude toward people with mental illness in our society'decreased from 92% to 85% and 'People with mental illness have for too long been the subject of ridicule' fell from 82% to 76% in 2009. It was also recorded that 'increased tolerance in the proportion agreeing mental health services should be provided through community-based facilities has increased from 75% in 1994 to 79% in 2009'. Differences by age, sex and gender revealed the following: 16–34 year-olds were significantly less likely to have understanding/tolerant attitudes on all of these statements. The only significant difference between 34–54-year olds and the 55+ groups was the latter were more likely to agree 'People with mental illness have for too long been the subject of ridicule'. In the DE social grouping were significantly less likely than ABs to adopt understanding/tolerant attitudes towards mental illness for all statements. Other significant differences include: a) C1s + C2s were less likely than ABs to agree, we have a responsibility to provide the best possible care; b) C2s were less likely than ABs to disagree that increased spending on mental health services is a waste of money; c) C2s were less likely than ABs to disagree that people with mental illness don't deserve sympathy. In terms of gender, there were differences between men and women in their attitudes in about best possible care with women at 93% and men at 90%. Women were more tolerant at 88% with men at 82%.	

Outcomes	**Summary of Findings – General contrasts with 1994 data**
<u>Integrating people with mental illness into the community</u> <u>Causes of mental illness and the need for special services</u> Since 1994, the proportion agreeing that there are sufficient existing services for people with mental illness increased 'steadily' from 11% to 24% in 2009. That 'there is something about people with mental illness that makes it easy to tell them from normal people' decreased from 29% to 21% 'fairly steadily' over the same period. Agreement that mental illness is mainly caused by a lack of self-discipline and will-power increased to 18% in 2009 from 15% in 1994. Differences by age, sex and social grade showed that 16–34s had the most negative attitudes towards mental illness and were more likely to hold these views than the other groups. Men had more negative issues towards mental illness than women. In terms of class, ABs were more positive in their attitudes than DEs. <u>Ways of Describing someone who is mentally ill</u> From a presented list of descriptions, respondents were asked to describe which they felt described a person who is mentally ill. Schizophrenia was the most likely to be selected (at 61%). 'Split personality' came next along with 'someone who has serious bouts of depression'.	

Table 2.7 Continued

Outcomes	General contrasts with 1994 data
Those who thought 'We need to adopt a more tolerant attitude' decreased from 92% to 85% and that 'People with mental illness have for too long been the subject of ridicule' fell from 82% to 76% in 2009. Increased tolerance was shown in that the proportion agreeing that mental health services should be provided through community-based facilities went up from 75% to 79% in 2009. Differences by age, sex and gender revealed the following: 16–34 year-olds were significantly less likely to have understanding/tolerant attitudes on all of these statements. The only significant difference between the 34–54 year-olds and the 55+ group was that the latter were more likely to believe 'People with mental illness have for too long been the subject of ridicule'. The DE social grouping were significantly less likely than ABs to adopt understanding/tolerant attitudes towards mental illness for all statements. Other significant differences include: a) C1s and C2s were less likely than ABs to agree that we have a responsibility to provide the best possible care; b) C2s were less likely than ABs to disagree that increased spending on mental health services is a waste of money; c) C2s were less likely than ABs to disagree that people with mental illness don't deserve sympathy. In terms of gender, there were differences between men and women in their attitudes in about best possible care with women at 93% and men at 90%. Women were more tolerant at 88% with men at 82%.	Fear and exclusion of people with mental illness In low levels of agreement, negative statements prevailed. Highest levels of agreement were accorded to statements such as 'Anyone with a history of mental illness should be excluded from taking public office' (22%) and 'Locating mental health in a residential area downgrades the neighbourhood' (21%). Acceptance of people with mental illness taking public office had grown since 1994. Differences by age showed those over 55 had the most negative attitudes. Women were less negative than men. Social grade DEs were generally more negative towards people with mental illness than those in ABs. ABs were more likely to agree that placing a mental health facility in a residential area downgraded the neighbourhood than DEs. <u>Understanding and tolerance of people with mental illness</u> Over time, levels of understanding and tolerance were generally high. 'People with mental illness have for too long been the subject of ridicule', was recorded at 76% proportion with 92% for 'We have a responsibility to provide the best possible care'. The proportion voicing tolerant opinions has, however, decreased from 1994 up to 2008, after which greater tolerance has occurred. 'We have a responsibility to provide the best possible care' increased from 89% in 2008 to 92% in 2009. That 'Virtually anyone can become mentally ill' was agreed by 89% in 2008 and by 91% in 2009. Similarly, 72% in 2008 agreed that 'As far as possible, mental health services should be provided through community-based facilities', and 79% agreed in 2009.

Outcomes	General contrasts with 1994 data
Integrating people with mental illness into the community Over time: Opinions on integrating people into the community were mixed. In 2009, 'No-one has the right to exclude people with mental illness from their neighbourhood'. 78% agreed, 'The best therapy for many people with mental illness is to be part of a normal community'. 77% agreed 'Mental illness is an illness like any other'. 66% agreed, 'People with mental health problems should have the same rights to a job as anyone else'. In contrast, respondents were less likely to agree that 'Most women who were once patients in a mental hospital can be trusted as babysitters' (only 23% agreed). 'Less emphasis should be placed on protecting the public from mental illness' only recorded 33% while 'Mental hospitals are an outdated means of treating people with mental illness' similarly recorded only 37%. In between these two extremes, two statements, 'Residents have nothing to fear from people coming into their neighbourhood to obtain mental health services' and 'People with mental illness are far less of a danger than most people suppose' recorded 62% and 61% respectively. In general, attitudes were significantly improved from the previous 2008 study. Differences by age, sex and social grade included the following: 16–34 year-olds were less likely than the older groups to be in favour of a) integrating people with conditions into the community; be less likely to agree people with a condition are less likely with the following statements – b) people with conditions are less of a danger than most people suppose; c) the best therapy for this group is to be part of a normal community and d) mental illness is like any other. Women were more likely than men to agree that people with mental illness are less of a danger than most people suppose and mental illness is like any other. AB respondents were most in favour of integrating people with mental illness into the community while the DE group were least in favour.	Difference by age confirmed that the youngest age group was less likely than the other two to have tolerant attitudes. DEs in social groups were less likely to have tolerant attitudes than ABs. Integrating people with mental illness into the community Agreement levels were high for statements in this section: 'No-one has the right to exclude people with mental illness from the neighbourhood' (79%); 'The best therapy for many people with mental illness is to be part of a normal community' (78%); 'Mental illness is like any other' (77%); 'People with mental illness should have the same rights to a job as anyone else' (66%). Contrastingly, respondents were less likely to agree that 'Most women who were once patients in a mental hospital can be trusted as babysitters' (23%); 'Less emphasis should be placed on protecting the public from people with mental illness' (33%); 'Mental hospitals are an outdated means of treating people with mental illness' (37%). Attitudes towards mental illness were significantly more positive in 2009 than in 2008: 'People with mental illness are far less of a danger than most people suppose' (agreement up from 57% to 61%); 'Less emphasis should be placed on protecting the public from people with mental illness' (up from 29% to 33%); 'The best therapy for many people with mental illness is to be part of a normal community' (up from 70% to 78%); 'People with mental health problems should have the same rights to a job as anyone else' (up from 66% to 73%); 'Mental illness is like any other' (up from 74% to 77%); 'No-one has the right to exclude people with mental illness from their neighbourhood' (up from 74% to 79%); 'Mental hospitals are an outdated means of treating people with mental illness' (up from 31% to 37%).

Table 2.7 Continued

Outcomes	General contrasts with 1994 data
Women were more likely than men to agree that people with mental illness are less of a danger than most people suppose, and that mental illness is like any other. AB respondents were most in favour of integrating people with mental illness into the community while the DE group were least in favour. Causes of mental illness and the need for special services Since 1994, the proportion agreeing that there are sufficient existing services for people with mental illness increased 'steadily' from 11% to 24% in 2009. That 'there is something about people with mental illness that makes it easy to tell them from normal people' decreased from 29% to 21% 'fairly steadily' over the same period. Agreement that mental illness is mainly caused by a lack of self-discipline and will-power increased to 18% in 2009 from 15% in 1994. Differences by age, sex and social grade showed that 16–34s had the most negative attitudes towards mental illness and were more likely to hold these views than the other groups. Men had more negative issues towards mental illness than women. In terms of class, ABs were more positive in their attitudes than DEs. Ways of describing someone who is mentally ill From a presented list of descriptions, respondents were asked to describe which they felt described a person who is mentally ill. Schizophrenia was the most likely to be selected (at 61%). Split personality came next along with someone who has serious bouts of depression. The least likely included 'someone who is incapable of making decisions about his or her own life' (32%) and 'someone who is prone to violence' (33%).	There was no overall significant change between 1994 and 2009, with the following exceptions: 'Mental illness is an illness like any other' (agreement 71% in 1994, 77% in 2009); 'No-one has the right to exclude people with mental illness from their neighbourhood' (76% to 79%); 'Mental hospitals are an outdated means of treating people with mental illness' (42% in 1994, 37% in 2009). The youngest age group were less likely than older groups to be in favour of integrating people with mental illness into the community. Women were more likely than men to agree that people with mental illness are less of a danger than most people suppose and that mental illness is like any other. ABs were most in favour of integration whereas the DE group were least in favour. Causes of mental illness and the need for special services A concerted increase in the proportion agreeing that there are sufficient existing services exists from 11% in 1994 to 24% in 2009. That 'there is something about mental illness that makes it easy to tell them from normal people' decreased fairly steadily from 29% in 1994 to 21% in 2008. However, there was a significant increase from 17% to 21% in 2009. Also, agreement that 'one of the main causes of mental illness is a lack of self-discipline and will-power' increased from 14% in 2008 to 18% in 2009 – a contrast with 15% in 1994. The youngest had the most negative attitudes towards mental illness with men having more negative attitudes than women. People in the AB social grade were more positive than DEs.

Outcomes	General contrasts with 1994 data
Women were more likely than men to select 'someone who has serious bouts of depression' (57% female against 51% male) and 'someone who is incapable of making simple decisions' (correspondingly 35% against 30% of men). With regard to age, 16–34s were less likely than older groups to select most of these statements. 55+ were more likely to select 'someone who is prone to violence'. Differences in social grades revealed that ABs were most likely to select each description and DEs were least likely. Types of mental illness Most agreed schizophrenia was a type of mental illness (69%) with bipolar disorder registering 60% in agreement. Depression recorded 82% but drug addiction only recorded 45% considering it was a mental illness. Attitudes to people with mental health problems Eight out of 10 agreed that mental health problems can be treated and that medication and therapy were effective treatments; 3 out of 5 believed recovery was possible but opinion about whether or not people with conditions go to professionals for treatment was mixed with 54% agreeing. Differences in age included 75% of 16–34s thought medication could be effective (against 80% of 35–54s or 81% of 55+); 83% of women agreed psychotherapy could be effective; by social class, 73% of DEs agreed with this, against 85% of ABs and 80% of C1s and C2s. Half of 35–54s thought most people with mental health conditions would see a professional, against 57% of 16–34s and 56% of those aged 55+. By social class, 40% of ABs were agreed with this, against 53% for C1s, 62% of C2s and 61% of DEs. Some 63% knew what advice to give a friend who had a mental health problem.	Ways of describing someone who is mentally ill From a list of descriptions respondents were asked to indicate which one describes a mentally ill person. 61% picked schizophrenia. Next was 'split personality' and 'serious bouts of depression' both at 54%. Least likely descriptions selected were 'someone who is incapable of making simple decisions about his or her own life' at 32% and at 33%, 'someone who is prone to violence'. Since 2003, there had been significant increases in the following: Someone who is suffering from schizophrenia – from 56% to 61%; someone who has to be kept in a psychiatric or mental hospital – from 47% to 52%; someone who is prone to violence – from 29% to 33%. There were significant decreases in the proportions selecting other descriptions: Someone who has a split personality – from 59% to 54%; someone who has to be kept in a psychiatric or mental hospital – from 59% to 52%; someone who cannot be held responsible for his or her own actions – from 49% to 45% and; someone who is incapable of making simple decisions about his or her own life – from 37% to 32%. Types of mental illness Questions were also asked about the extent to which respondents recognized that schizophrenia, stress, bipolar disorder (manic depression), drug addiction and grief are types of mental illness. Nine out of 10 respondents recognized schizophrenia as a mental illness, as did over 8 out of 10 for bipolar disorder and depression. The lowest proportion was for drug addiction, though nearly 50% thought it was a type of mental illness.

Table 2.7 Continued

Outcomes	**General contrasts with 1994 data**
69% agreed that 'Most people with mental health problems want to have paid employment'; 72% of C1 and C2s were more likely than 63% of ABs and 66% of DEs to agree with this statement. Personal experience of mental illness Asked about their experiences of people with conditions, respondents were asked if they had lived, worked, been a neighbour to or had a close friend with a condition. The most common experience (53%) was a neighbour with a condition. One in 5 said they had lived with someone with a condition. Four out of 5 indicated they would be willing to continue a relationship with a friend who developed a condition. Willingness to live with someone who had a condition in the future was lower at 57%. Some 58% recorded that someone close to them had a mental illness; 16% said this was a close partner or family member, 15% indicated it was a friend while 10% mentioned other family. Just 5% said they had experienced a kind of mental illness. In terms of age, 45–54 and 55–64 were likely to say they knew someone with experience while youngest and oldest were least likely – those over 75 were least likely to say they had had a condition. Asked what proportion of the UK population would have a problem at some point in their lives, a quarter thought 1 in 10; 13% correctly identified it as 1 in 4; 15% didn't know. Asked how likely it would be that they would go to a general practitioner if they had a condition 81% said they would; those over 55 were more likely to go than the youngest. Asked if they would feel comfortable about talking with a family member about their own mental health, 66% said they would and 23% indicated otherwise; the remainder did not know. Women were more likely to feel comfortable than men in this regard.	Attitudes to people with mental illness Eight out of 10 of respondents recognized that psychotherapy and medication can be effective treatments for people with mental health problems. Three out of 5 respondents agreed that people with mental health problems can fully recover. Opinions as to whether people with mental health problems go to see professionals for care was mixed with 54% in agreement. Knowing the right type of advice to give a friend who had a mental health problem – to get professional help – was recorded at 63%; 69% were in agreement that most people with mental health problems want to have paid employment. Personal experience of mental illness Approximately 50% said they currently had a neighbour with a mental health problem. One in 5 said they lived with someone with a condition. Over 4 out of 5 agreed that they would be willing to continue a relationship with someone who developed a mental condition in future; 7 out of 10 would be willing to live near or work with someone with a condition. Future willingness to live with someone was recorded at 57%. Some 58% of respondents mentioned that someone close to them had experienced a form of mental health condition – most usually a family member (16%). Respondents underestimated the proportion of people they thought might have a condition in their lives with only 13% getting it right; 8% thought it higher. Two-thirds would feel comfortable talking about mental health with a family member about a diagnosis and how it affected them. Women were more likely than men to talk about mental health with friends and family.

Conclusion

This examination of contexts has shown that the contemporary period is one of transformation in which there are major implications for mental well-being; and has illuminated the need for new information about representation development. Furthermore, the chapter has noted that with significant change also occurring across media, the need to discover how to develop mediations of mental health that facilitate community inclusion is imperative. These changes should ideally be led by people who themselves have experience of a mental health condition. After exploring a range of projects focusing on positive data, fundamental indications point toward undertaking a study that is cross-generic. They also suggest the need for a range of study participants, if contributions are to reveal the critical information needed for informing change in policy. Finally, in addressing these contexts, the study also takes useful advice about the promotion of mental health from David Seedhouse (1998). Whilst this thesis does not purport to be a mental health promotion project, such work engaging with the complexity of meanings, includes information which might usefully inform this study. Consequently, this chapter concludes with a look at how prior promotional approaches to mental health representation may provide useful bearings for the project.

Seedhouse

Seedhouse (1998) argues that any would-be mental health promoter must answer three questions in helping to inform understanding about mental health as a vital component for a balanced and healthy well-being. The questions posed are; What is mental health? How can mental health be promoted in this situation? Is this strategy ethically sound? Only the first question is addressed here.

Employing a fictional, though not unusual, case study about the young man 'Peter Murray', Seedhouse usefully lays out a social exposition of the subject's personhood, contributing a sense of realism. Murray, aged 22, has Scottish ancestral roots along with those of the Ngati Whatua tribe of Aotearoa. The family can pass as pure Caucasian and live among European New Zealanders. Whilst Peter has difficulties, with a history of small-time thieving and unemployment after leaving school (which he detested), he spends time with Maori mates complaining about the pakehas (foreigners), smoking cannabis, drinking and watching TV. One night after watching *Once Were Warriors* (a passionate story about the harshness of Maori life), Peter downs a considerable amount of alcohol and after donning his Maori shirt, heads downtown filled with anger about the treatment of the Maori. Booming out a *haka*, he squares up to a high street electrical store and after smashing its window, destroys the televisions on display. Cut and bleeding from the broken glass, he finds the police have arrived. After restraining him from his delirious state, they take him to hospital. After waking up from his sedation in the hospital, he has no idea where he has been or what he has done and is extremely upset. Because of his actions, he is perceived as needing a psychiatrist. Is he someone who might have benefited from mental health promotion?

In critically examining the first question Seedhouse presents two concepts of mental health in an attempt to facilitate understanding about mental health promotion. There is the 'mental illness' theory of mental health (that proposes mental health is the absence of the symptoms of mental illness) and the well-being theory of mental health (that mental health is positive well-being). Both have deficiencies which are thoroughly explored and lead to the putting forward of 'A Better Way'. Seedhouse offers the 'Foundations Theory of Health' as he proposes a way of helping Peter so that mental health promotion can be 'theoretically coherent, practically useful and socially responsible' (1998: 6). This study views this approach as useful in helping to understand the complexity of media mental health meanings.

It is proposed that in the mental illness theory of mental health there are two deficiencies; 'the assumption that clinically defined symptoms of mental illness are the only indicators of a person's mental health' and 'the belief that mental abnormality is an uncontroversial notion' (1998: 6). That this approach has difficulties for promoting an understanding of Peter's mental health can be related in two judgements. The first identifies that the 'assumption that mental illness symptoms are the only indicators of mental health is strikingly inadequate' (ibid.); the second confirms that 'The belief that mental abnormality is an uncontroversial notion is equally groundless' (ibid.). Each of the two positions are devoid of analytical exposition and yet, these type of meanings are ones which regularly surface in media. Rightly, these are exposed and identified as conceptually barren.

In examining 'the well-being theory of mental health', Seedhouse suggests it means precisely this: that you are mentally healthy if you have well-being. Identifying two deficiencies he states that there is 'ambiguity over the meaning of positive well being and related terms' and that 'the assumption that the promotion of particular interpretations of positive well-being is morally uncontroversial' (1998: 7). For the well-being theorist, there are difficulties in these approaches. First, it is possible to 'keep the notion of mental well-being ambiguous (which is what most writing on the well-being theory of mental health promotion does)', or 'define it specifically' or, 'permit subjects to define it for themselves' (ibid.). Seedhouse conveys that the first simply reinforces the status quo, whilst the second, makes 'assertions of value, and will inevitably make practical recommendations of the type; Peter should, the government should, Peter's family should, and so on' (ibid., taken from Downie, Fyfe and Tannahill 1990). The last choice runs the risk that Peter will specify in a way that, a promoter of mental health will be unable to agree with. A number of variations on this are possible but not preferred, as Seedhouse proposes his foundation theory developed upon his conceptual analysis of meanings of mental health. Useful to mental health promotion and helpful to media understanding, the foundations theory itself is suggestive but further exploration is beyond the scope of this chapter. The key aspect of foundations theory is that it shows, not only the complexity of meanings about mental health but also, that such health is connected to physical life and to the social. That people can become ill from excessive use of drugs is not just a mental health perspective but also social perspective since this activity is a socialized one. Clearly, 'mental health' in its promotion must be considered in relationships with physical health and the social world (Seedhouse 2002). It is mind and body which ought to be the focus instead of split specialism. A holistic approach bringing mental health into connections with other factors would help highlight these linkages. Media accounts could learn from this approach and the idea, not just of 'balance' between exercise, nutrition and mental health but that of a simple, honest approach to conditions, encompassing not just it but other contextual components. Just as Seedhouse proposes, the precise relationships with other connecting aspects require illumination for successful promotion about mental health.

If these conclusions and advice are suggestive, indicating possible ways forward in communicating about mental health, then previous studies (as presented by Secker and Platt 1996: 5–17) also illuminate why it is necessary to map out ways they have examined media and mental health, thus contributing understanding about this research field. The tables illustrate not only the approaches of the studies but also the trajectories they take toward the discovery of data eventuating in a situation of little social change. We need to, as Seedhouse proposes (2002: 3–31), look beyond the evidence. This is not to say that these studies do not have their uses in providing useful social data, or that their intentions were never valid. They most certainly are. However, this project recognizes a media and cultural studies research need to focus upon a real social problem to improve knowledge and understanding about an important topic for the community. It further recognizes that to explore ideas about social change in the general context of a group's existence, a range of groups with significant connection to the problem of mental health mediations must be included in the research process. Only by examining meaning-making in mediations about mental health, distress and madness will units of knowledge be exposed as integral elements of power in the relationship between a context, a producer and audience. Subsequently, a reception study (in Chapter 7) and processes from Theatre and Media for Development practices (see Chapter 8) are employed as new ways forward to address these issues and to develop indicators toward mental health mediation improvement.

Chapter 3
Historical Contexts for Popular Meanings of 'Madness'

The problem of mediations referencing mental health, and the case for needing new portrayals is established in previous chapters. This problem is, in part, due to a social and cultural history from which media take meanings of madness[1] laden with stigma. Centuries of instinctively assigned rather than thoughtfully worked out meanings have developed a complex of madness concepts that block exposition about mental health. Otto Wahl (1995) explores such notions in a range of forms including advertisements, cartoons, films and American television shows: Philo provides an array of words and phrases, as well as media portrayals, associated with mental illness and health (1996: 119–21). The aim of this chapter is to survey a history of cultural settings within which ideas about 'madness' have evolved, to capture a sense of their developing social character. By examining questions of social difference, identity, perceptions of 'normality' and also issues of fear and anxiety, the intention is to expose contexts from which contemporary society and culture have come to generate popular meanings about madness. Necessarily, a selection of cultural representations is also included in the examination as these inform the next chapter which explores, among other things how film came to variously portray madness. Several authors explore madness and historical contexts and therefore, the work of Roy Porter, Michel Foucault, Denise Jodelet, R.D. Laing, Sander L. Gilman, Thomas Szasz, Elaine Showalter and Andrew T. Scull are examined in this chapter.

The 'Long View'

Cultural meanings of madness have, in different historical contexts, become popularized in a range of genre forms, developing a complex of interconnections in images, dramatizations, scientific and artistic practices. Providing a rich vocabulary of supportive descriptions and mental landscapes, these contexts exist from the biblical period to the contemporary, constructing social meanings which Gilman (1982: xi) argues 'we have learned to see' in representations. He then raises the question: 'How do we learn to see?' (ibid.). Employing an early example from the Bible, Gilman looks at how we learn through Nebuchadnezzar about his

1 By madness is meant in this chapter a disruption to 'the "normal" social functioning of an individual, leading to strange and unpredictable behaviour' (Jary and Jary 1991: 364).

madness, that he was 'driven from men and did eat grass as oxen, and his body was wet with the dew of heaven, till his hairs were grown like eagles' feathers, and his nails like birds' claws' (Daniel 4:33). Through exposure to such language we learn to conceptualize 'a meaning' having broad connections with mental illness. Be they mobilized in language, image or sound, we learn to know of such meanings in various stereotypes.

> We learn to perceive the world through those cultural artifacts which preserve a society's stereotypes of its environment. We do not see the world, rather we are taught by representations of the world about us to conceive it in a culturally acceptable manner. It is not merely flora and fauna, sunset and seascape which are seen through the prism of culture. We also see man in his infinite variety through the filters of the stereotypical perspective. (Gilman 1982: xi)

Thus, historical contexts and cultural representations provide a range of meanings through which knowledge content about mental health has flowed, mostly referencing mental illness stereotypes[2] associated within the descriptive tag of madness. Culture has generated ill-understood knowledge about mental health which then, as a particularized projected meaning, has been recorded in a media form before being projected back into culture; where it has evolved as stereotypes[3] across time. Other exemplars which have significant implications for how we know about madness exist prior to the Bible.

Greek Mythology, Drama and Rationality

Porter (1987a) notes that during the classic period, the Greeks started looking at madness, trying to understand how it arose; trying to produce explanations. Examining Greek mythology and Homer, their narratives reveal 'archaic attitudes' towards madness; there is no sense of them appreciating the inner self and reflecting upon difficult experiences social life can present. Rather, as Porter records, 'Homer's Heroes are instead more like puppets, players at the mercy of forces essentially from Beyond and beyond their control: gods, demons, the fates, the furies' (1987a: 10–11). Characters are acted upon by forces that are mysteriously above them and out of their control. If initially heroes are the receptors of strange communiqués in dreams from the gods, the outcome is the hero's deterioration

2 By stereotype is meant an inaccurate, fixed value of attributes which are discriminatory and impoverishing not only about the identity of people with mental health conditions but also their condition.

3 In his study of stereotypes, Michael Pickering advises an approach as that taken here, where it is useful to understand not only 'the concept of the stereotype historically, but also to understand the *content* of stereotypes historically – to bring the repressed historical dimension of stereotyping back into the light of its analysis in the present' (2001: 8).

into madness. In a real sense, these social identities are special and their madness, magical in quality and causes, far removed from any identifiable mental condition.

Later, in the fifth century BC, Greek philosophy placed a strong emphasis on rationality – a key quality for civilized human beings needing to understand themselves through self-knowledge. Reason and unreason helped address the concept of madness but only served to render it more precisely, rather than 'solve' its problems. Following Bennett Simon (1978), Porter informs us that medicine was one tradition whilst drama, art and theatre were others that attempted to explain madness. In medicine, epilepsy, which had always been seen as a sacred disease, was subject to theorization by the Greeks. It became a physicalized problem, rather than an effect from something emanating from above; it was 'a product of the regular powers of nature' (Porter 1987a: 12). In drama, the genre of tragedy began to bring forward appreciation of the inner self that had previously been inaccessible. Civil wars of the mind in new heroes revealed internalized tensions for a public to witness in dramatic performance but in processes that were cathartic rather than seeking solutions through change. Unfortunately, as Porter usefully points out, 'Classical thinkers thus defined – but did not solve! – the problem of madness for future ages by elevating *mind*, by valuing reason, order and cosmic intelligibility so highly' (ibid.). And if Stoic philosophy illuminated the irrational as a focus of problems, then Plato's further confirmed the rational as having the 'rightful sovereignty' (1987a: 11) over the irrational. Thus, this historical moment produced a way of perceiving the world through a mode of differentiating between the rational and irrational. Most importantly, through this division, there developed not only ways of thinking about madness as something estranged but also of 'knowing' what was socially 'normal' and 'abnormal'. Plato's rationalism sees the world as ultimately a rational place. There can only be clear and determinate principles that give shape to the world and these principles, he called 'forms'. Peculiar to humanity for Plato is the rational mind's attempt to grasp a rational structure of the world – rationality. While this way of thinking has lasted until now, it is one which this book critiques in that the world in which the human condition exists is more irrational than has previously been given credit. In Plato's view, there can be no room for development between the irrational and rational which ultimately characterizes the human condition and mental health. While passion may be one element Plato's perspective does not accept, the nature of change in a person's existence in the times in which we live and which result in increasing rationality determined by technological developments is another. The non-acceptance of irrationality has major repercussions in the contemporary world in which we exist.

Also during this period Hippocrates (circa 460–370 BC) thought mental illness stemmed from an imbalance of the four humours of the body, in blood, phlegm, black bile and choler. He also believed hysteria was 'a uniquely female disorder caused by a uterus that wandered throughout the body!' (Gallagher 2002: 13) though Asclepiades (circa 100 BC) rejected this, stating that environmental factors were also significant.

Madness, Art and Security in a Developing Modernity[4]

Throughout the period prior to the Renaissance, the mad wandered the countryside of Europe; in the social hierarchy, they were above the lepers, who were housed in leprosariums. Law dictated containment for this social group in France when Louis VIII established leprosariums in 1226 (Foucault 1961). England and Scotland also had 220 lazar houses but toward the end of the Middle Ages such institutions became bereft of lepers as the problem disappeared. The vacant positions were duly filled by the mad, such places taking in small groups of people considered as disturbed. These people were not only located in static physical structures but also in ships on rivers, these being portrayed in literature and artistic works depicting the *Ships of Fools*. However, in the new age of modernity such cultural representations 'made strange' notions about the mad and madness.

Through such works as Sebastian Brant's literary work *Narrenschiff* (1494) and Bosch's *Ships of Fools* (circa 1498), these constructs of the mad began to be looked upon as deviant. The *Narrenschiff*, a mythical depiction of the mad being transported in boats, reflected a situation of its time. According to Foucault, towns and cities, especially in Germany, were for a long period wanting to rid themselves of wandering mad persons. Traversing the countryside, they were free to roam, but in urban areas they were marginalized to the outskirts: 'Frequently, they were handed over to boatmen: in Frankfort, in 1399, seamen were instructed to rid the city of a madman who walked about the streets naked' (1961: 8).

Bosch's *Ship of Fools* was connected not to Brant's novel but, as Linfert (1971) notes, to a Netherlandish poem from 1413. Precisely where its scene is located, and what it means, is open to a multiplicity of interpretations. If anything, it only makes for confusion.

> Everything becomes a sign alluding to something else: the swimmers, the fool on the mast, the man losing his dinner overboard, the one who crawls about in the bottom of the boat with a huge jug on a cord and over whom a woman is leaning – none of them can be taken as literal and real. (Linfert 1971: 68)

In the setting of the picture, the characters and scene only serve to bewilder. The ship is the only stable signifier, itself floating in a fluid substance, but as Linfert notes 'there are others in the picture, whose only message seems to be "that where ignorance is bliss, 'Tis folly to be wise"' (1971: 68). The characters appear to be free-floating signifiers as the mad and fools have 'no base, no ground to stand on: everything is in flux, the outcome unsure' (ibid.). Here, any notions of normality are evacuated; the meaning in the image is one of containment which appears

4 By modernity is meant that period commencing close to the Renaissance when, the development of new economies and societies gave rise to new ways of accomplishing actions. In a multitude of ways, structures began to impose themselves in society. This was the beginning of modernity that arguably continued into the last century.

to be taking place. Religion, in the form of a monk and nun is centrally located with those mad positioned around them. For Gilman, the work communicates 'the moral failings of society, a society seemingly adrift in its madness' (1982: 45) but certainly marginalization and confinement are making physical and symbolic boundaries. Ideas about the mad are in effect being taken to a new social position of being made into 'strangers', and various genre forms would develop these positions with Breughel the Elder's *Dulle Grete*, Hogarth's *Rake's Progress* (circa 1732–3) and later in William Blake's image of Nebuchadnezzar (1795). During the period in which Bosch painted, mainly between 1480 and 1516 (when he died), his work went against the grain of other artists; most stayed in alignment with the Church's views. The late fourteenth century in Europe was a period which Huizinga (1924) describes as highly disturbed, as the Black Death continued intermittently from its commencement in 1345. People lived in fear, not just of disease but of soldiers, who would rape and pillage. Nobles would please themselves in exploiting peasants without hindrance from any legal quarter. The Church also was particularly corrupt and cruel to peasants. It further extended 'borrowed' ideas which 'had always been part of medieval folk culture' (Harris 1995: 42), about the evil of the world, and re-cycled them for the same audience so as to sustain its own power. If the location of God and evil was confusing, then the Church, whilst considered holy, contributed yet more bafflement through its teachings. To contradict the church was to invite trouble. As Harris notes, Bosch was someone who believed the physical world was completely evil, created and controlled by Satan; Jesus, symbolized by light in a darkness devoid of spirituality, is either 'ignored or attacked' (1995: 49). Thus, Bosch's depictions of madness in the *Ship of Fools* were perplexing, most likely because of the power of religion. Visualizations of 'depictions of transportation' increased across the fifteenth century but, as Foucault observed, it was within this cultural setting that the face of madness was beginning to haunt the imaginations of the West.

In a new period of modernization, new buildings were to house the mad out of sight, removing the mad physically and displacing ideas about madness from rationalizing minds. Andrew Scull (1979), signals a changing response to the needs of the mad during the Renaissance. As the very existence of social and economic life changed, so too did the way of dealing with those deemed mad as exclusion was instituted as the way forward. The development of a single national economic market and a centralising political system led 'to the development of a state-sponsored system of segregative control' (1979: 48). The idea of authority structures imposing order and containment for those who appeared to need it became prevalent. Scull notes that as early as 1403–4, Bethlem was the only specialized housing for mad people; it housed only six mad and three sane patients. However, this small number was set to increase, accruing in total as society modernized: 'In 1632, for example, it was reported to contain twenty-seven patients, and in 1642, forty-four' (Jordan 1960: 189–90, cited in Scull 1979: 19). Thus, modernity began stratifying, ordering and structuring not only society but also perceptions of 'normal' in the social world. The identities of those deemed mad began to be occluded, and the nature of their social belonging, a political risk that authorities seemed unwilling to take.

As the Tudors (1485–1603) and Stuarts (1603–1714) reigned during a rise in the population, transformations in working practices and commercialization created not only new social groups searching for work but also greater needs for security. Plays such as *The Shoemaker's Holiday* by Thomas Dekker, although not completely accurate (see Dekker 1979: xx) in portraying social and economic life in the Elizabethan period (1558–1603) does provide useful indications of changes taking place. Craft guilds employed apprentices to learn their trade in ever developing economic structures, these working conditions contributing to a need for festive holidays where plebeian celebratory culture could often become unruly. Fear about behaviour that might unbalance the social norms grew, leading to new ideas about confinement. If this was broadly the case in England, in France it was further advanced when, in 1580, there was a popular uprising at the annual carnival at Romans with dire outcomes for its participants (Ladurie 1979). In a period where new regulations and taxes were but a few of the elements contributing to an oppressed existence, peasants, artisans, labourers and some bourgeoisie, formed a resistance to the then dominant culture. Catching wind of the intended rebellion, a coalition of other bourgeois and aristocratic groups massacred the uprising. Although, as Michael D. Bristol notes in his reflection (1985) upon Le Roy Ladurie's work, this was an isolated example and it communicated symbolic warnings to other European countries. A localized response to people considered broadly as 'deviant' developed, culminating in new institutions: Bethlem was later augmented by the Bridewell (a house of correction in 1555) and inhabitants of both institutions rose.

Securing More Sanity for Modernity

In France and England, more projects securing 'sanity' developed with the introduction of yet more new buildings. In 1656, the King of France proposed that several hospitals be opened in the provinces and Hôpitaux Généraux were built in 32 cities. Shortly after opening its doors, the Paris Hôpital Général 'contained six thousand persons, or around one percent of the population' (Foucault 1961: 45) and there commenced a state drive toward the confinement of those deemed mad. As the middle ages progressed, the mad were condemned as 'idle' (1961: 58) and in the sixteenth and seventeenth centuries were shut away. 'It was in this period that they began to "confine" or "intern" them, along with the entire population with whom their kinship was recognised' (Foucault 1961: 58). Modernity was in a political struggle of securing itself from identities it considered a threat. During this period, with the rise of commercialized agriculture, there was 'spawning a volatile "army" of vagrants, beggars, and idlers, no longer needed on the land. The threat that these groups posed to the power of the central royal authorities was heightened by the still precarious nature of the latter's control' (Scull

1979: 20). In England the confinement of people considered unwell in mind occurred away from urban centres, in the local parishes. Scull notes that, under the Poor Law Act of 1601, the care of those in poverty became a secular rather than a religious responsibility – and this included those deemed mad. Approximately 15,000 managerial projects became involved in regulating this heterogeneous group. Other institutions similar to Bridewell, such as workhouses, were built, 'destined to greater success' (Foucault 1961: 44). Porter, however, disagrees with Foucault's figures (see Porter 1987b: 8) for England (and Europe), discerning that if such a period of confinement existed, it did so not during the Georgian period (1714–1830) but after it. Whilst Porter dismisses talk of a 'system'[5] as misleading (ibid.), in a greater sociological context modernity was further imposing structures upon developing practices that were both systematizing and ordering in nature. There followed a greater differentiation[6] of people with mental health conditions from the community in a context of increasing social stratification; consequently, perceptions of the 'normal' increased with the so-called 'mad' being locked away, understanding of 'mental health' sealed up with them.

The Sixteenth to Eighteenth Centuries: Transformations in Treatment?

If the 'places of confinement' stimulated imaginations about the oddities of the mad, then treatments afforded them by doctors were also bizarre in character. From the Renaissance to the seventeenth century, treatments varied but one was consistently maintained. *Humoralism*, originally recommended by the Greeks, was passed down through the Middle Ages and beyond. Man was seen as constituted of four unifying basic elements of air, earth, fire and water. These embodied, to varying degrees, coldness and hotness, dryness and wetness. The correct balance of these elements produced harmony in the mind as did the four basic vital fluids phlegm, blood, black bile and yellow bile (or choler). Three procedures based around deficiencies or excesses of these criteria were seen as leading to recovery. These operations introduced sovereign remedies for the ill of mind: *bloodletting* involved cutting a vein which was thought to introduce and enhance recovery; *drinking an emetic* provoked violent vomiting which was believed to work wonders; and *purging the system* by submission to a laxative was believed to solve mental health conditions. Pathologies were solved in this way until the middle of the seventeenth century with more complex variations available for the rich but quite basic approaches for the poor. Thus, knowledge of dealing with madness mirrored its very condition, rendering healers as mad, but these images of madness found 'a medical discourse' even more keen to establish a new face of medicine.

5 Porter criticizes MacDonald (1977) for proposing that there was an 'asylum system' spreading 'throughout the nation' at that this time.

6 By 'differentiation' is meant that model proposed by Lash (1990) in which social stratification occurs between groups in processes of cultural change during modernity.

In the eighteenth century neurology developed, creating new methods of treating patients. These developments laid foundations for psychiatry to further reason about mental health conditions: George Nesse Hill and John and Thomas Mayo addressed the organic nature of mental health problems, providing 'graphic evidence of skull damage and brain tumours' (Porter 1987b: 183). The English medical profession, according to Scull (1975: 222), was composed of three separate groups: physicians, surgeons and apothecaries. Each of these occupations could enter the mad-business albeit with dubious qualification: physicians could acquaint themselves with a medical degree by way of social connections; surgeons had just separated themselves from the barbers' tradition and apothecaries were a wide ranging group of people potentially either semi-illiterate or highly competent. The new practice of psychiatry in the nineteenth century and the process of labelling and classifying developed despite controversy about the diagnoses of doctors. Arguments sprang from the new asylums that were to assist not only in housing the mad but in a few cases offering a new quality of care. Madness, it could be said, was gradually becoming identified as mental illness.

In 1796, William Tuke opened the York Asylum which started as a retreat only for Quakers but later opened its doors to all and became known for its more humane philosophy toward people with mental health conditions.

> On the outskirts of York, it was designed to be dwelt in as a large private house. Its atmosphere was domestic, and it was run along parental lines. The superintendent and his assistants were the 'family', and a spiritual bond was sought between staff and patients. 'There is much analogy' wrote Tuke 'between the judicious treatment of children, and that of the insane persons'. (Porter 1987b: 223)

During its early existence purposeful approaches were endorsed by its founders in the management of the establishment. Samuel Tuke was explicit when he said, 'The physician plainly perceived how much was to be done by moral and how little to be done by medical means' (ibid.). The new asylum at York represented all that was positive in the new profession of psychiatry. Resocialization was seriously attempted with particular direction toward the Quaker religion. Admiration and respect was acclaimed despite the occasional instilling of fear in pursuit of order. Other asylums of the time were not of the same calibre. Ticehurst and Brislington House, although under similar liberal regimes, provided inferior care – John Perceval, a patient in the 1830s, reported that the staff behaved 'as if I were a piece of furniture, an image of wood, incapable of desire or will as well as judgement' (Porter 1987b: 227). Bedlam in London further extended the notion of imprisonment and separation from society, where the new focus upon the mind was directed toward control, through policing within the 'self'. However, these transformations in resocializing treatment were all too rare.

The very fact that a psychiatric space was being arranged further encouraged difference between the main body of European society and those with mental health conditions. Social differentiations were also evolving in other parts of society in class and in national identity in relation to foreigners, as well as through myths about blackness and madness.

The Work of Clifford Beers in America

The history of mental illness and care of its people with conditions in the United States are not dissimilar from those in Europe. This history and documentation about care is concisely recorded in Deutsch 1948 and 1949. It is clear from his studies that many, locked away in institutions, were subject to punishing and gruelling treatments across many years. However, at around the beginning of the last century, reform of mental institutions took place with the work of Clifford Whittingham Beers having profound effect both there and overseas. Beers, born in New Haven, Connecticut on 30 March 1876, attended school there and later went to Yale University. According to Deutsch (1949), Beers as a young man was intent on a career in business but took a different direction when his brother experienced epilepsy. Gripped by fear that he would be susceptible to this condition, he gradually became obsessed during his undergraduate years at Yale. Three years after graduating and undertaking his business career, this fear led Beers to attempt suicide. Despite falling from the fourth floor of his family home, this attempt failed and Beers was later incarcerated in three different mental institutions across a three-year period where he was treated inhumanely by attendants with harsh beatings.

After his period of confinement, Clifford Beers dedicated much of his life to changing American mental institutions and to eradicating the abuse common within them. Beers also saw that the situations of people with mental unwell-being paralleled those of race after reading *Uncle Tom's Cabin*. He wrote his autobiography, *A Mind That Found Itself* (1907), a work that was to have profound impact in mobilizing reforms through the Mental Hygiene Movement (launched in 1908) which proved effective in bringing about change. This movement continued to grow; an international congress was held in Paris in 1937 and again in London in 1948. According to Deutsch:

> A major outcome of this congress was the birth of World Federation for Mental Health, to work closely with the United Nations World Health Organisation and U.N. Economic, Social and Cultural Organization. Representatives of more than a score of countries immediately joined as charter members of the Federation, dedicated mainly among promoting 'among all peoples and nations the highest possible level of mental health'. (1949: 329–30)

Prior to the work of Beers, the situation in mental asylums was also a cause undertaken by some journalists seeking to expose the maltreatment. The case of Nellie Bly was one such instance: she feigned madness to become incarcerated.

According to Deutsch, her story, *Ten Days in a Mad-House* 'bore the revealing subtitles, "Feigning Insanity in Order to Reveal Asylum Horrors; The Trying Ordeal of the *New York World's* Girl Correspondent"' (1949: 307). However, as Deutsch shows, such attempts disappeared from the newspaper columns as quickly as they had arrived, leaving the public no wiser. The work of Clifford Beers, however, made a lasting impression.

The Development of Psychiatry

The development of psychiatry and its tendencies to (mis-)diagnose mental illness led to yet more special institutions and hospitals as madness became a more common feature of everyday life in the nineteenth century.

> Around 1800, no more than a few thousand 'lunatics' were confined in England in all kinds of institutions; by 1900 the total had skyrocketed to about 100,000. In human terms, this increase of perhaps twenty fold means that during the nineteenth century a disturbed person's fate was likely – indeed, ever more likely – to end up as the story of encounters with organised psychiatry; in fact quite specifically, to be the tale of life and death within the asylum, encaged in 'museums of madness'. (Porter 1987b: 2)

Showalter (1985) shows that in the Victorian period (1837–1901) England was apparently amidst an epidemic of mental health conditions, the increase of asylums housing an escalating population of people. Women were casualties of these developments: 'By 1872, out of 58,640 certified lunatics in England and Wales, 31,822 were women' (Showalter 1985: 52), most likely misdiagnosed as well as mistreated. Men were able to secure a better class of asylum (privately run) but women were relegated to pauper borough and county asylums, and a significant fear was generated among women about mental health issues. Porter also notes that 'The Victorian era became the golden age of depression, nervous disorder and breakdown – witness the psychic health of Victorian intellectuals such as John Stuart Mill and Thomas Carlyle' (1987b: 283). More grandiose structures were built, in some instances monumental projects: Colney Hatch had an Italianate façade that was a third of mile in length (Showalter 1985: 23). But as they were built, so they were filled, at even faster rates (Porter 1987a: 20). By 1858, as Showalter notes, the madhouse had become 'the asylum' or 'retreat' and according to Dr Edgar Sheppard in the middle of the nineteenth century the members of such places were among the best treated in the land. This view must be balanced by the fact that patients could still be subject to restraint in numerous unpleasant ways. Manacles, body straps and various chairs for securing patients could also be applied, making them more like inmates and prisoners in a jail. But with psychiatry came a new language for mapping out and classifying the many 'illnesses' these 'doctors' thought they had identified, labelling every antisocial behaviour including depression or addiction. Those deemed mentally ill, if not physically incarcerated, could now become mentally typed through their medical records. Precisely what psychiatrists did with the mentally unwell was never clear (see Szasz 1962: 18) but their relationship to the sufferer was one of distance, what Szasz was to term a double standard (1962: 44). Toward the end of the nineteenth century, approaches in mental healthcare changed again with psychoanalysis advanced through the work of Freud (1856–1939), who studied under Jean-Martin Charcot.

In Paris, Charcot's work focused upon the treatment of hysteria through the method of hypnosis. His work is depicted in a famous painting by André Brouillet entitled *A Clinical Lesson at La Salpêtrière (1887)* in which he treats a female patient for hysteria before a group of (all male) students (the painting is critically examined in Showalter (1987) and Hall (1997)). Many sessions ended in a complete hysterical seizure for the patient but here the image depicts, potentially, the birth of two psychiatric approaches (Hall 1997: 53); one was psychoanalysis, a talking cure developed by Freud and Breuer in their pioneering work *Studies in Hysteria* (1895).

Freud, later examining the conscious and unconscious around the structure of the id, ego and superego advanced his developmental theory of personality as a tool for seeing human development as processual and socialized. Using talking therapy as a way forward in a dialogue with patients, each of the stages is explored with a view to solving adult behaviour problems of childhood origin. A number of followers, including Jung, took Freud's theories forward but it was Lacan (1901–81), who further modified his work to new levels to include language in the study of self and identity. His work also evolved what was already a problematic theory, further privileging the male. Altogether new ways of studying the human being and mental problems evolved but study of the mind which somehow retained an air of mystical distance prevented this new tradition and that of psychiatry from not becoming readily socially accepted.

Medical Photography

While artistic depictions such as *A Clinical Lesson at La Salpêtrière (1887)* provided an insight into the new workings of hypnosis by Charcot and, arguably, mental health, such representations were questionable. The parts played by subjects were 'theatrical'. Showalter (1987) notes Charcot's strong reliance on the use of imagery in lectures, with some of the women encouraged to nurture a performance. Performance was further extended in the use of photography by Albert Londe, employed to document patients in lectures at La Salpêtrière. This work at the hospital was 'an environment in which female hysteria was perpetually presented, represented and reproduced' (Showalter 1987: 150). Photography was to play a major role in representing mental patients which Gilman (1988) further addresses in *The Science of Visualizing the Insane: Charles Darwin.*

Figure 3.1 Hugh Welch Diamond (English, 1809–1886), Woman with Hair Standing on End, c. 1850. Albumen print, overall: 5 1/4 x 4 in. (13.3 x 10.2 cm).

Source: Sterling and Francine Clark Art Institute, Williamstown, Massachusetts, 1998.32.2 (Photo by Michael Agee). © Sterling and Francine Clark Art Institute, Williamstown, Massachusetts, USA.

Exploring unpublished correspondences between Charles Darwin and Sir James Crichton Browne, the focus upon the study of expression reveal inquiries that intertwined with that of Duchenne (discussed below). While interesting for the period, both imagery and correspondence belie a scientific tradition distanced from the people in its care and furthering another unhelpful way of how we have learned to see mentally unwell people.

Psychiatry quickly made use of new technologies in recording images of patients in France but, in England, Hugh Welch Diamond employed photography as an intended therapeutic tool. The mad and the asylum were no stranger to Diamond, whose father was a mad-house keeper initially in Sussex and then at St Pancras in London (Burrows and Schumacher 1990). Appointed physician to the female department at the Surrey Asylum in 1848 where he worked for 10 years, Diamond asserted that for women patients in particular, 'it was salutary to have this reminder of personal appearance, and to have the natural feminine vanity, dulled by disease, stimulated by a photographic portrait' (Showalter 1987: 86). He held the belief that photography was 'objective', offering the viewer clear and unequivocal insights into the patient's condition.

Woman with Hair Standing on End is a representation in which a definite pose is organized for the viewer. Often employing a subject looking to the side of the camera, these representations offer a 'tidiness' in the attire chosen for the image and a submissiveness in the posture patients took up. As Showalter notes, such images look like a voyeuristic examination of the inner world of madness. However, these constructions of madness are not accurate about conditions.

This image, a misrepresentation, offers a misguided spectacle that can only deceive, inviting us to think the asylum system was working effectively. With the contributions of other administrators such as T.N. Brushfield (at the Chester County Asylum) and Sir Charles Hood (at Bethlem), the new technology of the time was upheld as a marvel. What it really did was offer another distraction, to produce visual concepts proposing a good system of care. It did not present the internal dynamics of a condition, or what impacts it might have. Such experiences in their natural state were rarely shown. Far from the 'unerring accuracy' Diamond proposed of photography, myths multiplied through such representations. This mediation type added to the burgeoning contexts of seeing madness.

Medical photography further objectified the patient through the work of Adrien Tournachon (1825–1903), a French portrait painter commissioned by a neurologist, Dr Guillaume Duchenne. Tournachon photographed subjects in a supposedly painless experiment, in which electrical stimulation of muscles in the face would facilitate emotional expressions. The grounding of the work was based on 'the existence of one, discoverable mechanism to account for the whole vast range of human facial expression' (Younger 1991: 105). Drawings and caricatures had prevailed prior to photography but the photographic image like the one in Figure 3.2 was admired for its quality of 'accuracy'. But because of the multitude of these portrait genres becoming available to a developing medical profession, it would be seen as culturally acceptable by them and, later, by the public.

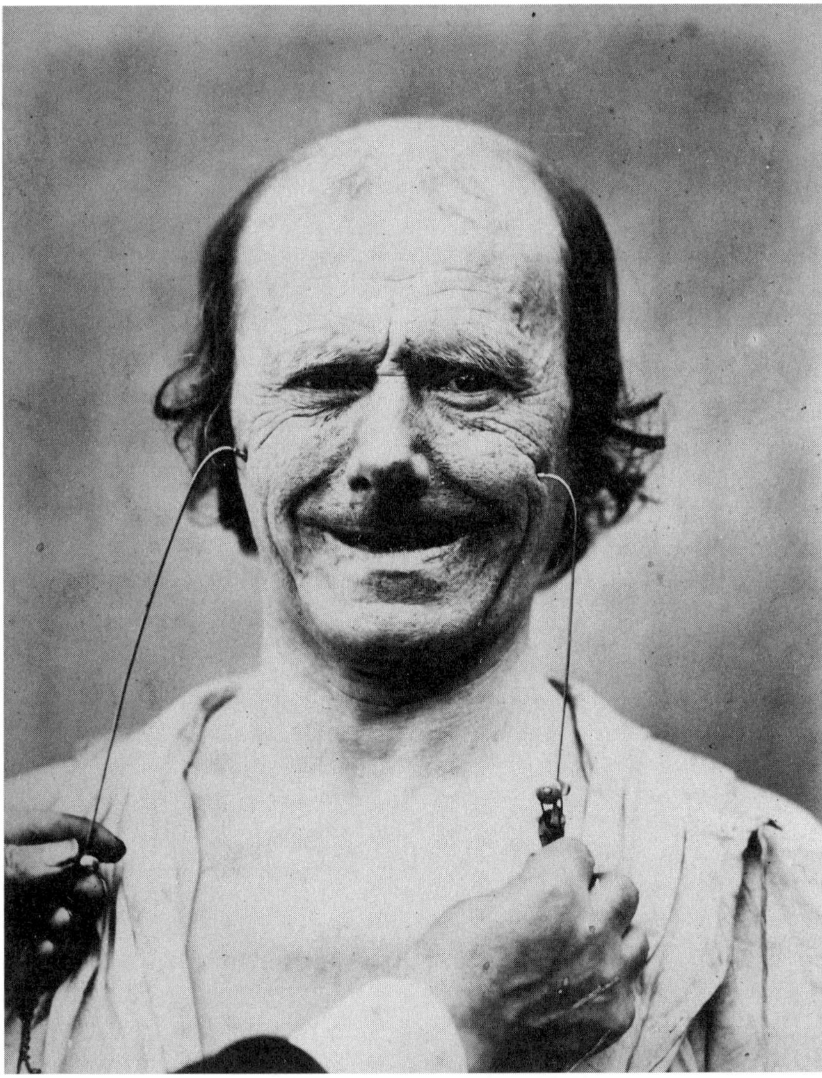

Figure 3.2 Guillaume-Amant Duchenne de Boulogne (French, 1806–1875), 'Plate 31: Excitation électrique un peu plus forte des grand zygomatiques: Rire faux', from 'Ch. 6: Muscles de la joie et de la bien veillance', in Icono Photographique: Mécanisme de la Physionomie Humaine, before 1857 (negative), published 1862. Albumen print, image: 4 3/4 x 3 9/16 in. (12 x 9.1 cm), sheet: 10 13/16 x 7 1/16 in. (27.5 x 18 cm).

Source: Sterling and Francine Clark Art Institute, Williamstown, Massachusetts, 1999.26 (Photo by Michael Agee). © Sterling and Francine Clark Art Institute, Williamstown, Massachusetts, USA.

The identity of people associated with mental illness in such imagery would be defined by the oddity of the procedures doctors were imposing upon them. Photography produced 'difference' about people with conditions for society and would certainly marginalize this group. The new technology for Duchenne and Diamond may have allowed for new techniques of recording and 'captured the contemporary imagination' (ibid.), but the distortion of imagery recording patients would only serve to confuse rather than inform the public. The use of the mentally unwell for experimentation and recording of such testing through the medium of photography would later be employed by Nazi scientists.

Anti-psychiatry: R.D. Laing and Thomas Szasz

From within the historical context of psychiatry, perceptions of the 'normal', even precisely what mental health or illness is, came to be questioned by R.D. Laing (1927–89) and Thomas Szasz (1920–). Both Szasz and Laing attempted to contribute a new humanism to a psychiatry located in positions of power and mystery. Laing carried out work with people suffering from schizophrenia and tried to unravel the mysteries surrounding the condition in his book *The Divided Self* (1960). Examined in radical ways, it was seen through a new perspective, as a condition that was prophetic and as a rational way of struggling with an irrational world. Removed from traditional psychiatry at the time, it struck a chord within popular culture of the 1960s in breaking away from oppressive shackles of past psychiatric practices. Laing's approach was also not easily accepted by psychiatrists, his work often antagonizing them. Radical in nature, Laing would make an impact not only in society but also in media, his work influencing the making of *Family Life* (discussed in the next chapter), a film about a mentally ill woman. Indeed, during this period mental health issues were given good airing: Ken Kesey's *One Flew Over The Cuckoo's Nest* was published as a play and then staged, travelling across America. However, it took 15 years from its publication to be produced as a film in 1975, when it also made a significant impact within the cultural setting of its time; a post-Vietnam period which saw a 'make love not war' approach in a popular culture, seeking to express liberation from oppressive governmental discourses.

Thomas Szasz (1972) notes how the concept of mental illness is freely used in media; how famous persons (e.g., Hitler) are identified as being mentally ill but without actual evidence qualifying as proof of a condition. Szasz also asks the question 'What is mental illness?' whilst showing it to be inextricably linked to another one: 'What do psychiatrists do?' Critical of his profession, the work was an important contribution to understanding of mental health and, perhaps more importantly, of how psychiatrists operated in their examinations of conditions. In arguing that mental illness is a myth, Szasz proposed that 'only bodies can be ill in a literal sense and that minds can only be sick metaphorically (like economies)' (see Pilgrim and Rogers 1993: 5). Focusing upon psychiatry, he demolishes the main substantives of contemporary psychological thought and asks of his profession what they would do without them and proposes the 'laying the foundations for a process-theory of personal conduct' (Szasz 1972: 18). If psychiatry was critiquing itself and attempting to reflect upon how it might renew its approach, feminism was also making a critique of its relationship to women.

Women and Madness

Elaine Showalter (1987) explores English culture, madness and women while Chesler (1972, 2005) examines American and English culture. Showalter critiques the role of men in psychiatry, in particular Laing's treatment of one woman, Mary Barnes, and her condition, schizophrenia. Having read *The Divided Self* and been turned down by Anna Freud for treatment, Mary Barnes brought herself to Laing's therapeutic community where she played a key role. A strong and impressive character, she told her own story – rather than allowing it to be told for her – in an account written with a contribution from her therapist, Joseph Berke. Consequently, Barnes' narrative of illness can be usefully compared with her male psychiatrist whom Showalter highlights; raising points concerning gender and the situation that women with a mental health condition experience.

Both Berke and Laing leave out certain elements present in the narrative discourse of Barnes. Central to her problems were frustrations other than sexual ones, which Showalter highlights as being missed by Berke through 'a number of narrow psychoanalytical ideas about femininity and female sexuality' (Showalter 1987: 235). As part of her behaviour was to withdraw into an infantile position, Berke surmized that this was an alternative integration of key psychic functions to a burning sexual desire and frustrations that could not be satisfied because of guilt she felt about incestuous feelings for her father and brother. Berke usefully got Mary involved in painting and exhibiting her work but incorrectly, in Showalter's view, diagnosed her psychological improvement in a way related to sexuality when the vocational was something clearly prominent in her – which Barnes had written about and apparently defined as 'masculine':

> What Berke sees as Mary's penis envy was rather her envy of male mobility, status, and independence. Ironically, Mary first achieved the success she craved by becoming the "Queen of the Schizophrenics" at Kingsley Hall, the main attraction of a psychiatric theater much like Charcot's at the Salpêtière. (Showalter 1987: 235)

Laing is criticized for fulfilling a male adventure of 'exploration and conquest – scarcely the reality of Mary Barnes's experience' (1987: 236); boyish ideals which were the stuff of earlier climbing exploits in Scotland. This approach, in trying to help the child-like qualities of Mary's personality was a process which Showalter raises as problematic. While also subject to critique from academia outside psychiatry, organizations such as *Survivors Speak Out* are significant in criticizing the nature of psychiatric care offered to people with mental health conditions. Similar criticisms are offered in Rogers, Pilgrim and Lacey (1993) with users of mental healthcare services damning professionals and other carers, one typical example relating 'I feel that I was treated too much as an object rather than a person' (1993: 50).

Phyllis Chesler in her examination of American culture finds similar situations for women to those identified by Showalter. In the United States, Chesler defines the institutions of the asylum, clinicians and society as inherently male with patriarchal infused power relationships privileging them. Exploring the 'patient careers' of 60 women her research is psychologically based, theoretical, a literary and philosophical discourse, and that of a clinician. From the 1972 and 2005 publication, Chesler documents English and American situations. In the first edition, clinical professions in America are male dominated as are theoretical approaches and therapeutic methods. This context is one in which the male view is calcified throughout this society but which she concedes is currently undergoing some transformation. However, Chesler cites Caplan and Cosgrove (2004), stating that bias continues to exist at the level of education despite this change. Quoting Autumn Wiley's review of 10 widely used undergraduate textbooks for abnormal psychology, she finds 'none included the feminist critique of institutional psychiatry and diagnostic practices; seven of the 10 texts included no mention of sex or gender bias; and none of the fourteen major feminist critics is cited in any of the books' (Chesler 2005: 15). Chesler's groundbreaking work further illuminates the difficulties of the American context of 2005 uncovering prejudice in decision making processes concerning women's mental health. This prejudice continues to prevail at conscious and unconscious levels, and favour the male at the expense of the female.

If early treatments were problematic then so too was the language of psychiatry. Emerging terms from both the USA and UK professions still contain past language that is the basis for some stigmatizing and maintaining of medical power over that patient today. In America, the *Diagnostic and Statistical Manual of Mental Disorders* (2000) still employs the word 'retardation' as early as the first page, a word which, in its varying forms finds its way into popular films and everyday discourse. In the social, the patient will be subject to such labelling and the implications of top-down power relationships that position the person at the margins of society. So too, the word 'schizophrenia' coined by Eugen Bleuler, initially termed by Bénédict Augustin Morel as 'démence précoce' and later medically classified by Emil Kraepelin as 'dementia praecox', carries stigma in significant ways through its shortened use as 'schizo' in today's tabloid press. However, while these psychiatric words and others like them have chequered histories, art and theatre is able to offer different languages conveying alternative memories.

Nina – ou La Folle par Amour[7] (Nina, or The Love-distressed Woman)

While numerous contexts have laid out a strong foundation for popular meanings about madness, a few depictions in theatre and painting have conveyed jarring representational images. One play called *Nina – ou La Folle par Amour* was also depicted in an engraving. Directed by Nicolas-Marie Dalayrac, this one act play was first performed on 15 May 1786 at the Comédie-Italienne in Paris. The libretto by Benoît-Joseph Marsollier des Vivetières was based on a story written by Baculard d'Arnaud and drew acclaim for the performance of its main actress Madame Louise Dugazon (1763–1821), who played the part of Nina. However, the performance was not undertaken without serious planning because of concerns about representational aspects connected with madness.

According to Hugh Noel Williams (1906) both Marsollier and Dalayrac withheld submission of the score to the Comédie-Italienne for fear that 'their attempt to depict madness on stage was too hazardous, and might expose them to the risk of a disastrous failure' (1906: 212). An experimental performance was produced at the private theatre of Mlle Guimard in the Chaussée-D'Antin and here Dugazon crafted her performance before a mixed audience. Purposeful in its depiction of sadness or melancholia through its association with love, audiences would acknowledge Nina's condition through her portrayal.

The narrative tells of how Nina's father, Count Lindoro (singing in a baritone voice), is against her relationship with Germeuil (also baritone). The father prefers another suitor who engages with Germeuil in a duel. Injured, Germeuil disappears and with Nina unclear as to his demise, she appears to lose her reason and at this moment, the aria *Quand le bien-aimé reviendra* – 'When my sweetheart returns to me', is sung. A representation of this theatrical moment from the operatic performance, the engraving by Francois Janinet depicts her sitting on a bench in a garden on the day of her wedding, waiting for her love to return.

In the Comédie-Italienne performances and with catharsis very much at the centre of its communication, Dugazon shared the feelings of the character Nina conveying an expression of feeling, about a felt pain and condition with which the audience could identify. Her bewitching looks and beautiful soprano voice hypnotized audiences through her characterization of Nina as a person depressed at the loss of her lover and for whose return she longed. Dressed in white, she captured the attention of the Parisian audience, reducing women and men to tears. One audience member in a letter recounts how Dugazon's performance was:

> with such enchanting grace, such sweet and delicate touches of sensibility and passion, as I never saw upon any theatre. It is the *sweet bells jangled out of tune*, but not *harsh*; no raving, no disorder of dress; but every look and gesture showed an unsettled mind, and a tenderness inimitable. (Ellis 1874: 161)

---

7 The author is grateful to Mark Ledbury at the Sterling and Francine Clark Institute (Massachusetts, USA) for discussions about this engraving and play.

Figure 3.3 Jean-François Janinet (French, 1752–1814) after Claude Hoin (French, 1750–1817), Nina, ou, La Folle par Amour, 1787. Engraving using aquatint on paper, image: 12 7/16 x 9 3/16 in. (31.6 x 23.3 cm), plate: 16 15/16 x 12 3/8 in. (43 x 31.5 cm), sheet: 23 9/16 x 12 3/8 in. (59.8 x 31.5 cm).

Source: Sterling and Francine Clark Art Institute, Williamstown, Massachusetts, U.S.A., 1955.2357 (Photo by Michael Agee). © Sterling and Francine Clark Art Institute, Williamstown, Massachusetts, USA.

Williams also notes the audience appreciation:

> The tears, the applause, baffled all description. Six times at the conclusion of the play was the 'sublime lunatic' recalled. The public could not applaud enough, and at each performance the enthusiasm increased; it seemed inexhaustible. … Madness became on a sudden the fashionable disease. In the salons a host of young women found occupation in playing the part of Nina, and some of them appeared to have worked themselves into a condition bordering lunacy. (Williams 1906: 213–14)

On Germueil's return, her reason is restored and the father, remorseful of his actions, allows the union to take place. Such is the moment of this aria that in making *Nina* a popular success, an Italian version of the libretto was also produced by Giovanni Paisello as *Nina, o sia La Pazza per amore* in 1789 and proved highly successful across Europe.

Edvard Munch – *Anxiety*

Another artistic representation unsettling to depictions of madness is that of *Anxiety* by Edvard Munch (1863–1944). He produced many paintings representing not only landscapes and portraits but also the human condition. The best known of his works, *The Scream* (1895), is internationally recognized for its referencing a sense of crises in the modern person, though arguably this was not what he intended. *Melancholy* (1896) and *Madonna* (1896), too, show how Munch as an artist was intent on using his emotions as a key resource for representing his view of the world. Howe (2001: 11) informs us that Munch, like his contemporaries van Gogh and Gauguin, sought 'to make his personal emotions and spiritual belongings the focus of his art'. The work examined here, known as *Anxiety* (specifically the 1896 lithograph, a reverse of the 1894 oil painting on canvas), is a significant image reflecting what a condition of mental health is and the title is representative of his intent to depict it. Anxiety is something most people can relate to, an integral part of human functioning. It is a very real experience and almost tangible thing for those seeing it in someone else. However, this image raises the question as to whether or not Munch is offering *Anxiety* as a representation of people in the image experiencing it or them seeing it in his self-identity.

As someone representing all aspects of life, authenticity and its fundamental truths were close to Munch's work. Beginning his artistic career as a realist Munch evolved with a new wave of Symbolists who 'distrusted reality as perceived through the senses, and sought other avenues of knowledge. The Symbolists demanded an art that was faithful to psychological realities as well' (Howe 2001: 14).

Figure 3.4 Edvard Munch (Norwegian, 1863–1944), Anxiety, 1896. Lithograph on paper, image: 16 1/8 x 15 1/8 in. (41 x 38.4 cm), sheet: 22 7/16 x 16 15/16 in. (57 x 43 cm).

Source: Sterling and Francine Clark Art Institute, Williamstown, Massachusetts, U.S.A., 1962.86 (Photo by Michael Agee). © Sterling and Francine Clark Art Institute, Williamstown, Massachusetts, USA.

Subsequently, the form and content of his work references pain in ways central to his personhood by representing the hidden phenomena within his own subjective psychology. In this regard, 'loss' was close to his experience, with his mother's death from tuberculosis at the early age of 31 and the subsequent fundamental change in his relationship with his father. With the loss of his wife, his father's religious beliefs shifted, but according to Øivind Storm Bjerke (1995: 20) a transformation into a manic depressive state occurred. While the original relationship with his father would change, it would be lost for ever with his father's death in 1889. He also lost his favourite sister Sophie in 1877 to tuberculosis and lost a younger brother in 1895. His sister Laura is said to have experienced a mental breakdown and Munch's own health was also punctuated by mental unwell health. Munch experienced a bout of alcoholism and depression which proved significant enough to ensure he referenced his knowledge and feelings in his artistic representations.

Also, Munch's sense of loss and his misgivings about the generation of urban environments were destabilizing. For Howe, the intention of *The Scream* and *Anxiety* 'were meant to communicate the loss of individuality and intense psychological unease the artist felt in the midst of an impersonal and congested urban environment' (2001: 156). The urban context was, for Munch, a disorienting experience in which people found their identity lost or dislocated. While *The Scream* is intended as a self portrait, it is unclear if this is the case for *Anxiety* which appears to be a mixture of two previous works *Evening on Karl Johan Street* and *Despair*. However, another reading is that Munch is viewing how other people see anxiety in him. The 1896 lithograph depicts the sky, a scene of Christiania fjord and houses in the background with a selection of men and women, almost confronting the viewer at the forefront of the image. Only three colours are employed in the 20 of 100 signed lithographs made and signed by Munch; red (in the sky), black (for the land and people) and the white of the paper. The collection of people is, similarly, heavily distinguished by the black except for their faces. Here we see faintness in depictions which offer the viewer a strong sense of the image's title. Of the four figures that are prominent in the foreground, eyes, nose, mouth and cheeks are slight in their marking, light sketching offering minimal detail. The eyes are set within the women's oval shaped facial expressions which contrasts with the thinner defined outlines of the men. Both sets are faintly visible within large sockets; mostly the pupils are prominent. Combined with corresponding mouths of each figure, the sense of angst is conveyed, supported by the even more angst ridden facial expressions of the persons in the mid-ground. These expressions propel the sense of gloom with the world around the subjects or in Munch himself, making anxiety the clear feature.

Symbolist aesthetics, for Bjerke, is a trend 'limited to pictures in which the content has been depicted in such as a way that the form substantiates the content' (1995: 89). Here, Munch's work is not depicting a biological or physiological mental health condition but rather the crises generated by the social world. This social world had a serious impact upon him and this is what constitutes 'mental health' in *Anxiety*; the relationship of people around him to society and also, with his own world. Today these works hold prophetic value in that admirers interpret their world as his appears. Their late modern existence is constituted of an endless array of signifiers within the information society they live in and to which they are beholden. In the expressions of the figures confronting the viewer, one question is: how are we people supposed to cope with all of this? Indicative of a shift in artistic meanings across modernity, Munch's later work occurred during a period in which late modern movements were gaining ground and contributing new interpretations of world.

The Late Modern – Popular Music, Literature and Talk Shows

In the late modern period, popular music provides a new space where meaning-making about mental health is more overtly expressed. The concept of mental illness has begun to become dislodged from a taboo subject to one commonplace in lyrics and has become a modern feature of popular music. With the development of new social movements in the early 1960s, new musical projects evolved with one band facilitating the transition from old to new ideas about a range of social issues – *Pink Floyd.*

While the old language of 'madness' prevailed in Pink Floyd's lyrics, the band's relationship to mental illness was close. Founding members of the band included Roger Waters, Nick Mason, Richard Wright and Syd Barrett, whose song-writing skills were highly original. Those who knew him made various claims that Barrett had contracted a mental illness. A strong theme of 'empathy for the human condition' drove Pink Floyd's music, and Barrett's contribution may have been more than just musical. While his behaviour was clearly erratic, his influence was profound. Two tracks of the album *The Dark Side of the Moon* referred to mental illness, and the album *Wish You Were Here* did so directly (it was originally entitled *Eclipse – A Piece for Assorted Lunatics).* Mason is credited with writing *Speak to Me*, a piece of music which merges with another called *Breathe.* In the midst of musical sounds, a heartbeat and other sounds, a roadie is heard saying: 'I've been mad for f***ing years, absolutely years, been over the edge for yonks, been working me buns off for bands', and then we hear: 'I've always been mad, I know I've been mad, like the most of us are … very hard to explain why you're mad, even if you're not mad'. Later in the album, *Brain Damage* again refers to mental illness; Barrett is said to have been a central focus of the song. This band in many ways accessed topics of the time and brought sympathetic concepts into the public sphere in an album that was to have marked impact, staying in the Billboard 200 album charts for approximately 741 weeks. Ushering in an openness to deal with social topics in accessible ways, Pink Floyd introduced a new representation to the popular consciousness, as something closer to the self.

Many bands have offered new representations and so too has literature. Late into the last century, bands like The Smiths and Madness produced an array of songs, the latter making albums like *Divine Madness*, *Complete Madness* and *Utter Madness*. Popular music forms have presented diverse meanings, offering alternative cultural values and ways of accessing concepts referencing mental health. Literature has also helped diversify meanings. Books by Solomon (2002) and Styron (1992) have helped bring the topic of depression more publicity and recognition, not only about the condition but also how it affects self-identity. A new set of contexts now exist, displacing old knowledge content with new and which also represent a forward movement in the production of new ideas and here, television talk shows have played an increasing role.

On television in both the UK and the USA, the proliferation of shows in which 'talk' refers to mental health is now considerable. In the UK, the relationship between public and private around mental health is frequently mentioned in programmes such as the BBC's *I Love Being Mad* (2006) which explores four young people overcoming their conditions. *Cracking Up* (broadcast on BBC2 in 2008) introduces former government media advisor Alistair Campbell talking about his depression while in 2006 on the same channel, *The Secret Life of the Manic Depressive* examined closely Stephen Fry's condition. In the United States, a number of shows have also addressed the topic; *Oprah* is one, while *Dr. Phil* has also attempted to examine it. In general, mental health is gaining considerable currency as a topic for broadcast talk.

Conclusion

These contexts and representations indicate a continuity and diversity of meanings about madness which, over an extensive period of time, have ossified into a conceptual complex, difficult to deconstruct. While there has been a small shift toward examining 'mental health', findings by Philo (1996) and Wahl (1995) of *violence* and *dangerousness* in popular cultural forms such as cartoons, newspapers and films are informed by this significant list of contextual 'madness' influences. Through the Bible, drama, literature and art, via axiomatic ideas about madness as synonymous with dangerousness and confinement, in a psychiatry critical of itself and being critiqued (to name but a few of the above examples), we have learned to see madness constituted as part of a category of mysterious stereotypes; as an amorphous mass of connotational and mythical significations with vague boundaries. All of these are in a mode of thinking which privileges rational thought at the expense of the irrational. Consequently, meanings about madness, commanded by these diverse influences, have become incorporated into the sediment of culture bearing little relation to the realities of mental health. Subsequently, when a story about mental health is communicated in news media or a horror film depicts madness, it is most likely to reference homicide and thus, representations of it, pulling in meanings from a knowledge reservoir of ill-informed understanding. A distorted concept is communicated for the public imagination, containing a problematic knowledge – a knowing absent of accurate information, communicating about ideas predominantly associated with dangerousness. Such questionable knowledge about mental health is evidenced in an interesting study by Denise Jodelet (1991) who investigated the way local people constructed identities of mentally ill people in a community at Ainay-le-Château, in France. The patients who lived there, in a 'family colony', had done so since 1900. Rather than being confined in an institution they lived as part of family units in the community. However, Jodelet determined that they were marginalized through the personally internalized perspectives of local people.

Jodelet reports that the population of the community welcomed those 'into its homes whom society normally hides behind walls of an asylum' (1991: 280) but only permitted 'to integrate an exogenous group without incorporating it' (ibid.). While the community gained strength from its actions and system of integration, it also felt it necessary to be a community on the defensive. Social protection may be one way of explaining the community's reaction but so too is a sense of a collectively shared defence in that the group had unified as a social body, mobilized with intent to retain its identity. Examining the manufacture of social representations and their constituents, Jodelet questions how these were 'produced and function within a delimited mental and social space' (1991: 283) as social communication as this was identified as key to the equilibrium of the collective for both well and unwell people. Jodelet went onto discover that at a number of levels the citizens of the community were fearful of contamination by the patient's mental health conditions and also fearful of dangerousness. The fear was so great that a taboo surfaced even about patients marrying non-patients. She found that:

> underlying the designation of the signs of the illness, we find a second set of constituents which refer to the values of the group and its lifestyle. Already the position of the pathological, alongside character, in the natural order, standing in contrast to the cultural order expressed by mentality and education, shows the intervention of the normative in the evaluation of morbid disease. (Jodelet 1991: 285–6)

If this was the situation in a colony whose project it was to care for people with mental health conditions, it raises questions about other discourses about madness or mental illness in society at large; for cultures who have no such concern. If, as in this collective experience, internalized schemas convened to consolidate a fear, and a fear based on a supposed infection from the 'mental', they not only marginalized the patients, they did, in effect, marginalize themselves from knowledge and understanding about mental health. This marginalization was, most likely, learnt through cultural and historical representations in archaic attitudes initiated in narratives – through Plato's philosophy and plays evolving from Homer's model. Through fixed narratives in art and from the medical profession, whose treatments were as much confused as its choice of who were 'unwell' patients, these factors contributed to public and meta-narratives informing this marginalization, through the constituting of 'mentally ill identity'. Somers and Gibson identify public narratives as:

> those narratives attached to cultural and institutional formations larger than the single individual, to intersubjective networks or institutions, however local or grand, micro or macro. … Like all narratives, these stories have drama, plot, explanation and selective appropriation. (Calhoun 1994: 62)

Metanarratives are '"master-narratives" in which we are embedded as contemporary actors in social history and as social scientists' (Somers and Gibson, in Calhoun 1994: 63). Thus, these narratives have over time come to inform not only the cultural order, as Jodelet intimates above but also, the media order: media forms playing a significant role in the continuation of these narratives.

I want now to ask questions of a more specific kind about contemporary representations – about the meanings of mental health produced and circulated by the media. What are these meanings and how have they been communicated? In answering this, I will draw in part on the historical legacy I have sketched out above. What has been its role in the construction of current portrayals and understandings? The book now moves to an examination of media genres, starting with film.

An Outline of the Case Studies

The following three chapters constitute Genre Studies 1, 2 and 3 and together comprise Phase One of a two phase project. (Phase Two, The Community Project, begins in Chapter 7 with a reception study, while Chapter 8 presents a production study.) Phase One analyses a range of communicative forms focusing upon madness, mental health and distress. Across these case studies form is defined as a 'crafted piece of communicative performance' to follow John Corner's description (Albertazzi and Cobley 2010: 35). It is an 'organisation of signs, sometimes simple, sometimes complex, sometimes seemingly spontaneous, sometimes highly considered and strategic, that constitute any specific (text or act) of media communication' (2010: 36). Commencing with an examination of horror film history, Genre Study 1 explores the way in which 'horror film' variously presents depictions of madness and then it examines three very different films depicting mental health from within different kinds of realist perspective. Chapter 5 will explore non-fiction looking at news genres and a documentary while the study in Chapter 6 will examine broadcast dramas and a comic strip.

Genre Studies: Mediation Selection, Genre and Meaning-making

Phase One counters a strong tendency in past research to focus upon negative portrayals. Its selection of mediations from between 1886 until 2009 includes texts which are either sympathetic toward mental health 'problems' in the way they depict them without stigmatizing them, or simply 'progressive' insofar as they not lend themselves to reinforcing prejudice by projecting themes of dangerousness whose final effect is to stigmatize whether intentionally or not. Enabling a wider selection for the project's cross-genre focus, the selection includes mediations from literature, film, theatre, television and radio.

Focusing upon genre as a key component, this critical analysis seeks insight into differences in mental health meaning-making across non-fictional and fictional forms. While the division is never definite, recognition of it makes for a sensible way forward because although certain principles connected with fiction apply to non-fiction too, differences in the way in which they work to position, inform and 'move' the viewer are significant. By identifying the knowledge properties stemming from each form, a more decisive analysis of mental health meaning is sought. As noted in Chapter 1, there are different levels of referentiality, modes of address, forms of propositional or more associative symbolic discourse and the presence/absence of indicators which mark the two areas into distinctive realms.

This division of genre enables Phase One to pose its main analytical question about the interactions between generic forms and the constructions of cultural meanings about people with mental health conditions more critically: how do forms depict the social life of this group through meaning-makings that produce particular relationships of power, in the process either accepting or denying social agency? By looking at form, these chapters probe how meaning-making in image, language, sound and music is selected and organized to: a) construct a mental health space; b) produce relationships about cultural realities and identities; c) address spectators; and d) provide the means for language and dramatic elements to play a role in representations. It is from these analytical positions that Phase One also seeks to produce a broad typology of mental health conditions and identities. Consequently, the framework for examining mass media texts about 'mental health' employs a critical theoretical approach with representation, realism, stereotypes, performance culture, various dramatic modes and narrative systems constituting the key analytical elements.

Chapter 4

Phase One, Genre Studies 1: Film

Film carries significance in the popular mediation of mental health because of the wide range of generic and sub-generic formats either broadly, as in horror films about madness, or, specifically, in the special examples examined below. Historically, film representation has addressed the spectator through the dominant theme of 'dangerousness' and the positioning of the stereotypical 'mad' identity. Problematic knowledge content in film has implications for the relationships which the spectator has with the topic of mental health. Specifically, the problem is the relationship between mental concepts and signifiers about mental health and/or madness which lie at the heart of 'representing'. With meanings about mental health as 'dangerousness' common across cinema and now replicated in entertainment sites like Hulu.com and Netflix.com, the opportunities for meanings to proliferate through social networking sites like Twitter and Facebook are numerous. Thus, the potential for social knowledge in the cultural form of film to misinform as well as entertain remains significant. Also, the appeal at the box office of films such as *The Silence of the Lambs* and its follow-ups clearly influence film producers and their products. The potential for film-makers to creatively organize and multiply meanings about madness increases not only in terms of the process of making new meanings but also in film's long life as an imaginative artefact. Such films will also impact significantly through what Raymond Williams called the 'dramatisation of consciousness' and maintain meanings about its topic across a potentially broad sphere of social life. Shown initially at the cinema in a public place, repeated on television (most likely) within the confines of a home and made available either for purchase or rent on video or DVD, the shelf-life of meanings about madness is lengthy.

Analytical Framework

Seeking understanding about the patterns of pleasure-meanings in fictional texts, this first genre study employs Neale's (1980) theory about genre, narrative, realism and the special component of psychoanalysis.

In the making of any film genre, its production process is ultimately social in its practices. Various personnel help make representational decisions not only about what these meanings *are* but also *how* they are communicated. 'How' meanings are communicated for our seeing, hearing and reading play a part in *what* is known from them. This leads us into understanding about the consequences of representations and how they can locate and specify cultural identity and mental health realities. Subsequently, in the analysis of meanings, the Barthesian couplet of denotation and connotation is used in conjunction with myth, a component at work in many mental health texts. This leads to the suggestive work of Stuart Hall (1997) being used throughout this chapter with regard to meanings and how the languages which produce them are augmented by dramatic communicative components. In appraising how drama plays a significant role in meaning-making as a thematic focus of the fictional form, a different analytical approach to the non-fictional is required. A key focus of this analysis is *how* such components contribute to that part of a character's existence whose conscious agency is representationally undermined (as in the horror form), hindering any ability to function. In the examination of desire and pleasure in film representations, the spectator–text relationship is explored to offer explanations about identifications the spectator has with the camera's view. The psychoanalytical method does have limitations which some analysts see as the vague nature of interpretations that emerge in theorizing about human subjectivity. However, the psychoanalytical approach is widely acknowledged as a useful tool in the study of identity for both analysts and directors of films and TV Series like *The Sopranos* (see Chapter 5), in explaining a character's condition. Linking with these elements, other theoretical work examines identity stereotypes (Sander L. Gilman and Michael Pickering) and stigma (Heatherton et al.). This analytical framework first grounds each film with a description before critical analysis of its meaning-making as a practice illuminates the social character of its representation.

Film Mediations of Madness, Distress and Mental Health

The last chapter argued that social contexts and cultural representations across a broad historical sweep left a diversity of negative meanings about madness culturally available. Small surprise, then, that in the contemporary moment mainstream cinema represents *mental illness*[1] mostly within the indistinct category

1 Throughout this chapter, the term 'mental illness' can variably mean 'transitory episodes of anxiety or depression (i.e., neuroses) which interfere with normal daily living through mood changes involved' or, 'psychoses which may require in-patient psychiatric treatment to control the severe changes in mood and behaviour associated with them', (Jary and Jary 1991: 391), these purposefully constructed as real-life behaviours for the public imagination.

of *madness*,[2] meaning-making processes referencing it to realisms[3] of *violence* and *dangerousness*. Selected knowledge content and film form combine according naturalness to themes portraying the world of the 'mentally ill' as constituted of the criminal and the mysterious, these depictions arranging pejorative systems of knowledge and beliefs. Otto Wahl (1995: 56–86) offers an informative account identifying an array of mis-selected knowledge content in media 'madness' forms across history. Also recognized are the few films which explore 'mental illness' but relate to murder, such as *Silence of the Lambs* (1991) and *Sleeping with the Enemy* (1990). Even more rare are those which specifically identify and explore it sympathetically: Wahl cites *Gaslight* (1944), *Miracle on 34th Street* (1947), *The Three Faces of Eve* (1957), *One Flew Over The Cuckoo's Nest* (1975), *Rain Man* (1988), *Angel At My Table* (1990) and *The Fisher King* (1991).

In contrast to mainstream cinematic form, the two films *Angel Baby* (1995) and *Family Life* (1971) resist dominant representational treatment; their form and content explores the topic of mental illness but avoids stereotypes. *Angel Baby*, a drama-romance genre, tells a story about the loving relationship between two people suffering from schizophrenia and their eventful social circumstances. *Family Life*, a conventional drama, is a probing examination of a young woman's experience of mental health difficulties. These films represent a rare sample exploring mental illness, making them worthy of analysis. Examining characterizations, narrative and dramatic discourses as constituent elements of generic form, this chapter first investigates the qualities which put *Rain Man* in mainstream cinema and then *Angel Baby* and *Family Life*, looking at how their representations reside outside dominant cinema form. Exploring the three films, this chapter analyses the different types of mental illness meaning-making produced, making (where needed) appropriate comparisons with those of madness. In seeking these comparisons, this chapter first explores a brief developmental history of meaning-making about 'madness' in

2 In this chapter, 'madness' means nebulous behaviour(s) with vague connections to mental illness about which producers of a media artefact organise significations, portraying it as a disruption of 'normal' behaviour from usual social functions within a person. These lead to new, strange, unpredictable and even violent actions purposefully constructed as *more than* real-life behaviours for the public imagination. Therefore, part of the work of this chapter is to alert the reader to the above distinctions, an intention of the following analyses being to reveal mediation differences.

3 The term realism, as Corner (1992) shows in his discussion about its use in television studies, accrues much in the way of confusion and demands an exposition. In this chapter, I employ a useful distinction he makes in order to maintain clarity of explanation in depictions: that of thematic realisms, which, in this context refers to the 'normative plausibility of characterisation, circumstance and action (*i.e., the relationship of what a film about mental illness or madness is to reality*) as well as being shaped within particular national and political pressures towards such categories as the "socially ordinary", or the "socially problematic"' (1992: 100, my italics); and formal realisms, 'conventions of staging, directing, acting, shooting and editing' (ibid.), i.e., the way a real-seemingness about the look of the world of mental illness or madness is represented.

film and the ways in which it has evolved, necessarily giving significant emphasis to the horror genre.

Several authors, notably Ross (1972), Tudor (1974), Derry (1977), Wood (1979), Cook (1985), McCarty (1993) and Wahl (1995), explore the origins of the horror genre and its development. This chapter examines broadly the development of generic elements, discursive features and also a range of theoretical paradigms in order to provide a set of foci from which to examine selected films.

From Literature to German Expressionist Film: Transformations in Meaning-makings about Mad Characters

Prior to the eighteenth century, tales of horror in fairy tale literature focused upon meanings of evil located within mythical animals or monsters; these ideas developed from Greek mythology (see Chapter 2). McCarty (1993) points out that in these stories animals usually preyed upon humans, generating notions of fear and dread. Stevenson (1886) broke with this convention, this literature merging monster-with-man. In the character of Dr Jekyll, an intelligent man who realizes there is a dark side to his nature, creates a potion to purge what he views as his own internalized poison. Consuming this intended remedy he accidentally constructs a character with two identities, his other identity (Mr Hyde) being a killer. This new character convention, acclaimed by readers, was noted by an actor-manager in America, Richard Mansfield, who 'saw in the dual roles of Jekyll and Hyde the acting challenge of his career' (McCarty 1993: 14). Playwright Thomas Sullivan adapted Stevenson's book and a theatre production of the story opened in Boston in 1887 and attracted large audiences, as it did in London in 1888. Unlike the book, where Dr Jekyll's transformation to Hyde is revealed at the end, in the stage production metamorphosis was the play's focus. Thus, mythical meanings established and maintained in literature were dramatized for theatre with Mansfield creatively organizing a new credible character for audience imagination. Medicine proved a useful site for media to take problematic themes about humanity and make stereotypical[4] identities; forms of social exorcism which Sander L. Gilman (1988) sees as part of myth-making made necessary by a human need to control the world. In this new entertainment form, audience

4 By 'stereotypical' here I mean that characterization of an identity which, as Michael Pickering puts it, are 'characterisations of others, and as a general process, stereotyping is a unilinear mode of representing them. While they occur in all sorts of discourse, and can draw on various ideological assumptions, stereotypes operate as a means of evaluatively placing, and attempting to fix in place, other people or cultures from a particular and privileged perspective' (2001: 47). In this sense, the mad doctor becomes a figure into which all negative fears and things that could be constructed about a doctor are assumed as part of a group's worst foreboding in a fictional character, so as to have these fears to expelled in the dénouement of a mainstream narrative.

could still recognize aspects of itself in a developing society, these *more than* real life behaviours here perhaps a wider reflection about the negative side of human nature.

Silent film nurtured themes about mad characters and transformations before, during and after World War I. Peter Byrne (1998) identifies several films popular with spectators; some were variations on 'the chase movie' but which framed characters resembling a 'lunatic on the loose' pursuing people. These included *The Escapees from Cherenton* (1901) by Georges Méliès who also made *Off to Bloomingdale Asylum* in America and, in the UK, *Off to Bedlam*. In 1908, *Where the Breakers Roar* by D.W. Griffiths produced a mad character escaped from an asylum which, Byrne notes, linked lunacy and dangerousness together. Similar Griffiths films included *Money Mad* (1908), *The Maniac Cook* (1909) and *The Cord of Life* (1909) again linking lunacy and dangerousness. Byrne sees a brief respite in demonic views of mental illness but excludes the Jekyll and Hyde films which touched upon madness-as-mental-illness. In 1913, *Dr Jekyll and Mr Hyde* with King Baggot playing both roles was one of seven thematic adaptations between 1908 and 1920 (see McCarty 1993: 16). Films like *Trilby* (1915, directed by Maurice Tourneur) and *Der Januskopf* (1920, directed by F.W. Murnau) were versions of the Jekyll narrative also helping to make violent themes. John S. Robertson's *Dr Jekyll and Mr Hyde* (1920) consolidated the transforming dual-personality through John Barrymore's critically acclaimed dramatic performance, but it was *The Cabinet of Dr Caligari* (1919–20, directed by Robert Wiene) that developed the mad doctor stereotype. Employing techniques from German Expressionism, this film exposes an identity whose high scientific intelligence, combined with subconscious instinctual base behaviours, constitute him as a classic version of the 'crazed killer'. A development from this film was *Dr Mabuse, The Gambler* (1922), directed by Fritz Lang.

Dr Mabuse The Gambler – Consolidating Madness Through 'The Look'

In *Mabuse*, Lang further constructed the enigma of the dual-personality character theme, developing it through formal image components in the 'look' of madness. Aided by German expressionism and using dramatic codes in facial expressions, Lang employed 'point of view' camera shots portraying a subjective new mad world – an inner mind state that was corrupt and perverse. In the story, Mabuse arranges a stock market collapse and then, a boom, making an immense profit. Moving to extract fortunes from unsuspecting gamblers through use of his psychoanalytical powers, Mabuse's use of disguises are exceptional; privileged through careful camera treatment of facial expressiveness. Fertile significations in 'looks' of madness and visual formal conventions generated a multiplicity of themes about subjectivity, the 'point of view' frame referencing odd realities about the internal world of mad characters.

Focusing on subjectivity while also discussing narration, Edward Branigan explores 'how depictions of character subjectivity in film narrative may be related to the spectator's perception of the material on the screen' (1992: 142) and this is key to understanding portrayals of characters, in horror images for the public imagination.

> the point of view shot actually *limits* what the spectator can easily know about the character. Though a POV shot may appear simple and straight-forward in comparison with 'objective' narration, it actually requires the spectator to hold together a great number of assumptions – corresponding to the descriptive assumptions of *all* of the levels of narration above it – and hence is more restrictive than higher-level narrations. For example, the specific *angle* of view on the object is normally irrelevant to our comprehension of the object in space – any one of several angles would suffice in nonfocalized narration. However, in a POV shot the specific angle of view is importantly tied to the attention and awareness of a specific character and thus the angle must be captured and held in the working memory by the spectator. (Branigan 1992: 157)

Point of view shots of Mabuse, his angle of view, and unfolding content in his relationships with characters invoked a socially problematic persona with a potent, mysterious power. As he plays with human fates at a series of fraudulent events, deceptions are caught in the framing of his face. On one occasion in a special box at a theatre, views of him are carefully arranged as he hypnotizes Edgar Hull, the unsuspecting son of a rich industrialist. In the theatre, Mabuse sits opposite Hull in a theatre box looking at him through binoculars, a darkened area around its double eyepiece revealing this view for spectators; this viewing field again reduced by a singular circular opening of Hull's image. As a dancing performance including bizarre expressionistic figures concludes, applause begins, and with it Mabuse's hypnotic gaze falls upon Hull. From an angle of view almost straight-on to Mabuse his eyes hold a cold stare. One close-up frame capturing in his subjectivity an intense expression of concentration followed by another image revealing Hull suddenly stopping his clapping; suggesting for spectators through POV shot that the hypnotism is making its pejorative impact. Another image of Mabuse's stare only serves to compound ideas about his controlling power as Hull feels overcome and leaves the special box to meet with Mabuse. His hypnosis induces Hull to go to 'The Incognito Club' where gambling takes place and Mabuse swindles him. Thus, via the POV shot, visual coding and dramatic actions, Mabuse's 'looks of madness' communicated a consistent behaviour, an identity typed with evil intent and a focused ambition. Soured with connotational qualities of criminally transgressive behaviours, his mental state is simultaneously seen as impoverished while generating mythologies about madness (by displacing the category of mental illness). The formal and thematic attributes of Lang's madness realisms were the very basis for which his reputation was to endure; in particular, with remakes like

Testament of Dr Mabuse (1932) and *The 1,000 Eyes of Dr Mabuse* (1960), both directed by Lang.

Universal Studios: Iconizing the Mad Character

Despite the end of the expressionist movement in the late 1920s, character qualities like those in Mabuse and Caligari evolved in Universal's gothic horrors like *Dracula* (1931, directed by Tod Browning) and *Frankenstein* (1931, directed by James Whale). This period saw the introduction of sound in 1927, which combined with imagery to create new aesthetic qualities. 'Looks' of madness were soon to be supplemented by language and new special effects. Carl Laemmle Jr produced films which stemmed from literature – Bram Stoker's *Dracula* and Mary W. Shelley's *Frankenstein*. In *Frankenstein*, Whale employed make-up artist Jack Pierce whose facial creation of Frankenstein proved very effective. Lugosi's portrayal of Dracula on a staircase in front of a massive spider's web proved so convincing that, with his white face and broken English accent, the performance proved an economic saviour for Universal Studios. Repetitions and variations of these films and their concepts of madness were remade with sequels by other producers but Universal's most successful development was *The Bride of Frankenstein*, significant for its dramatic sparking images and noisy machinery. If previously the 'look of madness' communicated most strongly in the face, then new conventions were about to rivet terror more comprehensively in the non-human image. A set of conventions stabilized in horror form which Murphy catalogues as follows:

> men turn into werewolves only but always on nights of the full moon; vampires always dislike garlic, cast no reflection in mirrors, and can be destroyed only by having their hearts pierced with a wooden stake; and it is the nature of Frankenstein's monster that he can never be destroyed. (Murphy 1972: 34)

The nature of the mad subjectivity born into film had evolved into a new stereotypical value. This time the previously identifiable human being had once more transformed into the permanent physical distortion of one. Emerging from history, a stereotype of man transforming into something animalistic and mad, or an already beast-like mad being, became an even greater site of denial because, as a mythological element, it was able to produce barriers. As Michael Pickering has put it, 'stereotypes operate through myths because both involve the combined repression of politics and history' (2001: 48) thus perpetuating exclusion and consequently denying understanding.

1950s Science Fiction and Monster Madness

Like Universal needing financial success during the 1930s, economic problems for Hammer Productions in the UK across the 1950s demanded it investigate new ways of film making. Once more, the confluence of science with madness proved a highly successful cultural formula, leading not only to science fiction films but also monster movies. Evolving from early horror film, the development of narrative had maintained similarities with classic narrative structure in terms of equilibrium but also made contrasts in character and enigma: these elements were to prove significant attributes for the new form.

Neale's Horror Narrative: Enigma and Character

Stephen Neale (1980) argues that horror narrative produces contrasts in character and enigma with a classic narrative structure. In classic narrative structures, enigma is a 'problem' defined around a story which requires resolution. Clearly, early horror form confirmed the central character *as* the enigma/problem. Caligari, recognizable by his human characteristics, was mysterious in possessing invisible monster or monstrous qualities. But in science-fiction form, a new main character appeared, signalling a departure from previous forms: these were introduced creatures with visible protean qualities. In the very popular film *The Quatermass Xperiment* (1955), a fungus returned from space with the last remaining member of a three man space crew: other shape changing creatures were to follow.

For Neale, horror narrative follows a version of classic narrative structure. Disturbed by a character like a vampire or a werewolf, the condition of ordered and/or disordered elements making narrative equilibrium is agitated by disrupting relationships of coherence across time and space. Enacting savage and murderous actions upon the civilized human order, the enigma breaks the rules of the social world with the unthinkable seen and the unbelievable happening. Thus, science fiction characters and monsters contributed to a disequilibrium reigning across the horror narrative, problematized significations requiring resolution and restructuring that are *only* possible by a gifted agent with ownership of special character powers. Developing story in a logical way, the agent's motivations accomplish restoration returning a sense of normality and resolution through appeasement and/or removal of the monster/enigma. In the end mythical aspects are solved, the violence removed, and a normal psychological profile restored to the world. But in this narrative structure, as with other forms that preceded it, spectator expectation and feeling for it would eventually tire, the institution of film needing yet another new stimulus to keep its spectator. Neale explains that:

> genres institutionalise, guarantee coherence by institutionalising conventions, i.e. sets of expectations with respect to narrative process and narrative closure which may be subject to variation, but which are never exceeded or broken. The existence of genres means that the spectator, precisely, will always know

> that everything will be 'made right in the end', that everything will cohere, that any threat or any danger in the narrative process itself will always be contained. (Neale 1980: 28)

The pleasures of this closure can give way to staleness over time. While resembling classic narrative, the horror narrative of the 1950s enjoyed a high degree of closure but with spectators wearying of its narrative predictability, new forms were sought.

From *Psycho* to the Contemporary

Psycho (1960), directed by Alfred Hitchcock (and assisted by Saul Bass), was significant in meaning-making about madness through its new character stereotype. Anthony Perkins, playing the part of Norman Bates, substituted the scientist and doctor for the psychotic, inaugurating frightening new paradigms of violence and danger. Derry (1977) and Neale (1980) also identify *Psycho* as a critical moment for the horror genre.

The 'Not Quite Right' Personality

Derry's insights into the new character indicate that it is the meanings of the monster and the monstrous which pose problems and offers a psychological explanation; that normality is key to argument about character. The horror of personality is something 'not quite right' in the human being where common-sense perceptions of what is 'normal' in everyday experience is contrasted with what is not. The characterization of Norman Bates as a 'not quite right' personality is achieved through his portrayal as a motel manager, enacting a socially ordinary occupation which contrasts with another side to his personality, as one who dresses as his mother and then kills. The nature of the killing is the worst imaginable, that of a woman murdered in the most brutal way, by a character whose dark outline is all what we see and which is viewed mostly from a voyeuristic, and sometimes the victim's, point of view. Neale in his examination of horror offers an alternative theoretical view with particular reference to the elements of narrative and fetishism.

Narrative and Fetishism Genres are components of the machine within which 'orders of regularity' (1980: 18) underpin practices. These 'orders' are instruments for regulating while regularity is resident in different genres and also operates in different spheres of practice. Particular genres are primarily regulated by specific elements such as narrative and fetishism. Exploring narrative, Neale considers that:

> the violence and the sexual ambiguity of the monster, whether gothic creature or deranged psychotic, the hovering of the horror film around the abnormal and taboo, far from representing a release of the repressed and a challenge to the

> patriarchal status quo, simply offers a fetishistic feast in acknowledgement and perpetuation of the perversity on which patriarchy is founded, the simultaneous fascination with and the disavowal of female sexuality: 'The horror film is concerned … not only with curiosity, knowledge and belief, but also, and crucially, with their transgressive and "forbidden" forms.' From this, he argues, arises the dominance of religious, or religio-scientific forms of explanation within the horror film and of critical accounts of the genre 'rooted in mysticism and other forms of irrationalism'. (Cook 1985: 104)

Psycho proved distinctive in many ways – not least because its closing revelations revealed a man at times thinking he was his dead mother. In contrast to many previous films, this aspect of sexual difference was an elaborate and complex development made all too puzzling and vague through the appearance of the monster in the famous shower scene. However, this fetishistic substitute while playing a significant part in theory about horror film at the level of sexuality becomes more complex when it also represents a fearful Other with significant relationships to mental health.

In *Psycho*, the figure of Bates offers a sense of mental diseased-ness in his identity. Rather than being a momentary release of the sexually repressed, at the level of psychology, Bates cues anxious and fearful reflection in the spectator subject. Through film, portraying a mad Other in the external world, albeit fictional, tensions are raised in the relationship with the internalized self which culminate in the need for further control and repression. All that is offered at the level of mental health is anxiety about dangerousness in 'the self' when fully represented. Thus the question is raised, 'Are we sane or are we not?' The film raised psychic structures of anxiety and fear, which, like fetishism, leads to powerful pressures mobilizing stereotypical Others.

Anxiety Characters and Narrative Fear

Gilman proposes that art, whatever form it takes, is 'an icon of our control of the flux of reality' (1988: 2). Thus *Psycho*, as an art form, is a controlled opportunity for pleasures in a fictional reality but, unlike previous horrors, it is located in a geographically and temporally immediate frame. In its character and narrative it offers a sense of carnival through experiences in a controlled 'loss of control'; an orderly and safe sense of disorder, which, by the film's dénouement returns safely to a sense of social order. 'Diseased' meanings about a mad Other are propelled in the film, these external images of disorder, momentarily tantalizing not only as elements of danger but also potentially threatening to internalized feelings of security about the self. In *every* human psychology, deep structures of stereotypes reside about things we fear or glorify. Where anxiety and fear reign, a potentially destabilizing effect to our sense of self-security demands *self*-protection from dangerous fears.

According to Kernberg, during the early moments of human development, the world is just an extension of the self, where 'The organization of intrapsychic reality [is constituted] in terms of love and hate' (Kernberg 1984: 237). Humankind is both anchored to and driven by these two constituents. Initially, a sense of security is seen as coming from the world in the shape of love, warmth and food and is felt as an extension of the self, security and expectation. Soon, however, difference with the world is produced in the child as s/he becomes more accomplished in distinguishing between 'self' and 'world' and during early stages of development a sense of identity begins to take place through 'difference' determined through experiences of the child with the world. Also, at this time, anxiety about perceived loss of control of the world is raised through adjustment of the child's mental picture of people and objects in it. Combating this anxiety evolves through defeat in dealing with conflicts in the child's world via attempts to make adjustments through replacing a mental picture of objects and people; so they appear good even if they are perceived as bad. Through this mode, the child's sense of self is styled even more to accommodate this way of being but across time it eventually splits between a good and bad 'self'; this single splitting stage is the root and route from which all stereotypical associations will eventuate.

At the beginning of the split, the good part of the 'self' is in complete control of its world and is free from anxiety. The '"bad" self however, is unable to control the environment and is thus exposed to anxieties' (Kernberg 1984: 17). As a child matures, not only do its increasingly sophisticated and complex perceptions of the world but also, the abilities to differentiate between goodness and badness,

> so that by the later oedipal stage an illusion of verisimilitude is cast over the inherent (and irrational) distinction between the 'good' and 'bad' world and self, between control and loss of control, between acquiescence and denial. (Kernberg 1984: 17)

As further development takes place, so too does structuring about stereotypes as the self continues to seek a sense of security and order or, as Mary Douglas puts it, 'a yearning for rigidity' (1966). The continuation of further splitting of 'self' and 'world' into good and bad 'objects' results in the bad self becoming further located and distanced along with mental representations of bad objects (see Jacobson 1964 for a more in-depth explanation); this an act of projection allowing the avoidance of confrontation with internal and uncomfortable contradictions in a sense of self desiring processes of integration between its parts. In this way, our sense of our 'self' and 'world' becomes constructed upon illusions about our self and the world. Divided into two camps of 'us' and 'them', these elements can only be either good or bad and as further human development occurs, the complexity of illusion becomes even more intricate. Within ever deepening structures of self the potential for anxiety about the 'them' is still linked to a sense of illusory integration but the still very real separation is all but lost to recognition due to layers of structures developed in the self across time. In Gilman's view, the adult's sense of order is held like the structure of order which comes before the earliest stage of individuation. It is:

> an unconscious sense of symbiosis with the world, a world under the control of the self. Anxiety arises as much through any alteration of the sense of order (real or imagined) between the self and the Other (real or imagined) as through the strains of regulating repressed drives. (Gilman 1985: 19)

With regard to madness or mental illness and adult development, there is an unconscious and inherent need to maintain a unified and coherent sense of self and identity. When viewing a horror film yields uncomfortable meaning about madness, however real or imaginary, it does so to an individual's self and through his/her own internalized representational filter, with that meaning 'infected' from its own societal context. Of significance here is that disease is a seemingly random element in an indeterminable world from which we want to distance ourselves. Where madness-as-mental illness is concerned this is particularly pertinent: 'For illness is a real loss of control that results in our becoming the Other whom we have feared, whom we have projected on the world' (Gilman 1988: 3). In the psychological thriller form, the control of an 'uncontrolled reality', albeit a fictional one, poses the problem of madness-as-mental-illness for the spectator subject. Diseased representations of madness are deeply disturbing to the self, even in a fictional reality. As Mary Douglas wrote, the 'idea of society is a powerful image' (1966: 115) and in it, there are all powerful symbolic boundaries which maintain social inclusion, and by implication, exclusion through its ordering. Disorder can spoil the image of society and the disordered such as the 'mad' can be threatening. The idea of a loss of control culminating in a serious and extended sickness raises anxiety and governed by a self-imposed imaginary line of the self, illusions about the world may occur. Where fear of the mad Other threatens, this imaginary line, as something always active, moves with the 'shifting relationship of antithetical stereotypes that parallel the existence of "bad" and "good" representations of self and Other' (1966: 18). With fear of a mad Other threatening the division, the psyche is put under stress, internalized processes causing tensions in relationships between the self's internal world and its connection with external social realities. Whether what is at issue are real or imagined diseases, the level of tension is upped during a scene of violence, inducing a danger to the maintenance of the line and also, to unity and coherence of self. In order to protect the self, the stereotypical Other comes into service.

The Shower Scene in Psycho*:* *How We See in Madness What We Know as Mental Illness*

As structures of self develop, ever resident stereotypes become layered over by other experiences constantly calling into question our 'self', continuously mobilizing a need for a sense of difference. Whenever threatened, the bad object mobilizes the Other, commencing a process of self-protection through a sense of *difference*, resulting in the creation of a stereotype. From the first dominant angled image overlooking the naked woman enjoying her shower, it is this monster and what we know in its madness signifiers that are important. Neale proposes that in mainstream cinema, the drives of fetishism and scopophilia[5] are complemented by another, that of epistemophilia – 'the desire to know, to find out' (1980: 42) and this too, as a central element of narrative carries implications for knowledge and belief. Some versions of the thriller, Neale argues, are prominent because of their overt and 'insistent hermeneutic structure: the restoration of narrative equilibrium is conditional upon the establishment of a knowledge as to the cause or causes of the event initiating the narrative in the first place – a murder' (ibid.). *Psycho*, in making conspicuous the disappearance of people near the Bates Motel, invokes a narrative process investigating their absence; with its title and genre form raising expectations about the potential demise of the missing. The film spectator constantly assesses significations for solutions to the mystery seeking an answer, eventually supplied to the original enigma. While the drives of fetishism and scopophilia are at work, that of epistemophilia similarly operates like the structure of fetishism; in desire and denial to know about madness signifiers. Neale argues:

> This is no accident: disavowal and the desire to know are displaced in order to preserve the fissure supporting/necessitating the fetish. Indeed it might be argued that fetishism itself is the product of the articulation of both these instances together, that it is a structure founded upon the modalities of the epistemophilic drive: the desire to know *and* disavowal, together, articulate a desire to know something else, a substitute for what in fact is at stake. The process of finding out is thus represented in relation to that which one wishes to avoid knowing. (Neale 1980: 42)

Thus, as the curtain obscures the monster's entrance to the shower room and its human body is only apparent as a dark outline, we see a view of madness through the form of an ambiguous, out of control personality, minded toward violence but through a code of darkness performing a function in that it

> not only signifies concealment, invoking an unknown and unseen presence within it (thereby simultaneously invoking the desire to know and the desire to see); it is also a figure of absence and lack. Darkness is the edge between presence (that which it conceals) and absence (that which is), and its ambiguity in this respect is reflected in its status *vis-à-vis* the cinematic signifier on the one hand and the diegesis on the other. (Neale 1980: 43)

5 For Stephen Neale, this term means 'a drive which has the look as its object of desire' (1985: 33).

As the curtain is wrenched across and the monster's body is lit revealing only a human form through a dark outline, imagery presents not just a non-gendered human being but an absent mentality in the dark void; functioning as a vacuum for the generation of mythical meanings, making strong links between madness-as-mental illness. Shot from several angles, one from over and behind the bath, the figure is privileged with an imposing dominance. Another from the victim's point of view includes imagery of a slashing knife cutting diagonally across the screen, this combined with repetitive shrieking sounds and knife-entering-body effects producing not only a singular moment of horror but also the exit of the monster's physicality as a signifier of madness. Thus, this formal dark void becomes a vacuum, generating meanings of a sick and enigmatic subjectivity connective with mental illness. In its new visual-aural codes and character conventions, *Psycho* organized 'regimes of credibility' (Neale 1980: 37) organized through its own pathological themes about madness-as-mental illness. As a consequence, this and later scenes support notions about madness-as-mental illness being synonymous with violence and danger.

Where pathology is concerned, meaning about mental illness is all powerful because it directly confronts the self and identity with its own potential loss of control. As Gilman relates, it raises the frightening (also thrilling) possibility of a 'loss of control over the self, and loss of control is associated with loss of language and thought perhaps even more than with physical illness' (Gilman 1985: 23). The antithesis of this is order and control of the self and so, coming to know pathological meanings through seeing the dark unknown character performing sudden violent actions and the ambiguity about the character's mentality triggers anxieties. In order to save the illusion of control over the self and world in which it exists, myths and stereotypes occur. Self-esteem is linked to images of the self which, in their own society, need status and meaning for the individual, and also models of control over the self are linked to structures of society, the maintenance of self are a pre-requisite for the individual self and the values about a topic will constantly be resonating with meanings in the social world. Subsequently, denial and disavowal preside. The horror in the image of madness coupled with social meanings of mental illness in society, perhaps as seen via media depictions, also produce stigma. In a conflict between perceiver or target position, the maintenance of the self always opts for the perceiver position and the giver, rather than the receiver of stigma.

Madness as Mental Illness: Simply a Split Personality Again?

Withheld until nearly the last scene, the identity of the killer is revealed as Bates who thinks he is his mother. There follows a scientific (and banally funny) explanation by a psychiatrist – a preliminary lesson in mental health conditions. Hitchcock's exposition of madness is a 'split-personality', the physical duality of Jekyll and Hyde traded for the abstract form of an abnormal psychology. Occurring during childhood, the seeds of Bates' internal disturbance, alluded to during an earlier conversation with his victim Janet Leigh, are fully displayed through the camera's slow and objectifying zoom out. The visualization of Bates, the man, conflicts with a dominant and domineering voice of his mother, language and image colliding in a gender/health disparity. A man who looks like any other but is internally possessed by his mother, this person appearing to perform normal everyday actions is actually responsible for many murders. Yet again, the transformation had taken place, though this time it was made invisible to the spectator, in a new and different way. That a 'change' had taken place, could take place without being seen culminating in such terrifying outcomes promoted a symbolic fear about the potentially problematic mental health of humans. This knowledge effect about duality in the human mind and its causes is a scary event made all the more fearful by Bates in this last scene. Omnipresent in his cell, the mother's bitter voice finally resonates, 'why, she wouldn't hurt a fly' with an unexpected frightening expression of Bates' piercing eyes radiating out from his dipped forlorn figure. Complemented by a casually growing smile, this image mixes with a brief nearly indistinguishable fade to the mother's rotting head, her teeth superimposed over his mouth seeping through. This 'look of madness' and final fade to the car being dragged from the marsh, marks a connotative signification, a turning point for the horror film. Madness, rather than being a separate element as in many previous films, is here fused with a specified mental illness making them both one and the same component. Derry concluded that films like *Psycho* and *Diabolique* (1955) were raising concerns and questions about: 'Who, then, are the true crazy people? Or are we all?' (1977: 21). *Psycho* because of its radical generic conventions denied usual narrative closure, instead leaving questions unanswered about the psychological, about personality and what it contains.

Evidence of this stereotype can be found within *The Silence of the Lambs* (1991) and subsequent follow-ups. Portraying a madman and also, a psychiatric expert, Lecter advises from his prison cell on how to catch other 'mad persons' at large in society committing horrific acts on women. Lecter's personality is very close to that of the everyday person; another exposition of normality, but with a few quirky facial expressions to cue the potential for the deviant and the monstrous.

Mediating Distress and Mental Health: *Rain Man*, *Family Life* and *Angel Baby*

In mainstream cinema, informative portrayals of mental illness such as *Rain Man* are rare and films like *Angel Baby* and *Family Life*, that contrast with mainstream representations, even more so. Their form and knowledge content in exploring mental distress are distinctive in narrative, character(s) and dramatic discourses, distinguishing them within a very small group of films. *Angel Baby*, a drama-romance genre written and directed by Michael Rymer and produced by Timothy White and Jonathan Shteinman, won seven Australian Film Awards including

'Best Picture'. *In Two Minds*, a television play (1967) written by David Mercer, provided the basis for *Family Life*, a conventional drama, produced by Tony Garnett and directed by Ken Loach. EMI/Kestrel shot the film in Technicolor. The intention of the analysis which follows is to illuminate representational components not only concerning the distinctiveness of *Rain Man* but to emphasize further the significance of *Angel Baby* and *Family Life* as mental health portrayals: Examining each portrayal, a brief description is offered before moving to an analysis. *Rain Man*, written by Barry Morrow and directed by Barry Levinson as a melodramatic comedy was based upon the life of the late Kim Peek, and is considered first. This film won four Academy awards (including Best Picture) and presents some interesting differences with classic narrative structure.

Rain Man *(1988): Description*

In the film, Tom Cruise, who plays Charley Babbitt and Dustin Hoffman, Raymond Babbitt, are brothers brought together after years of separation through their father's death. Both were together when very young but have never met or communicated since then. The story tells of their encounter and is dedicated to the events of their meeting. Raymond has autism and Charley is a luxury sports car salesman which leads to a story, sometimes fraught with moments of tension and poignancy, as a lost brother's relationship is discovered. The drama which follows between the two takes place within what is largely a form of road-movie genre.

1. Nearing completion of a major sale of sports cars, Charley and his girlfriend depart for a holiday but news of his father's death interrupts their vacation. Charley has to visit the family attorney to find out about the settlement of his inheritance.
2. Discovering he is not to receive a $3 million fortune from the family but instead just an old sports car and some roses, Charley, tries to ascertain, unsuccessfully, from the attorney who is the trustee of a brother he never knew. Instead, after some of his own research work, he discovers his brother is in a mental institution.
3. Eventually, after difficulty in getting to meet Raymond, Charley is reunited with him but decides it is in his interests to abduct him so he can share, as his guardian, in the trustee money. The story takes the brothers across America where Charley learns of Raymond's special attributes, as well as his frailties.
4. Across the period of the journey, unfolding events mean significant developments that change the nature of their relationship. Charley's yuppie morals alter, leading to a realization that money isn't everything but his brother and the new understanding they have in a 'relationship' is far more important.

Analysis: Melodramatic Comedy Form: Examinations of Brotherly Tensions and Humorous Rituals In *Rain Man*, melodramatic comedy form is structured around the examination of interactions between two brothers which generate relationship tensions and humorous rituals originating from the character of Raymond. The stimulus for these tensions and rituals emanate from the character of Charley as he struggles to resolve his financial problems. In the drama of the unfolding brotherly relationship, Raymond is seen as 'the threatened party' subjected to the greed of his brother; his actions are seen as synonymous with a money-making world and the spectator is led to take up a moral position. From this moment, the interactions across the remainder of the film give rise to dramatic tensions. Knowledge content is arranged to present Raymond's condition as a key focus in the film but in a dialectical tension with his brother's financial escapade – a dialectic that gives rise to the development of their relationship.

The Character of Raymond Babbitt and the Language of Autism In the narrative, Raymond's character contrasts with classic structures in similar ways to that found in the horror form. In classic narrative, the enigma is located in the narrative system but in the horror form, it is often located more narrowly within the character. So too in *Rain Man*, Raymond's character is enigmatic, his mental health condition facilitating mystical idiot and magical savant, intellectual abilities. In so far as his agency is concerned, he is gifted in one sense while socially restricted; he can only do certain things which fit into a scheduled and fixed routine. His special attributes are displayed mostly through his use of language.

Language is utilized as a significant tool in portraying a special mental health identity, dramatic qualities achieved through 'vocalizations' (Elam 1980: 79) helping differentiate Raymond's everyday social use of American English; as his life is ruled by rituals and routines, securing his world from the dangers he perceives outside it. Practising recitations of facts and figures is important to him, this language particular to his condition. Taking generic structures from news and sport media, his own speech genre is one employed to bar anxiety or anxiety attacks that might take hold. For the spectator, this is at first a confusing but later humorous discursive practice. However, it is these vocalizations that indicate a 'mental illness' as closer to notions of helplessness and different from dangerousness, thus demanding sympathy and understanding. '*Who's on first base?*' is a line taken from the comedy show *Abbot and Costello* and is employed when rituals and routines are likely to be fundamentally undermined. Levinson, in researching the condition, determined that such a line would be like a mantra to cover up an autistic person's anxiety. Other 'vocal qualities' (Elam 1980: 79) include a consistent monotone pitch of voice, except when feeling threatened. When an anxious high pitched 'vocal segregate' (ibid.) of 'Oh!' followed by a lower 'Oh!' to make, 'Oh, Oh!', signifies he thinks he has done something wrong. These vocal features help to convey a character with vulnerabilities and who exists within an enclosed world of insecurity but who clearly has qualities of high intelligence but with restricted social ability. Other vocal indices reveal that when made to do something he doesn't want to do, hollerings of derision are very loud, as when a visit to the airport to catch a plane to Los Angeles sends Raymond into a high state of anxiety. Raymond will only fly Qantas because of their safety record, forcing Charley to switch plans and use the trusted Buick. Thus, we see mental health represented not only in sympathetic ways but also cognitive ones allowing the viewer potentials for learning about conditions free of stigma. Information is forefronted and dramatic situations usefully made humorous.

A 'Moving' Narrative When Charley drives the Buick across America, he appears as the motivating force of narrative as he seeks to strike a legal deal. However, as much as he appears to move his project forward, his brother's needs pull him in other directions, actually taking control of him. The outcome is in interactional tensions, mostly for Charley, as Raymond's care and needs continually surface. The final outcome of these narrative tensions is the development of a relationship between the brothers and a commitment to its continuation.

The film's narrative serves to develop Raymond's abilities in an orderly exposition of meanings that compound steadily, increasing illumination about his mental state and unique qualities. Events present his special abilities, first of all, in a diner, at breakfast when waitress Sally Dibbs (identifiable by her name badge) arrives to take an order. Raymond automatically recites her telephone number '461 0152' from a phone book he previously read. Then, an event in a mid-west psychologist's office further emphasizes his abilities. Raymond's condition is examined and the psychologist applies some arithmetical tests that he knows only a calculator can achieve quickly. Raymond achieves them in as quick a time and through brain work alone. This test is repeated and again with stunning, accurate results revealing incredible intelligence, seeming to construct the identity of Raymond as a genius. However, when asked the price of a candy bar, and then a new company car, to both questions he responds: 'About $100': the forming label of genius is dispelled but intrigue about the condition is encouraged.

Across their journey, layovers in motels allow for moments where the two brothers get to know each other better. One occasion allows for a distant childhood memory to re-surface for both, realizing that at one important moment, they shared a song and were together. Charley is significantly moved by this event and later, despite winning $85,000 at a casino in Las Vegas (through a series of Raymond's shrewd mathematical calculations), turns down $250,000 from Raymond's mental healthcare trustee. The trustee wants him to leave Raymond alone but Charley now wants custody of care, to look after him. Charley, realizing he has a new treasure in his relationship with Raymond, attempts to resolve matters so as to continue it but finally, the professional care offered is accepted and the film's dénouement sees their parting. The struggle for acquisition of money also concludes, replaced by the value of a relationship heralded as something more special that anything money might buy. Full narrative closure is denied in an ending that offers knowledge the two will meet again in a relationship set to continue, albeit at intervals but with much less sustained intimacy.

This film's specially designed humorous moments, underpinned by research, portray autism through character traits and mental attributes that supersede the intellectual ability of the average person. A vulnerable identity is exposed, augmented by the special gifts associated with the condition. Through the interactions of a brotherly relationship, *Rain Man* introduces popular culture to a condition without the negative influence of stigma. The audience is allowed to see Raymond as a person, not just a condition.

Family Life *(1971): Description*

A conventional social drama, *Family Life* depicts mental illness in a middle-class family. A development from an earlier BBC Wednesday Play, *In Two Minds* (1967), it drew 'heavily on the work of the radical psychiatrist R.D. Laing' (Petley in McKnight 1997: 32). Like other Loach films, *Family Life* was experimental and naturalistic in its approach to dramatization, its processes of re-presenting actual settings and employing method acting (where an actor attempts to 'become' the character rather being a representation of it). Thus, location and character are coded in ways that are 'natural'. The narrative focuses upon a young woman called Janice exploring a problematic relationship with her parents, Mr and Mrs Baildon, and its damaging effect on her mental well-being.

Developing around her mental health, the story examines both Janice's initial problems and her potential rehabilitation. It then follows her deterioration, attempting to promote concern about mental illness in the society and culture at the time of its making. It also tries to expose two approaches to her mental healthcare treatment; one seeking solutions to her problem via therapy while the other is dedicated to medication and containment. At the time of making *Family Life*, debate about mixing non-fictional with fictional forms was at a height, Loach's work feeding fuel to an already established fire. Following success in films like the drama documentary *Cathy Come Home* (1966), critics were concerned for viewers about the fusing of the two genres; *Cathy* had raised serious questions about housing and although *Family Life* was principally a drama both in generic design and execution, it also generated serious concerns about the 'real issue' of mental health in society.

1. Janice's need for psychological assistance is established as during the opening scene a young male doctor (Dr Donaldson) inquires about her parents. A range of flashbacks follow, a sense of her plight is related through her despair working at a clothing store and also, her removal from an underground station concourse by a concerned official. When she returns home, she is offered little understanding by her parents but medical assistance is identified. Therapeutic methods follow in group situations. Janice is viewed with patients and then individually, discussing problems and working out solutions.

2. News of Janice's pregnancy introduce other scenes depicting family tensions; and Janice is subjected to an unrelenting patronizing parental discourse. Undermined further by her parents, the stigma associated with having a child out of marriage is raised, as well as advice about having an abortion. Mr Baildon visits Dr Donaldson to discuss family relationships, talking of his wife. It is clear that his sexual relationship with his wife is unfulfilled and his daughter has always been denied development by his controlling wife.
3. Janice's boyfriend, who figures as the only consistent character (besides the doctor) caring about her welfare, discovers news of the abortion and tries to persuade her to leave home: she refuses. Locked out, they return to Mike's flat on a Vespa motor scooter. Returning the following morning Janice tries to apologize to parents but angry at their lack of response, she screams at them violently and threatens her mother with a knife. The father intervenes to restrain her before the mother again offers more blame. The parents decide that hospitalization is in Janice's best interests. Both parents visit the doctor for advice.
4. Janice is admitted to hospital and receives psychotherapy from Dr Donaldson. Her rehabilitation continues but she feels she has sinned through hurting her parents.
5. The renewal of Dr Donaldson's position as Registrar arises but a review committee decides against retaining his services. From this moment, the nature of treatment changes to more traditional approaches; using drugs and also electroconvulsive therapy. Advised by another doctor that Janice has a form of schizophrenia, the parents are informed she will be returned home soon with medication.
6. Janice returns home and later meets with her boyfriend at his art college where he unsuccessfully tries to present her with a new painting. They engage in a critique of her parents, family life and society as place for the mindlessness of working every day. Later, at a family gathering a dispute with Janice's sister leads to a blazing row and a scream from Janice concludes the meal. In the middle of the night Janice comes downstairs and carves a message in the dining room table. The parents take her back to the mental institution.
7. Befriending a gardener (also a patient) she eventually has sex with him. When advised against the relationship by a nurse, Janice demolishes her bedroom but is administered drugs and electroconvulsive therapy. Slowly her condition deteriorates. A meeting between her and her parents at the hospital only worsens the situation but her old boyfriend arrives and smuggles her out of the institution. In the middle of the night a doctor arrives at his flat with ambulance men who 'section' her, putting her back in the mental institution. The final scene depicts her as an object of science presented before medical students, the object of their academic inquiry.

Analysis: Form and Thematic Development: Some Dimensions of Significance – The First Flashback Commencing its operation across a series of scenes, the first flashback provides for spectator contemplation on a part of Janice's social history; the first of several privileging knowledge content about the mental health of characters. With the view of the store and Janice, Dr Donaldson's voice-over is heard raising the question 'Does it upset your mother that you have had so many different jobs?' Her fragile voice-over accompanies, following depictions of her on the shop floor as an assistant, behind a counter.

> **Janice**: Oh yer … she says I am irresponsible but I mean sometimes I go to lunch not come back again. I wanted to be a hairdresser once … I had a Saturday job for a while in this place called Eva Roma … down the high street … I never really did any hair you know … just sweeping up and things like that.

Later, she is seen sitting on a tube station platform from which she is assisted by a station guard. Amid scenes of rush hour chaos, she is viewed as a person whose disposition is delicate, the weakness of her subjectivity further substantiated in later moments in a police station where a woman officer tries to help Janice. Maintaining silence, she is resistant to requests until another officer finds her address in her personal effects. This found, so too is her voice, small pleas reconciling with officers that she is okay, only fear of parental discovery about her situation mobilizing concerned cries for independence. Taken home by a WPC, Janice is subjected to a parental inquiry verifying suspicions raised in the therapeutic session – that her parents are a contributory factor to her mental distress.

Parents as Pariahs Whatever Janice might try to do in explaining herself, the ordering of dramatic discourse and visualizations diminish her character in discursive exchanges which help to qualify not only her character as a conventional element of naturalism but also as the subject of parental oppression and stigmatization. As an example, her father refers to her as 'mad'. As with the main character of Cathy in *Cathy Come Home*, she is like a sacrificial figure or, as George McKnight (1997) suggests, she is a character acted upon, not an instigator of actions. A significant moment in the film, this scene presents a disturbance in the family's affairs, generating a tension in narrative that requires resolution. It also serves Loach's intention of constructing a tension for development across the drama, arranging linguistic content into a conflict between parents versus youth and old versus young.

Development towards Decline Examining naturalism from Zola to Loach, Deborah Knight indicates that one of its goals has been, 'to reflect upon – not just reflect – the circumstances of socially disempowered individuals and groups' (McKnight 1997: 61). Recalling Zola's insistence that he is determinist and not fatalist, Knight explains the purpose of this and Loachian style:

> The whole point of the literary or cinematic experiment is that it should carry through, inevitably, the consequences that are inbuilt in the initial conditions of the narrative situation. Part of the emotional force of these narratives is the result of just this sort of inexorable narrative structuring. (McKnight 1997: 75)

After the first therapy session and flashback, other flashbacks follow, providing opportunity for contemplation not only upon the main character as a socially disempowered individual but also the agency of her parents. At the first therapy session with Mrs Baildon, rigidly fixed ideals are revealed more by accident than by design. During her interview a knock at the door signals the entrance of a secretary who addresses the doctor as 'Mike' and offers cups of tea. Afterwards, Mrs Baildon objects to the first name terms, remarking that this is a lack of respect in maintaining social standards, her values connoting snobbery belonging to a conservative middle class. Her stated view is that people all have a place; they should know it and stay there. As framed through the therapeutic interview, signifiers of class are aired for audience reflection.

Between therapeutic scenes, juxtaposed flashbacks of Janice's social and family life expose cultural differences between daughter and parents. Concluding the first scene with the doctor and Mrs Baildon, the mother's last line delivers social concern about youth and their sexual values: how we may all end up 'living in the jungle'. In contrast, the flashback scene presents a group of young people including Janice and boyfriend sitting in a circle singing a popular song accompanied by a guitarist. This hardly harmful situation is followed by another significant moment when lying on her bed after an argument with her parents about her pregnancy and its potential termination, she draws a picture of her baby on her abdomen. The baby slowly becomes clear with a body, face and then eyes. Tears are then drawn falling from the eyes, an indicator that the pregnancy will soon be terminated. Subsequent to another therapeutic scene between the father and the psychiatrist, the termination of the pregnancy is confirmed in a flashback where Janice reveals this information to her friend Mike. Visiting him, she reflects that her mother is trying to kill her because she is, in her mother's eyes, bad. Her baby was bad, her mother having made her have an abortion has made her bad too. Distressed and crying, she needs consoling but then raises the question, 'Do you think I'm mental?' Quickly her friend responds, 'I don't know what being mental means', and so she changes the term to 'peculiar'. That we are all a bit peculiar in some way is his view and there follows a mediating account from the boyfriend that we all, at some point in our lives, experience a frame of mind different from the way we usually are. Thus, 'therapeutic' sessions develop as narrative conventions, allowing space to examine the mother's and father's values, exposing these as a source of conflicts, through juxtapositions with Janice's social and family life.

Sin, Control and Responsibility Amidst what appears to be the potential for liberation, spectators are treated to an exposition of what really is happening;

confirmation of Janice's suspect parental treatment and a feeling that she is close to some sort of rescue. In another scene, Dr Donaldson suggests to the mother that what is actually happening is Janice's attempt to stand on her own two feet, to gain 'responsibility', but this is being frustrated by parental over-involvement. Liberation appears even closer in the next therapeutic scene where the nature of dramatic action in the therapeutic space changes. This time, Dr Donaldson, with back to camera, is kept in frame, his voice more personalized with Janice's face located in the bottom right hand corner. With the nature of social relationships changed through distance to only one metre, the doctor's posture is one of leaning forward toward Janice, as if eager to tell her things. In terms of spatial relationships, spectators are offered a new situation about Janice's mental health. (**Dr D.** = Dr Donaldson; **J.** = Janice)

> **Dr D.**: … and when your feelings are involved as well and your feelings about being – at all – not just about whether it's nice or not – then in a way being mad and cutting yourself off from the world is the only place that you can really be private …
>
> (*Here the image cuts to Janice in her kneeling position before Dr Donaldson, her face one of a learning and realisation about her life-world.*)
>
> **J.**: Mmm – you mean – it's like – it's your – own little bit of safety …
>
> (*Then cuts back to the previous framing of Dr Donaldson.*)
>
> **Dr D.**: … yer … one of the things is that you really can't stand your parents' disapproval – actually – it upsets you so much that you feel you've either got to do what they say or else it throws you into confusion and you've got to be able to – I mean – we've got to find a way to help you – both stand up to them and not hate them for disapproving of you either – this takes time.

This positive image and language signals a turning point in a narrative where its inbuilt initial conditions are brought to a head. The emotional force of narrative structuring located in the temporal present is now set for a turn for the worse. Together these components portray the how and why of mental illness as experienced by Janice, the cause of parental problems neither recognized nor remedied. The plot of narrative opens out for each character's mental health disposition and the cause and effect of Janice's situation. With themes of hope produced, the narrative looks like it may move in a positive direction, the therapy sessions offering space for rehabilitation. However useful this may have been, Loach designs for his characters a move away from 'things are getting better' to 'things are going from bad to worse' in a plot with no solvability. Donaldson's departure signals the oncoming of tragedy and the narrative's final descent.

Advancing Narrative Backwards Naturalist narrative, having made headway, looks set to undo everything it has achieved when Dr Donaldson is dismissed by the Hospital Board. With the doctor's departure go his effective treatments, replaced by old fashion approaches to psychiatry including electro-convulsive therapy and medication. The potential for health that existed at the beginning of the narrative is wrenched away and the remaining plot is used to limit Janice's character further. Janice is subjected to the medicine of containment and given a new diagnosis of schizophrenia which might be seen as the final stage of the film but for one, in a catalogue of disastrous events. Smuggled away from the mental institution by her boyfriend, she is located and removed by orderlies to become the object of student medical analysis in a lecture theatre.

The film's dénouement in presenting Janice as an 'object' of medical inquiry resists classic closure. Through this approach there is no resolution but rather a continuance to problems in the story. There is no gifted agent with ownership of special powers and if anything the disturbed equilibrium that existed at the film's commencement is further destabilized to the extent that incarceration and regression replaces progress. Depictions contribute to a form and content destined to decline, with any positive developments doomed to failure. The purpose in Loachian fictional naturalism is not to show the injurious qualities of mental illness and scope for 'treatment' but to highlight social realities and cultural causes. It does not suit his purpose to have a positive resolution, since this contradicts his broader diagnosis. Knight points out that for Loach:

> Naturalism is on the side of a cultural or social psychology, one which sees individuals as constructed and constrained through their socio-cultural environments. As such, the function of Loach's naturalist fiction generally, and certainly the function of Loach's naturalism in particular is to examine that interaction between socio-cultural environment and various characters. (McKnight 1997: 73)

In difference to classical narrative in mainstream cinema, this main character is purposefully portrayed with little in the way of agency. The first person positioning of viewer in Janice's situation arranges the viewer–text relations to see stigmatization at work in the family. However, it is only her character to which the viewer is aligned but we are not allowed into her head (in contrast with Cathy in *Cathy Come Home*). We see her problems and the causes of them, in fact so clearly that the diagnosis of schizophrenia is questionable. As a broader sociological vision, this film types her mental distress and identity as a consequence of the institutions of family (as in parents) and state, in both instances bereft of adequate care or understanding.

Angel Baby *(1995)*

Angel Baby is a story about the relationship between two young adults, Harry (played by John Lynch) and Kate (by Jacqueline McKenzie), both of whom suffer schizophrenia. Set in modern day Australia, the film is a drama-romance form, its narrative constituted of comparable generic rules in that, they meet, fall in love, live together and Kate later becomes pregnant. However, complications develop in the pregnancy resulting in implications for the couple, their conditions and Harry's family (his brother, Morris played by Colin Friels and Louise played by Deborra-Lee Furness). The nature of their mental health later undergoes significant change resulting in deteriorations with tragic consequences. Amid turbulent events in their quest for love, an intense drama occurs as they struggle to seek resolutions in a film which contrasts in many ways with *Family Life* and *Rain Man*.

Angel Baby resists a poetic liberation tale for realisms more identifiable with sufferers of schizophrenia and also, denies a 'happy ending', unlike highly praised predecessors like *Shine* and *A Beautiful Mind*. In contrast to other films examining mental health themes, its drama-romance generic structure imposes a strong focus on 'the emotional' in a relationship connecting with their conditions. High peaks and deep troughs are produced are in a narrative momentum of extremes.

1. At the family home of Morris, Louise and their son, Sam, Harry sits at the kitchen table talking with his brother. Joining them, Louise sits down to listen about Harry's new girlfriend but when Morris asks where she is from, he is met with a slightly embarrassed response from Harry; indicating that he hasn't even talked to her yet. Harry later puts Sam to bed, drawing a magic chalk circle around it, as Sam is scared of monsters at night. Sam is convinced but for a picture on his bedroom wall of a clown with piercing, looking eyes which Harry takes down and throws out the window. Sam, now convinced, goes to sleep while Harry goes to the bathroom to take extensive medication.
2. Harry meets Kate at a group therapy session; she is a newcomer and he is a longer term member. She notices Harry looking at the underside of her wrists disclosing scars running across her veins rather than down them. Annoyed at Harry's attention to them, she covers them up. Afterwards, she gets on a bus but alights swiftly, because she feels uncomfortable about Harry's following her. She quickly runs off with Harry in pursuit. Confronting him, she wants to know what he's playing at, but slowly, they get to know each other. Realizing she is late, Kate runs off. Arriving at a bus stop, angry and blaming of Harry, he takes her to a new place to view her favourite TV programme, *Wheel of Fortune*.
3. Kate takes down the words and numbers gaining messages via her guardian angel 'Astral'. Transfixed by the whole event, Harry becomes involved, deciding this a good time to tell her about his interest. She reacts angrily but she soon has to change her mind as the message from the show is 'You

are my special angel'; Harry and Kate get closer, the spinning wheel of fortune signalling a change in their personal fortunes. They quickly fall in love and soon, love-making takes place out in the streets of the city in a heavy downpour.

4. They move into a flat and Harry finds a job with a computer firm but lies at the interview about his medical history. Then, during one evening spent together, Kate tells Harry she's pregnant; this news determined by interpretations she makes from *Wheel of Fortune* and later confirmed by a private obstetrician. Unfortunately, the pregnancy brings her into conflict with the healthcare authorities who don't want to take into consideration the wants of the couple. The couple withdraw from taking their medications and reject any further medical help.
5. Later, on a bridge, Harry appears despondent but Kate mimics the cries of flying seagulls around them. Taken with her actions, Harry is lifted from his depression and joins in. At home, they throw out their medication for the benefit of the forthcoming baby but negative consequences occur as the health of both deteriorates. Harry's manager finds out about his condition and fires him, this leading to a deeply upsetting reaction for Kate and Harry. Eventually both are hospitalized.
6. Harry is told in hospital that Kate doesn't want to see him. His feelings still strong, he visits her in hospital only to find her heavily medicated. Following the words and numbers in *Wheel of Fortune* he later tells Kate about them in hospital. Informing Kate of their reunion, the birth, and how they must run away together, he smuggles her from the secure ward and they hide in a set of flats under construction. With support from their friends in the therapy group, they obtain a television but waiting to view *Wheel of Fortune* one night, they find it excluded from the schedule. Both distraught, Harry telephones the company but the series has concluded its current run. Bewildered, he returns to his brother's home in order to find his medication but his brother discovers him there. When he takes Harry back to the squat, Kate suddenly finds herself about to give birth.
7. Rushed to hospital, complications arise as she has lost a lot of blood. Her situation stabilized, the obstetrician states the problems concerning potential bleeding but the couple refuse a caesarean. Kate gives birth to a little girl but then dies after severe haemorrhaging. The obstetrician then tells Harry he can see his baby but at this moment, the body of Kate is wheeled passed. Harry viewing his baby then breaks down into tears, saying to his brother that he must get some air.
8. Unknown to his brother, Harry returns to the bridge where both he and Kate had mimicked seagulls. Standing on the railing and amid an increasingly loud music, Kate, as if by a ghostly magic, reappears. Simultaneously, both screech their seagull cries in unison with the vocals of the music and wave their arms. In concluding, the final image cuts to black complemented with a piercing scream and a crashing musical crescendo.

Analysis: Dramatic Form in Angel Baby *– Characters and Relationship as Story* In *Angel Baby* the characters of Harry and Kate and their relationship are the focus of the story. Two further elements make significant contributions. The first is, *The Wheel of Fortune*, a television entertainment programme watched by the couple for its significations of prize money totals and phrases containing messages sent from *Astral*. *Astral* is the second element, directing actions they should undertake in their relationship. On one hand, *The Wheel of Fortune* operates as a symbolic signifier, standing for notions about life as a 'game of chance' while on the other it directs the paths Harry and Kate take. It also functions as a guide for spectator expectation. The sense of chance is sometimes made all the more unpredictable in its linkage with the figure of Astral; a fictional goddess figure (for spectators) in a photograph but a psychical reality for Kate, as she confirms programme interpretations. Throughout the story, characters and relationship develop as if in a mutual process of cause and effect with the programme: their falling in love, Kate's pregnancy, experience of mental health difficulties, the loss of Harry's job and sufferings are explored. These events and actions shape a dramatic form that will eventually lead to tragedy. Often, the combination of the spinning *Wheel of Fortune* with experimental modern music initiates fantastical if sometimes unstable qualities to its form, veering from one emotional moment to another. As a convention it creates an effective vehicle for communicating not only about their lives but also their mental health conditions. In short, dramatic form is emotional and transitory, sometimes stable, at others fluid, veering from one mood to another at unexpected moments.

Characterizing Harry: Themes of Sensitivity and Medication Early in the film, three consecutive scenes arrange knowledge about Harry as being kind and sensitive but also dependent on medication. Stigma, together with notions of dangerousness are circumvented to produce a caring and sentient character.

In the first scene, Harry sits with his brother Morris at the breakfast table, his infatuation clear as he says: 'She's beautiful … she's fiery … she's mysterious … and I worship her'. But when questioned about her, he discloses he hasn't even met her yet, thus disclosing an avuncular side to his persona. In the second scene, a symbolic discourse also portrays Harry's identity as the *evictor* of monsters, simultaneously absenting him from being one. After drawing a line of protection around Sam's bed, a static camera reveals the room from a view across it. Sam is positioned at the bottom right corner of the frame with Harry standing to its left and on the wall, a picture of a clown with piercing looking eyes is visible between them. The chalk circle completed and protection from 'monsters' achieved, Harry gives the magical chalk to Sam. But for the picture on the bedroom wall, Sam is nearly at ease but says that it still disturbs him. Harry simply removes it, throwing it out the window and with Sam feeling safe, he lies down in his bed. Notions of monsters for Sam are expelled through the window, and with them any connected notions for the spectator about Harry: his character is framed as that of a guardian protector.

Next Harry is seen at a horizontal level incorporating a near frontal angle, entering the bathroom. From within the mirror inset in a bathroom cabinet, his face is momentarily visible before the mirror door is opened revealing shelves upon which items are stored. To the right, a medication list is placed recording tablets to take for breakfast, lunch and dinner. The function of the horizontal level and near frontal angle is to 'involve' viewers (see Kress and van Leeuwen 1990: 35–6) with the character, aligning them with subjectivity and privileging his point of view. This is apparent in the next shot which locates the view from actually within the cabinet, again at a horizontal level but fully frontal in contrast to the previous shot. First, Harry is in sharp focus, the shelves with medicine containers blurred but a pulling of focus converges upon the bottles, his face now blurred itself (through its positioning outside of the new focal point) as he takes a selection of tablets for consumption. Viewers see tablets disappear into the vague outline of his face, this portrayal elevating medicine as a dominant factor, significations of medicine dominating his life. This sequence of scenes arrange content about Harry's character and actions, within a context of the socially ordinary and who, like anyone else, can be attracted to another human being. However, his identity, an unwell one, is in need of medication and though the actual nature of his unwellness is not yet fully disclosed, the knowledge effect of these scenes for the spectator, reveal a person with a dependency – certainly not someone representing any epistemophilic threat or fear.

The Character of Kate: More Therapeutic Sessions and Stigma As in *Family Life*, the therapeutic session in *Angel Baby* is functional, introducing spectators to Kate's character, a potential relationship and a range of characters with conditions. Unlike *Family Life* where each character's social history is exposed in depth for spectator understanding, here the therapy session is a vehicle, acquainting spectators with mental health at a general level; Kate's condition and identity is afforded only slight attention. Located in a rehabilitation centre, the session presents a space where stability in people's conditions indicates forward movement in seeking solutions, this, foregrounded through psychotherapeutic discourse.

Kate's exuberant nature and condition is assisted by the portrayal of her appearance and physical posture; she has longish length ginger hair, wears colourful clothes and, like Harry, smokes. Sitting rigidly, with a sense of defiance, her make-up includes heavy eye shadow. In a defensive posture she presents an indignant and glaring expression, her attention mostly focused on lighting her cigarette. The doctor continues, 'When we have someone new join us we like to offer them the chance to say a few words so – if you feel comfortable with that – that's fine and just take your time'. Taking her time, she looks around with a hard stare and after a very long pause, says, 'Kate – my name's Kate', this response revealing paranoia.

Kate meets with Harry after the meeting. He has followed her from the bus she was taking home and each find out about the others past history of self harm; characterizations and dramatic action playing key roles in communicating themes about schizophrenia. That both need psychological assistance is apparent from their presence at the therapy session but mental health aspects previously withheld from spectators are now revealed. These allow spectators to examine reasons for Kate's condition, her stigma and self-harm. Now knowing his amorous intentions toward her, she confronts him by asking if he usually follows women. Knowing his interest is discovered, he admits it is his first time but her response is that she doesn't usually hang around with 'psychos'. Still in a state of surprise from her catching him, he replies he isn't one but she again accuses him of being 'a psycho' like the others from the clubhouse. So he responds by saying he is nothing like that; rather, he is like her. Being seen as mentally unwell carries a stigma for Kate; denial of her own condition is expressed through her stating she isn't 'a psycho'. This depiction of suffering stigma is rare, as it allows an alternative look at what it means to a human subject and how it operates. It exposes how Kate tries to 'cover' (see Goffman 1963: 125–8) her identity, knowing it as socially spoiled but simultaneously shows her denying her own condition.

Unstable Narrative and Character Agencies Early in the film, interactions with *The Wheel of Fortune* and *Astral* develop instability in the narrative and character agencies. Where the prime motivator of action in classic narrative will usually be male, Kate's fiery nature makes a strong impact, her pugnacious identity a key component. However, both character agencies are influenced by the television programme through messages apparently communicated from *Astral*. They function as devices not only for messages directing the path the relationship takes but also, in organizing viewer–text relationships about their mental health realities.

Using subjective character shots interwoven with close-up images of the programme's spinning wheel, spectator attention is directed to themes of chance and risk, the accompanying experimental music adding mystification to the way these components constitute everyday realities. Returning to her hostel late, Kate is let in by a disgruntled warden. In her room, she lights several candles at an altar-like shrine to Astral. A slow pan from left to right introduces close-up large imagery of odd regalia and iconography, with modern experimental music slowly becoming audible. The iconography includes a small gold-like statue of an Egyptian pharaoh and a teddy bear with a picture of a woman (Elise Mayberry) with light coloured hair, her head surrounded by lines of Scrabble letters emanating from her head. A close-up view of iconography combined with inaudible utterances and wailing vocals is underscored by a disrupted drumming rhythm. This meaning-making produces a supernatural, metaphysical spiritual space, a sense of magical causes and effects for the spectator constitutive of new regimes of credibility (different from *Psycho*). These symbols constitute Kate's belief systems, making Astral appear credible. This is confirmed when she requests of the figure, 'Please Astral – tell me – so I can know for sure – is he the one? Cos this is very scary for me'.

The music also contributes to a mêlée of free floating signifiers, developing a tribal aesthetic reminiscent of Aboriginal wailing voices at a corroboree.[6] Music, as Malcolm Budd (1985) shows, maintains significant relationships to the emotions and a tribal vocal form combines with a modern popular drumming style to produce a connotational code. As a non-diegetic element, these codes represent instinctual themes reminiscent of fundamental human rituals and construct a spiritual reality for text–viewer relations.

Characters in Fear and an Anxious Narrative: How We See What We Know as Schizophrenia Later in the narrative, juxtaposed scenes of Harry and Kate's independent schizophrenic experiences are cross-cut edited to contribute to a unique representation. This concomitant double-take of schizophrenia is also accomplished by acting and music which helps build dramatic form into an intense viewing experience of realisms referencing themes of distress. It begins when Harry is fired by his boss at work and simultaneously Kate, in a laundry, realizes this impending bad news through her *Wheel of Fortune* interpretation.

After a zoom out from large size dots on a television screen to reveal the *Wheel of Fortune*, viewer–text relations are initially arranged by a close-up of Kate's face viewing the television left of frame; in the background and to the right, machines spin-dry clothes. Kate's expression is one of concern as a contestant wins $750 filling in missing letters of a phrase '. . R S T . . S . S . . . . R . .' which will turn out to be '*WORST CASE SCENARIO*'. Cross-cutting to an upper mid-shot of Harry shows his hands over his face in a silver coloured elevator. As the camera tracks around him facial expressions reveal him stricken with anxiety as audible whispering but inaudible words increase in volume; hearing voices is causing him anguish. Kate is next seen phoning Harry's office via the same previously framed shot; the laundry dryers rotate adding a disorienting sense. Alarmed, she twice asks: 'Hello, can I speak to Harry Goodman please – thank you', leaving viewers to imagine that what happens next cannot be good.

Cutting to the next scene, a low angled long shot exposes a long plush restroom with sinks and mirrors diminished in size due to their location at the far end of the room. A blue rinse colour makes the space seem cold as Harry walks in, his stature lessened by perspective.

> The perspectival image compels the viewer to become, together with the institution that has produced the image, an 'us' with respect to a 'them' or an 'it' – that is, with respect to the participants represented in the image. (Kress and van Leeuwen 1990: 32)

Next, a close-up of Harry's face fills the frame as he looks into the mirror, bringing viewer–text relations to see him directly; giving spectators a sense of

6 The aboriginal native gathering or dance (as at a festival or war ceremony) that uses voice as a key communicational tool.

his experiences. This scene is also strongly connected with that mirror scene at the film's beginning when medications are taken, only this time he is in severe withdrawal from them. This frontal horizontal angle encourages spectator involvement with Harry's subjectivity and his unwell health. Looking down he turns on the tap and a pan down shows gushing water, this accompanied by the sound of loud hissing water. Cutting back to a close-up of the drier rotating, its dizzying nature is prolonged by a slow zoom out showing Kate in the laundry room. Increasing high and low musical notes add to a sense of chaos as Kate slowly replaces the phone, her facial expression of shock steadily emerging. She foresees that the *worst case scenario* is about to transpire. The dramatic action increases with her pulling clothes around her and anxiously biting her nails.

Cutting back to Harry in the restroom, his look of internal torment increases with his voices in a flow of images that helps to convey a disoriented sense of reality, contrasting to that which he usually experiences. Briefly, memory from the elevator scene returns in two shots. First, the camera rotates around his body before the same shot is repeated but in reverse rotation. With his voices even louder but still indecipherable, a dissolve to a new image takes up Harry's point of view, seeing the silvery elevator spinning around him. Another cut to a long shot of Harry in the restroom leaning over the sink is followed by a big close-up of his contorted face. Turning away from the camera, he walks out of focus blurring spectator vision of him. Partially visible, he begins to spin around, his mental experiences causing him turmoil as his hands grasp his head. The next cut conveys an image of Harry in the expansive space of the restroom floor, his voices increasing in volume and number. Tearing at his hair, the intensity of his voices is portrayed by him placing his hands over his ears, this posture communicating that the voices might be external as well as internal. As he revolves, the camera rotates the other way with Harry screaming, 'I don't want this' repeatedly. After kneeling on the floor, another cut sees him turning around on the floor in the opposite direction, again the camera rotating the other way. Repeatedly he screams 'I don't f***ing want this', while the experimental music grows. With a faster editing rhythm increasing the sense of uncontrollability of his condition, he utters: 'I don't want this in my f***ing head'.

The next cut reveals a floor, orange in hue, with a slow upward pan revealing Harry's brother, Morris, arriving at the couple's apartment. Background music 'My Special Angel' (performed by the Vogues) plays as Morris walks in slowly. The apartment looks unkempt with clothes hanging from every conceivable place; Kate has lost control and thrown things around. The camera follows Morris as he searches the room, calling 'Kate' several times. Furniture is up-ended and the television is on the floor, its screen emitting a fuzzy image and a hissing noise. Prominently, the lyrics 'You are my special angel' continue as the camera's long pan around the room returns to Morris who then exclaims 'Jesus' when he discovers Kate underneath some of the tossed clothes.

A swift sequence of fast edits follows. One cut reveals a 'point of view' shot from Kate, lying on the floor with her view of Morris looking down at her; imagery of Morris is blurred, this coded mist effect conveying that Kate is delirious. With this cut, a sudden increase in sound level brings the lyrics of 'You are my special angel' closer. Morris departs in search of help and the next cut shows a paramedic team arriving at an elevator with Morris. As the doors close, a new cut reveals a different set of opening doors at a hospital. Harry comes in in a wheelchair with orderlies around him and he looks bewildered. Another cut sees the medics with Morris in the apartment, Kate now locked into the bathroom. The medics break in to find her fully clothed but in bathwater looking confused. A cut to Harry in his wheelchair shows him perplexed at what is going on about him. Next, we see Kate in the bath asking for Harry as the medics try to tease her from the bath. Finally, a cut to Harry shows him looking completely confused as the song ends in an upward crescendo of 'Angel! Angel! Angel!' Through editing, acting and music, two episodes of schizophrenia in separate spaces but in simultaneous time unify a form that conveys a dizzying sense of time and space for text–viewer relations, a reference to the condition. Realisms produce themes about schizophrenia through creatively composed formal elements to show it as a confusing processual condition characterized by extreme experiences.

Conclusion

The horror form has developed unchecked concepts about 'madness' and functioned as a significatory vehicle to introduce, evolve and manifest, irregular themes that reference mental health with ambiguity, providing little or no understanding about it. Few fictional films deal with mental health in an informative or entertaining way to dislodge mad concepts, but those that do use a range of conventions and codes to illuminate meanings useful to mental health understanding. In *Angel Baby*, formal properties work to convey rare realisms and strong themes representative of the schizophrenic condition, classifying people's identities in original ways. In *Family Life*, a naturalistic narrative critiques the institutions of mental healthcare, family and state, objecting that the needs of the citizen are not adequately met. In *Rain Man*, the melodramatic comedy form helps type qualities associated with autism accurately; this film proves to be an iconic text for popular culture in terms of its representational qualities. These broadly allow for a factualization about mental health in a fictional form. Indeed, these mental health genres operate to effectively portray mental health at the expense of madness.

Chapter 5
Phase One, Genre Studies 2: News and Documentary

Introduction

Peter Dahlgren, in his discussions about the public sphere, notes that it is 'a major societal mechanism for the formation of individual and collective subjectivity – for the production and circulation of culture – which frames and gives meanings to our identities' (1994: 4). However, from the accounts cited in the first chapter by people with mental health conditions and researchers, it is clear that a considerable group of people, wary of media portrayals of their identity and social stigma, choose not to participate fully in society. With regard to this non-participation it is useful to examine Dahlgren's point concerning the relationships between subjectivity and identity when he states:

> At first glance, subjectivity may seem like an odd category as a dimension of the public sphere. It may seem to hover within the realm of personal and private experience, the precise opposite of what the public sphere is concerned with. But if we bear in mind subjectivity in general has to do with what goes on in people's heads and that much of this is of obvious relevance: opinions attitudes, values and norms, knowledge and information, frames of reference and schemas of relevance, world views, and so on, certainly are all pertinent for the public sphere. And I would go one step further by suggesting that subjectivity also includes a particular aspect which is of importance for the public sphere, namely that of identity. Our sense of who we are, to ourselves and to others takes on relevance for the public sphere because it shapes the way in which we participate and may well determine if we participate or not. (Dahlgren 1994: 4)

Following the last chapter's examination of fictional genres, this chapter explores selected non-fictional forms which depict the condition called schizophrenia. These are noteworthy mediations specially chosen for their representational qualities as three avoid themes of 'dangerousness' to communicate about 'mental health', and another is included with themes of 'dangerousness' selected for sub-generic elements integral to its form. Three are broadcast news programmes (two from TV and one from radio) and one is a television video diary documentary. The intent of the analysis is to explore the ways in which mediations make meanings about mental health, subjectivity and identity in values, norms, knowledge, information, etc., portrayed for a public sphere constituted of people of both mentally well and unwell-being. Another intention is to explore circulated meanings questioning if they would encourage participation by the person with unwell mental health in society.

Non-fictional forms are analysed as crafted works of communicative performance with the aim of evaluating generic developments as in recent years news media institutions have sought to capture audiences, cultivating genre as the means to secure them. News and documentary forms have evolved, utilizing more sophisticated patterns of imagery, sound and language with various aspects of drama manufactured into these significatory systems. This drama is significant for the ways in which certain kinds of knowledge are framed for audience. At a general level, news studio sets look visually panoramic with large screens and larger graphics enabling dramatic impact in referencing story topics. Introductory music is more striking in its seriousness by way of electronic enrichment. More specifically 'performance culture', employed in conjunction with spoken language in news story-telling, has moved from the formal to a more personalized direct/indirect speech address and voice-over. Broadcast news is set up to be a dramatic event and the topics contained in it seem to require the qualification of being dramatic, certainly in headline stories. In documentary, numerous techniques (editing, camera usage, etc.), determined at preproduction, production and post production levels, capture what is, in essence, drama – the human condition in a tense struggle to resolve situations relevant to her/his context. This has also emerged as a focus of news recently where the dramas of an individual person or group in a tragic situation make for 'good television', at least from a producer's point of view. Something contemporary news producers want is dramatic imagery or the expectation of it in a long running story, like the build-up to a Gulf War or an oil disaster in the Gulf of Mexico (as in 2010). Dramatic stories and images like these are the premium choice, obviously more so than the 'happy story' that often ends a news programme. And it is also *how* what is recorded that adds to the drama and the ways in which it directs the audience to make meaning from the form. While aspects of drama studied in non-fictional forms are varied, taking place in discourse as well as topic types, these communicative characteristics are evaluated in representations.

News Genres and Mental Health

Although research outcomes about mental health mediations have been largely static as the review in Chapter 2 showed, themes of dangerousness have maintained a consistency in type as have the dramatic nature of news story topics. The most commonly identified stories about mental health in the UK are reports about killings related to schizophrenia, by an individual whose condition has gone unchecked – like Michael Stone or Christopher Klunis. Such stories have previously focused upon the policy called Care in the Community reporting on contexts surrounding policy failures. This UK trend, mentioned by Philo (1996), is not uncommon. Similar trends are found in the USA, as studies by Steadman and Cocozza (1977) and Nunnally (1957) have determined (see K.A. Neuendorf in Ray and Donohew 1990). However, a trend in American news stories is to cite a person whose behaviour causes concern as having 'mental health issues', a formula now occurring in the UK. Little if anything is addressed beyond this other than story content. Only in cases like that of the Texas, Fort Hood shooting by a Muslim psychiatrist in 2009 is mental health explored with questions about how this could have happened. Subsequently, the first three mediations analysed reflect the frequency of schizophrenia as a news story but focus upon news mediations about suicide as well as homicide.

Analytical Framework

In this analysis of non-fictional forms, the framework is designed to focus upon how each mediation is shaped as a crafted piece of communicative performance. The aim is to determine different types of mental health produced as information for public knowledge and to reveal how components construct representations that: allow or deny social agency; construct a mental health space; address audience and employ language – all of which culminate in the absence or presence of stigma, stereotypes and myths.

Examining television and radio mediations, a different analytical approach is used to that of fiction. In news programmes, studio and location modes of address employ the presence of institutional representatives (e.g., presenter or reporter) making it a distinctive communication. Meanings are made in a predictable storytelling structure for audience expectation, of when a topic will be introduced and reporting will occur. In recent documentary, meaning-making can also be distinctive but within less predictable storytelling structures. According to Bill Nicholls, while the direct address of narrators or characters in interview forms speaking to camera have dominated the 1990s, self-reflexive forms with observational pieces and interviews are more current (see Rosenthal and Corner 2005: 18). Also, in examining drama, this component is given special consideration in exploring how it plays a different creative and varied role to its counterpart in fiction. It does this while analysing the formal organization of significatory components of images, language, music and sound, and the integral elements of set, personas, performance, technology and discourse.

Set

At the beginning of any communicative form, a key element is the idea of *set*. An important factor in any news or documentary genre is its opening moments and *set* is central to directing audience expectation about what meanings they will receive. *Set* governs how generic elements, particularly language, 'open' and is of generative significance. The concept is taken from perceptual studies in psychology and contended here is that in any mediation, *set* directs an audience who have prior experience of mediations toward one collection of meanings rather than others. '*Set*' is when:

> The effect of experience … is to establish in the perceiver a *set* or readiness for some stimuli rather than others. As a result of differential experience he is *set* to attend to some stimulus characteristic rather than the others when stimuli are ambiguous. If perceived, the perceiver will think first of the 'probable' words (*images, sounds, music*) (that is the words *images, sounds, music* which have been frequently encountered in the past and therefore encountered again) in trying to fit a word, *image, sound, music* to the partial information derived from the stimulus. Only if 'probable' words, *images, sounds, music* are found unsatisfactory is s/he likely to consider 'improbable' words, *images, sounds, music* as possible identifications. (Taylor et al. 1970: 295, my italics)

Thus, in broadcast forms, audiences see or hear the opening moments such as the distinctive elements of news and are cued for probable meanings and style of mediation experience. Subsequently, when a story begins an audience is *set* by the parameters of linguistic (or other) content in its early stages which guide and structure anticipation of signification, stimulating and organizing perception. Frequently, these parameters are offered by a *persona* using performance skills.

Personas, Performance and Technology

Writing in 1956, Horton and Wohl introduced the concept of persona in their commentary on the changing nature of television and radio during that period; a concept which resonates in news even today. Then, the delivery of news and documentary language in the UK and the USA was characterized by more formal qualities.

> Sometimes the 'actor' – whether he is playing himself or performing in a fiction role – is seen engaged with others; but he often faces the spectator, uses the mode of direct address, talks as if he were conversing personally and privately. (Horton and Wohl 1956: 215)

These actors could:

> claim and achieve intimacy with what were literally crowds of strangers, and this intimacy, even if it is an imitation and a shadow of what is ordinarily meant by that word, is extremely influential with, and satisfying for, the great numbers who willingly receive it and share in it. (Horton and Wohl 1956: 216)

Then, television and radio personalities were able to offer 'gestures, conversational style, and milieu of an informal face-to-face gathering' (1956: 217) to create a *para-social relationship*, an illusion of intimacy from a distance. Today, the devices of persona and performance are fused with more sophistication. From the *setting* of a story, new intimacies are an offered 'experience' for an individual and collective audience. Via enhanced performance skills in voice, gesture and cultural demeanour, a new contrived closeness is played out in a process making a persona socially attractive and someone who will be accepted by a predetermined target audience.

Boal's (1979) discussions about theatre (examined in Chapter 8) parallel how drama is viewed in this framework. He views theatre as something that once belonged to the people until it became the property of the ruling classes. Divisions were introduced between actor and spectator, and later between classes of spectator – cheap seats versus more expensive ones. Yet drama is something we can relate to immediately and not something we just see at the theatre or on television via the web. It takes place between people every day in different ways and at varying levels; drama is around us, even in the most mundane of situations. To varying extents, we are all involved in performance of sorts during our everyday lives. Moreover, a news presentation is a heightened performance when an individual audience member knows that others are simultaneously experiencing this constructed discourse away from her/his space which involves the ideological, the economic and the political.

Therefore, this new form of intimacy is examined with the propositioned social relationship given special focus because of its impact in partnering content. In this befriending relationship, elements like voice, facial expression and general demeanour, as well as class, gender, sexuality and race matter in *how* we receive information. These components matter because Horton and Wohl wisely call personas 'actors'. Today journalists are like actors engaged in crafted social actions that show them attempting the pretence of 'a relationship' into which the all-important quality of *trust* is established in projects based upon facts and truth claims. Through language, stories are told with relating, the foundation for belief and trust. With intent and purpose, reporters and presenters/anchors craft their practice by drawing upon dramatic and non-verbal communication skills. Directed to bring alive news content in sometimes controlled and less-controlled situations (like live breaking-news moments), news personnel employ vocalization within informal discourse coupled with facial expressiveness to make meaning from a script; the intent to get their message across effectively. Scripts are often co-written for the studio and reporters in the field often recall from memory to talk to camera while studio presenter/anchors talk from a prompter.

While a number of authors use Goffman's (1981) animator/author/principal model to view what happens in the process of presentation/reports, this is now complicated by new technology. For instance, television news editing systems like Avid Newscutter and iNews used in conjunction with servers allow for multi-user simultaneous usage. Today, these applications enable several contributors to co-develop a script to which author, editor and journalist, and animator/presenter contribute, complicating Goffman's model. Examining news in this way, while having its merits, denies a full analytical scope.

In other non-fiction mediations like documentary, drama as a component operates in different ways. While some documentaries do have an institutional representative, the analysed vérité observational style reveals tensions, stresses and successes in a human relationship. Therefore, significations expose struggles in which two people seek resolutions to disturbances supplying drama in that context. Drama in this sense is when those disturbances in human affairs generate struggles in action to resolve them. Story and editing techniques are also creatively used to produce a less predictable form that can serve to support particular points of view over others. These help shape a more varied communicative form to that of news where discourse is also subject to more formal influences with regard to performance.

Discourse and the Performative

In this study of non-fiction, discourse[1] is defined as the language employed to make meaning and is considered a constituent element of form inextricably linked to diverse and shifting dramatic qualities which are always part of communicative performance. The relationship between discourse and performance across forms contrast as each project is different; one is intended for informing and educating and the other to entertain. Yet, in (inter)national news whether CNN, BBC, SKY or FOX, some studio spaces resemble more a theatre stage and some, like that of ITN, are even cinematic. In these spaces otherwise mainly associated with fiction, language uttered will be subject to creative inputs within constraining and creative influences; legal issues about what can and cannot be said as well as economic ones connected to ratings. Discourse is also subject to personas enabling linkages to 'intimacy' which is considered as action but only when fully completed by performative qualities.

Montgomery (2007: 24) notes that while 'actions depend completely on language for their performance they are also underpinned by social content and structure'. Using the example that if we promise, apologize, or insult, he argues that it is difficult to conceive how else this could be done except in words though notions of information-value conveyed in vocalizations are overlooked. The point

1 Historically, the study of discourse analysis is viewed as a linguistic concept. Foucault popularized discourse but his method has been criticized as vague. Several theorists including Diane Macdonell (1986) and Sara Mills (1997) produce helpful analyses but the term still draws debate. For contexts to this, Norman Fairclough (1992: 12–61) produces a useful 'discourse analysis history' before his explanation about textually oriented discourse analysis and Martin Montgomery also offers a critical examination in his linguistically oriented discourse analysis of broadcast news (2007: 20–37). Notably, these two linguistic approaches (also Fairclough 1995) examine news discourse analysing language as a social action, exploring it in connection to personality and performance in media texts. They discuss the inseparability of the linguistic from 'the social' which is relevant for this framework.

is, if conveyed with varying dramatic inflections, each process will be more fully and socially complete as 'action' than if simply uttered in monotone. Furthermore, participants other than news or documentary institution representatives are now also practised in media talk and performance. Indeed, interviews with these skilled (often public relations) people provide contrasts with those who are not. Such indirect address moments expose struggles for power in meaning, setting news institution discourse apart from those participants contesting a subject, as well as information-offering experts. When practised by a presenter or participant, information-values in discourse used in conjunction with non-verbal communication can shift power in numerous ways.

Connecting with discourse are components that inform it, which this framework limits to: a) discourse practice, b) discourse type, c) discourse domain and d) orders of discourse. Discourse practice refers to the practice of a particular discourse such as that of a judge, a doctor or a police officer and it follows a newsreader or reporter. In this way, a type of talk integrates power relationships relative to the nature of that work. A sense of equality occurs with a doctor that will likely be absent with a judge. Language is also constrained by the practice in terms of rules, ethics and laws peculiar to it. Discourse type is the style of talk and again, this may involve particular conventions such as sentencing by a judge or apparent care offered by a doctor in a dialogue with a patient. Discourse domain is, as Montgomery defines it, 'an institutionalised area of social life dependent upon recognisable distinct discourse practices and genres' (2007: 26) which include the areas of law, health and broadcast journalism. These all qualify as domains in which language becomes limited by factors such as producer guidelines, laws and previous significant events that govern what to do and what not to do in broadcast talk.

Orders of Discourse

The final component is the order of discourse. Fairclough proposes that the order of discourse in the social institution of media is formed by the tensions between contradictory public sources and private targets. Thus, institutions like news producers form a text for a chosen audience ordering discourse from public sources in ways appropriate to its purpose to secure a specific target audience. Fairclough speaks of 'discursive practices of a community – its normal ways of using language – in terms of networks … "orders of discourse". The order of discourse of a social institution or social domain is constituted by all the discursive types which are used there' (1995: 55). Subsequently, in news media its orders of discourse are constituted by all the discursive types employed in it, like the BBC, FOX, PBS and *Channel 4 News*. Styles of talk from presenters and/or anchors, formed by editors and producers differ with each institution defined from the other. In this domain, institutions work to shape mediations distinctively. *Discourse* is *ordered* to meet social criteria that match readers' needs, continuously 'forming' information for reception. This implicates not just linguistic content but in this framework, the ways in which discourse is ordered by drama[2] and which can facilitate variances of power relationships about knowledge.

Vocalizations are linked not just to presenter/anchors speaking and their ability to turn content into an accessible form for consumption but also to the ways in which meanings in words and phrases can be shaped by all participants. Broadcast discourse in news and documentary is as much about struggles for power concerning relationships and identities as it is about constructing new meanings. Modifying Fairclough's order of discourse (1995: 56) this approach includes the elements of generic configuration and discourse both linked to performance. Here, Fairclough's generic configuration is extended to a 'use of language with employed performance qualities facilitating the practice of news presenting/anchoring', linking it to ideas about persona. Discourse, the second constituent component, is 'the language used, constituted of dramatic elements employed from the producer's point of view' (ibid.). In this ordering of discourse, implications arise for public knowledge in modified frames of reference as broadcast news discourse publicly names the world, the people in it and also, what they do. In the examples that follow, analyses are organized around the conventions of studio and location modes of address. The diagrams shown highlight different models of news with linguistic elements in examples from television and radio. *ITN News* at 5.40pm, *Channel 4 News* and BBC Radio Four's *Today* news programme are examined along with a video diary entitled *Mad, Sad or Bad.*

ITN News at 5.40pm

Description

The focus of the ITN story broadcast on 6 March 1996 is a man, Anthony Smith, convicted at Nottingham Crown Court for murders he committed after being released from hospital. The report examines the consequences of his neglected condition, the situation of his family and the hospital's response to his conviction. Working through the presented *ITN News* diagram (see Table 5.1), generic elements are examined in the studio and location modes of address. Exploring newsreader John Suchet's mode of address, this first section looks at how he begins to tell the story about Anthony Smith. It examines direct address focusing

2 Neither Fairclough nor Montgomery views media discourse as an element correlated to a more general process of producing drama, which can for example occur by way of story sequencing or editing, as well as discourse. Drama and its relationships to other components has become sophisticated in media forms particularly in news but meanings are embellished sometimes purposefully as a produced feature and at other times as a spontaneous by-product of communications. Either way, the implications of the effect of drama make this prominent feature of contemporary media worthy of analysis.

upon how discourse, shaped by dramatic qualities and persona help to produce a schema that results in a quite specific knowledge yield. It should be noted at the outset that while a presenter offers the information for public knowledge, that person is simply a conduit through which preparers of a script, news editors and presenters collectively shape news. Indeed, John Suchet (hereafter JS), who used to present this news programme, has campaigned vigorously for help in understanding and combating dementia, a condition his wife Bonnie contracted. As Montgomery states about presenters, 'In delivering the news, theirs is the voice not of an individual in their own right but of the institution on whose behalf they read' (2007: 69).

The Studio Mode of Address

A mid-shot image of Suchet starts the studio mode of address. Behind, above and to his right, a picture of Smith is inset. Piercing eyes stare out of a police 'mug shot'. In the interplay between image and following speech, a 'narrativisation of the subject' (Kress and van Leeuven 1990: 47) develops as Suchet briefly enunciates what the man did (see lines 1–3). Viewing him at a downward angle, Smith's identity is constructed as an object of *oddity* rather than someone extremely unwell, thus marking him as abnormal and strange. So commences a stigmatizing of the person, a 'target' for following content. Facing the camera, the newsreader's delivery is coded with guarded resonances of 'serving', combining confident tones of 'authority' as he presents a brief résumé of three of four stories *setting* headline frameworks of reference. Then, the lead story is presented.

Table 5.1 *ITN News* at 5.40pm (time continuum follows along the sequence outlined below)

Generic Structure: Visual Codes and Conventions	Opening titles reference channel identity and programme time.	Studio scene of presenter waiting to deliver news to the audience.	Studio direct mode of address. Audience perceptually 'set' to receive information within specific frames of reference.	Studio Mode report begins.
Visualization/ Auralization	View of studio set and blue graphics of ITN 5.40 News. Opening music with pronounced bass levels; horns and strings.	Code of blue background for aiding communication. Convention of presenter seated behind desk.	Studio direct address with presenter offering viewer headlines.	Presenter direct address. Inset photograph of man with piercing eyes above and to left of presenter.
Language and Dramatic Components	Written language displaying channel identity, time and presenter voice-over in a deeply toned male voice saying 'From the studios of ITN "The News" with John Suchet'.	As music fades, presenter is introduced to camera in formal dress code. Facial expression indexical of subordinate relationship – as a server of news.	Pleasant greeting followed by serious expression for news delivery. Headlines (usually a set of stories). Sentence 1,2,3,4, (summary sometimes followed by quotation).	Vocally (male) denoting a personal level but also deep tonal characteristic of connotational values. 'The father of a paranoid schizophrenic …' Enunciation of sentencing is short and offering a simplistic schema.

Table 5.1 Continued

Location Mode filmed surveillance sequence.	Location Mode film sequence.	Location Mode film sequence.	Location Mode film sequence.	Location Mode filmed sequence followed by return to Studio Mode and next story.
Footage of exiting defendant with warders at court in procession to security vehicle. Defendant viewed through an ellipse to aid identification.	Establishing shots of defendant's family home and kitchen where action and event took place.	Still photos of mother followed by those of son (both victims of the attack).	Mid shot of interview with father, then new establishing shots of hospital followed by interview with doctor.	Reporter to-camera speech in 'stand-up' position.
Reporter voice-over with voices and public discourses. Fluent and authoritative tones in voice of reporter descriptively informing of details.	Reporter voice-over with story; graphic details of gruesome murder at home. Expressive in paralinguistic codes and rhythmically fast.	Reporter voice-over with information of how man then had bath after the attack. Tonally settled to maintain consistency of monologue. Further characteristics of previous two sections present.	Father chastises 'so-called experts' referring to doctors and then doctors discourse presented. Resigned tone to events in formal dress for court appearance. Doctor in formal dress with codes of epistemology (i.e., books behind).	Journalist ties up report presenting his identity: 'Eric Macinnes for ITN News at Nottingham Crown Court'. Formal dress codes leading to indicative tones of speech genres associated with end of monologue.

Note: This table should be read from left to right across both pages.

Presenter's Generic Configuration, Voice and Gaze

Integral to news genres are the ways in which direct speech address is ordered across discrete moments of programme time and space. In recent generic configurations of presenting, levels of the emotional have crept into news through the greater deployment of a persona's use of gaze. Michael Argyle (1988) quotes Kleck and Nuessle's (1968) study which found that interactors looking into camera 80% (rather than 15%) of the time in a film were judged by viewers to be friendly, sincere, natural, mature and self-confident. Indeed, Suchet's eye contact and controlled concerned facial expression are highly accomplished in seeking to achieve closeness.

1. **JS**: The father of a paranoid schizophrenic who killed his mother
2. and step brother said today he was barely surprised it had
3. happened. The son, Anthony Smith had recently been
4. discharged from hospital. A judge at Nottingham Crown Court
5. ordered him to be detained indefinitely and demanded an
6. inquiry. Eric Macinnes was in court.

Channelled at a personal level, Suchet is persuasive in communicating about family loss but it is *how* the opening moments of his discourse is ordered that make this delivery significant. From lines 1–6 Suchet's crafted performance is one that links to ideas concerned with the 'public colloquial nature of the style' (Fairclough 1995b: 72) rewriting boundaries between public and private to create a hybrid speech address. His generic configuration is constituted of simple 'informing' with that of 'telling tales'. By this is meant that vocal resonance associated with the telling of a misdoing by another, as a chosen speech style imported from a social order of discourse into the generic configuration of professional presenting. Taking 'discourse' as a constituent element of orders of discourse, the words used in the opening sentence are declarative. The words 'paranoid schizophrenic' are linked to dangerousness by the relative pronoun of 'who' connecting with the verb 'kill'. This highlights a choice to characterize stimuli with words that frame Smith's identity as someone who is generally extremely violent, rather than someone who contracted an extremely complex health condition. Discourse also helps *set* the tone for the following report with codes of exasperation vocalized in 'barely surprised' (line 2) adversely affecting notions about schizophrenia. From lines 3 until 6 codes of frustration tinged with sadness are employed. Contained in the remaining address are connotations of 'loss' constructing a theme of sorrow for the family but there is also an impression of a situation that could have been avoided. This ordering of discourse helps set story parameters to align sympathy with the family but frame Smith's identity as dangerous and requiring incarceration.

Also, Suchet's facial expression as 'barely surprised' (line 2) is uttered, a long blink coincides with his change in gaze as well as tone. Facially, his concerned gaze resembles a sense of 'not again!?' which, with the tones of frustration (noted above) imbue a sense of futility in the government policy of 'Care in the Community'. Produced is an impression in the opening statement of 'Oh no, it's happened again! You'd think they do something about it, wouldn't you!?' Schizophrenia begins as a stigmatized concept from early in the studio mode.

The Location Mode of Address and its Discourse

The expansion of the schema in the location mode is delivered through actuality footage, photographs, a filmed sequence of locations in the house where the homicides, interviews with the father and then, a hospital doctor. All of this is accompanied by a voice-over from Eric Macinnes and his final reporter-to-camera segment ending the address. Throughout, Macinnes maintains a medium-pitched voice, his generic configuration constituted of bold and uncompromising vocalizations. Moving forward, his exposé presents vivid detail about action and event, but in this address the sense of persona is diminished to that of the studio, the open and public space lessening the potentiality for intimacy.

The first visualization is the departure from court by Anthony Smith. A voice-over from Eric Macinnes at Nottingham Crown Court works this footage exposing the man's departure from a rear entrance to a waiting police van. The area at the back of the court is one in which admittance to the general public and media is prohibited. Attainment of televized pictures demands cameras located at an elevated level in order to see over the court's walls and into the secure area. This elevated angle integrates a code of surveillance in which there is a stigmatizing power produced in image (see Kress and van Leeuwen 1990: 40); 'high angles tend to diminish the individual, to flatten him morally by reducing him to ground level, to render him as caught in an insurmountable determinism' (Martin 1968: 37–8, Theo van Leeuwen's translation). As Smith leaves the court house, surrounded by warders, a digitally imposed ellipse is set over his face, making him more easily identifiable. This visually constructs a sense of a target for the viewer augmented by heard information. Morally reduced, he is assigned the identity of *the other* adding to the marginalization initiated in the studio mode. Purposely picked out from those around him, he is framed as a freak. This feature of the reporting deprives understanding through a visual framing which enhances spoken notions of 'dangerousness' about Smith as Macinnes starts his discourse (see lines 7–10).

Constructing 'Dangerous' Identity

The second visualized sequence in the location mode records the tragic event and actions in a chronicle revisiting the spaces where the murders occurred, augmented by a narrated re-enactment. The voice-over of Macinnes (coded as **EM**) further elaborates the schema of events proposed in lines 1–6 and rather than constructing a discourse about a condition, Smith's identity is categorized through the widely used label of 'paranoid schizophrenic'. The voice-over develops meanings of dangerousness as the next scene cuts to an establishing shot of the family house quickly followed by a close-up of a door entrance which then opens up to display the kitchen where the event occurred. Expectation raised about dangerousness is confirmed in lines 7–10.

7. **EM**: Anthony Smith killed his mother and step-brother instructed
8. by voices in his head. His family today claimed that their
9. voice was ignored by psychiatrists who released him from a
10. mental hospital ward, one month before the killings.

Clearly, some knowledge about schizophrenia on the part of the journalist is understood, if only from the court proceedings in terms of 'hearing voices'. The usage of the word 'voice' is employed in line 8 but is used again in line 9 to frame the family as victim through ironic value. Their 'voice' was not heard and a strong and implied tone preferences the family.

In an almost fictionalized replay of event and actions, the interplay of linguistic elements with visualizations communicates a graphic detailing of danger that generates stigma. First, the kitchen where the mother's death occurred is revealed by the suggestive opening of its door before the camera. The audience see where the homicides took place, this visualization resembling a dramatic setting-of-the-scene for them. Through a zooming lens, the image moves into the space disclosing the kitchen. In this way, imagination is left to re-work the reported actuality described in lines 11–14.

11. **EM**: Smith was taken back to the family home but one afternoon he
12. walked into the kitchen and stabbed his mother Gwendolyn 45
13. times; he had threatened her before. Next he turned on his 11
14. year old brother David, killed him, then went upstairs for a bath.

The reviewing of locations in the house is almost cinematic in its revelatory mode through language synchronizing with image; bringing into the viewing imagination a constructed sense of *how* the deaths occurred, a reconceptualizing experience of the action and event. As the name 'Gwendolyn' is mentioned, values about the *loss* of the mother are mobilized, through words like '*stabbed*' used in conjunction with a family photograph of her. Loss is further emphasized as the brother, a young boy of 11, is portrayed like his mother. A family photograph displaying depictions of youthfulness synchronize with the words '*turned on* his 11 year old brother David, *killed* him'. This mix of language with image generates significations of tragedy for the audience, still photographs connoting tragic death and simultaneously organizing relationships of sympathy for the family. Originally framed within Suchet's opening introduction, the reporter's discourse about 'paranoid schizophrenia' correlates with 'dangerousness'. Thus, this discourse recontextualizes (van Leeuwen 1993) the studio introduction foregrounding murderous events and actions in preference to other knowledge. Words like 'kill' are used four times and reinforced by the graphic nature of 'stabbed' (line 12), allowing a sense of the uncontrollable to prevail. The fulfilment of perceptual parameters about schizophrenia is completed in line 14 with 'nonchalance' connoted with his apparent action – 'killed him then went upstairs for a bath'. The knowledge content produced here is that Smith's everyday social practice is one consistent with essentialist notions of dangerousness and is misleading.

In the remaining sequence of interviews between lines 15 and 30, the determining of blame is arranged by the reporter's discourse locating responsibility for the events with a hospital.

15. Anthony's father says there's no such things as Care in the
16. Community. He claims the doctors did not heed the warnings.
17. **Anthony's father**: If I can spot it why can't the so-called experts, if that's what
18. they like to call themselves … they knew he was a ticking
19. time bomb, they just let him out.

20. **EM**: An internal hospital inquiry now recommends that patient
21. risk must be considered before discharge. (Cut to doctor in
22. his office). Though the doctors say that they didn't know
23. about Anthony's threats.

24. **Doctor**: With hindsight a longer period in hospital might have
25. helped but we need to remember that Anthony was well for
26. quite a while at home after his discharge.

27. **EM**: The judge said that Smith's release from hospital into
28. the community had to be looked at with great care. He said
29. the full facts must be known and lessons learnt.
30. Eric Macinnes. ITN. Nottingham.

The doctor's short interview mildly references the changeable nature of the condition but we are left uninformed about schizophrenia. Subsequently, the brevity of his contribution and edited information suggests the report sides with the family and legal ruling. Created is a sense of 'us' with the institution's story as right and 'them', the medical profession as wrong.

Strongly affective visual generic and linguistic components combine in a story to promote a stereotyped identity of Smith as dangerous; stigma is likely to prevail. Smith's identity is therefore subject to pejorative values and what Pickering terms 'social exorcism' (2001: 38), denying social agency. This combination within a small component of the news story pulls it in the direction of fiction, something uncommon in the character of news. Within a large UK community of people with unwell mental health, these properties in portrayal components would likely inhibit someone with any condition to be open about their condition. Certainly, the 'well' public will likely find only content about schizophrenia typed as dangerousness with little information about mental health.

News and Suicide

Before analysing the next two news stories, it is prudent to explore the relationship between news and suicide. Examining suicidal behaviour and the media, Williams and Hawton (2001) advise that storytelling approaches be considered with great care and purpose. When someone completes a suicide, there is a profound impact on the family and surrounding friends, with the risk of copycat suicides becoming a serious concern. Indeed, useful advice is now offered by the government organization SHIFT (see http://www.shift.org.uk/) in the *What's the Story* document on how to report on suicide. Prior to this document there have been some examples of excellent reporting on this topic and the two examples that follow are each worthy of close critical analysis. One *Channel 4 News* programme and another *BBC Radio 4 Today* news item present alternatives showing sensitive ways of dealing with this difficult subject. The way in which the following stories are *set* linguistically, focused upon suicide, structured in terms of storytelling, discursively and performatively arranged, hold special interest.

Channel 4 News: 'Community Care Criticism'

Description

The *Channel 4 News* example was broadcast on 18 April 1994. Lasting nearly an hour, this programme allows for a considerable duration of story treatment. Studio and location modes offer in-depth analysis and commentary across a range of items. However, this story is an example of how a programme can produce a lengthy report facilitating detailed examination of a topic. Lasting 13 minutes, the 'Community Care Criticism' story is the first of a two-stage 'special report' communicated over two days. Referencing a Commons All Party Committee Report to be published the following day, the story characterizes how news agencies plan ahead in preparation for such events and for reaction to them. The story critiques the new policy in an extended location based report with contributions from experts, parents and users of mental healthcare services.

The Studio Mode: Presenter–Viewer Relations and Personality

The 'Community Care Criticism' story begins (after a commercial break) with presenter–viewer relationships initiated around an inset image (in the top right corner of the frame) and presenter Jon Snow. Known for his colourful ties (and socks), Snow adopts an intellectual approach to storytelling in an unsentimental style of talk in a generic configuration drawing little from public orders of discourse. The delivery is styled objectively rather than reactively with intimacy traded for critical distance. The image chosen to represent the mentally unwell frames two men casually dressed, standing against a wall, looking relaxed in posture, their facial expressions suggesting a lack of interest. As the presenter speaks of people like them, the social relationships constructed to view this social group are established through themes in Snow's discourse. Snow's (hereafter JS) discourse *sets* schema for compassionate consideration in the first line.

1. **JS**: The care of the mentally ill within the community is expected to be
2. sharply criticized tomorrow in a report from the Commons All Party Committee
3. on Health. Health workers have told the committee of their profound
4. concern over the way in which mentally ill people are released from hospital
5. into the community. One new study reveals that the suicide rates among newly
6. discharged mental patients is more than 200 higher than for the rest of the
7. population. Our Home Affairs Correspondent, Robert Parker, reports
8. now on how the neglect faced by mentally ill in the community can
9. all too often have tragic consequences. *(Pause.)*

The word 'care' (line 1) spoken with an inflection of concern, sets parameters around the first theme, 'concern for the mentally ill released into the community'. These concerned tones continue with the next theme: 'a major suicide increase within mentally ill people' (lines 3–7). A shift to more sombre vocalizations then makes clear the direction the report will take, when a third theme, 'tragic consequences', is mentioned (line 9). From these themes and inflections, a serious space is produced focusing upon 'life and death' ideas about mental illness that evolve across the report. However, the words 'mentally ill' used with 'release' imply that this social group requires incarceration and introduces stigma. Many people living in society experience unwell mental health and far from requiring separation, play significant roles in the community.

The Location Mode: Performative Discourse and Imagery

If the studio address introduces an informative report with a sense of the profound, then the location mode commences a story through a distinctive voice-over with *moving* moments. Robert Parker's voice is a 'detached' generic configuration and sometimes 'concerned' vocalizations about schizophrenia. Overall, the ordering of his discourse adopts a slow pace, in a voice-over relating simply but with the culminating effect of a delivery contrasting significantly with accessed voices, especially the mother of a young schizophrenic man.

Parker's voice-over (hereafter **RP**) and first interview carry dramatic impact supported by photographs of Mark Beith (lines 1–4). This imagery functions denotatively and connotatively for the view before the mother's voice-over (hereafter **Mrs B.**) begins in line 2. The photographs are iconic, denotative significations simply referencing the person but turn connotational as the mother is introduced. Questioning community care she then unexpectedly reveals that the previous year Mark took his life.

1. **RP**: Mark Beith developed schizophrenia five years ago when he was just 18.

2. **Mrs B.**: I cannot think of anything he didn't try in the community … this is
3. called community care? Hostels, streets, *(Jean Beith fades into view)* prison,
4. bed and breakfast, hospital and his own flat.

5. **RP**: Just over a year ago with his condition worsening his parents managed
6. to get him accepted back at Napsbury Hospital near St Albans where
7. he had been twice before. *(Pause.)* But last August he was taken to this hotel in
8. North London as part of a plan to begin caring for him again in the community.

9. **Mrs B.**: He was taken up to a room, put his little things in a locker,
10. went down to the kitchen, said he was hungry, made a sandwich,
11. said he was off to the day centre, given 30p for a cup of tea and left the
12. building … so within … about … an hour and a half of being left there he had
13. jumped off a car park and was dead.

14. **RP**: The car park from which Mark jumped was within
15. a stone's throw of his old flat, and in the heart of the very
16. community in which he was being looked after. *(Pause.)*

Parker initially directs expectation toward a probable medical story but offering informative content, frames schizophrenia as a condition *evolving* during early teens.

A dissolve in line 6 sets the rural scene of Napsbury Hospital with signs indicating ward names and imagery of a hostel. The mother's voice is reintroduced in line 9 as her image returns and after informing of her family's tragic death, she closes her eyes and dips her head in sorrow (line 13) and with this second viewing of the mother, the sense that this is a shared public address is established. The unexpected dramatic moment also addresses audience with emotional power encouraging of sympathy. However, a following close-up image of a stark concrete structure is the aforementioned car park referred to by Parker, a slow zoom out revealing the location. However, his 'detached' voice-over allows only the possibility of reflection (rather than imagination) about the tragedy, as to what caused the tragedy.

Location Report, Story and Expositional Development

In the location mode, the form of the extended report is organized around its story incorporating a thesis, antithesis and synthesis with two dramatic moments (the first described above). The thesis criticizes 'care in the community', arguing that 'the mentally ill released into the community' need better treatment. By introducing Mark's life and then revealing his suicide, a following critical examination of statistical research about suicide establishes concern. This leads to the second theme, 'a major suicide increase within mentally ill people', and the instituting of the antithesis which cites the example of another young man with schizophrenia, Alex, at a new centre in Bournemouth. For Alex, the policy has worked and his introduction is made as a comparative value with Mark's identity to advance story criticism. Mark's identity even when absent is very much the focus of the story, its expositional development (even his absence) occurring at human interest and informational levels. Finally, the synthesis introduces implications about policy directions in another dramatic moment highlighting how 'tragic consequences' for Mark's family could have been avoided.

The mother's opening account is moving but effectively functions as a focus for following indirect expert discourses that explain situations like Mark's. After a torrent of troubling statistics about suicide, another academic's research contributes more information about the implications of current policy. A National Schizophrenia Society representative then offers supporting evidence from his agency. He says that the practices of the mentally unwell are presented as simply unfamiliar behaviours to a society ignorant about mental health issues. The confluence of three 'expert' sources helps expose why people with advanced conditions end up in prison when the system that is supposed to support them fails.

However, a turn in the story begins with a change in Parker's criticism and an upward directional tone symbolizing a turning point: the beginning of an antithesis advancing the situation of Alex (from line 1 below). He is seen coping well in a Bournemouth hostel, where (we learn) no suicides have occurred. However, his introduction contrasts with the still strong signifier of Mark's absence. Alex is used to drive home a reflection on 'what might have been'.

Table 5.2 ***Channel 4 News***

Generic Structure: Visual Codes and Conventions	C O M M E R C I A L	Channel 4 logo with introduction to the news. Music accompanies. Scene of presenter and studio. An oblique angle introduces viewer relations to this news of institution.	Cut to Snow introducing new viewer-relations prior to speech of *involvement* in the studio mode. The implications of the shot are similar to relations of portraiture codes.	Snow commences his direct address.
Visualisation – Auralisation	B R E A K	Channel identity through the number '4' is presented on a black border with the accompanying music. Jon Snow is introduced to the viewer, seen sitting behind a desk.	The visualization of Snow is organized through portrait, organizing personal viewer-relations channel for the delivery of language and visualizations.	Snow speaks facing camera, his mode of address organizing relations of *involvement* for the viewer. His discourse ends with a viewed expression signalling an emotive account about mental illness.
Language and Dramatic Components	C O N C L U D E S	No language communicated except the number 4.	No language is used in this section.	Language begins: 'The care of the mentally ill within the community is expected to be sharply criticized tomorrow in a report from the Commons All Party Committee on Health'. See text.

Table 5.2 Continued

Location mode of address begins. Robert Parker's voice-over in the form of a direct address employs a distanced style.	Dramatic moment: The mother announces suicide of her son after the system has neglected his case.	Thesis argument begins, working through criticism of *Care in the Community*. Facts, statistics from experts clarify and qualify the argument about the state of the government's policy toward the mentally ill.	Antithesis begins after the new hostel is seen at Bournemouth. A turn in the tone of the report signals a new slant about *Care in the Community* working.	Synthesis concludes with photos of Mark Beith. Mother concludes story with a question for the government in a moving moment.
Photographs of Mark Beith communicate his appearance/ identity without immediate notification of his absence through suicide. Mother's voice also heard talking about him.	Mother seen in grief. The shot is followed by a view of the car park from where Mark Beith died. Image pans down the building.	Run down hospitals and mentally ill people living on the street are viewed but not communicated with. Experts interviewed detailing 'suicide' levels in a study undertaken by Dr Michael Goldacre.	A selection of shots provides interesting shots of service-users in the hostel taking part in everyday activities. Alex, sufferer from 'schizophrenia' speaks.	Final visualization of the angry mother questioning action over the policy. The scene is one of understandable anger, and a moving moment.
Parker's voice-over works in a style 'distancing' the story and this order of discourse works across the report.	Mother's voice in direct relating mode but tinged with emotion at announcement of her son's passing. Parker's discourse verifies the young man's death in conjunction with the visualizations.	Parker continues to effectively refocus visual portrayals. Community Care is seen to be *not* working.	The discourse of everyday life in the hostel works its way through the contribution of Alex. The hostel, a rare example, is seen to be working assisted through tonal inflection.	Angry and anguished tones fill the last scene of the mother criticizing the government: 'when will the government listen? My son is dead'.

Note: This table should be read from left to right across both pages.

Parker's voice-over refocuses visualizations, with Alex's discourse (lines 3–5 and 7–8, see below) depicting people with schizophrenia as simply in need of care. With the condition illustrated as deeply complex and conveyed without stigma, his story of success is traded for the other; one of sadness.

Mental Health Identity and Reality:
Constructions of a Condition Called Schizophrenia

Parker's lighter tone maintains its 'detached' feel but coupled with hostel imagery and accessed-voices infuse new hope, this turn of information bringing about new constructions of schizophrenic identity and reality. The selective but highly productive choice of Alex shows another side to the community care system. He is similar in age to Mark, and his interview works powerfully as an intended but not overt comparison of how two similar situations can turn out differently. Alex is seen talking about suicide as a key element of his condition and made real through his identification of symptoms that lead toward 'tackling the problem early'. Parker introduces him:

1. This former student had made several attempts on his
2. life before he finally got a place at the centre.

If previously sufferers were not heard those in the hostel now are; two members, including Alex are viewed entering the hostel and greeting each other. Depicted walking upstairs and into their rooms they are subjectivized as 'ordinary', albeit in slightly contrived enactments. This 'reality' view helps build a strong sense of condition 'actuality' as Alex is seen as someone with a debilitating health condition in need of specialized medical and social care. A succession of shots of other residents reveals their practices before the imagery returns to Alex.

3. **Alex**: I could see my friends around me finishing
4. College, going on to University and this sort of thing
5. and … that for me was just like there was this void in my life.

6. **RP**: Do you think that is less likely to happen here?

7. **Alex**: I would say so yes … because the staff can see
8. it happening and they can nip it in the bud.

Alex (in lines 3–5) informs his life as a '*void*', presenting alternative values about the evolution of his condition. This direct portrayal and voice-over help clarify his experience as seen in the context of other social figures (i.e., that of friends, now students). Being a college student is an identifiable practice in many societies and with the suicide theme being reversed (see lines 7–8 above), Parker's voice-over continues with imagery depicting a number of people in activities. Imagery augments Parker's information as to how clients live in the centre before a familiar photograph returns audience attention to Mark Beith and the story's synthesis. Art he produced before his death is introduced across the remaining dialogue, but a final dramatic moment employing Mrs Beith signals the story's end. As the last person to speak, her irreplaceable loss and pain is clearly evident and the focus of the story's strong ending. Her final question demands action about the lack of resources and neglect that contributed to her son's situation. In this last moment, communicatively engineered to instil sympathy, meanings made about bereavement serve to make poignant her plea for answers.

Through clear phases of inquiry Care in the Community is criticized with meanings about schizophrenia evolving from two categories; academic data and real-world situations. These help to type it as a medical condition requiring critical care. By placing two dramatically moving moments at the beginning and end of the report, audience are anchored in a real world situation viewing story content through the 'family' point of view. Utilizing these dramatic moments effectively, the intervening generic structure is constituted of a carefully constructed argument with critical research content, experts, accessed voices in a report delivery conscientiously vocalized. Social agency is enabled through the discourse and imagery of Alex, his schizophrenia also typed as an evolving and complex condition. With little stigma generated, few stereotypes emerge and subsequently, viewers with unwell mental health will likely be encouraged by this report and those with mental well-being are likely to discover something new about the subjectivity of people with schizophrenia.

BBC Radio 4: *The Today Programme*

This BBC Radio 4 'Today' mediation was broadcast on 4 February 1997. An established programme, its formal characteristics have changed little in recent years. With a mix of styles employed by its news presenters and announcers, the programme is very popular with listeners. Each presenter undertakes interviews in a discursive practice that can be described as searching and sometimes 'combative' in stylistic configuration. Presenters can also convey feelings of relaxed, good-humoured address in an established tradition of in-depth inquiry. The analysis which follows explores selected modes of address with contributions from Sue MacGregor, Niall Dickson and reporter Mike Thompson. Like the Channel 4 exemplar, this story focuses upon Care in the Community and suicide, using aspects of dramatic performance in its communicative processes.

The Today Programme *as a Form of Knowing*

The form of *The Today Programme* consists of discursive conventions which oscillate between broadly formal/informal styles of discourse delivery (see Table 5.3 for generic structure). By convention, a presenter introduces the programme's headlines in a mostly formal style. This is followed by a continuity announcer who formally presents headlines, sometimes with story contributions from reporters in the field. Then, an informal discourse within an interview and/or report occurs before a new presenter addresses another topic and so on. Toward the end of every half hour, sport is reported in an informal way and after every half hour, a shift to the same pattern of formal/informal delivery is repeated. Audience know when styles of talk change across a programme and expect different deliveries from journalists as well as from politicians, experts and accessed voices. For each formal/informal style, different relationships with audience are organized via different interpretative demands made upon listeners.

Studio Modes of Address: Discursive Conventions and Discourse Types in Today

Midway through the sub-headlines, the opening segment for this story is read out by continuity announcer Charlotte Green (hereafter **CG**). Voice, according to Crisell (1994), provides a human presence in radio news and is an indexical signifier of identity. Green's generic configuration fosters a personable and warm yet formal deep toned voice, her identity also known as that of a 'friend' to some listeners (Elmes 2007). Always clear, topic details are mostly denotative presenting just literally the words and sentences in a vocalization with the barest of vocal value. Her delivery is simply a declaration of headlines and the presence of her voice reflects that albeit paced quickly as she delivers a list of topics.

a. **CG**: Proposals for improving care for the mentally ill are to be outlined by
b. ministers today in a green paper. It'll set out several options for reform
c. of Care in the Community, including the creation of new joint health and
d. social service authorities.

In this opening segment, 'green paper legislation' is the key focus and so mental health is assigned a legal status because of linkages to a parliamentary procedure. Words, particularly 'proposals' and 'the mentally ill' retain a literal quality, contributing as shapers to following content. Operating as a generic anchor, they cue expectations about mental health as schema constituted of healthcare and legal qualities before a shift to another discursive convention.

> The amount of human 'presence' must be enough to make reading the news expressive and interesting, but not so great as to make us more conscious of the reader than of what is being read. Hence when a change of voice occurs in radio news it must be dictated by the logic of the news itself – by a change from one headline or story to another, or from one aspect of the story to another, including the transition from the actual text of the bulletin to a correspondent's report. (Crisell 1994: 105)

Green's presence holds interest for headlines only, but when this discursive convention resumes at approximately 7.30am another series of sub-headlines are formally offered but the story about mental health is absent. Sub-headlines concluded, the story begins, signifying the end of formalized discourse and the beginning of an informal yet direct style demanding greater listener attention and interpretation. Opening the story two minutes later without notification, MacGregor's generic configuration is constituted of Received Pronunciation in a relaxed style, her vocal tones resembling a friend in a fireside conversation. Mentioning the green paper, she next introduces Niall Dickson but unlike television where edited interviews provide evidential qualities in the 'viewings' of interviewees, in radio news it is *hearings*, though here vocal data introduces resembles a 'between friends' configuration.

A level of disquiet in MacGregor's voice reveals unease in her introduction illustrated in 'failings' (line 2), the combined words and language *setting* a sense of, '*well, why should it have failed?*'. Codes of concern invite further listener curiosity about why reform is needed with lines 1–3 configured in a formal style but from line 4, the talk changes to a discourse type more associated with a trusted friend. What follows is an alternating dialogue between the two.

1. **SM**: The government unveils its plans for mental health today and what
2. it plans to do in an area where there have been some high profile failings.
3. Our Social Affairs Editor Niall Dickson is on the line.
4. Niall, the Government has admitted – Mr Dorrell has admitted –
5. that all is not well in mental health care – hasn't he?

Dickson responds in a similar 'friends' configuration but also like a person resigned to relating about a bad situation that occurred at work. This exchange is probably a result of preproduction planning intended to frame the topic in a certain way. The contrivance of the conversation is not so apparent as to appear pretentious but comes across as something just happening and demanding a listener relationship akin to, but just short of eavesdropping.

6. **ND**: Yes he had – and in a sense this document is an admission that care
7. in the community – an old policy really dating from the early sixties and
8. shutting down these large asylums is not working for everyone as it
9. should – in spite of a long list of government inspired initiatives. I think
10. today the document will concentrate on the fact that the links between
11. social services and the health service is sometimes poor – and that
12. sometimes the service offered is not safe and it's not efficient so they're
13. identifying both managerial and organisational failures.

Confirmation by Dickson to MacGregor is made through agreement not just in words but also in vocalizations. In line 6, '*Yes he had*' is pitched upwards with a presupposed sense of all that follows is accepted fact, his remaining discourse

Table 5.3 BBC Radio 4 *The Today Programme*

Time → Generic Elements ↓	On the hour	Post 7+8am (immediately after time signal)	At approx. 1–2 mins past the hour and at the half hour
Generic Structure	Time signal initiates programme cycle.	Broadcast journalists read out four or five headlines before introducing newsreader.	Continuity announcers read story with reporter contributions. Headlines increase to approx. six to eight, sometimes more.
Discursive Conventions	No language.	A set of approx. four headlines and communicated in a serious tone indicationg the gravitas of news content. The newsreader is introduced by name.	A wider range of headlines are presented in deep voice tones typical for both female and male newsreaders.
Auralization	Five bleeps prior to the hour signify a five-second countdown, the last signal indicating the time precisely.	Only one voice heard against silence.	Combination of continuity announcers heard against silence and 'on the scene' reporter sometimes with external noise.

Table 5.3 Continued

At approx. 7–8 mins past each half hour in-depth examination begins	**At approx. 7.25 and 8.25am**	**At approx. 7.30 and 8.30am**	**Some 7–8 mins prior to the hour signal**
New stories follow on from previous headlines with broadcast journalists developing topics with a series of interviews which address range of interview types.	Sport is introduced near the half hour.	Sub-headlines are repeated though varying in number and selection.	'Thought For The Day', Weather, Radio 4 Programmes across the day, road conditions etc. are communicated from about 15 mins to the hour.
Conversationalized discourse is encountered through the interview genre.	Sometimes triumphant, sometimes woeful tones of sporting results. Interviews carried out with players, managers and other parties.	Again, a set of approx. four headlines communicated in a serious toned voice indicating the gravitas of news content. A newsreader is again introduced by name.	A selection of people introduces these topics before the main newsreader returns to introduce the time signal.
Combination of broadcast journalist and interviewees, also accompanied by reporters, interested parties and at times, associated sounds from the scene.	Sound of sports journalist in a less serious tone reporting the sporting events. This includes atmosphere of the event, sometimes the sounds of sporting crowds.	Voice set against silence.	Change in the normal voices heard across the hour signifying change of information for weather, traffic and eventually the time signal once again.

Note: This table shoud be read from left to right across both pages.

also vocalized in explanatory tones. Notably absent are notions about killings or suicides and instead, a focus extending to policy and managerial issues are addressed without any reference to dangerousness. This *friendly* discussion continues with MacGregor questioning if new institutions will replace old ones. Economic considerations are also examined but after evidence about 'hot bedding' is mentioned, where patients in communities share facilities in overcrowded hospitals, more useful information is revealed. In line 14 her vocalization is *concerned* but in 15 and 16, transforms to a questioning style pitching upwards, drawing upon *common sense* type of discourse to question that if this is obvious – why has no-one done anything?

14. **SM**: But just briefly, as you indicated at the beginning Niall,
15. people will say why on earth did it take them so long with all these
16. high profile cases some of them ending in death?

17. **ND**: I think that's a fair charge – there's no doubt that this policy under
18. successive Governments has proven much more difficult than either the
19. health professionals or the social service professionals realized – or indeed
20. policy makers have done. Secondly, I think there is a recognition it has
21. remained a Cinderella service – it was David Owen when he was Health
22. Minister who first said mental health needs to be a priority in ministers –
23. frankly have been bleating that ever since – and lastly, the demand is rising:
24. there are more of us who are mentally ill, more of us who are sick.
25. The stresses of modern life means that the pressure on the service is
26. actually increasing.

27. **SM**: Niall Dickson, thank you.

MacGregor's opening question focuses upon government responsibility to resolve the situation. By choosing the word 'death', this meaning conflates homicide and suicide to introduce tragedy rather than fear usually associated with dangerousness. Avoiding such themes, Quinn agrees in this conversationalized mode that admissions about making the policy work have proved challenging. But it is through this 'between friends' type of talk that a personal space for discussing mental health makes it accessible. It is made yet more relatable via personal relationship with the topic further facilitated by Quinn's mention of Dr David Owen's views about the system requiring overhaul. The use of 'us' (line 24), in a societal sense, becoming unwell also draws listeners into the notion that it is as much about *them* because modernity is fraught with pressure. Through this concerned tone and carefully used language broadcast discourse avoids stigma and instead, includes everyone in the address. Mental health is typed as an official 'well-being and health' responsibility of government but also as something that should concern everyone. Following this examination, another studio and location report occurs in the following half-hour segment.

Location Mode: Story, Interview and Discourse

Constituted mainly of reporter discourse, a range of voices edited prior to broadcast augment the story. However, contained across this report, alternating discourses between Thompson and Hurley enhance a drama during its opening through a sequential intertextuality, 'where different texts … alternate within a text' (Fairclough 1992: 118) as the voices of Thompson and a mother develop story. Here, the unique aural qualities of radio allow audience to imagine anguish rather than see it, as in the Channel 4 exemplar. MacGregor introduces the story.

28. **SM**: The Government's publishing its ideas today on how services for
29. the mentally ill could be improved. There's been a great deal of concern that
30. the care in the community idea has been failing, so that the Green Paper is
31. expected to concentrate on ways of improving co-ordination between
32. health authorities and social services departments – a lack of proper
33. communication is being blamed for some suicides and even killings by
34. psychiatric patients. In a moment we will be talking to the health secretary
35. Stephen Dorrell, but first Mike Thompson reports.

After *setting* a legislative context again, MacGregor's discourse examines the issues of suicide and homicide but in a way rare to news. Suicides are mentioned first (line 33) making it more the dominant issue rather than homicide, this sequence uncommon in news. As the adverb 'even' is vocalized in surprised tones and followed by 'killings' an intended comparison with suicides is invited, introducing the notion that homicide is less common event, a rare accuracy in this form. This guides expectation that what will follow is different to the norm of news stories which usually reference homicide. Journalist Mike Thompson's voice (hereafter **MT**) starts the report but another voice, that of Joy Hurley (hereafter **JH**), provides dramatic impact. Thompson's voice is calm in manner, embodying levels of concern and also irony.

36. **MT**: Care in the Community in Joy Hurley's view didn't amount
37. to very much care at all for her 25-year-old son Paul who
38. suffered from schizophrenia – she said that since leaving hospital he
39. continued to struggle mentally but was lucky to see his local psychiatric
40. nurse more than once every six weeks – and then for just a few minutes at a
41. time – and when he suffered serious and often frightening relapses he, like
42. many other patients, was offered only fleeting stays in hospital.

'Care in the Community' (line 36) is vocalized pointedly via Thompson's emphasis on 'care' and contains a questioning value (line 37) which falls slightly short of sarcasm. One meaning of the word care, as intended here, is to 'look after' or 'provide for', but this strong vocalization organizes intertextual relationships of irony between word meaning and policy practice. Thus, care for those with unwell mental being is organized in a poor relationship to *Care in the Community*. Highlighting this inadequacy, Thompson next portrays Paul's identity as in trouble, one who 'struggled' (line 39) and 'suffered' (lines 38 and 41) to receive appropriate medical assistance. Subsequently, his identity subsumed within Care in the Community's poor care is framed as the subject of neglect. Next however, the mother's testimony is vocalized in a distraught but emphatic voice. (Italics represent emphasis in vocalization and bold italics, emphasis with raised voice.)

43. **JH**: They will not keep them in hospital – they send
44. them straight back *to the family* – they are left to their own devices to
45. take the medication prescribed – ***and of course they don't***

46. **MT**: Paul recently told Joy that he felt psychotic and violent and was
47. worried he'd hurt her or himself if he didn't get emergency help quickly

48. **JH**: *Paul wanted to go to hospital that morning – he was screaming to go to*
49. *hospital. [Pause.] I* ***told*** *them and* ***told*** *them – but nothing was ever done*

50. **MT**: Ten days ago Paul committed suicide. Since the dawn of care in the
51. community in the mid 1980s numerous asylums and psychiatric units have
52. closed and with them 150,000 beds. Professor Chris Thompson, Registrar
53. of the Royal College of Psychiatrists, said this has made helping people
54. in Paul's condition increasingly difficult.

Lines 43–45 and 48–49 provide windows of experience into dealing with the community care system, the mother's graphic accounts retaining powerful human presence within Thompson's story. But these imagined encounters for listeners resonate within Thompson's discourse which organizes these elements as tense moments of conflict for the mother. Her discourse further critiques the system by her twice use of 'they' emphatically (line 43), this third person plural and a subjective pronoun delineating boundaries between her family and authorities. Emphasis in the word is provocative but its further use (lines 44 and 45) references patients suffering the same condition as her son. Here, her vocalization changes switching from values of *explanation* to *exasperation* at two points her generic configuration transforming to almost screaming as codes of injustice emerge as well as grievance. Subsequently, Thomson represents the mother's discourse supplying a personal history of her son's experiences and as he concludes, so she begins drawing upon her personal testimony. As she concludes so he begins increasing the sense of neglect about her son's care within the interview. From lines 43 to 49, there is nothing to suggest Hurley's son has passed on but the story is constructed for the dramatic disclosure revealed in line 50. Resonating neglect, the mother's tones of distress add authenticity to a story of patient abandonment.

From Green's literal discourse to a 'friends' discussion and through another effectively employed dramatic arrangement, the topic of mental health is arranged in a careful sequence that results in accessible information. Facts relative to 'care' are mostly associated with administrative and organizational matters and by doing this, the story bypasses stigma. Story structure used in Thompson's discourse, like Parker's in the previous example organize a dramatic moments to give a focus to seriousness around life and death themes. Likely, viewers with experience of a mental health condition will find it accessible as a depiction and without stereotypes usually found in news language. The listening public too will likely be interested by knowledge content.

Documentary Form and Mental Health

A number of documentaries have examined mental health, most notably Fred Wiseman's *Titicut Follies* (1967), a fly-on-the-wall documentary examining a Massachusetts State Hospital for the 'criminally insane' in Bridgewater which was later closed. Controversy surrounded this film when it showed the internal workings of the facility, which saw staff taunting and bullying prison occupants. A lengthy legal battle ensued over whether patients' rights to privacy had been violated and the case even went to the United States Supreme Court, but in 1992 the film was legally shown. Also in the USA, *No Ordinary Joe: Erasing the Stigma of Mental Illness* (2004) explores the life of teacher Joe Laurencelle, an athlete and coach was diagnosed with bipolar depression at the age of 22. Joe took his own life at 26 but the documentary celebrates his relationships with friends and discusses mental illness. Other UK documentaries include Michael Apted's *Up* films, a series which began in 1964, and *The Hurt Mind* (1957, see Chapter 2). One *Up* mental health depiction examined depression and *The Hurt Mind* examined a range of conditions with first person accounts.

More recently in the UK, self-reflexive forms with observational pieces and interviews have prevailed. Stephen Fry's *The Secret Life of The Manic Depressive* (2006) shown on BBC 2 illuminates useful knowledge about the condition. Also, Alistair Campbell's *Cracking Up* (2008) explores depression during an earlier part of his career. These last two films are characteristic of a period in which there have been considerable efforts on the part of some mental health charities and media institutions to get celebrities to use their public prominence to encourage open discussion about mental health issues. However, as Caprani (2009), who worked for the charity *Rethink* (on the *Time to Change* campaign) notes, the media appear reluctant to cover the issue without celebrity endorsement. Such projects while worthy of getting the subject into the public eye, do so without showing the situation of the many (without fame) who experience conditions. Stories about ordinary people experiencing stigma are few and far between, indeed, documentaries referencing schizophrenia in this way are rare but for the following example.

Mad, Sad or Bad

Mad, Sad or Bad is a BBC *Video Diaries* production (13 September 1994), a vérité observational documentary form about a young woman, Sharon, who suffers from schizophrenia. The programme won a Mental Health Media Award for its portrayal. Popular in Britain at the time, *Video Diaries* was an access programme promoted by the BBC Community Action Unit which provided camcorder equipment to individuals who desired to make their own programme. Participants retained editorial and content control over the programme's production process. The form's success came during the early 1990s and rejuvenated documentary when a lurch toward hybrid forms was underway. The infotainment value was considerable but dependent on the person whose diary was being told, their personality and topic. The diversity of these diary formats was as wide as the numerous people and ideas offered for examination.

Description In this diary, Sharon, who has been diagnosed as schizophrenic, attempts to confront what she terms as 'the roots of her madness' in order to rid herself of the voices which daily plague her. Born to a white mother who had a brief relationship with a black man, and from a family of six children, Sharon was abandoned at birth and given away for fostering. As the fostering process failed her, she was sent into mental institutions and later prisons. Eventually she was released into the community, became homeless and lived on the streets but was plagued by her voices which were her only company. The programme acts as a vehicle for Sharon, who seeks to find her mother with the help of a social worker. Living in the Manchester area with her boyfriend Mick who also experiences schizophrenia, Sharon's journey begins in a tensioned struggle to resolve situations relevant to her condition. Living in a flat, the couple's existence is one which involves everyday meetings with people using mental healthcare services and also, events which bring Sharon into contact with the official discourses of institutions such as psychiatric and social services. Another intention of the film is to try and show what the reality of life is for those who live behind the schizophrenia label in society and reveal the politics of their existence.

Knowing through the Video Diaries Form The generic qualities of *Mad, Sad or Bad* makes its form a vérité observation type as the film is an intervention between the topic and filmmakers, Sharon and Mick; they are directly involved in making observable themselves as characters informing about their condition. The generic structure is also shaped in a form similar to the way in which someone might skip through the pages of diary booklet but in an aural and visual way. Days are selectively presented becoming minutes with only relevant conversations communicated in disjointed ways with editing a significant definer of story flow. Conventions common to the series involve edit cuts depicted by white noise with intentionally produced screen interference, signifying location, event and story changes for viewers. A less predictable form of knowing to that of news, audience also come to know 'visually' through a camera, sometimes on a tripod while at other times handheld. Sometimes they view Sharon or Mick through direct address or hear Sharon's narration. With indirect addresses, overheard speech and long takes offering extended views of time and space, there is an orderly 'disorder' across the form, which has structural implications enforcing a fragmentary aesthetic.

Analysis Opening imagery depicts Sharon lying on her bed, her discourse overheard as it evidences that all is not well in a vocalization resembling someone feeling sick. Uncluttered by directorial devices, this discourse conveys an apparent natural quality, giving the documentary a real-time rhythm and feel. The pace of the programme requires audience work at the identification of communicative elements as human behaviours occurs through an 'as-it-happens' reality. One example is Mick, seen moving into frame to sit next to Sharon who *is* in some discomfort. Mick comforts her in a gentle manner but in this vérité mode he *sometimes* interacts with the camera while at other times does not.

Mick: It's Friday … Monday 27 July and we've just started filming in the bedroom and see what we're getting and Sharon is a bit upset. I'm sorry.

Sharon: *(Distressed.)* I don't want to do it *(referring to the film)*! I'm tired!

Mick: Can you explain what the problem is? Sharon! Please!

Sharon: I'm tired!

Mick: I feel like I'm torturing you! *(Indicating that he is only trying to help.)*

Sharon: I'm sick of this film … I want to go to sleep.

A fade to black occurs, then a picture of the sky is shown and the titles 'Mad, Sad or Bad' fade up.

This opening scene *sets* visual and linguistic perception within ambiguous parameters. Instead of a steady flow of direct address, as in news, a long take characteristic of the form introduces Sharon. Viewed in what appears as non-compliance with the filming, unclear boundaries are established. She appears to go against the grain of the documentary's purpose by not offering any point of view. Her indirect and apparent muddled address 'I'm tired' followed by 'I'm sick of this film … I want to go to sleep' shows her unhappy psychological state but precisely what the matter is remains unclear. From social orders of discourse, her generic configuration resembles the person who *might* be medicated but the apparent lack of action initiates a greater expectation about precisely what will be forthcoming.

Thus, the development of a structure of anticipation about potential directions is left blurred with the only real conveyed sense being that she is troubled. The space produced is a confused one but leaves viewers to discern their own construction of what is happening.

After the opening titles Sharon and Mick are seen at a park enjoying the slides and swings though both are cognizant of their part in attempting to set something up for the film. Sharon's voice-over then begins, breaking up any notions of external production values, her personal voice highlighting that this is not something she regularly undertakes. However, there is agency through a felt strength in a voice with intention.

> *You probably don't think you'll crack up – the chances are you might then you'd be a nutter like me – a doctor will give you a label that sticks to you for the rest of your life. Mine was schizophrenic. Making this diary was hard, sharing all my secrets, but I really wanted you to see me – the person I am behind the label. Most of my life I've spent in institutions until I met Mickey. He's a schizophrenic too. Now we live together in Manchester – Mickey, my two cats and my voices, echoes from the past. This is the root of my madness.*

This opening address is significant since previous cues as to what the programme might be about are now dispelled. First, audience are challenged by a vernacular mode of expression in 'cracking up', the (in)security of viewer well-being questioned and with this, the politics of mental unwell identity brought to the fore. Presenting her own mental label, this disclosure qualifies as a huge political decision to expose her difference before a national audience. The idea of living with difference is a central choice by Sharon, to challenge viewers about prevalent stereotypes. Moreover, she seeks to offer a new conceptualization, that of the person and not the label. Her subjectivity in all its normality, her strengths and weaknesses are unveiled for examination making for an exceptional knowledge yield.

Authenticity about stigmatized identity is also revealed in Sharon's discourse when she calls herself a 'nutter'. This usage of the word shows her reclaiming the language of dominant culture, to employ the stigmatizing nominalization of perceivers and her enunciating this word, she is again celebrating her difference from society, a point Cross (2010: 147) also identifies. However, her discourse also draws viewers to her sense of linguistic action about stigma, demanding from them greater thought about it. Embracing this position she communicates about the politics of living with a 'schizophrenic' label, her voices and also her love for Mickey. The term 'schizophrenic' is also examined by Mickey as something he doesn't like, this personal mode of address again, a significant component exposing cultural boundaries about the label's pejorativeness. For him, this stigmatizing removes mentally unwell people from any social position connected with culture, exorcizing them in the most extreme ways possible. Also, the words 'mental illness' are impregnated with a diseased-ness, but Mickey's candour while illuminating, it is difficult listening to the painfulness of the term revealed by him. Clearly, negative values associated with these linguistic elements are significant and real to both.

After an edit of produced screen and sound interference, a scene depicts how the reality of schizophrenia is governed by medication. Sharon's condition is supported through psychiatric advice about what she should take, but a critical review by Mickey before she visits her drug cabinet reveals the extent of her situation. With prior experience of the mental healthcare system and medication, he critiques the service they use, his personal testimony not complimentary. Mick is seen in the kitchen washing up, mid-shot from the side. While the documentary's opening may have been perplexing, the scene's actions gather pace as he talks about Sharon's medication history.

Mick: 1. When I first met Sharon, she was very over medicated
2. cos she was on tons of tablets and things, she was
3. basically … she could hardly f***ing move and er …

(Sharon, in the background, calls.)

Sharon: 4. … you said I,
5. I got all the Ventolin.

Mick: 6. Yer, I did say that Sharon would get better and she's
7. on a bit less medication now.

If Mick implies that things are better, the ensuing imagery and discourse challenge that suggestion. Sharon is depicted (mid-shot) standing by an open bathroom cupboard filled with an array of medicine boxes in different shapes, colours and sizes. She takes a packet out and presents it to camera. From this point forward, her personal testimony changes between direct and indirect address to a camera placed close to her face. The social space afforded the viewer is one inviting closeness with her views. While her discourse sounds tired, likely because of medication, she is very able in communicating feelings and thoughts.

Sharon: 8. These are my tablets, I'm on eleven a day. I'm on this
9. one, Carbamazepine, which is for a mood disorder and I
10. take this one three times a day. *(She puts it back.)*
11. And it makes me feel tired. I also take Procyclidine
12. for the side effects of the injection. That's four
13. times a day. *(She returns this bottle to the cabinet.)*
14. What else? … I'm also on these tablets for migraine
15. called Migralieve, Prothiadine, yer, that's an
16. anti-depressant and Largactyl which is, er, its full
17. name is chlorpromazine hydrochloride.

(Mick, still in the kitchen, hollers:)

Mick: 18. It's an anti-psychotic ...

Sharon: 19. It's an anti-psychotic and I take that at night. *(She puts*
20. *it back and picks up another one.)* And another,
21. Mellerill … this is Mellerill. *(Opens the box to extract*
22. *capsule packet.)* No, that's Largactyl, well Mellerill
23. and Largactyl are similar and I take four of these a day.
24. *(Puts it back.)* And that's about it. *(Closes the*
25. *cupboard.)* I feel drugged up most of the time!

In this testimony and through a close-up, face-to-face angle, Sharon's revelatory discourse about her medication dependency is firsthand information offered through first-person experience for viewers. This imagery formulates a personal space enabling the viewing of a woman with a complex condition in a struggle to just try and live. As the increasing number of prescription names likely confuses most viewers, this also works to authenticate her situation. Their frequency of usage and side-effects of fatigue also contribute to a sense of bewilderment about how many tablets a person *can* take. While agency is present in her commitment to make the documentary, her power to function as she would like is inhibited by medication making her tired, as conveyed through her voice.

Two other contributions make this a significant depiction. First, through her diary viewers are afforded an opportunity to know about the 'voices' Sharon hears and that of other people with schizophrenia, at a Hearing Voices group. She is aware that her voices originate from her past whereas another group user vividly describes how hers occur only when she is angry. Quite purposeful on the part of Sharon as camera person, she ensures her point of view and that of another person is seen and heard by their inclusion. In direct and indirect address, discourses of other people with schizophrenia elaborate different situation and causes of the condition. Thus, through imagery showing Sharon and her friends, the mechanisms that cause voices are exposed, this inclusion helping to dispel myths. The second contribution is the relationship between Mickey and Sharon. Representations of schizophrenia usually mobilize stigmatic knowledge about violence, denying notions that people with such conditions can maintain relationships. However, in one depiction of Mickey in a lounge with a friend, he complains about a recent violent event. He quips the violent offender should be locked up. Sharon, again unwell, interjects to question if she should be too (because her condition stereotypes her as violent) but he responds very quickly that she doesn't need locking up; rather she needs lots of loving. A clear targeting of this stereotype which stigmatizes people with schizophrenia by Sharon makes this moment singularly meaningful. Myths about this group as 'dangerous' to society are single-handedly addressed through a self-effacing humour which effectively dismantles powerful ideas about violence. If her previous testimonies and imagery of medication induced tiredness communicate anything, it is far from being a danger to anyone. Rather, her identity is affected by social, health and medical discourses that cannot quell her ebullient persona or agency.

In *Mad, Sad or Bad*, meanings made support ideas about social realities and identities which inform about schizophrenia in knowledge content not usually found in broadcasting schedules. Ideas about individuals struggling to survive complex personal histories prevail to result in a counter discourse disrupting of themes about dangerousness. Schizophrenia is typed as constituted of unsettling processes which significantly impede balance in a person's wellbeing; something most people take for granted. By having it explained directly by people who have schizophrenia, not only is stigma absent but also knowledge about the impact on the person is improved.

Conclusions

In these non-fictional forms, a range of mental health types and identities are produced for the public sphere from different communicative performances. While a variety of representational outcomes occur, from themes of dangerousness to more medical models, it is useful to bear in mind now (before the Reception Study in Chapter 7) what people who have the subjectivity of experience of a mental health condition might read in these mediations. Questions arise about what people with unwell mental being make sense of 'who they are?' and/or 'who they might be?' and also, the variations of stigma in these mediations.

In the ITN studio mode concepts about 'dangerousness' are set up with language stating facts that a '*schizophrenic ... killed*'. The location mode report further magnifies the murder event with representational elements of selected footage and graphic language combining to frame schizophrenia in a segment resembling horror film depiction. In this briefly fictionalizing moment the audience are offered a re-imagining of action with dramatic value in a report with words like '*stabbed*' etc. Subsequently, through its form the mediation mildly fictionalizes producing relationships to horror form and stereotypical identity. Such meanings do not encourage useful knowledge about mental health or people with unwell mental being to participate in society.

The Channel 4 exemplar employs different aspects of drama as its studio mode of address exchanges emotionalizing the issue for an unsentimental delivery. Dramatic effect is employed without warning at the beginning of the location report but with some expectation of it at end, while the intervening 12 minutes is employed as a critical space to focus upon data about the need to reduce deaths. Through presenting academic data to critique Care in the Community and by employing the absent young man as a comparison with another for whom the system is working, a strong argument is made to increase similar care. Parker's performance is crafted through well-structured storytelling and in a formal 'reserved' configuration. These components and the careful choice of language serve to encourage understanding about the condition making mental health an accessible concept for the general public while mostly also avoiding the generation of stigma.

Similarly, *The Today Programme* creates several spaces conducive to knowing about mental health. A convivial space enables accessible information for listeners to learn about mental health which, while legally framed is also socially inclusive for all. The second space is similar to the Channel 4 exemplar's focus upon suicide in relation to schizophrenia. Empathetic consideration is encouraged through an emotive mode of address in which the bereaved mother's statements position the audience to know *personally*, information about her loss. The words 'suicide' and 'homicides' are replaced by 'death' shifting focus from action taken to loss.

In *Mad, Sad or Bad* first person accounts offer first person experiences about schizophrenia. Its generic form replaces institutionalized performance for ones natural, allowing for a point of view from the person(s) with the condition. Sharon and Mick inform about their own history and relate about the impact of medications in a view of schizophrenia that is largely unfettered. The unravelling of Sharon's existence exposes tensions of how personally difficult the condition of schizophrenia is to negotiate. Its depiction as seriously disruptive to a person's consciousness and its requiring different types but significant quantities of medication, ensures knowledge about well-being, is effectively conveyed. The drama played out is not imagined but real, Sharon's personality is able to engage in close relationships with other people; a relationship which is not only lasting but also meaningful.

Chapter 6
Phase One, Genre Studies 3: Drama

Introduction

The following chapter about fictional forms critically examines drama and its representational qualities. Two forms are comedy dramas from television; the first, *Takin' Over the Asylum*, is produced at BBC Scotland for BBC 2 and second, *The Sopranos*, is produced by HBO. A third, a comic strip produced by Chester Brown entitled *My Mom Was A Schizophrenic*, undertakes a serious treatment of schizophrenia. Each example has as its imaginative centre a place and particular set of people. One is the asylum and its patients. Another is New Jersey and two families while the final one is Chester Brown, Toronto and historical discourses. The foci for analysis in the forms are the imaginative pleasures produced for audience/reader–text relations. The aim is to examine how portrayals construct spaces about mental health, enabling identities to speak and produce knowledge content in various realisms. Of note are drama's propositional and/or symbolic discourses, and claims each mediation makes in communicating something about mental health.

Analytical Framework

This framework is designed to analyse different types of meaning-making about mental health and associated identities in the patterns of pleasure in fictional forms. In this framework, drama is defined as the examination of human interaction at its roots. The key focus is *how* drama's significatory components contribute to representations, especially about a character's condition and identity.

Identity is also studied in a changing television drama context. As Thornham and Purvis (2005) note in writing about Stuart Hall's (1987) work, television dramas are prolific as primary generators of narratives producing identities for contemporary culture. They write: 'It is this fact which has produced anxieties about "saturation", fear that firm identities and points of value are being lost, and the desire to rescue for serious critical attention that which is *not* fluid, unbounded and over-involving' (2005: 28). With each television mediation employing the forms of drama and comedy, and the comic strip composed of humorous but also serious elements, the analysis questions what these mediations say about mental health identities not only in a television drama context but also a societal one. It also questions the implications of each mediation concerning fears over saturation.

The framework also examines relationships between drama and comedy, because humour has a role in society for undermining dominant, serious ideas through communicative forms. Brett Mills shows that theory about humour has traditionally been split into three categories. The first is *superiority*, where laughter reinforces positions of power; the second is *incongruity* in which humour 'results from the clash of incompatible discourses, which are themselves socially constructed and learned' (Creeber 2001: 63). The final category is *relief theory*, which has its roots in the psychoanalytical approach; this explores humour as a 'vent for repression and, by extension, questions social norms' (2001: 63). Subsequently, the framework examines these forms and the resemblances they have to these categories. Finally, in studying the TV Series *The Sopranos*, a broad philosophical view is also adopted for its focus on the main character.

Takin' Over the Asylum[1]

Takin' Over the Asylum was written by Donna Franceschild, produced by Chris Parr and directed by David Blair. Franceschild's motivation for the work originated from personal experience, her intention to critically challenge accepted views about mental illness. With considerable research undertaken, much of it was translated into the fiction's characterizations. As Henderson notes (see Philo et al. 1996: 35), the writer worked with mental health organizations to secure important information but also had a strong production team. Made into a serial of six programmes, these won awards for its depictions from Mental Health Media, English BAFTA for Best Serial and Best Editing and Scottish BAFTA for Best Serial and Writer; it also won a Royal Television Society award for Best Writer. With a supportive producer and BBC 2 controller sympathetic to the production, and with both cognizant of the potential for relatively low viewing figures, a risk was undertaken in its scheduling at a time when ratings were increasingly sought after. From her interviews, Henderson also notes, the subject matter was seen as the reason why audience numbers were, in fact, low. *Takin' Over the Asylum* was, in effect, a special scheduling event but also special to draw critical acclaim and to be given a second airing.

Description

The focus of the comedy drama is a psychiatric hospital in Glasgow, Scotland. Eddy McKenna (played by Ken Stott) is offered an opportunity to develop a radio station in the hospital after being nudged out of his former radio station position. Across the serial, four characters who are patients in the hospital play significant roles in relation to Eddy and have clearly defined conditions which

1 Some arguments and material from this analysis have appeared in another form (Birch 1996).

are explored below. Fergus (Angus Macfayden) is a former electrical engineer; Francine (Katy Murphy) is a young woman, a little reclusive but the subject of Eddy's later romantic advances; Campbell (David Tennant) is a youthful and exuberant participant in just about everything at the hospital and finally; Rosalie (Ruth McCabe) is a middle aged woman separating from her husband. The fifth episode, chosen for analysis here, starts with a tragedy that ended the previous programme. Fergus Mackinnon who experienced schizophrenia and took his own life, is buried. Patients leave the hospital to visit a cemetery and pay their respects to a charismatic friend who longed to leave the confines of St Jude's. Each episode is named after a popular song: the first is entitled *Hey Jude*; in this programme 'Rainy Night in Georgia' opens the story.

Knowing Through the Comedy Drama Form in Takin' Over the Asylum

Significant to *Takin' Over the Asylum* is the way in which its form treats the subject of mental health and portrayals of all people's identity, regardless of their mental health experience. As the terms 'comedy' and 'drama' indicate, the serial's form is organized through systems of signs and tacit agreements in a mix of seriousness with humour. Its depictions are also organized by advancing two social contexts of the world organized through juxtaposition. Thus, imaginative pleasures are produced by portraying the world as consisting of two worlds of madness. Depicted from the first episode onwards, this juxtaposition serves to highlight humour and tragedy about aspects of mental health peculiar to each world. It allows for critical comparisons to be made between them and is indicative of a clash of discourses to come. In the fifth episode, sadness is evident through grief on faces around a graveside and further stressed through the popular song *Rainy Night in Georgia*, imagery and music helping set parameters around a tragedy, signalling a sombre mood. However, in keeping with this basic form, the moment soon moves to brighter spaces established in earlier episodes, including the asylum and the headquarters of a double glazing company.

Analysis

Two Worlds of Madness

Madness as a concept is employed not only as a domain through which to portray popular expectation about those identified as mentally ill but also for those who might be termed 'well' in the so-called normal world. The two distinctive worlds are organized, one inside the mental institution of St Jude's, the other outside in the social world, in a double glazing company called Twin View Windows Ltd. Emphasis is afforded to St Jude's as the dominant place and to its people as the main cultural focus. They are cultural insiders and the rest of the world are outsiders; part of the programmes' purpose is to challenge popular conceptions of the social world as normal. Thus, usual understanding of the social world is inverted and the psychologies of all become subject to microscopic mental health examination. Concepts of normality and madness are transposed and everyone is 'investigated', raising questions about character. Scenes in the mental institution present a range of people with expressions, gestures and interactions unlike those found in everyday life. These contrast with scenes of people from the world in Twin View Windows Ltd., where equally bizarre actions are performed at the behest of an idiosyncratic managing director for whom 'the company' is the be all and end all of life.

The significant connection between these worlds is the character of Eddy. Reticent about being a double glazing salesman, he is enthusiastic for his part-time job as a radio DJ, his devotion stemming from an encyclopaedic knowledge about popular music. An accessible character for audience relations, his slippage between the two worlds provides a critical point of view through which the audience may see the madness in the so-called normal world and the normality in the so-called mad world. Thus, questions are raised in each environment about mental health contexts and identities.

Languages of Madness

Supporting the notion of two worlds of madness, comedic circumstances within each world collide through manic chants. 'Sell! Sell! Sell!' is chanted by employees in the Twin View Windows company headquarters and 'We are loonies and we are proud' is chanted by the patients in St Jude's, producing two languages of madness. Viewing both worlds through Eddy, we can see the futility of selling double glazing on a commission basis in a recession, as well as observe the unwell who are seeking to gain some dignity in their lives. We are also able to decide which is the more valuable. Eddy is unimpressed with selling, but has a real passion for running a hospital radio project for people. Thus the comic element of the genre, with its scope for exaggeration and farce, illuminate attributes of both worlds whilst the dramatic component operates as a check and balance; its structure temporarily collapses social boundaries.

Characterizing Mental Health Conditions and Identities

Depictions of mental health conditions are informative, their propositional discourses offering simple, single quality identifications of each character and condition attributes for audience. Thus, Rosalie undertakes repeated actions in ways presenting a condition as one continually compelled to ensure her internal conflict is comforted – portraying her as an obsessive compulsive neurotic personality. Francine's past abuse and its manifestation within a withdrawn and reclusive individuality is portrayed through mood shifts and self-harm – her subsequent depression is informatively depicted. Campbell's manic depression is also usefully characterized, his subjectivity following the highs and lows representative of his condition. Thus, characterizations hold significance for the audience, who know the conditions of the characters. Expectations about conditions are directed not only toward understanding but also, interest in where the next scene/episode will take them and what may or may not happen in that new context.

Dramatic Circumstances and Conditions

The analytical focuses here are dramatic circumstances between Francine and Eddy, in dramatic scenes which craft meanings about mental health. By building upon three scenes, knowledge content is developed through formal and thematic realisms arranged across the two worlds of madness. Here, the focus is more on the portrayals in the mental institution than those located in the world outside it.

In the first scene, a long shot of a bench in the grounds of the hospital shows Eddy joining Francine, sitting on a bench. It is evening and fading light contributes an intimate aesthetic. As a patient Francine is now beginning to show positive signs of recovery. Eddy inquires, 'Are you waiting for McTavish?' (McTavish is a cat about to have kittens.) Addicted to alcohol, Eddy draws out his whisky flask but is gently admonished by Francine. He says it makes him feel free and that's why he does it. Expanding on his reasons, he recounts a narrative from a previous moment in his school life when he had to recite a poem in class. Drink helped him to do it because he had to feel 'free' to be able to and in this moment a personal flaw is revealed. Through extended close-ups of Eddy's facial expression, this desire for freedom is emphasized as a poignant truth with which Francine is likely to relate. In turn, close-up visualizations of Francine's facial expressions not only show an attractive woman but allow a glimpse of someone with her own psychological difficulties. These moments allow a space to see personal situations connecting to issues of mental well-being and evidencing romantic interest between the couple.

Next, Eddy returns home to find his grandmother packing her belongings; she wants to sell everything and return to Lithuania where she can die with her people. Berating him for not having a wife, she commands he come to the Lithuanian Club night with a beautiful woman, so as not to embarrass her. Returning to the hospital, Eddy sees Francine hassled by two youths near a shed where McTavish lives. Confronted, they flee; Eddy and Francine admire McTavish's newborn kittens. Eddy asks Francine to join him as his 'pretend' girlfriend at the Club night; she agrees. Another scene portrays the development of a pilot radio programme which Eddy and Campbell have created and which is accepted by the BBC but with one reservation: management are dubious about letting a person with a 'mental health problem' on air. Disgruntled, Eddy leaves the studio, warning that if there's no Campbell, there's no show.

In the second scene, at the Lithuanian Club night, a good time is had by all; later, Francine is driven home by Eddy. As a romantic encounter starts to take place in the car, they are interrupted. The two boys are up to no good again and have doused the shed where the kittens are located with petrol, set light to it and run off.

Sounds of screaming take the scene from a warmly romantic setting into confusion as Francine, yelling loudly, makes her way through the fire to the kittens. Eddy extinguishes the fire. Music during this scene further raises emotional levels as Francine cries: 'They're no safe! They're no safe! They're no safe!' Eddy, trying to calm her, says the boys have run away but is met with a further confusing response: 'Not from them, from Uncle Frank. He'll come for these, they're no safe, we're not safe!' It appears that Francine has become dissociated from present space and time to a past world, the power of dramatic representation showing the susceptibility of her condition as she reverts to a past traumatic event.

In the third scene, Eddy, after securing a big contract, returns to the hospital and ventures into Francine's dimly lit room. This low light allows a degree of intimacy in which close dialogue can take place. We hear the kittens meowing and Francine discloses to Eddy that they have been put in a drawer by her bed. She knows 'the rules' but says she had to bring them to her room as McTavish did not return. Eddy voices his concern but she replies, 'I know but I'll be getting out (of the institution) soon, I've been really well eh!?' As Eddy talks to Francine, a series of close-ups in reverse angle shots allows the audience another look at the psychological well-being of each, in particular Francine. These close-ups function as a device to assist a 'revelatory discourse' about Francine's personal history and help introduce knowledge about her condition. Her disclosure begins after Eddy inquires about who Uncle Frank is. After avoiding answering the question, she says he was just someone who used to hang around the house, but then she reveals, 'After Ma died Uncle Frank use to come round a lot to see my Da, he used to buy me lots of presents. On Saturdays they use to play cards and get absolutely steamin' … and Uncle Frank would stay over and sleep on the settee except one night he didn't sleep on the settee'. Eddy, guessing what comes next, says: 'He slept with you'. Encouraged by Eddy's supportive dialogue, Francine continues: 'I was nine years old. I was nine. [She begins to weep.] Uncle Frank never slept on the settee again … I used to hide sometimes … or when I was asleep I used to call out for my Da. I would hear him snoring but he never came to help me'. Picking up a kitten, she says, 'He was my Da and he should've kept me safe but he never seemed to notice'. The kitten meows. A big close-up view of the kitten against Francine's chest, being administered milk from a pipette, is followed by another of Eddy's face. Eddy: 'Until you got pregnant!' Francine: 'He never believed me when I told him! I was 15! I messed myself when Jamie was born. The mid-wife said lots of women do that. [She smiles.] Don't know. They gave him to me to hold, Eddy. He was just that beautiful!' Eddy reassures her and then a two shot as she puts the kitten back in the drawer and then big close up of Francine. 'I had to let him go so that he could be safe'. She bursts into tears and a mid-shot of both on the floor opens out with Eddy comforting her.

The language of the scene and the dramatic way in which it is vocalized construct productive knowledge about the context of Francine's mental health condition and her identity. Portraying her past treatment as directly informing her present life, her narrative unfolds as one in which, she, as a young girl, lost her mother. This fact and her young age elicit useful knowledge content when accounts of sexual abuse are brought out into the open, offering reasons for her mental unwell-being. The words 'rape' or 'abuse' are not used but their meaning is evidenced by Eddy when he confirms that the uncle slept with her and that she became pregnant. Formal realisms via close-ups, of frail facial expressions assist thematic realisms about emotional and psychological disruption in Francine's childhood. Other close-up shots of Eddy also contribute strong emotional appeal. Her fixed gaze reveals a state of reflection about her past and the word 'safe', used in the earlier fire scene, makes prominent the notion of security, something all children should rightfully have. Francine's deprivation invites our understanding. As she reveals her past, a kitten is seen clutched close to her chest suckling a pipette filled with milk but this is more than just an animal: it is a form of symbolic replacement for her lost child. An underlying associative discourse in the scene is the right of motherhood to nurture a child, giving it warmth and security. For Francine, however, a kitten is a replacement for the child which she could never have, the nature of her situation signalled for the audience as second best.

Later, returning to the hospital, Eddy and Campbell celebrate the broadcasting of the radio show. All the patients join in the now conventional chant synonymous with the series, 'We are loonies and we are proud!' However these chants in the corridors are brought sharply to a halt when Francine sees a man in an SSPCA (Scottish Society for the Prevention of Cruelty to Animals) uniform walking down the corridor, carrying her kittens away. Her excruciating howl reverberates around the room as her main emotional investment in life is taken from her. It appears also that her mental well-being is being stolen, the screams continuing as she pursues the kitten's captor. In the final scene, Eddy sits on a bench in the grounds with his bottle to feed his addiction, his contrast of mood reflecting the life-opportunity that has been missed through Francine's sudden relapse. A soul ballad in the background assists this mood as the episode concludes, the capacity of the comedy drama and dramatic licence to 'shift mood' evident in this generic mechanism, working to *invert* meaning.

In this development of character conditions and identity, the form offers more reassurance than anxiety through exposure about why a person is, who they are and how they came to be that way. Where previously dangerous identities may have prevailed, this portrayal is a welcome change showing that at very least with explanations both medical and social in mental health typing; older representations have clearly occupied shaky ground.

The Sopranos

Created and produced by David Chase, *The Sopranos* was broadcast by HBO (Home Box Office) across six highly successful series. Originally intended as a film, *The Sopranos* was slated for production with FOX. However, HBO took the production and made it into the most popular series of the late 1990s and early

2000s. It was nominated for and won Primetime Emmy awards for Outstanding Drama Series in 2004 and 2007. While drawing many other awards, it continued to dominate other fields including Outstanding Director, Actor/Actress, Supporting Actor/Actress and Best Writer across the life of the show.

A hybrid form consisting primarily of family and gangster genres, its narrative tells the story of mob boss Anthony Soprano's (played by James Gandolfini) life and his crises over both his families' futures. One is his natural family; the other family is a New Jersey mafia organization he heads. Both are subject to serious treatment through drama but with humorous components exposing comedic moments of characters and their situations. The narrative's main foci are Tony's relationships and psychological issues uncovered through psychotherapy with Dr Melfi (Lorraine Bracco) his therapist. These mainly concern his biological family, particularly his mother (Nancy Marchand), sister Janice (Aida Tuturro) and his late father. Across the series, therapy sessions expose psychological landscapes in the life of the main character and significant others, profiling a range of conditions such as anxiety and depression. Other conditions examined include his uncle's dementia, his son's depression and Christopher Moltisanti's addictions. Of note is that Chase openly tells that much *Sopranos* content is informed by his own therapeutic experiences and relationship with his mother. The episode analysed is entitled *Cold Cuts* (from the fifth series) directed by Mike Figgis and is chosen for its 'anger' issues and dramatic and comedic techniques.

Description

During this *Sopranos* episode several storylines operate. The one given greater attention here focuses upon 'rage'. Beginning with an example of 'sports rage', viewers see two soccer moms at a match coming to blows, one of whom is Janice. Pressured to address her anger problems in therapy she does so honestly and makes progress. However, Tony's own deep rooted problems are viewed for all to see when he subjects his sister to his cruel nature. Running parallel to therapy scenes about anger, a second narrative focuses upon a trip to upstate New York made by Tony Blundetto (Steve Buscemi) and Christopher Moltisanti (Michael Imperioli). They visit Uncle Pat Blundetto at his picturesque country home to remove three buried bodies as a new property development is likely to find them causing legal complications. All are eventually located and unceremoniously disposed of in a lake. Within a reflective mode, the two recall painful childhood memories from their times in this area. Part of the representational value of these scenes is the contrasting rural, calm aesthetic running parallel to angry happenings occurring in urban New Jersey. This narrative offers examinations of the painful childhood antagonisms surfacing in adulthood, the other, and the one examined here, searches for the causes and mechanisms. Prior to undertaking these analyses, the first episode opening moments are briefly examined so as to offer readers a context upon which to understand Tony Soprano.

Analysis

Knowing through The Sopranos *Drama-Comedy Form: Episode One, Opening Moments* The first scene of the series introduces viewers to Tony Soprano waiting for and then meeting psychiatrist Dr Melfi in her office. This therapy scene is the first of many that function as a convention, offering audience a psychological view into Tony's fears, anxieties and depression which revolve around 'family' and fears about things coming to an *end*. During the first dialogue with Melfi several flashbacks with voice-overs in Tony's first person narration describe the lead-up to an anxiety attack. Flashbacks also occur later in the series, featuring as a device to explore Tony's life narrative but also clearly showing that he feels stigma in seeing a psychiatrist.

The first flashback depicts a family breakfast where Tony visits his swimming pool expectantly seeking a paddle of ducks. His voice-over disdainfully reveals that unlike his father's times, opportunities are becoming increasingly difficult; Melfi notes that many Americans would agree with this. His joy at seeing the ducks return is not shared by his children who, at the father's request, dutifully walk out to view them before quickly returning to their breakfast. Preparing for a barbecue some time later, Tony sees the ducks momentarily return before they flap their wings and fly away, this departure precipitating the panic attack. His subsequent collapse and a minor explosion of fuel ignited on the grill signals a dramatic event, but it is the ducks' departure which holds the greater symbolic reference – about anxieties for his 'families' in the future. The remainder of the series is based on these fears and on his visits to a psychiatrist. Therapy sessions provide critical insights into Tony's past relationship with his mother (and father) as well as past events which offer audiences voyeuristic pleasures as they recognize how these experiences resonate with their own. Other Family meetings as well as those from neighbouring New York gangs provide moments in which plots thicken, and as a new mobster arrives another disappears, probably murdered. Most of all, Tony's anxieties about relationships with friends and both families offer audience relatable angst, making *The Sopranos* unique because of its generic and cultural verisimilitude.

Generic and Cultural Verisimilitude

Christine Gledhill (in Hall 1997) writes about Steve Neale's distinction between generic and cultural verisimilitude in relation to realism (this latter term is covered in Chapter 4). *The Sopranos* is recognized for the genre it is through its gangster and family forms composition. Each generic structure consists of its own rule-governed history with *The Sopranos* conforming to previous gangster film forms like *The Godfather* and *Goodfellas*. By convention there are soldiers and captains, people who serve the illegal interests of a godfather. Also, conventions align *The Sopranos* with family-based dramas in which marital relationships are one focus as too are transgressions within them; children and their development are also a generic element. However, originality in this series lies in the difference of its generic verisimilitude with other forms through the realisms produced about its main character's frequent therapeutic visits. It is also this latter point that refers us to cultural verisimilitude.

Todorov points out from literary works that verisimilitude is a reality which lies between what readers *believe* to be true and a discourse. He notes that 'The relation is here established between the work and a scattered discourse that belongs to each of the individuals of a society but of which none may claim ownership; in other words, to *public opinion*. The latter is of course not "reality" but merely a further discourse, independent of the work' (1981: 18–19, taken from Neale and Krutnik 1990: 84). While the regimes of credibility in this hybrid genre are mixed, they allow for a degree of play within the form's parameters, facilitating audience pleasure from that which they believe to be true outside the genre in cultural knowledge about mental health. In representations of therapy, audiences find themes that parallel their own experience, a common feature in western societies, from which to draw part of their pleasure.

Neale and Krutnik also note about the concept of verisimilitude in comedy, that by convention it is 'concerned with "low" or "inferior" characters, classes, and life. It also enables us to address the role of stereotypes in comedy, and the idea that comedy is inherently subversive' (Neale and Krutnik 1990: 3). Meeting with Melfi, Soprano informs his occupation is 'waste management consulting', a livelihood that allows viewers accessibility to a character's experiences and attributes. However, amusement is in the 'low' character stereotype of an Italian Mafiosi with whom few would compare themselves as he sometimes manages the 'wasting' or killing adversaries. This irony around 'waste management' as an occupation produces generic verisimilitude in the form as it:

> specifies adherence to socio-cultural norms as the condition under which the characters portrayed and the actions depicted in any instance of representation can be considered both probable and proper. It also specifies adherence to aesthetic norms and conventions as the condition under which any representation can be both generally recognizable and aesthetically appropriate. However, comedy necessarily trades upon the surprising, the improper, the unlikely, and the transgressive in order to make us laugh; it plays on deviations both from socio-cultural norms, and from rules that govern other genres and aesthetic regimes. In the case of comedy, therefore, generic conventions demand both social and aesthetic indecorum. (Neale and Krutnik 1990: 3)

Thus, the genre offers expectation about Soprano's apparently legitimate, day-to-day activities, family goings-on etc., which provide one set of causes for his anxieties but it is his illegal, improper and transgressive activities in the other Family that are a burden. Killing enemies provide yet more stress but the haphazard way in which this sometimes occurs, offers pleasure through social and aesthetic indecorums and which also transpire in therapy sessions.

In the first therapy session Soprano is about to inform of a meeting with someone in debt to him, when he is counselled as to what he cannot say; Melfi does not want to know if someone got hurt because ethically she must report him. With a gentle smile he says 'Nothing! We had coffee'. While coffee was involved, audience learn it was the debtor with a friend, who, shocked at seeing Soprano and Moltisanti suddenly arrive in a car, made him drop coffee cups in alarm and then run. Soprano drives after the man, runs him down, physically hits his wound and then co-beats him with Moltisanti. Audience pleasure is in the humour of hearing one thing from Soprano about 'coffee' but knowing a list of other connotations it bears. The humour for this moment is completed when Melfi's naive and relieved acceptance is affirmed in 'So you had coffee!' With this first therapeutic session also functioning as a device to introduce main characters who cause Soprano stress, the unlikely practice of a Godfather seeking serious therapeutic help is depicted, with humour revealed in flashbacks showing his social indecorum and indiscretions. Indecorums further occur in two therapy scenes that follow and which facilitate a space for reflection about anger.

Cold Cuts*: Tensions as Soccer Moms Come to Blows*

In *Cold Cuts*, Tony's problems increase when two mothers come to blows at a soccer match. Janice has an argument with another soccer mom over an apparent foul upon Sophia (Janice's step-daughter) but it is how anger is introduced and explored that offers the audience serious and humorous discourses through which to understand it. Initially, both are viewed watching and vocally supporting their respective girls play but when Sophia is tackled, harshly in Janice's opinion, a confrontation ensues. Other parents holding camcorders are seen filming the developing brawl as a change from normal camera mode to home-movie footage within an inset frame positions the audience with the onlookers. The instability of handheld camera-work conveys rawness in imagery, according with the brawl's chaotic nature. As Janice gets the better of her opponent, she is restrained by a match official and spectator before audience next see Carmela in normal camera mode calling Tony to tell him of Janice's arrest.

Soprano is then seen sitting down to view the incident on local television news but this time the audience watch camcorder footage within the usual televisual mode. Now positioned with Soprano's point of view and privileged with knowledge of the preceding events, they see a factual form parodied within one fictional. As Soprano sees a news anchor quipping that a woman arrested in Essex County is connected with the mafia, the anchor names 'Janice Baccalieri', as sister of mob boss 'Anthony Soprano' getting arrested. He jokingly asks if the 'other mom better go into the soccer mom protection programme'. Through this fictional form viewers enjoy the twisting of a factual genre, part of the form's pleasure, the linguistic play on work of law enforcement. As footage is replayed, 'sports rage' is re-introduced for indulgence in the magnification of the incident; audience knowing how making the tale public will intensify Tony's anger. Seeing his rage incandesce, their pleasure is intensified through a new image of Janice tackled rugby-style by a Verona policeman. The reporter jests this is a 'mafia related hit' causing the anchor to chuckle before introducing psychologist 'Bela Kakuk'.

Drawing again upon news conventions, this 'expert' is viewed delivering 'specialist' knowledge supported against a background of bookcases. With regular cut-backs showing Tony's steadily increasing anger, the psychologist says, 'It's a growing problem in our society. Psychologists are finding that certain individuals are particularly prone to rage. Almost any frustration … er, inconvenience or perceived inconsideration will set them off'. Proving the psychologist's point and concluding pleasure for this scene, the expected explosive reaction arrives with Tony screaming 'motherf*****'. Later, an angry encounter occurs when Tony meets Janice with her husband Bobby. He persuades her to receive treatment and this introduces viewers to a group therapy session.

Therapy Convention 1: Group Session and Anger

At a group session Janice sits in a circle with participants all prepared for discussion when the therapist walks into the room. The camera follows him as he stands in front of the write-board with the words '*Anger Scripts – Emotional Triggers*' viewed behind him; eye level imagery positioning audience with group members who are there to learn more about anger. Reminding participants he previously requested they write down one or two situations or people that trigger anger, the therapist volunteers Bradley, a quiet man, to start.

Bradley begins to say that his partner often parks in front of his car, but then Janice interrupts. Dominating the room, she identifies her problem but a bizarre if humorous interruption occurs when Janice let's everyone know her stepchildren leave their bikes in the garage. Then, a man screams, 'Doris, can't you keep Billy's bike out of the driveway?' A series of quick edits show group members confused at the outburst followed by a close-up shot of the man explaining calmly, 'It's a famous commercial from the 60s. Bufferin. Guy has a headache and he takes it out on his wife'. Here, comedic meanings are made through seeing an acted, 'angry' intervention offering a humorous point of reference with a more serious moment that follows.

The therapist requests information about Bradley's physical sensation of anger but again Janice interrupts, annoyed at his situation. But, referring to the words on the whiteboard, the therapist clarifies that the triggers of anger within us are controllable and asks why Janice should be annoyed. He notes, '"It" does not make you mad.[2] You make you mad' – a point about responsibility made clear for Janice and the audience. Moving the discussion forward, the therapist questions what Janice's physical response is. Her response is that she would like to punch him in the face. However, she becomes embarrassed when he points out her clenched

2 The meaning of 'mad' in the American vernacular differs from British English in that it often means 'angry'.

fists and complains he is provocative but denial of her anger is clear. Evelyn, able to occupy a position of reflection and compromise, intervenes telling Janice it *is* others who provoke, many of us taking on other people's feelings and carrying it on. Janice's final expression shows realization of the therapist's view that other people's situations *do* get to her; she later modifies her behaviour. For viewers, serious and humorous meanings are contrasted to produce dynamic points of reference allowing them to see the mechanics of anger at work in relationships and as a component of society.

Therapy Convention 2: The Individual Session – Depression is Rage Turned Inward

> The human being is a spirit. But what is spirit? Spirit is the self. But what is the self? The self is a relation which related itself to itself ... A human being is a synthesis of the infinite and the finite, of possibility and necessity, of the eternal and the temporal. In short, a synthesis. A synthesis is a relation between two factors. Looked at in this way, a human being is not yet a self. (Kierkegaard 1980: 284)

In a meeting with Dr Melfi, a serious tone is set as Tony's anxieties are addressed. This session about rage is juxtaposed with the previous one, about anger. Writers David Chase, Robin Green and Mitchell Burgess use the therapeutic space to explore Soprano's self-identity and his angry relationships within the world. Simultaneously they offer audience a view into his psychological situation, his likeable character, a safe site to harbour common conditions. He also represents a parallel spirit who, as Kierkegaard puts it, is a 'self ... not yet a self', an identity struggling with existential anxieties; a person with whom audience can identify but also safely maintain distance from because of his morally repugnant occupation.

In this session Tony's anxieties are not just representations of pressures an audience can relate to but also *avoidances* of painful issues. When Janice's 'soccer' temper is mentioned, Melfi joyfully says 'Excellent! Let's talk about that'. Trying to avoid the topic Tony says, 'What?' and Melfi then mentions 'rage'. Tony again sidesteps with 'Why?' and she then states, 'Depression is rage turned inward' before questioning the Soprano temper. As Tony reflects that it was John Gotti's temper (a former New York mobster) that cost him his freedom he also notes that the older gangsters always waited and got even later. He says, 'Revenge is like serving cold cuts'; this sort of awkward gaffe is a regular component of the genre and typical of many *Soprano* characters in the show. Correcting him, Melfi states, 'I think it's, revenge is a dish best served cold'. Quickly moving to focus upon his personal code of conduct, Melfi asks, 'Why revenge all the time? Where does it come from this insatiable anger you and your sister share?' Getting annoyed, he exclaims: 'I was wondering how long it was going to take for her to come up'.

As behaviour in adulthood is informed by practices learnt in childhood, Melfi moves to discuss his mother and father. Experiencing traumatic events like seeing a man's finger being chopped off at a young age rather than expressing feelings, Tony's response is shame at his family's association with this violent heritage. By virtue of the fact he is talking with Melfi, Tony wants a more whole self-identity but it is his failure to confront internal conflicts or avoidances that hinder development. However, Melfi denies such evasion when he attempts to ignore discussion about his own impatience. Clutching at ideas to explain his feelings about loss of self-control he loudly says, 'Thank you for holding. [Gestures he is holding a phone.] Your call is important to us. If it's so f***ing important to you answer the f***ing phone!' Referring to the common frustration of recorded telephone voices replacing a real person to answer account queries, Melfi encouragingly says, 'Stay with it'. He responds angrily, 'It's just a level of bull****, bull****, bull****! Every f***ing new idea they come up with is supposed to make things better – it makes things worse'. Melfi encourages more but in using a line from a poem 'The Second Coming'[3] she shows her educated background while exposing Tony's lack. 'Okay right I agree. The centre cannot hold. The falcon cannot hear the falconer' (referring to a society in chaos). Confused, Tony complains, 'What the f*** are you talking about?' She points out to Tony (and the audience), 'We live in a time of technological and spiritual crisis but you feel you're above all of it, certainly above any inconvenience or annoyance and if things don't go your way, instead of being merely disappointed or inconvenienced, you blow'. Half-heartedly wanting to make progress, he reflects upon a recent conversation with Janice: 'My sister, she's taking anger management classes … Maybe she's on the right track'. Melfi inquires, 'Is this something you'd consider?' He firmly responds 'No!' Knowing Janice has found a way, Tony knows he *could* but avoidance of dealing with his painful issues wins over a synthesis of 'possibility' with 'necessity'. Taking the easier way, he says, 'But I'll admit it's not good for me all this f***ing agitation … wears me out … f***ing exhausted all the time'. Reaffirming the psychology lesson about anger, Melfi asks, 'Where did we start off?' Tony, sulking, answers, 'I don't know', so she states, 'Depression is rage turned inward' and he grumbles 'OK'. With two juxtaposed therapy sessions focusing upon 'anger', the audience are afforded a critical exposé of two characters beset by anger issues. One develops while the other is unable to look at the possibility of a new self and therefore, does not evolve; this confirmed in two following scenes with Janice and Tony.

3 The poem, written by Yeats in 1919, can be interpreted as part of a chaotic society after World War I. Arguably reflecting upon the need for a second coming of Christ, Melfi is referring to lacking societal connections.

Jealousy

After one of Tony's gibes, Janice apologizes for her recent behaviour and reveals her joy about the sessions, this scene exposing her as a potential agent of change. Janice announces she feels better but Tony is surprised to learn that she is not taking medication. Edits between Janice and Tony reveal her process of self-learning and his surprise at it. She further reveals that you have to take responsibility for your own anger by recognizing such feelings and dealing with them. With every remark Tony makes, Janice evidences her successful advancements and openly states, 'It's like a great sadness is beginning to lift'. Tony jealously asks, 'Sadness?' – recognizing not Janice's situation but his own. His own burden is not being lifted so when he states he is happy for her, he lies hiding his own jealousy and unhappiness at his inability to tackle problems.

The fixedness of Tony's self-identity is revealed in the final scene when he sits down to a meal with his sister, her husband Bobby (Stephen R. Schirripa), and his two children. Janice's advancements are clear when a telemarketer's calls are met with her patient, assertive discourse. Correlating with Tony's earlier outburst about telephoning companies, audience are offered a rare angelic view of Janice's newfound patience. Amid Tony's interventions, she calmly concludes the call to convene the meal with Tony looking astonished. Unable to contain his jealousy, Tony seeks to undermine her progress and inquires after the sensitive issue of Janice's long lost son Harpo. In her earlier travels across Europe she married a Québécois man and bore a young son. Without Janice to care for him, he was last heard of living Seattle but claiming disability benefit. After referring to his French-Canadian heritage, Tony inquires if Bobby's family know the song by Phoebe Snow called 'Harpo', after which the son was named. Seeing possibilities of winding up Janice, he quips, 'I wonder what's French-Canadian for "I grew up without a mother"' and then sings in a poor French accent, 'Sacre bleu, where is my mama?', taunting Janice. His gibe hits its mark. Her anger explodes and she gets up to chase Tony with a fork but is restrained by Bobby with the children, gleefully looking on at adults in anger. As if to extol Tony's ego, selfishness and singular narrow-mindedness the episode ends with him walking away from the house and the Kinks popular song, 'I'm not like anyone else' playing out his departure. Audience pleasure is reaffirmed centred upon knowing the character's inability to change in previous episodes.

Through this hybrid form, therapeutic scenes juxtaposed with angry events reveal an overt psychoanalytical typing not just about anger but also depression though this approach is shared with the conditions socially framed. Character psychologies and actions are explored across serious and humorous levels in flashbacks showing social indecorums and deceptions. Pleasures include 'relief' humour as a vent for repression but there is also an acceptance that the representation of Soprano's character is of someone who ultimately cannot change and who will never fulfil his search for a complete self. Central to his character are the failings most represented in the human condition with jealousy and revenge, top of the list.

My Mom Was A Schizophrenic

The next mediation is a comic strip called *My Mom Was A Schizophrenic*[4] created by Chester Brown, a Canadian comic artist and cartoonist. As the title indicates, Chester's mother had the condition of schizophrenia and provided his motivation for the work. It is critically concerned with how we have come to know about schizophrenia from psychiatric sources and media information, and also the knowledge that results from those discourses. Taking a comic and historical approach, it also offers an alternative perspective through taking an anti-psychiatry stance. Its initial publication process is also unconventional and different from the usual book form. Seeking to make more immediate public understanding about schizophrenia, Brown left copies of the comic around the city of Toronto in bus shelters and telephone booths.[5] Consequently, Brown's approach to publishing about a serious health issue is a direct intervention with the public to inform about schizophrenia.

Knowing through the Comic Strip Form

How we come to know content through the comic strip form is based upon the sequence of meanings in imagery and text. Will Eisner describes sequential comic art as 'a means of creative expression, a distinct discipline, an art literary form that deals with the arrangement of pictures or images and words to narrate a story or dramatize and idea (2008: xi). Scott McCloud notes that comics are 'Juxtaposed pictorial and other images in deliberate sequence, intended to convey information and/or to produce an aesthetic response in the viewer' (1993: 9). Whichever definition is employed, through this sequencing of imagery and words as a communicative form audience come to know stories through a distinctive reading experience unlike other mediations. Eisner points out that in reading such a text, a range of visual and verbal interpretive skills are brought to bear, 'The reading of a graphic novel is an act of both aesthetic perception and intellectual pursuit' (2008: 2). Thus, the form of *My Mom Was A Schizophrenic* resembles most other comics as it contains a series of repetitive images with writing.

---

4 The author is grateful to Chester Brown and publishers Drawn and Quarterly for use of this comic strip. © Copyright Chester Brown, all rights reserved. Used with permission.

5 Emulating the approach taken by Jack Chick whose work focuses upon Protestant evangelism, Brown employs his art form like Chicks' in a direct engagement with the public.

Figure 6.1 ***My Mom Was A Schizophrenic***

Source: © Copyright Chester Brown, all rights reserved. Used with permission.

Figure 6.1 Continued

Figure 6.1 Continued

Figure 6.1 Continued

Figure 6.1 Continued

Figure 6.1 Continued

These depict Brown himself, conventional and radical psychiatrists, significant writers and thinkers as characters, with graphics in a sequential artistic representation about schizophrenia.

Frames form the spaces into which imagery and writing are placed and which contain a given meaning. After the first frame, others follow orienting the reader's eye to move left to right, then down, and to repeat this sequence until a new page requires a repetition of this reading pattern until the story is concluded. A small division of space separates each frame which in the case of this strip retains this convention found in most comics. Others can forego the containing box and adopt a number of creative variations such as circles or even forego an enclosure altogether, this affecting the eye's reading orientation. Within a space, calligraphy of a given type can also accompany graphic imagery of selected style. Through this form, a comic strip artist will tell a story and employ any number of symbols to convey their tale, often communicating expressive features within contained figures.

Description

Conforming to conventional comic strip form, Brown's cartoon tells about schizophrenia but as a label produced for the public in a society which discards people whose belief systems do not fit within societal norms. To that end his work questions what is meant by the word 'schizophrenia' and the experiences the medical profession propose that people with the condition live through. He employs in his questioning, psychiatrists and psychiatry's own critics about schizophrenia as a process; he also uses past writers and thinkers. Subsequently, the comic strip uses contributors, some living and some dead, to donate their views through a series of constructed dramatized testimonies in narratives encapsulating their points of view. Set against several discourses elaborating on drug-induced as well as non-drug-induced states of consciousness, schizophrenia is critically assessed in light of these perspectives. Society's relationship to the condition and indeed society's own so-called normality is critically questioned.

Analysis

In *My Mom Was A Schizophrenic*, the interplay between fact and story, knowledge and imagination, and reference and textuality provide insightful reading. In its sequence of imagery and text, opening frames dramatize historical perspectives about the origins of the term 'schizophrenia' and the consequences of its contemporary meanings for those who must live either with the condition or with a person experiencing it. This is accomplished through a discourse offering the reader a critique of media portrayals as well as a critical contestation of psychiatry's contribution in a story with intent to identify the complex nature of a condition. Over history schizophrenia has accumulated numerous influences making claims to know it, but which mostly fail to help the sufferer or elaborate useful ways to inform society about it.

After the title frame, the first image depicts a television with text viewed emerging from it, stating that 'Schizophrenia is an organic disease of the brain'. It offers a three dimensional space with the television set against a light background with shadows around it, as does the figure of Brown standing beside it; the space could well be a room in a house. His features retain a serious look and his posture, apart from three frames, remains the same across the strip. His fashion and hairstyle also indicate that 'time' in the cartoon belongs to the contemporary. In the next frame, Brown's language and action combine to dispute the knowledge it communicates and here, kinesis or movement occurs as the television is pushed. Indeed, the challenge to the dominant view is completed in the third frame as it portrays an outright dismissal of message and medium, with the television viewed fragmenting. Consequently, an alternative argument commences from this image onwards, with the comic strip's first character, Brown himself. These people are either presented to make contributions saying things about schizophrenia or set up to address this topic.

Historicizing Schizophrenia: Narrative, Characters and Condition

Initiating a broad chronological history of psychiatry, the first character begins a listing of how psychiatric contributions came to frame schizophrenia in the way we currently know it. With the discourses of media also critiqued from the second frame, later imagery depicts other significant characters donating their ideas but the central character across this work is Brown. Standing against a wall, he offers critical evaluations about how schizophrenia came to be viewed.

The story begins with a succession of figures from psychiatry that have direct historical relationships with either how the term came to be known or with criticism of its development. The character of Kraepelin begins his discourse, set against a black background, a signifier of 'time' passed, a flashback. Introduced as static figure, he is joined by Bleuler who follows in the next frame. Both are positioned close together making meanings of sameness not just in terms of their professional occupation but also in psychiatric perspectives that show how the word 'schizophrenia' has historical origins in a scientific race to identify the condition. However, it is one not backed up by evidence. The choice of the phrase 'horned in on Kraepelin's act', presents an 'imagined competition' taking place in the past, Brown portraying the first two scientists through criticism from psychiatrist Thomas Szasz. He enters dramatically from left of frame lunging at the two, to begin a challenge that they 'invented' schizophrenia rather than discovered it. From this point, Szasz's anti-psychiatry discourse is established and added to by his well publicized criticisms. With 'beliefs' emboldened, his characterization takes on more dynamic features than Kraepelin and Bleuler[6] with three frames dedicated to strengthening his argument. This he does in direct fashion by revealing knowledge as beliefs without evidence, equivalent to invention. The introduction of Szasz also offers readers a professional's intervention into the anti-psychiatric argument.

More Modern Day Perspectives

Brown further critiques psychiatry in contestations over the State of Ontario's Ministry of Health list of schizophrenia's 'signs and symptoms' which he interprets as 'beliefs and behaviours'. Written on a board and intended to help readers 'Understand Schizophrenia' this ends up the same way as the media messages, ejected to the left of the frame with a criticism by Brown. It is at this point where again, schizophrenia is not 'medically' diagnosed but rather framed as 'socially unacceptable beliefs and behaviours'. This is a revelation for the lay person whose knowledge about the condition may be limited compared to that of a doctor. If the 'times' of Bleuler and Kraepelin's psychiatric diagnoses have not moved forward by 1995 (the time of this cartoon's publication), then Brown's judgement is a critical indictment. He makes further commentary distinguishing that the nature of scientific information does not clarify schizophrenia with sound evidence but rather, even by this day and age, intimates things have not moved forward.

Next, Brown parallels the treatment of the schizophrenic with that of the homosexual which as a practice and social group was ostracized before 1973 in America. Only from this date did American psychiatry remove it from its academic texts as an illness. This comparative analysis about the way in which homosexuality has been pejoratively viewed reaches a new expositional phase. A series of images and text depicts society by showing alleyways, buildings and a car, in a discourse that suggests gay people were negatively viewed as people with unwell mental health; their identity, like that of the schizophrenic, immersed in a fearful culture. Here, a sequence of significations portrays old dilapidated walls, with steps, a vent, cans and a car that show spaces empty of people depicting little value in terms of human inclusion. This portrayal is a broad reference to the stigmatization of the homosexual, marked out and absented from the social through myths obscuring this group's identity. It is through these images that an imaginative reference is made, that this social group was stigmatized as having a 'mental illness', by way of Brown's written text, culture and society is critiqued for its phobia; the parallel with the way in which people with unwell mental health is clearly made.

6 In his notes at the end of the cartoon, Brown notes that Bleuler did an about turn indicating that psychiatric determinants are 'forensic' rather than medical.

Civilizing Bodies and Minds

The comparison of the schizophrenic's situation with that of the homosexual approximates to Elias's analysis of European processes about civilizing 'bodies' and Bourdieu's view of the body. The notion of the body serves as a site of evaluation over history for social constructionist approaches in identifying developments in differences about identity but here, in relation to health. By making his comparative analysis, Brown proposes by the absence of any 'body' from imagery, that like the homosexual, the mentally unwell are nowhere to be seen, not just out of sight and therefore out of mind but disregarded for the betterment of the well who cannot or do not want to deal with the matter. While the homosexual was made to feel 'they were sick' the implied message is that, so too, this same situation prevails for people with conditions, particularly the schizophrenic. Societies in their process of civilizing excluded those it could not understand.

In addition, Shilling (see Woodward 1997) notes in his work on Elias that during the Middle Ages there was a lack of prohibition on behaviours. It was only from the Renaissance onward that more self-control over emotions occurred across Europe as a matter of required observance of personal codes of conduct, especially in courts. While behavioural codes changed, so too did notions of what was acceptable behaviour and appropriate practice. Distinction amongst people, and later, classes meant 'do's and don'ts' 'helped to internalize behavioural codes' (1997: 96), with the mind now a site for civilizing. This increased personal psychological censoring and increasing systemic pressure upon culture and society across Europe would normalize standards of ways to behave and ways not to. In particular, later Victorian society would further strengthen social stratification and while this receded over the last century, strong societal influences still persist in various parts of the world. In what are mostly consumerist societies, not only is the 'body' now a site for physical and cultural capital but so too is the mind. Attainment of lifestyle products has previously avoided mental well-being in US commercials. However, as people are now classed as consumers[7] and, with depression and anxiety recognized because of high population sizes, pharmaceutical companies aggressively advertise medications for these conditions.

Further Psychiatric and Writer Perspectives

Next in the comic strip, several significant writers and/or thinkers are introduced to make commentary about what Brown frames as 'intentionally' induced psychedelic states. Aldous Huxley is referenced as he took and wrote about various drugs like peyote, mescaline and LSD. The prolific writer Joseph Campbell also confirms LSD as an 'intentionally' induced schizophrenia before

7 The subtitle of Otto Wahl's (1999) book which focuses upon American mental health experiences employs the word 'consumer'.

Terence McKenna contributes his own view (influenced by Aldous Huxley). Shamanism and the person who practises it is mentioned by Campbell but it is Farber (in McKenna 1991) who maintains that 'Yesterday's Shaman is today's schizophrenic'. Contending that differences exist within shamanism, McKenna proposes his views with Stanislav Grof's perspectives, adding that the difference between intentionally reached psychedelic states of mind with those of non-drug psychedelic states of mind are 'indistinguishable'. This helps Brown arrive at a position in which a set of experiences can introduce readers to schizophrenia not as a medically induced condition but as one 'accidentally' arrived at. His posture incorporates a critically distanced perspective that searches for a way of explaining to readers in order that they can get a handle on what the condition is. What is more significant about the way in which the comic strip facilitates this is the social criticism that is facilitated by the introduction of R.D. Laing (see also Chapter 2). The comic form proposes that the condition of schizophrenia is largely feared by culture.

Its final argument is made that culture and society in its self-situated 'normalcy' is in fact problematic because we have driven ourselves into a confined space and also one of security that we cannot move beyond; what is now an alienated position with regard to how we see things like schizophrenia. Taking a Laingian perspective around the self and the 'other', Brown argues that those who think they belong to the normal are repressed or in denial and therefore protective of our supposed sense of 'sane' self. His argument is that having adopted media's 'monotonous rhythms and repetitive tasks', these have made us comply with the dominant strain of ideas and beliefs proposed about a topic like mental health. The culminating situation is that now the 'normal majority' is the real 'alienated'. Taking conclusions from this is not so much the distance that the so-called normal have with the so-called 'alienated', rather it is a journey of schizophrenia we now need to travel, to really know what 'schizophrenia' is and thereby understand the place we have arrived at – that of an alienated normality.

Through a form combining serious historical treatment with comedic aspects, Brown addresses psychiatric, media and literary discourses raising questions about schizophrenia and society's relationship with it. Well researched knowledge content together with profound personal knowledge help type the condition of schizophrenia through an approach employing a collision of different discourses. Viewed as an uncared for and neglected condition, he suggests that society is mentally unwell and advises it is now time to address this ignored identity. Consequently, anxieties about the saturation of identities require allaying as it is media, culture and society which have fixed ideas about schizophrenia and so change is encouraged.

Conclusion

In the fictional forms examined, meanings made in drama are creatively combined with comedy in varying measures to critically expose original discourses about mental health. Pleasures about mental health are imparted in representations by positioning ideas across seriousness and humour, which enables reflection and then, critical appreciation. Thoughtfulness *after* critical research helps provide a depth and breadth of information allowing each mediation to say something insightful about mental health identity; these are often socially as well as medically framed. *Takin' Over The Asylum* compares and contrasts two societies through critical comparisons that produce irony; clear character portrayals probe who really is *normal*. Its creative performances depict being 'unwell' offering relatable reasons for the human condition losing mental well-being and also sensitively portrays what transpires in the process of unwell mental health. By way of its representing prowess, the form helps convey the need for greater mental health understanding. *The Sopranos* introduces the increasing commonality of conditions like depression and anxiety. In the consistent convention of therapeutic spaces, audience expectations generate interest and curiosity to discover more about conditions in characters and to compare generic with cultural verisimilitude. If comparisons with conditions are insightful in the two latter examples, in *My Mom Was A Schizophrenic* Brown's purposeful collision of conventional with radical psychiatric opinion, makes for strong critique about the disparate discourses that cloud rather than clarify mental health understanding. However, all three mediations combine forms of drama and comedy to produce deep resonances about mental health and society. Far from producing fears about saturation these hybrid forms allow for new ideas about identity.

Chapter 7
Phase Two, Part 1: The Community Project: Reception Study

Introduction

The impetus for this media reception-production study is concern over stigma generated in mental health mediations across the community at large. Completed in September 2002, the study consisted of a two-part process. Part 1, the focus of this chapter, is a reception study which aims to discover new knowledge about the circulation of mental health meanings in the community. Part 2, which begins in Chapter 8, is an experimental production study that intends to develop useful indicators towards alternative practice for policy makers. Evolving from Parts 1 and 2, a third part of the inquiry is developed, depending on a group's progression and choice. Within this overall design, this chapter investigates what participants read in four items of mediation as well as pursuing questions of research design, interpretation issues across genres, the process of analysing data and, finally, influence and effect.

Part One: Exploring Response

Conceived broadly within the framework of Corner, Richardson and Fenton's (1990) *Nuclear Reactions: Form and Response in 'Public Issue' Television*, the reception study explores responses to meaning-making. Four mediations about mental health are examined by three special groups in three different communities. The purpose is to discover useful information about the ways in which Group A, people with experience of a mental health condition, read mediations and how they are constituted by them. It also aims to determine what Group B, media personnel and Group C, mental healthcare professionals, make of meanings in mediations.

Analysing both non-fictional and fictional forms, the study explores mental health meanings read by each group, examining relationships between specific forms and response.

Table 7.1 Community Project, Part 1: Groups and Locations

Groups/Locations	Cornwall/Devon Community
Group A – People with Experience of a Mental Health Condition Participants: 15	Five people participated, two men and three women. All indicated they did not want their names used; these have been changed. The group included: Robin who was involved with a local mental health charity and an activist in mental health matters. Anne, William and Julie came from local mental health centres; one undertook part-time maintenance work, another part-time hairdressing, also helping out at her local church; Anne was seeking work whilst William worked as a gardener. Finally, Petra, a student at Falmouth College of Arts, was undertaking a degree course. Mental health conditions across the group varied. One person lived with '*a post traumatic stress disorder*' caused by a car crash, this '*manifesting as depression and disrupted sleep ... This is a constant state of affairs with 'lapses' into worst scenario from time to time (acute depression and either no sleep or constant sleep)*'. One experienced '*depression*' whilst another suffered from '*severe depression, severe anxiety, SAD and Post Traumatic Stress Syndrome*'. Another declined to answer.
Group B – Media Professionals Participants: 20	Eight professionals. One was a print journalist for a local newspaper. Broadcast journalists included one from the local radio station BBC Radio Cornwall, two from BBC Plymouth and four from what was formerly called Carlton Westcountry. Six described themselves as mentally well and two did not respond.
Group C – Mental Healthcare Professionals Participants: 55	28 professionals: care assistants, nurse educators, mental health nurses, a lecturer in mental health, a psychiatric medical secretary, a training manager, employment placement advisors for a mental health facility, community psychiatric nurses, mental health workers and 12 students of mental health nursing. One respondent said 'Well, I think!' Another said 'Well state of mental health' while others indicated they were 'okay today', implying that their well-being was changeable.
Total Participants: **90**	Area Participants: 41

Table 7.1 Continued

Hampshire Community	Liverpool Community
Three women and two men. All declined to let their names be used; these have been changed. Carol, in her mid twenties, previously a student with a degree, was out of work and participating in various mental health service activities. Roger was also out of work though well qualified, his condition incapacitating him; he is in his forties. Julie, also in her forties, was a shop assistant, cleaner and worker. Jane, in her fifties, was a bar worker and also a support worker while Malcolm, nearing 50, formerly in the army, worked as a waiter. He also undertook an active part in the community, promoting mental health issues. Of the mental health conditions, one person suffered from '*anxiety with depression*', another from '*schizophrenia*', one from a '*schizo-affective disorder*'. The two remaining declined to answer.	Six people initially participated and then one left, leaving the group all male; all were from mental healthcare centres across Liverpool. One member of the group gave permission for his name to be used, the remainder declined and therefore, four of the five names have been changed. One group member, Daniel, was an activist, undertaking a busy role in the local community. Alan, previously an HGV driver, had been involved in a horrific crash, his mental health condition a direct result of this event. Mark had taken drugs to help keep working in his youth, these causing a deterioration in his mental health. James' condition occurred across his life, drugs also playing a role in later exacerbating his unwell health. Arthur's condition developed during his late teens while Don (his real name) suffered from his across the later years of adult life. The range of mental health conditions amongst the group varied; two people suffered from *schizophrenia*, one from a *post-traumatic stress condition* and two from *depressive* conditions. Many in this group were taking medications, which at times were remarked upon by them as inhibiting their project work.
Five broadcast journalists. Concerted attempts were made to involve the print journalists from a newspaper in Southampton but these lengthy efforts failed. Three were from the independent sector and two BBC broadcasters took part. All described themselves as mentally well.	Seven participants from independent radio and television stations, as well as from the BBC. Six described themselves as mentally well and one did not respond to the question.
A college counsellor, four lecturers in mental health nursing, a student placement facilitator and five mental health project workers. All worked in and around the Southampton and Winchester areas. Respondents mainly talked of feeling 'well'. One mental health project worker said he would 'pass as normal' with another indicating she was 'well at the moment'.	16 professionals. A large section of the group were occupational therapists and mental health support workers and some were day care centre managers. Generally, people said they were in 'well mental health' with one saying 'well as far as I am aware'. Another said she was 'well but a little stressed' while one person claimed to be 'okay at the moment'.
Area Participants: 21	Area Participants: 28

Note: This table should be read from left to right across both pages.

The study compares structured critical reflections of Group A with Groups B and C. The aim is to help inform a sense of location about the cultural issue of mental health concerning 'public knowledge' (in news/current affairs) as different from 'popular culture' and dramatic pleasure (in soaps). It also aims to clarify the interplay between non-fiction and fiction while addressing the issue of hybridity. Across groups the study is alert to when stigma is identified in responses not only by way of mention but also, as a construct; it also notes when stigma is absent. Finally, the study's data calibrates the need for developing measures that would lead to or enable a better understanding in mental health mediations in the wider community.

Research Design

Groups: Triangulated Samples and Communities

The research design integrates three special sample groups in a methodological triangulation (Denzin 1989) across three communities: Cornwall and Devon; Hampshire; and Liverpool. Each comprises three participating groups, listed in Table 7.1. Each group has a special relationship to mental health and is formulated around engagement with mediation form and content; people with a mental health condition have personal experience to offer and the remaining two groups employ professional practices which address mental health. The rationale for structuring the sample in this way is because of the potential research benefit to both media and mental healthcare professional communities. The generation of empirical research data is also useful information for subsequent policy change to encourage more enabling attitudes in the community.

Limitations of the study revolve around a) small sample sizes; b) claims made at the macro level from its micro level study; and c) a largely non-fictional form in mediation selection. While focusing upon the groups' occupations, it does not address d) age, gender, race, class or geographic focus in detail. Group participation meant that only small sample sizes could participate, which restricted outcomes – and this study was conducted only in the UK. While limited in particular frequencies, the triangulation component assisted validation of data across groups. Claims made about the relationship of the micro-context with that of macro require critical attention but where similarities occur between groups, critical comparative analysis assists.

Group Recruitment

Group A recruitment was accomplished by proposing the Community Project to managers in local mental healthcare centres. Following disclosure of reception and production study processes agreement for participant inclusion was secured and flyers advertising the project were left on centre notice-boards. The flyers asked potential participants if they viewed 'media images about mental health as a problem' and inquired if they were interested in making new media images. A follow-up meeting was arranged with interested participants, staff and managers. A presentation by the researcher furnished interested people with a broad project description (including reception and production study details) focusing upon mental health mediations as a problem because of stigma and themes referencing dangerousness. One week after the presentation, participants were invited to express their interest through the centre manager and by agreement, joined the project. This time lapse was intended to determine if a participant was comfortable with undertaking the project's five-day process (see Chapter 8 for a timetable of the project) and content.

Group B were contacted by telephone at their area institutions and included independent journalists as well as public service broadcast journalists. As a qualification for the project, participants had to have worked in some way with stories associated with mental health. BBC Spotlight (Plymouth), formerly Carlton Broadcasting West Country, BBC Southampton and Meridian, BBC Radio Merseyside, Radio City all agreed to participate. Local newspapers included the *West Briton* and the *Liverpool Daily Post and Echo*. Despite repeated efforts a Southampton newspaper did not respond to invitations to participate. Group C were approached through contacting a range of professional mental health agencies in each region. Flyers were sent to institutions; interested parties contacted the researcher by telephone. The entire recruitment process was managed from (then) Falmouth College of Arts.

Questionnaire Design, Opinion and Confidentiality

For all groups, one qualitatively standardized, structured, self-administered questionnaire was designed, organized in two sections; the first section sought data about mediation opinion, the second was a background questionnaire. Each group was allowed three hours to read and write up their responses; Group A were given more time if needed.

The study sought to establish opinion from each group's reading practice, this process constitutive of a cultural practice which couldn't be directly observed. It represented a range of 'group views' held about mental health from a belief system; a special knowledge culminating in thoughts or judgements. It was also preferred as it could elicit balanced data for commentary and analytical comparison. Consequently, the reception study could illuminate each social actor's perspective, especially that of Group A, and provide useful data for interpreting their struggle with portrayals; it would also supply data about reading practice with mediation form.

All three groups examined the same standardized questionnaire, this common information-base making critical comparisons possible between groups. The questions were structured in two parts: the first four led the respondent into the mediation, three were closed-ended, and the last was open-ended. The intention here was not to reveal remaining open-ended questions as the ones in which a coding system was organized. The first set of questions was: 1) Are you familiar with this programme? 2) Do you watch/read this programme/newspaper regularly? 3) Can you recall seeing this television news programme before? 4) Do you recognize any of the people in the story as having a mental health condition? If so, who, and what condition do you think they have? The second set of questions was designed to elicit data about mental health meaning, the role of drama in making meanings and identities. They were also sequenced to lead respondent inquiry into representation and accuracy with opportunity provided for offering other comments. They were constituted as follows: 5) What do you understand about mental health and mental illness from portrayals in this programme/newspaper? 6) How is drama playing a role in your understanding of meanings about mental health and/or illness? 7) How is drama helping you understand the identity of people connected with mental health or mental illness? 8) How accurate do you consider these portrayals of mental health or illness?

A background questionnaire filled out *after* viewing mediations was requested from each group with information inquiring about social and demographic details such as name, age, gender, ethnic origin, mental health, location and cultural factors. Group discourses prevail in vocabulary usage, providing further information on values and assumptions. Therefore, a standardized inquiry of mainly closed-ended questions was created for the background questionnaire. Another question concerning mental health status was also asked and, in line with advice, was located well down the list of questions due to sensitivities connected with this topic.

The self-completed questionnaire was chosen because of the practicalities of participant availability. Convening broadcast and print media journalists for a three-hour period was an impossible goal due to their work demands and concerns of editors/programme controllers through whom access was obtained. Obtaining their inclusion was not easy, so this approach was considered the best option. A video and photocopy of a newspaper article was posted for completion across a two-week time frame. For the remaining groups, screenings at an educational institution cited or mental healthcare facility were considered the best option as a controlled environment. The situational context of reception (Corner 1991: 278; Wilson in Sapsford 1996: 97) was considered and the researcher visited these locations to manage the process and discourage group discussion. Participants were instead requested to ask for clarification about questions from the researcher. Because of the technological demands of the production study, Group A attended a designated educational institution which was chosen because of accessibility to production facilities. The reception study was conducted in the studios or room used and the researcher acted as a facilitator to talk in a supportive atmosphere.

Confidentiality about individual identity within Group A was also a key concern; stigma meant privacy and anonymity about a participant's identity required safeguarding. According to Ferriter and Butwell (see Cordess 2001), confidentiality in mental health research can be viewed at two levels. There is a responsibility 'to protect the interest of their patient/client and the quite different moral and social responsibility to use the information imparted by the patient or client ethically' (Cordess 2001: 159).

During both parts of the research, the study's priority was to protect Group A's interests. A key project element focused upon the real concern of identity and non-disclosure became a crucial element in negotiating participation. A formal consent form was constructed allowing the researcher to carry out the research and assure participants that the information retained confidentiality about them in the study and in the event of publication. The consent form was shown to centre managers and distributed through them to participants for signing. Confidentiality was also extended to Groups B and C in the background questionnaire.

Mediation Selection, Sequence and Description

Decisions influencing mediation selection and sequence were determined by the following criteria: 1) they contained portrayals linking significant relationships about mental health to the main study group; 2) there was as varied a range of portrayals about mental health as possible but reflective as a sample of mediations available for UK public consumption; 3) fictional and non-fictional mediations used employed dramatic components in varying communicative ways; 4) the project sought to be constitutive of a sample broadly representative of Philo's (1996) research which shows two thirds of media references relating in some way to violence but which would not upset. In addition, before each mediation was presented to Group A, a brief description was offered to apprise and advise participants of general information about material *before* viewing. Mediations were sequenced to allow respondents a comfortable introduction: a) a five minute *BBC News* example was followed by, b) a longer news form in the *Daily Mirror* text (see Figure 7.1). Next, c) the radio documentary *Scapegoats* followed, this lasting 30 minutes. The final exemplar, d) *EastEnders*, was 35 minutes in length. An optional break of 15 minutes was offered after completion of the *Mirror* questions, so as not to fatigue respondents. In the descriptions that follow in each story development, themes and imagery are broadly illustrated.

Television News: *BBC Six o'clock News*

Description

Broadcast 12 February 1998. This non-fictional form commences with Martin Lewis' headline announcements for four stories and includes the story about Care in the Community, the second in the schedule. In the studio mode of address, the story is presented by Moira Stuart introducing the report and addresses investment by the government of the day as the main topic: there will be £500 million for funding mental health services. Following this, the location mode of address with Fergus Walsh extends this theme in more detail. Here, there are several interviews with users of mental healthcare services accompanied by a voice-over and reporter-to-camera address from the journalist, with one delivery, a pre-arranged walk-and-talk to camera, in a rehabilitation centre. Beginning the story, a camera located in the back seat of a vehicle offers visualizations of London streets, a voice-over identifying the car's occupants as a mental health worker outreach team. The journalist is next seen walking through the rehabilitation centre and speaking to camera, reporting about the current funding situation. Next, users of mental healthcare services and their testimonies include two people talking about their experiences. Imagery involves old Victorian buildings with views of windows with bars across them. High walls are also shown before returning to the centre where the journalist concludes the report. Focusing mainly upon the economic aspects of mental health, the news narrative story also emphasizes stories about dangerous people, noting previous reports of threats to society.

Tabloid Newspaper: *Daily Mirror*

Description

Two separate stories depict two men suffering from schizophrenia on page 5 (26 September 1995, see Figure 7.1) each man having committed a murder. Both report *Care in the Community* as failing, framed through cases criticizing it. The first story is about Stephen Laudat and reports from an independent inquiry; the second is about Jason Mitchell and is from Ipswich Crown Court where Mitchell's sentencing took place. In the main story about Laudat, both he and a day patient, Bryan Bennett, are framed in oval portraiture shapes set in a black background, these set apart from each other so as to hold an enlarged headline 'Scandal of Schizophrenics Freed To Kill'. Between the two portraitures, a direct quote in large print states 'My father was stabbed 82 times'. Underneath the portraits are the titles of VICTIM and KILLER. The articles follow below as Case One and Case Two. In a similar vein to the first case, an oval portrait frame in the second is placed in a column. Again, words in block capitals precede actual names with DAD, KILLED and KILLED employed for all of the individuals whose lives Jason Mitchell has taken. Mitchell is portrayed in a large square shape with greater surface area, with the caption: 'HANNIBAL FAN: Killer Jason Mitchell'. Tattoos of a skull and snake are given prominence.

DAILY MIRROR, Tuesday, September 26, 1995 PAGE 5

Don't let Sky buy top soap

MPs last night vowed to stop Coronation Street being hijacked by satellite television.

They are angry at Sky TV's plans to buy Britain's best-loved soap — enjoyed by 18 million fans.

A cross-party campaign has been launched with MPs complaining the move would be "like selling the Crown jewels".

And they want watchdogs to prevent the soap going the same way as live Premier League football and the Ryder Cup — covered exclusively by Sky.

Fans

The deal would stop fans watching the three-times a week serial unless they get pay-as-you-view TV.

Granada is considering Sky as an alternative to continuing the Street's 35 year run on ITV.

But Labour Heritage spokesman Chris Smith said: "Forcing 18 million people to pay a subscription is unacceptable."

Lib-Dem MP Liz Lynne stormed: "To sell it off to satellite and deny its many fans from seeing it is just not right."

Schoolboy survives 120ft fall

A MOTHER yesterday told of her teenage son's "million-to-one" escape as he plunged 120 feet from a viaduct into three feet of water.

Jonathan Windross, 14, was sitting on the edge of the railway parapet throwing stones into a river when he lurched forward and fell.

He landed in the shallow water but escaped with a dislocated shoulder and severe bruising.

"He's damn lucky to be alive and he knows it," said June Windross, 40, at her home in Harrogate, Yorks.

Harrogate District Hospital last night said Jonathan was "comfortable".

He was playing with friends on the rail bridge above the Nidd Gorge at Bilton, two miles from his home, when he fell.

Timetable of blunders

RAIL chiefs could be forced to issue a new timetable after suspected blunders in corrections to earlier mistakes.

Despite a 246-page revision yesterday to the 2,100-page winter guide — which already has a 57-page errors supplement — experts claim Railtrack has still not got it right.

They believe about 15 per cent of entries in the original £7.50 timetable gave wrong arrival and departure times.

AC SPARKS PC

COMPLAINING women got "men at work" signs covered up as an all-male team of electricians toiled at Norwich council offices.

SCANDAL OF SCHIZOPHRENICS FREED TO KILL

'My father was stabbed 82 times..care in the community isn't working'

VICTIM: Day care patient Bryan Bennett

KILLER: Psycho knifeman Stephen Laudat

FAILED

By MICHAEL STREETER Whitehall Correspondent

HEARTBROKEN Kim Bennett wept yesterday as she blasted the community care blunders that led to her dad's death at the hands of a freed schizophrenic.

Tragic Bryan Bennett was butchered by fellow day centre patient Stephen Laudat eight months after the knifeman was released from hospital.

Kim, 34, sobbed: "Why was this man allowed out? My father was stabbed 82 times, 27 times in the face. My brother and I had to witness this to identify his body.

"It's time the Government realised their policies of community care are not working."

The killer's father Angelo, 53, from Walthamstow, East London, stormed: "My son and

CASE ONE

Mr Bennett were both victims of a community care policy that has failed both those in need of care and the wider community."

Laudat, 26, served a jail term for armed robbery and was sent to Kneesworth House private hospital in Cambridgeshire in 1992.

Stopped

He stopped taking medication without the local health authority knowing.

In December 1993 a social worker and a ward manager cautioned against his release.

But he was freed as a care in the community patient.

Laudat was being treated at a day centre run by Newham Council in east London when he attacked 56-year-old Mr Bennett in July last year, believing his victim was the jailed gangster Ronnie Kray.

The killer was later sent to Rampton top-security hospital.

Yesterday an independent inquiry found that a breakdown in communication between health and social workers meant Laudat failed to get the help he needed after his release.

The report concludes the killing could not have been predicted.

But inquiry chairman Len Woodley QC told a news conference: "We believe that at the time Stephen Laudat committed his first criminal offence in 1991 he was mentally ill."

The Laudat case follows a string of other care in the community tragedies, including the killing of 27-year-old Jonathan Zito by a schizophrenic in London in 1992.

Yesterday's report, commissioned by Newham Council and the East London and City Health Authority, makes more than 60 recommendations for improvements. The authority has promised to provide more care in secure units and hire more medical staff.

Attack

Last night Zito's campaigning widow Jayne said: "Some people who are severely mentally ill need long-term in-patient care."

Health Minister John Bowis said the report highlighted the need for better liaison between caring agencies. Labour blamed the Government for getting rid of 50,000 psychiatric hospital beds in the last decade, without supplying proper community care to replace them.

● Comment – Page Six

Breakdown in communication

Poor communications led to "the right hand not knowing what the left hand was doing.

Inquiry chairman Len Woodley QC

No sign of level of violence here

There was nothing which could have indicated the level of violence which took place

Deborah Cameron, Newham, director of social services

BLUNDERS THAT LED TO SLAUGHTER

DAD: Robert Mitchell

KILLED: Arthur Wilson

KILLED: Shirley Wilson

HANNIBAL FAN: Killer Jason Mitchell

SILENCE Of The Lambs killer Jason Mitchell slaughtered three people after a legal blunder led to him being freed from mental hospital, a public inquiry heard yesterday.

Mitchell, 24, was given three life sentences at Ipswich Crown Court, Suffolk, in July after he admitted three manslaughter charges.

He killed Arthur Wilson and his wife Shirley, both 65, at their home in the village of Bramford, Suffolk, then strangled his father Robert, 54, at his home nearby and chopped off his legs, arms and head.

He boasted to police of strangling his victims and claimed he had wanted to eat them – like Hannibal "The Cannibal" Lecter in his favourite film.

The grim details were revealed at the start of an inquiry into the case

CASE TWO

chaired by QC Sir Louis Blom-Cooper.

The killings happened after he fled a hospital in Ipswich, where he was a voluntary patient.

He had been sent there following his conditional discharge as a compulsory restricted patient at another hospital.

But counsel to the inquiry Oliver Thorold revealed that the discharge followed two "legally flawed" mental health review tribunals.

The first said he could be freed if he lived in a hostel and that his medication could be stopped.

His behaviour deteriorated the Home Office ordered second tribunal.

But there was confusion over what its decision meant and he was freed after "a sequence of misapprehensions", said Mr Thorold.

OUCH!

Feeling pinched by your car insurance?

Call for HOME INSURANCE too

TOUCHLINE

A better deal at your fingertips

0800 207 800

8.00am–8.00pm Mon-Fri, 9.00am–2.00pm Sat

Not available in Northern Ireland, the Channel Islands or the Isle of Man. For the Republic of Ireland ring 1800 332211 DMR 175

Figure 7.1 ***Daily Mirror* 26 September 1995, page 5**

Note: Reprinted with permission of *Daily Mirror*/Mirrorpix.

Radio Documentary: *Scapegoats*

Description

Scapegoats was made by independent production house Forsyth Productions for BBC Radio 4. Presented by Hugh Pryor-Jones, this production examines several socially outcast groups across a series of programmes. Lasting 30 minutes, it follows the pattern of a voice-of-god documentary and focuses upon the changing historical definitions of mental illness/madness across 500 years and is very well researched. The presenter's discourse is accompanied by expert witness testimonies, these in turn complemented by one user of mental healthcare services intervention. Throughout the programme, soliloquies, small dramatizations and folk music are employed to enhance depictions of mental distress and madness. Across its generic structure, random sequences of dramatizations, interviews and folk music serve to segment historical moments for the listener's imagination, generating ideas about society at a given time and location of the mentally ill people within it. Consequently, this ordering exposes different ways in which each period treats health conditions.

Soap Opera: *EastEnders*

Description

A soap opera made by the BBC, this popular fictional form produces imaginative realities about the cultural practices of working-class people living in the East End of London and explores social relationships between its peoples in their everyday life. Supplying a range of stereotypes including hard man Phil Grant (played by Steve McFadden) and his mother Peggy (played by Barbara Windsor), a number of settings such as The Queen Victoria (the local pub) and various domestic scenes provide a view into different relationships and how meaningful they are (or not) for the people involved. Continuous struggles in situations, people and events provide a rich social fabric into which audience can examine conflicts, tensions and their resolutions and non-resolutions. At the time of this episode, the character of Joe Wickes, a young man, is beginning to experience early symptoms of schizophrenia, starting some 20 minutes into the omnibus edition. It is clear that the experiences for Joe and his family are particularly difficult with Joe bewildered and frightened of his mother's intentions despite his father's attempts to console him. Supporting characters consist of a community psychiatric nurse who appears twice with advice to offer, and then with medication. Despite taking the prescribed drugs, Joe doesn't appear to improve. He begins to wrap electronic goods in silver foil and also cuts the phone cord; a mobile phone is also damaged beyond repair. The intention seems to be to cut all communication into and out of the home. At times, he withdraws to the security of his bedroom in which he locks himself; this causing a growing suspicion in his father. The last scene shows the father discovering the contents of the room, this dramatic exposition revealing a secret space full of news headlines referring to Joe's reality. Newspaper headlines about 'dying' and 'desperation' adorn the walls of the room, generating questions about why they are there.

Interpreting Response: Meanings Made across Genres

A lack of precision within recent reception studies has led to a variety of problems in the interpretation of meaning. With this in mind, the study employs the idea of 'frames' with regard to interpretation and 'levels' of meanings, while differentiating between genres. Frames of understanding inform respondent interpretation and the reasons they evaluate mediation form and content; they are also a way of organizing criteria for evaluation. For instance, mental healthcare respondents approach responses through their professional frames but could employ criteria for evaluations focusing upon concern about stigma. People with conditions respond from their unique frame of experience while media personnel respond via an objective frame relative to their profession. Hopefully, these 'frames' will become apparent across the following responses as will the character of responses and interpretative positions which are also examined.

In the interpretation of meanings, Corner's (1991) advice about 'levels' of meaning is employed to achieve clarity.[1] When interpreted meanings require clarification, 'levels' are sometimes used to illuminate key analytical moments. The first, a Level One meaning, is associated with denotation; this is where 'a word, image or sequence's primary signification is recognized and comprehended' (Corner 1991: 271). These meanings might be generally exemplified by a label such as Alzheimer's which carries little in the way of pejorative connotations. The second level is of particular importance. It might previously have been identified as a connotation but this term requires careful consideration. It is:

> a word, image or sequence's secondary, implicatory, or associative signification … This level will vary according to the character either of the signifier or the signified or a combination of both (i.e. named or visually depicted entities) will vary in their degree of symbolic/metaphoric resonance … the secondary signifying force of each verbal phrasing or articulation of image will be dependant in part not only on its local elements but on their organization within the larger textual unit which is being attended to. (Corner 1991: 271–2)

1 These levels are employed in order to differentiate awareness. Rather than being applied rigidly and sequentially, they are employed here as useful exploratory categories when needed.

Examples of these might be 'nutter', 'psycho' or 'schizophrenic' which can, for example, impart level two meanings of dangerousness or violence depending on their symbolic/metaphoric resonance in the organization of the text. In the third level, listeners, readers and viewers:

> attach a generalized significance to what they have seen and heard, evaluating it (perhaps in relations to its perceived presuppositions and entailments if it has propositional force) and locating it within a negotiated place in their knowledge or memory where it may continue to do modifying work on other constituents of their consciousness (and indeed, of their unconsciousness). (1991: 272)

Here, the term 'preferred reading' can be used. Where a text may not immediately communicate a definite meaning, it may be 'held in abeyance' until clarification of it takes place, or even revision, following from encounters with texts or experiences. Finally, categorizing responses within a genre helped assign a designation while simultaneously teasing out hybrid components.

Analysing Questionnaire Data: Process, Reduction, Explanation and Theory

Data was analysed using quantitative means and a coded system (see Lindlof 1995: 215–44). Employing an action of 'processing' information followed by reduction and explanation, data was coded and conceptualized. *Processing* information requires placing respondent data from questions into meaningful categories. *Reduction* is the further physical placement of paper responses into meaningfully coded groupings. From this physical processing it becomes possible to identify concepts requiring explanation. *Explaining* concepts made through reduction processes necessitate further interpretation of respondent opinion, so there is a continuous task of selecting, dividing and interrelating material with other group data. These preliminary readings are used to categorize codes and develop 'concepts and themes' which appear as *italicized* and <u>underlined</u> items – and qualify where two or more respondents mention the same idea.

In the graphs below, questions of accuracy according to genre are formulated into three sections: 'accurate', 'inaccurate' and 'incomplete responses'. An 'accurate' response reflects consideration of the mediation as a truthful representation whereas 'inaccurate' indicates to the contrary. Incomplete responses reflect either a divided opinion over accuracy or a declined response. Where a divided opinion occurs critical responses are addressed. The use of 'accuracy' graphs is intended as a complementary device with qualitative data drawn from questions.

Theory Used

As noted in the Introduction, the history of studying effects in media research is long and complicated, and the 'hypodermic model' is now discredited. Yet this work chooses not to ignore effects particularly with regard to stigma. Influence is also a focus in understanding outcomes as Corner et al. indicate in their reception study, 'images can exert a "positioning power" upon viewer imagination and understanding' (1990: 105); mediations carry important implications for 'who a person is', 'who a person can be' and 'who a person wants to be'. Subsequently, across group results, perspectives include social psychology theory about stigma from Heatherton et al. (2000) and their 'perceivers and targets' framework. Somers and Gibson's work on narrative and social identity (Calhoun 1994) is employed, exploring how the identity of mental health respondents as an ontological condition is storied across time and space. The politics of identity is a significant theme, as the purposes of self-identity are constantly at play 'in the context of internal and external relations of *time* and *place* and *power*' (Calhoun 1994: 65). Tied to these ideas are those of Anthony Giddens (1991) about security, danger, trust and risk. Exploring human experience as a mediated phenomenon in which language acquisition plays a crucial role, living with a mental health condition becomes politicized in culture and society, 'Language and memory are intrinsically connected, both on the level of individual recall and that of the institutionalisation of collective experience' (1991: 23). Across the contours of modernity, time and space figure significantly for ontological security and how these elements connect with what it is like to live in this moment. In the case of people with conditions, what is existentially troubling is a key analytical focus, with language a special element of interest and how it relates to the sense of security about the self. The study now turns to the reception project opinions.

Television News: *BBC Six o'clock News*

Group A – People with Conditions

Cornwall/Devon Through personal frames this group read themes about mental health as <u>*dangerousness*</u> evaluating with concern how the public may be fearful of mediation content. From the location report: <u>*Outlaws-on-the-Loose and the Lawmen*</u>: *the shot of the car cruising the streets looking for people who had slipped through the care in the community net suggested that they were looking for escaped convicts* is read as dramatic imagery. For Petra, this is a <u>*Misunderstanding*</u>: *Public safety mentioned first ... that the public might be 'at risk'*. Respondents are resistive to resemblances of *Western* and *Cop* genres embedded in a non-fiction form as it references fictitious ideas about them as 'criminal'. These are powerful values known to the community and as such, undermine the trust respondents feel they have with society. As Anne notes: *the general public watching would feel very unsafe and under threat and would therefore develop a very negative attitude toward people with problems*. Respondents are concerned about stigma generated through an imaginative rather than factual story content in what Crocker and Quinn (2000) term 'collective representations' and which have links to effects upon self-esteem. These representations are:

> sometimes broadly known and shared by both stigmatized and nonstigmatized persons, sometimes shared by individuals with a particular social identity but not people with another social identity, and sometimes shared by only some of those individuals with a particular stigmatized identity. (Crocker and Quinn 2000: 159)

Two respondents view the potentiality for themes like *Cultural Outsiders – 'No Goods' and Non-Entities* will become activated in perceivers (the non-stigmatized) which can undermine trust and self-esteem for people like her (the targets). Supporting this view, Anne and Petra view words such as '*vulnerable, acute, stabilized, murderer, suicide*' as producing *Negative Language and Tone* for self-esteem. Petra notes such language is persuasive: *it suggests the negative whilst the 'factual reporting' appears to be just that – clear, factual, rational, 'normal'*. All see the mediation as inaccurate.

Hampshire Themes of *dangerousness* and *safety and security* are also read through personal frames with respondent concern and about how the public perceive them. Problematic language and images shot from the back of a car draw criticisms: *the constant use of the words 'safe' and 'secure' gives the definite impression that mental health patients are dangerous*. Also 'dramatic' delivery codes trigger comment: *the newsreaders' tone of voice – almost 'disapproving' or with a sense of warning, at times, words like 'secure', 'threat', 'suicide', 'self-harm', 'severe' being used. Also links made – in words and pictures – to prisons/crime (etc.)*. Two respondents complain about mental health identities portrayed as '*outsiders*' and '*a threat*' from which the public requires protection. Again, participants identify that language and imagery target respondents as 'criminals' undermining social relations of trust and complicate ontological narratives: 'The stories social actors use to make sense of – indeed, in order to act in – their lives. Ontological narratives are used to define who we are; this in turn is a precondition for knowing what to do' (Calhoun 1994: 61). Potent values in the news narrative produce concern because they conflict with their ontological narrative – who they are, and what they do; it wrongly *frames* them as being capable of bad actions. Again, fictitious and stigmatizing themes of 'criminalization' are critiqued. Two regard the mediation as inaccurate, one is unsure and two decline to answer.

Liverpool Themes about *Security* and *Negative Tone* are read through personal frames with respondents resistive to the story. James initially views the mediation as hopeful: *it was about people needing and getting help. New centres would replace old hospitals, people with mental health problems can get help to get better*, but this later takes a negative turn, his view aligning with the other's concerns. *The video showed bars on the window which was intimidating. The images of the bars on the window gave the impression that anybody with mental health problems would be caged.* Daniel notes it: *is not very helpful in helping me identify people with the illness, it is usually far removed from the truth.* Alan complains, '*It was about people being locked up and the key thrown away*', while Don is critical because it *portrayed wrongly ... not explaining mental health.*

Again, respondents criticize references to 'the criminal' because these conflict with their self-identity, these responses indicative of 'bypassed shame'. Giddens (1991) notes that a person's ontological security depends on maintaining the key unconscious element of trust, the important lynchpin between identity and society. However, when trust is compromised by visual language as it is here, implications arise for self-esteem. Quoting Helen Lewis, Giddens writes that by-passed shame 'consists of repressed fears that the narrative of self-identity cannot withstand pressures on its coherence or social acceptability' (1991: 65). Exploring the work of Kohut (1971), Giddens examines 'the ideal self' as a key component of self-identity aligning it with a trajectory of what it, as a 'self wants to be'. Thus, stigmatizing content undermines ontological narratives to produce 'bypassed shame' because identity is indirectly shamed and this is risky because it tends to register to the fore 'as a feature of psychic organisation' (1991: 69) undermining the coherence of the ideal self, complicating its intended trajectory. Three indicate the mediation is inaccurate, one says it is and another declines to answer.

Group B – Media

Cornwall/Devon Two sets of opinions are formed through objective frames, one accepting of content, the other critical of stereotypical imagery and language. This first small constituency relates to knowledge content as fact about Care in the Community read at face value: *care is not enough, integration not happening, mental illness contributes to suicide and murder, more security needed.* Another respondent notes: *those with a mental health condition are 'ordinary' people, not so different from those who consider themselves healthy.*

The remaining set of opinions reveal Level Two meanings about identity in imagery from bars on windows. Respondents view these as potentially stereotypical with controversial perceived portrayals about confinement. Four note dramatic language: *conveyed the brutality of some aspects of old style care – and of locking people up 'out of sight and out of mind'.* There was: *emotive language to reinforce the scale and seriousness of the current problem – 'too many vulnerable people were left to their own'.* One views the story as '*measured*' because *murder and suicides were at the end of the report, after we had seen patients behaving and talking fairly normally.* Broadly, these readings disclose awareness of stereotyping but not stigma.

Examining the relationships between stigma and stereotypes as individual entities, Biernat and Dovidio (in Heatherton et al. 2000) explain that stigma may not be identified because a member of society may only know stereotypical information. They propose that people encode, store and retrieve data through socialization and personal experience. Following this line of thought implies that Group B is no different to other people. In their role as providers of public knowledge, they draw on interpretative frameworks containing already stereotypical knowledge and language but with little choice available for alternative representation, they perceive a 'neutral language' in the mediation designed for 'balance'. Its intent not to offend is recognized: *I think the piece intends to be balanced but actually gives a very sterile negative picture. No expansion of what the lady from MIND says that there are examples of success in care in the community*. Four find the story accurate but three are undecided though user identity is recognized as 'ordinary' when accessed voice is employed. One finds the story inaccurate.

Hampshire Through objective frames respondents read Care in the Community Fails the people it is supposed to serve. The Headline 'Care in the Community Failed' and Bars on Windows are remarked for their use to create 'impact'; this perhaps is indicative of concern about stereotypes perceived from 'collective representations'. A sense of objective balance in evaluations continues with the St Bernard's centre and its new-looking gymnasium drawing comment about Leisure and Normality: *the bright colours of the new centre illustrate a more modern approach* and, *the gymnasium where the boys were playing volleyball helped me understand how some people with mental health problems live and are treated.*

Imagery helps respondents perceive people with conditions as appearing just like anyone else otherwise there is no convergence of other responses. Some note those seen as unwell in the report are not directly asked questions. Two respondents consider it as 'accurate'. One says it's 'partly accurate' while two decline clear decisions, one (of the two) commenting about 'balance': *the problem for me is that the BBC said Care in the Community had failed, based on Frank Dobson's quote. The MIND angle was that it had worked and there had been a few failings. This was buried in the report and should have been brought to the surface.*

Liverpool Responses in the Liverpool group contrast with the other Group B respondents in that mention about stereotyping and stigmatizing is absent. Read through an objective frame, little information is provided except for 'supposed' factual themes about Dangerousness and Too Many People were creating a Problem for the Government; this group accept knowledge content in the form. While other groups note pejorative stereotypes, this group does not, instead reading a Level One meaning in a theme of Normal People vs. Supervised People – suggesting that the latter *are* dangerous. The other half read that The Asylum and its Treatments had moved on. Contained in these 'commonsense' themes are ideas reflecting an 'order for society', to alleviate a perceived chaos because the unwell are perceived as a nuisance. All think the report accurate except one who doesn't answer.

Group C – Mental Healthcare

Cornwall/Devon In Group C, 13 respondents read the theme Dangerous Murderers through a professional frame evaluating it with concern. The term '*personality disorder*' is criticized as worrisome, one respondent noting: *the programme suggests these sufferers are not safe in (i.e., for) the community ... it gives the impression that mental health sufferers are potential murderers*. Imagery is also excessively dramatic for six with one respondent critiquing: *Mental health and illness are part of the same continuum*. Seeing mental health as a confused concept in this mediation, professionals ask how the public can ever know anything useful about it; in a general sense, concerns focus upon a lack of clarity. Misinformation can only perpetuate stigma rather than change public attitudes, and here opinions form around concerns about what Merton (1948) termed a 'self-fulfilling' prophecy but in relation to stigma. A self-fulfilling prophecy is when an initially erroneous social belief which carries stigma leads to its own fulfilment. These responses characterize professional apprehensions about what the public may learn from the mediation.

The relationship of this group to the form is constituted once again of concern as Schizophrenic Stereotypes encourage stigma. One respondent asked if: *the mentally ill are permanently and seriously disordered and a risk to society*? Another said: *I do think the piece focused heavily on the criminal side of the disorder with the final focus of the man who murdered two people, being pushed to the fore, this I believe was highlighting dangerousness rather than therapeutic values of in-patient care*. Another person made it clear that *it doesn't try in any way to explain or educate about the issues of mental health*. If myths about mental illness prevail then the public will only have fictitious information about mental health to perpetuate already problematic ideas. Ten respondents remark that Dark Lighting is Not Helpful though the *MIND segment is useful*. Like Group A, the CPN portrayal draws criticism in observations about meanings in: *Scenes of the two out-reach CPN's gave images of hunting people with mental illness down*. Thirteen see the mediation as inaccurate, seven view it as accurate and eight record mixed views.

Hampshire Through a professional frame, respondents are critical of Negative Portrayals reading imagery of 'out of control people' and 'prison bars' with concern: *one tends to get the impression that there are a lot of out-of-control people at large in the community*. Another complains: *the first image of the hospital came across like inmates of a prison, that's how it looked and felt, there is no evidence of people doing well, it all portrays the need to control these people*. 'Dramatic' statistics about suicides are questioned raising concerns about misleading information: *the reference to 25 murders and 1,000 suicides were dramatic. It tends to reinforce the stereotypical views of mental illness as being potentially dangerous phenomena from which the public need protection.* Generally, remarks indicate how problematic statistics can generate stigma. Six identify representations as inaccurate, two indicate accuracy and the remainder are unsure.

Liverpool Through professional frames respondents read themes of <u>Dangerousness</u> with concern. One questions: mentally ill people are dangerous and 'at large' in the community? Another probes a statistical disparity: 25 people may commit crime a year but how many people commit crime who do not have a mental illness? Also, suicides aren't afforded the same attention as murders even though they significantly exceed them. Similar to Group A concerns, dramatic imagery of <u>*Touring the Streets*</u> and <u>*Mug-shots*</u> are noted for complicating mental health identity: Images reminiscent of The Bill [a UK cop series] and mug-shots used aren't helpful, these develop stigma. Professionals worry about misleading information for the public but do identify <u>*Good Use of Patients*</u>. Eleven think the programme inaccurate; two think it is and three are undecided. An occupational therapist says it is inaccurate: because mental illness happens to people who are brothers, sisters, parents, partners, sons, daughters, colleagues.

BBC TV News Genre – Group Summaries

Group A respondents read the news form through personal frames with themes of dangerousness evaluated with concern. Generally, the character of group responses reflect that the news story targets their identity as 'criminal' because they have mental health conditions; no-one sees their actual self-identity in what is identified as an imaginative rather than factual mediation. Criminality themes from fictional forms like Cop and Western genres constituted in imagery shot from the back of the moving vehicle and linguistic components facilitate simplistic good versus bad meanings; this is strongly affective and produces stigma. Such meanings are potent, embedded in society as part of collective representations known to both targets and perceivers; they come from the past to produce strongly subjective responses. These readings are indicative of how relationships about security of the self and trust within society – two key components for feeling included – are compromised. Specifically, tonal styles of linguistic elements in the studio mode misrepresent identity to indicate cultural division and feelings of shame. Knowledge reflecting mental health realities about the unwell person is largely absent. 66.6% of respondents find the mediation inaccurate.

In Group B, all group interpretative positions are characterized by mostly surface meanings read through objective frames; two of the three groups mention pejorative stereotypes but not stigma. With themes of dangerousness not read, as in Group A, these participants relate to the form as containing facts and knowledge with two groups sensitive to problematic language and controversial dramatic imagery referencing confinement. However, they are unaware of the affective negative properties in imagery from the car as read by Group A. These emerge as potentially stereotypical evaluated through criteria about balance of content and participants are questioning of the story. However, the Liverpool group read everything at a surface level equating mental health with dangerousness and accepting knowledge content as presented, while unmindful to stereotyping and stigmatization taking place. In contrast to Groups A and C, 60% think the mediation accurate with some not answering.

Through professional frames Group C interpretations are characterized by criticisms about 'dangerousness' themes and problematic information. Dramatic significations are potently affective in misrepresenting the unwell as 'criminal' and obfuscate useful mental health information, as do imagery of bars on windows and notions of out-of-control people; these are imaginative at best, not facts. Producing self-fulfilling prophecies, professionals view this mediation encourages stigma, misleading the public about who an unwell person is and what they are really like; it places limits upon who they can be. Dark lighting is identified as a representational problem. Suicide isn't afforded attention commensurate with figures associated with murder. 55% view the mediation as inaccurate. This largely accords with data from Group A along with critical commentary about the seepage of meanings crossing over from fictional forms into non-fiction. Thus, the interplay between imagination and knowledge is controversial space containing many questions from this group. 'Accessed voice' is regarded as helpful. 20% consider the mediation accurate and 55% inaccurate.

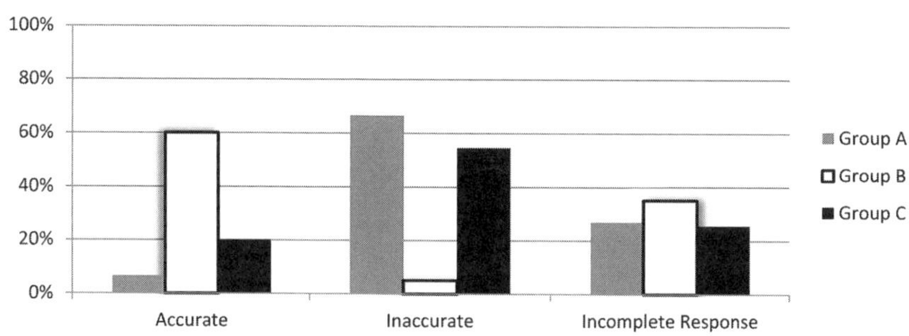

Figure 7.2 Television News Genre–Group Comparison

Newspaper Form – The *Daily Mirror*

Group A – People with Conditions

Cornwall/Devon Respondents read a theme of *Sensationalized Killings* through personal frames criticizing imagery as all strongly resist the mediation, citing words like '*violence*', '*danger*', '*butchers*' and '*out of control killers*'. These contribute to the 'killer' label about which respondents are sharply critical; mediated identity and their own are simply miles apart, the difference being one is imaginative fiction and the other is fact. For Giddens (1991: 18), 'abstract systems' consist of 'symbolic tokens' coupled with 'expert systems' and together they are also 'disembedding mechanisms'. If newspapers produce symbolic tokens or meanings which disseminate standard negative values about mental health, then, when self-identity is symbolized in such ways, issues of trust, danger and risk emerge for respondents. As Giddens notes:

> Where, for example, a person interprets – correctly or not – a response from another as indicating that her assumptions about others' views of her are false, the result might be to compromise a whole set of trust relations which has been built up. (1991: 66)

One person suggests: the public would be easily influenced by powerful, anti-social images and easily impressed by violent personalities. Petra criticizes framing the unwell person as 'a killer' saying: It is damning by association, although in this case, the specific incidents are tragic and horrendous, not everyone with a mental health condition will be this extreme. The story not only conveys stigma but is destabilizing in terms trust relations in society; how she views others viewing people like her. Giddens further notes:

> Attitudes of trust, in relation to specific situations, persons or systems, and on a more generalised level, are directly connected to the psychological *security* of individuals and groups. Trust and security, risk and danger: these exist in various historically unique conjunctions in conditions of modernity. (1991: 19)

For Petra, this mediation affects trust relations between her and society and also the psychological security she would normally feel as an integral member of society. Thus, headlines with *Sensationalized Detail* and *Emotive and Dramatic Language* are undermining to the psychological security of self-identity, this mediation reads similarly in the Hampshire and Liverpool groups. Words like '*schizophrenic*' and '*kill*' are also censured because when employed with the film character Hannibal Lecter, produce negative relations to mental health.

Hampshire The interplay between story and fact again raise significant criticisms. Through personal frames four of five people evaluate with strong criticism themes of dangerousness; they negatively connect with cultural memories from the film *Psycho*. Roger complains: *the paper bandied the words 'schizophrenic' and 'psycho' to the villain of case, without explaining the words ... The word 'psycho' conjures up the Alfred Hitchcock film 'Psycho' where a man makes a frenzied stabbing of victims.* Jane rejects the text because of its stigmatizing linkages with fictional film characters. She is concerned the public may draw problematic conclusions from *'Schizophrenics slaughter'* – *'Schizophrenics are silent as lambs'* – *'No schizophrenic should be free'*. Dramatic references stigmatize *all* unwell people including those experiencing schizophrenia producing mythical information challenging to respondent self-identity. As Giddens proposes that in everyone, the ideal self 'is a key part of self-identity because it forms a channel of positive aspiration in terms of which the narrative is worked out' (1991: 68) here, identity-as-an-ideal is contested when the representation compares the self to a killer from horror film. All reject the portrayal as inaccurate.

Liverpool A theme of Dangerous Killers is recorded through personal frames with respondents evaluating with strong criticism, portrayals of identity. Alan's question: *people in mental health institutions are being let out into the community, to kill people?* Respondents are critical of the tabloid because they see misleading information communicated as 'fact' for public consumption. News narratives such as this are disliked not only for the conflict produced in ontological narratives but also because of how they enter into the fabric of society to become what Somers and Gibson term 'public narratives'. These are defined as:

> those narratives attached to cultural and institutional formations larger than the single individual, to intersubjective networks and institutions, however local or grand, micro or macro. Like all narratives, these stories have drama, plot, explanation and selective appropriation. (Calhoun 1994: 62)

Once disseminated, these narratives can gain cultural acceptance and unless checked, have stigmatizing consequences. Four consider representations inaccurate and one does not respond.

Group B – Media

Cornwall/Devon Respondents identify the theme People Who are Mentally Ill are Killers through an objective frame evaluating the mediation with distrust. Opinions are split critically between level one and two meanings. Some read level two meanings about a threat requiring 'containment' while others question ideas that: *people with mental illness kill?* Three interpret themes of Killer versus Victim in imagery and distorted notions of monsters. Other themes about 'threat' surface through dramatic language with words like '*Psycho Knifeman*' and '*slaughter*' identified as misrepresenting identity. Four view large-font headlines as unhelpful. Five consider the report inaccurate, two are undecided and one views it as accurate.

Hampshire Through an objective frame the theme of *Mental Illness with Dangerousness*, three respondents viewing that *Powerful and Emotive Use of Language* misrepresents identity. Also, *Language Constructs Dangerous Identities* incorrectly, that unwell people are murderers. Language is more '*deliberately used and given prominence*', *e.g., psycho knifeman, slaughter, heartbroken* and '*psycho killer*', '*Hannibal Fan*' *is very emotive*. *Stabbed 82 times* is identified as a problem and the word 'schizophrenia' is wrongly synonymous with 'killers'. However, the group discerns this content typical of tabloid journalism. Three consider it inaccurate with a fourth stating it is: *factually accurate but giving a totally mistaken impression*. Respondents know that story and fact are in-play but this and the remaining media groups are resigned to its 'incorrectness'; this is simply what tabloids do. While the meanings are understood to be inaccurate respondents are unaware of stigma. Across this group there is also an acceptance that like other professional people, they are in psychologically 'motivated performance situations' (see Blascovich et al. in Heatherton 2000: 319), that demand they achieve goals. They are motivated to produce their work focusing upon facts known to be true (at the time). One does not respond over accuracy.

Liverpool In contrast with their previous BBC TV News reading, this group questions portrayals that people with schizophrenia are *Dangerous* through a objective frame. This includes criticism of stories that offer *No Explanation* about schizophrenia. Respondents see *Dramatic Language* as problematic: *the Headlines are very influential in the understanding of mental illness – 'scandal of schizophrenic freed to kill' 'My father was stabbed 82 times', 'FAILED'*, hinder understanding. Imagery is viewed as unhelpful and four consider the item inaccurate though one notes it is accurate saying: *the reports are based on fact and are obviously correct but they definitely are worded to be emotive and could give the wrong impression that ALL mental patients are dangerous to readers*. One participant does not respond.

Group C – Mental Healthcare

Cornwall/Devon Through a professional frame 19 workers read themes about *Schizophrenics are Murderers* and are *Dangerous to the Public* evaluating these with critical responses. Three cite *No Information for the Public about Mental Health* and 13 note that overly dramatic headlines such as '*Stabbed 82 Times*' and '*Failed*' emotionalize story content. One respondent notes about linguistic and visual properties:

> *Most newspaper reports sensationalise cases such as these – key words = Scandal of Schizophrenics Freed To Kill. Stabbed 82 Times. FAILED.*

> *SLAUGHTER. PSYCHO. Also photographs of victims are always shown smiling where perpetrators are always scowling or looking aggressive ... Schizophrenia is frequently painted in a very negative way.*

Four are concerned that the photographs stigmatize and four complain that the story is symbolic of only the worst case about mental health getting reported. Respondents question why stories about 'schizophrenia' prevail at the expense of other conditions. Some may be less newsworthy but are equally, if not more important, when it comes to informing public knowledge. Thirteen opinions record identity as <u>*Negatively Portrayed*</u> and seven view schizophrenics, unnecessarily stereotyped as <u>*Evil*</u> and <u>*Dangerous Killers*</u>. Twenty-three consider the articles inaccurate, three do not respond and two think it accurate.

Hampshire Through a professional frame respondents evaluate with concern <u>*Mental Health is Dangerous – People with Mental Illness are Killers and Vice-Versa*</u>. The report's content only advances fear and this mediation is viewed as detrimental to public knowledge. Readings include: *Very little is described in the way of illness and symptoms ... Very negative of portrayal of someone with schizophrenia ... to the public it might add fear*. Respondents show concern that 'making strange' the identity of anyone with a condition through <u>*Dramatic Language*</u> is undermining, let alone someone with schizophrenia. Phrases like '*stabbed 82 times*' are persistently mentioned by respondents with words like '*slaughter*' and '*blunder*' as advancing stereotypes rather than knowledge. Eleven think the mediation portrayals are inaccurate.

Liverpool Respondents read themes <u>*Schizophrenics Kill and Fear*</u> through a professional frame evaluating the mediation with strong concerns. Fourteen register the reports are inaccurate and two decline answers. People suffering from schizophrenia are not dangerous, so this report generates <u>*fear*</u>. One says: *very little information was given with regard to the person's mental illness*. Another notes that the portrayals wrongly say that: *mentally ill people are all killers/psychos, are criminals, should be locked up – make reference of being freed rather than discharged, are young/male*. Respondents present strong emphasis that by constructing a criminalized identity which distances 'well' culture from 'unwell' is very unhelpful. Half identify the <u>*Language of Dangerousness/Horror/Mug-Shot*</u> as instrumental in arranging negative perceptions with '*82 Times*' and words like '*Psycho*' and '*knifeman*' frequently cited as the cause. Two identify font size as dramatic and exacerbating perceptions. Four view film references as problematically associating violence in words like '*killers*'. Respondents also read themes of <u>*Violence, Black and Mad, Blame, No Understanding*</u> identifying racism and stigmatization. Two remark that no useful knowledge is available in the reports.

Daily Mirror – *Group Summaries*

Group A interpretations are characterized by strong complaints about themes of dangerousness and stigma read through personal framings. Recurrent dramatic themes about cultural identity directly linked to film characters from *Psycho* or *The Silence of the Lambs* and mis-selected knowledge are singled out for devaluing of identity. Horror film references contain potently affective properties in negative words like 'schizophrenia', 'killer' and 'psycho' and produce strong symbolic/metaphoric resonances confusing any possibly useful information about mental health. Misinformation offered to the public concerns the group as it promotes the possibility of fuelling already problematic public narratives that can only increase the impact of stigma. The portrayal is viewed as inaccurate by 93%.

Sceptical of knowledge content, Group B question themes of dangerousness. Most respondents read the mediation as a problematic portrayal. Others opine that while 'facts-are-right', the actual actions and events offer the wrong impression. They also know this form denies mental health knowledge. Headlines and language used are identified for how they discourage understanding and dramatic language is accepted as problematic in the construction of identity; respondents agree the mediation draws heavily on imaginative fiction but any identification about stigma is absent. The Liverpool group response changes from their first mediation to see dangerousness themes as negative. Some 15% view the portrayal as accurate, 60% it as inaccurate while 25% see it as partly accurate or inaccurate.

Group C's interpretative position is unanimous. They are concerned that the report produces no useful 'mental health' knowledge to inform public about schizophrenia or the many other conditions that exist. With no references to mental health, they are also concerned that demeaning unwell people undermines self-identity.

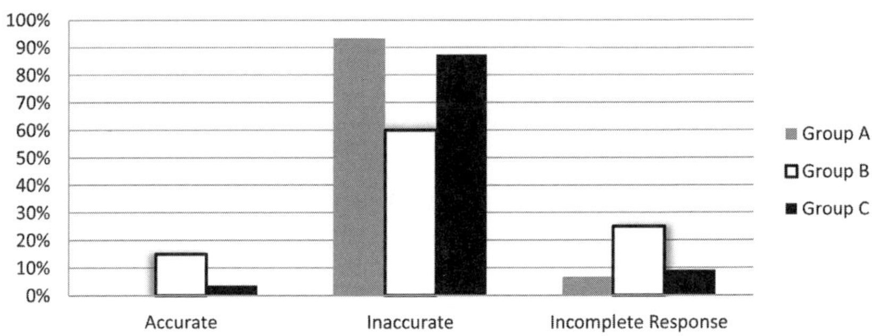

Figure 7.3 Newspaper Genre–Group Comparison

If meanings about madness characterize the unwell as killers and produce negative stereotypes mobilizing stigma, there are implications for people with unwell mental health. Dramatic language, headline size and report content constructs problematical public information when referenced with fictional horror film characters. Potent values in imagery generate stigmatizing meanings when health and race are represented in pejorative ways. Some 87.3% find the mediation inaccurate.

Radio Documentary – *Scapegoats*

Group A – People with Conditions

Cornwall/Devon Respondents read this form through a rejecting orientation in a strongly subjective frame, with history central to most of their objections. The indications are that historical re-enactments make for a complex relationship as they produce stigma. Robin criticizes re-enactments because they are '*making us all look mad*', they shock via stigmatizing stories from the past. Petra voices her disapproval: *history equalled stigma equalled yesterday* and Anne similarly criticizes content, saying that:

> *from early times, mental illness has been considered to be not human, people suffering from any form of it are no better than animals, they are punished for being different, whipped and otherwise ill treated ... are shameful, dirty, have no place in so called normal society – and thus were isolated from it.*

Stories from the past for all respondents reference problematic facts which, when dramatized, draw upon an already distorted history. Petra views re-enactments as '*unhelpful*'. Anne says the documentary while '*a factual account*', views its songs and dialogue as giving a sense of historical period but the documentary references suggests unwell people as: *strange but on the whole good to laugh at – except the mention in the* (Bedlam) *song of the murder.* William and Julie do not respond to the questionnaire but when asked '*Why?*' they simply say they do not like the programme. Anne makes a critical distinction, that: *perhaps most importantly of all, was the use of people's own testimonies – that of Edna Higginbottom sticks in my mind, her account of the reason she was locked up and her treatment was terrible*. Two do not respond and the remainder note divisions over accuracy and inaccuracy.

Hampshire As with the Cornwall/Devon group, nearly all respondents read the mediation through a subjective frame rejecting it. Malcolm observes: *the fear of the public in general, of the mentally ill persists today as it has always done: But perhaps concealed more below the surface ... Mental health in general has a very negative history*. Again, anxiety about the public holding generally negative views about people like him emerges. Using subjective frames, three read stigma in Demeaned Others:

> *The words used, the music and dramatic depictions all contributed toward portrayals of mentally ill people either as mad, bad, stupid, immoral, 'frantic', delusional, criminals or some negative connotation. Carol notes: Largely very inaccurate, born out of the past (and perhaps present to a lesser extent) ignorance and fear of 'mentally ill' people and, The programme concentrated too much, too heavily & too dramatically on these 'false' representations, ... words like 'idiot', 'mad', and 'defective' stick in the brain.*

Again, emphasis upon history in words and songs prove negative as four view such portrayals as stigmatizing identity. Respondents voice concern stigma that stems from history with Carol re-emphasizing: *Mental health has been misrepresented frequently and quite horrifically in the past – the programme makes this very clear. Yet the idea of 'the mad/the insane' (i.e., psychotic?) persisted throughout, it was hard to tell if the producers refuted this or not.* Here, concern is with how much awareness producers actually have about the implications of labelling the unwell, with tags like 'mad' or 'insane'. One respondent views the depiction as accurate, three as inaccurate and one records an incomplete response.

Liverpool Four read negative meanings about Treatments through a subjective frame. Mark informs: that through the years many different treatments have tried, most of them, all of them were in my eyes wrong. The programme was at the extreme, and through history, totally at the experimental stage of (madness) treatment. He objects that the portrayal of treatments contributes to the formulation of bizarre notions distorting cultural identity: the questions are linked to the extreme side of mental illness and therefore they are bad portrayals of mental health. Why are we portrayed in this media item treated as freaks? While four respondents indicate portrayals are inaccurate, Alan notes the tale of Edna Higginbottom is positive dramatic exposition with: the story of the narrative by a woman who had a sexual relationship had a right to speak up but this helped things in understanding. One sees it as accurate.

This set of Group A responses indicates that narratives from history in the form of re-enactments, language and folk music challenge self-identity. Here, theory about intertextuality from Kristeva (1986), and the concept of the looking glass in Crocker and Quinn (2000), are helpful to understanding these responses. The looking-glass self is based upon the reactions of others, that 'Other people provide the 'Looking Glass' in which we see ourselves reflected' (2000: 155). Here, 'Other people' can be interpreted in two ways. First, producers of mediations provide a 'looking glass', their text is a lens through which mental health is seen. Second, and importantly, 'the public' are also a 'looking glass'; for this group they represent an important entity through which respondents perceive themselves seen. Once communicated, narratives provide mostly distorted knowledge about which people with conditions perceive, the public are partially or completely in receipt of about their identity. In the views above, history is a problem because stigmatizing meanings compound already negative knowledge in collective representations. Problematic concepts embedded in narratives, language and songs merge with negative information from other texts across history. Concepts fuse with others in an intertextual sense to gain persuasiveness. Thus, across time problematic meanings in texts become 'taken for granted' and gain an 'accepted-as-right' status as mediations multiply without correction. As Kristeva writes of intertextuality, it is 'the insertion of history (society) into a text and of this text into history' (1986: 39). To paraphrase Fairclough (1992), meanings become reworked, reaccentuated and in this instance reinforced, increasing in their hegemonic influence. Once in the public domain, meanings add confusion not clarity, to knowledge about mental health for both stigmatized and non-stigmatized persons. Based upon the symbolic interactionist theory of Mead (1934), in which he argued that how others see us is crucial to how we see ourselves, Crocker and Quinn (2000) explain that, 'Those "others" may be either the specific individuals with whom we are interacting or a "generalized other"' (2000: 155). In this instance, Group A respondents are reflecting about what the public are imagining about their identities in re-enactments, in that they see their self-identity as an individual and as a collective, misrecognized.

Group B – Media

Cornwall/Devon

Group B responses contrast with Group A. Read via an objective frame, themes of <u>*Pleasure*</u>, <u>*Mad=Bad*</u>, <u>*Madness as a Force of Nature*</u> and <u>*Mental Illness=Punishment*</u> are evaluated through a criteria about balance. One respondent notes the programme allows a context for what he is writing about, that *Attitudes towards Mental Illness across the Centuries had Changed*. This implied admission of 'not knowing' also extends across the remaining media groups with a sense of learning taking place. Two identify songs in the play *King Lear* as <u>*Sympathetic*</u>. *The use of 17th century and 18th century folk songs dramatically illustrates how some in society realized the injustices of using mental illness as a way of getting inconvenient people out of the way or punishing contrariness*. The use of scenes from a play and folk music not only appear to assist here but also (in contrast to Group A), draw out a theme of <u>*pleasure*</u> for this group.

Twice, style and programme content are mentioned as sophisticated and subtle, though 'old English' style language is negative; words such as *lunatics*, *mad* and *insane* are identified unhelpful. However, 'accessed voice' is significant for four respondents: *Edna's firsthand account is more powerful than a description of her experience from another person. She sounds lucid, articulate and 'normal', so her account of her treatment, when she is labelled mentally ill is shocking.* Six find the documentary accurate, one is undecided and one declines a decision. Comments include: *well researched ... longer – more in-depth ... put across in an entertaining way*. As a non-fictional form with re-enactments, there is an acceptance of facts and knowledge content as correct, if a little negative in places.

Hampshire Read through an objective frame and evaluated through a criteria of balance, this group reads programme themes focusing upon mental illness and society, about *The Mentally Ill as Shunned and Shut Away*. Exploring 'facts' one journalist asks: *mental illness is a reflection of the current society and what constitutes a 'mental illness'?* Re-enactments are useful, one respondent saying he learns from dramatic expositions like *King Lear* and music, saying it is a good way of relating about mental health. Narration about cultural identity is criticized as terms like '*mentally ill*' and '*insane*' make '*them out to be a homogeneous mad, rather than a collection of individual people*'. Another says through frame of civic responsibility: *it seems that mental illness was often used/abused as an excuse for authorities to clear the streets*. Two view the mediation as accurate while three answer it can be seen both ways. The case of Edna Higginbottom is sad and moving but all agree the programme is well researched and interesting. In this non-fictional form, its references to history are unquestioned but mention of stigma is absent.

Liverpool Opinions from this group are few but people with mental health conditions are read as outsiders who have been treated differently across the years. One respondent notes: *how fear lies behind our reaction to mental illness, historically nowadays*. Other themes include *Outcast Group* and *Different Treatment* with one remarking that, *society blames others*. Songs and dramas play an important role but information offered about dramatic elements is minimal, as is data concerning identity. All think the programme accurate, one noting it helpful as there are: *different voices to back up the claims in the report*. Another agrees it is: *because it accords with the general knowledge I have of the subject*. Several note the documentary as *being a good constructed story* and the programme is well made.

Group C – Mental Healthcare

Cornwall/Devon Read through a professional frame and evaluated through occupational knowledge, 16 observe *Ideas about Mental Illness have Changed* across history in economic, social, gendered and linguistic ways:

> *1) Understanding of madness has changed over-time having previously had positive connotations i.e., religious. 2) Coming to be known as 'lunatics' meant who could be punished as a form of correction, i.e., beating and ducking. 3) Age of reason, 'mad' known as 'bad' – building of houses of correction. Public attitudes hardened. 4) The state in 18th century took responsibility for looking*

> *after lunatics due to increasing numbers in the asylums. 5) In-patients severely abused by staff in the asylums. 6) In the 1960s, it was thought drugs would be eradicated. 7) Recently public tolerance became decreased.*

Four view history as problematic, viewing '*language as a problem*': words like '*insanity*', a legal term and '*defective*', need replacement with new, improved representations. Five consider re-enactments *Usefully Portray* identity but 13 register generally *Negative Views* this, indicative of stigma: two mention concepts of *Mad Axe Murderer* and another two, *The Dysfunctional Fool*. Three view such concepts as a *Damaging Influence*. Concerns also focus upon themes about the unwell feeling *Segregated from Society*. Here participants view linguistic content with concern questioning how unwell people can recognize their self-identity as with this comes the risk of self-exclusion.

In contrast, *Edna Higginbottom* is significant for seven who identify her voice as helpful in understanding the context of past incarcerations. One notes:

> *The 15 year old girl – locked away for having sex ... she would be tamed like a lion, whipped with a towel. It provokes images of sorrow for girl, anger toward the nurse. I think the issues bring understanding of mental illness, the drama (in this case) strongly reinforced my understanding.*

Another notes:

> *In a social context it highlighted strongly for me the history of wrongly admitted people – the lady who discussed her life was excellent in showing how people are labelled due to others beliefs on their behaviour being socially acceptable, or not.*

While 17 say *Scapegoats* is accurate, it is broadly critiqued as '*historically correct*' but '*generalized*'. Nine view it as inaccurate and two are incomplete responses.

Hampshire Read through a professional frame, critical and complimentary remarks reveal evenly split opinions. Respondents are critical of language portraying identity negatively. One notes: *again words like unstable, threats, deficient, lunatic etc.* and another informs that the language is:

> *A clear historical over-view which was informative and detailed on legislation etc. and to some extent on public views and prejudices. The language used e.g., mental deficiency, tacitly supported a negative view of mental illness. The documentary style gives it historical veracity also.*

Opinions about Edna Higginbottom's portrayal are prominent when set against other dramatic expositions though views are split about dramatic conventions and music. Her inclusion is a '*useful device*' but drama and its role in communicating 'identity' makes for problematic language. *The 'mentally ill' were viewed as a group and only one isolated individual was made available for comment*. Opinions about accuracy in this group are evenly split.

Liverpool Through a professional frame, respondents read themes about <u>*Medicalized Society, Religious Madness and Containment*</u> based upon occupational knowledge. Concepts about madness are viewed as constructed by society as it develops and, society sees madness in varying ways depending on the period; sometimes viewing containment as a requirement. Respondents find <u>*Styles of Reporting/Songs and Sketches/Emotive Language*</u> significant. Words used are a problem because a story can encourage stigma, if not in antagonistic then in 'humorous' ways; professionals are concerned about denigrating someone's life as meaningless by way of belittling identity. Opinion is evenly divided about whether or not songs and sketches are a good or bad influence. Bad influences are: *the terminology used, affects the general public perception. It highlights prejudices of the fickle public*. Good influences are the '*light hearted*' feel though fewer people respond to the question concerning drama and identity, one indicating <u>*Drama Helped*</u>: *it helped the focus and, broke stereotypes*. Eleven think portrayals accurate, three do not and remaining respondents do not respond.

Scapegoats – *Group Summaries*

Group A interpretations generally reject the form because re-enactments and folk music contain affective language and narratives from history which produce stigma. When such content is represented as an 'objective' truth through acting intended to authenticate the past, it is more influential in its marking properties which are doubly powerfully and persuasive. Again, what the public make of these meanings is a concern. This generic component of folk music containing stories is rejected through a strongly subjective frame. Personal testimonies work well however, especially that of Edna Higginbottom but respondents are again concerned with what the public may make of distorted knowledge content as linguistically extreme descriptions denigrate identity. While 13.4% see the form as accurate, 46.6% see it as inaccurate. However, 40% are divided over this question revealing a tension about representational components. The interplay between produced story and what group members see as fact and knowledge are poles apart.

In contrast to Group A, Group B's relationship to this form centres on their view of knowledge content containing interesting information. The character of responses is consistently reflected in remarks identifying it is a pleasurable and well made programme. Switching between objective and civic frames, the story for these respondents is clearly about how society views of mental illness have changed across history. There is also a sense of learning about the study's topic taking place. Re-enactments are viewed as useful with 'King Lear' informing a sense of identity about the unwell.

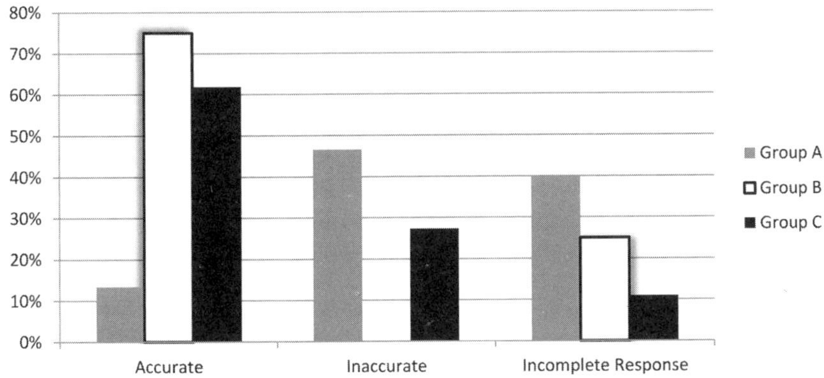

Figure 7.4 Radio Documentary Genre–Group Comparison

Mostly read through a critical working frame, some recognize language as unhelpful but recognizing notions of history as synonymous with stigma or stereotypes is largely absent. With admiration for the quality of information, the use of accessed voice appears to alert respondents to another facet of mental health detail. In contrast to Group A, 75% of Group B view the mediation as accurate with none seeing it as inaccurate and 25% divided over the question. Group C read through mostly professional frames with some accepting, others resistive to the form. Historical content in the form of language and dramatic re-enactments, while viewed as accurate, are unhelpful because they view these produce stigma, though opinion is divided over this. The documentary form offers veracity in presented knowledge content but is not helpful because data misleads, and in some ways is a concern. Most say it is accurate through its historical perspectives but this information type is simply not as useful as the kind which offers useful mental health knowledge. The voice of Edna Higginbottom is identified as helpful and effective in conveying a positive mental health message. 61.8% say it is accurate while 27.3% say it is not. 10.9% do not answer the question.

Television Soap Opera – *EastEnders*

Group A – People with Conditions

Across Group A responses, relationships between form and response contrast to previous mediations. While there is generally no criticism of the form, similarly, there is no significant shift in disposition either. Instead, in this fictional form many respondents view the story referencing factual data in improved ways but the soap's textuality through its use of lightness and darkness to imagine unwell identity is critiqued. It appears there is a critical yet cautious compromise over this mediation.

Cornwall/Devon Themes of Mental Distress and the Family are read through personal frames but several cautiously evaluate the mediation. Robin thinks Joe's acting is '*strong*' and '*played well*' usefully exposing the family's torment and Petra notes that mental distress:

> *Affects the family as much as the individual ... someone with a mental health condition can display a variety of symptoms one minute and six hours later may appear to be 'totally normal' ... someone with a mental health condition is still a handsome, loveable young person – who appears to be confused, delusional, withdrawn at this time.*

Anne says:

> *I understand that mentally ill-health is largely misunderstood – Joe's father David Wickes, at first gives me the impression that he thinks Joe is just being moody, it's a phase he's going through, and will snap out of it soon.*

Previous concerns of how the public might view the mediation are absent for *EastEnders*. Petra observes: It was an accurate portrayal of a single possible situation, experience, individual … you cannot homogenize mental ill-health or conditions – each one has its problems, merits, symptoms, idiosyncrasies etc. Two think dramatic representation of 'hearing voices' is helpful to public understanding but does not fully alleviate stigma. Two register the soap as inaccurate, two view it as accurate and one does not respond.

Hampshire Through a personal frame this group read that Joe is a *Danger to Himself* and his character is a little stereotyped through the use of darkness in setting up a space to learn about mental health. Opinion is split about *EastEnders* with Jane stating: *this was the best but I felt it still left a lot to be desired and in some respects I pondered if it did more harm than good.* Malcolm notes:

> *The producers had done some extensive research into the subject and the scriptwriters did have some qualified mental health advisors available to them.*

But he then says:

> *Most of the scenes in which Joe appeared are very dark and gloomy. I take it that this was intentional as the mentally ill are inevitably associated with dark and gloom. By the way in my experience this association is a misconception.*

EastEnders' portrayal goes some of the way to diminishing the sense of social exclusion and concern over how the public might be viewing things as stigma is not mentioned. This story introduces, at very least, a new narrative for public knowledge which respondents appear to trust. Malcolm and others question The Punctual CPN?. *It gives a false impression of real life. One telephone call and a CPN arrives like a genie out of a bottle!* Opinion about accuracy is mixed with two indicating accuracy, two non-responses and one indicating inaccuracy.

Liverpool Four read that *Joe's got a Problem* through a personal frame, referencing his situation as relatable. There are no concerns mentioned as to how the public may view the depiction. Instead, Alan notes: *mental illness was treated sympathetically, promoted understanding of the condition ... how he* [Joe] *could improve or drag people down*. Mark says: *mental illness had taken a grip of this lad Joe, that without treatment he wasn't getting any better and that, his family weren't coping any better.*

Respondents indicate that the Soap Drama Helps and Opens up Understanding. Daniel (who lives with the condition) views the form as helping illuminate the condition: ... *pretty true to life and reasonably accurate. EastEnders was helping me understand the way he is, in himself, and he seems that he is very confused. He is also needing help*. Don notes it might help people to: *learn to treat people with mental health problems as normal and with respect ... it is reasonably accurate, people can identify with the character and it can lead to more empathy with sufferers*. Two say it is accurate, while one says it is not and two record incomplete responses.

Group B – Media

Cornwall/Devon Respondents present diverse set of opinions through objective frames. One dominant theme centres upon *The Family*'s difficulty in coping with Joe's behaviour. Others include *Fear*, Changing Moods and people with mental illness doing Bizarre Things. One respondent notes the drama stereotypes Joe: *'staring eyes', paranoia, 'unkempt' – gives a very negative and scary view*. One views his parents as: *worried and fearful and – especially his mother is alienated by her son's behaviour – reflect the difficulties for those close to mentally ill people.* A general opinion is that people like Joe just simply do these strange things, their mood generating a fearful quality for audience. However, no associational meanings are read leaving only surface values.

One respondent is critical of the fictional form as a provider of public information.

> *'EastEnders' seems to be trying to fulfil a quasi-educational role in bringing 'issues' (of a serious nature) to a wide audience in a light entertainment programme. In fact there is very little understanding for audience when you compare it to the role's entertainment value.*

In contrast, two note the last scene with David Wickes and the family as significant. Coping with schizophrenia is viewed as very difficult and the portrayal of his identity is admirable. Choosing a young person for raising awareness is a good idea with most respondents pointing to this story as a new public narrative. Five consider *EastEnders* accurate, two think it is not and one is undecided.

Hampshire Through objective frames respondents read themes that Schizophrenia Affects the Family with dramatic expositions facilitating concepts about the condition and the family. *The Last Scene* produces strong themes, when Joe's room with newspapers and silver foil on the walls show his condition. However, it isn't easy to comprehend. Its complex nature is identified as frightening, connected with moods and perplexing for all. His portrayal as *A Handsome Male* is identified as useful this aspect of identity helpful to accessing his character but one critically questions: '*How do you deal with it effectively and sensitively?*' perhaps revelatory of a personal quandary about representational difficulties over this issue. The character played by David Wickes is thought to be a useful device through whom the audience can identify: *the viewer sees things from David's perspective, and learns through him, what it would be like to have a family member with mental illness*. The last scene is: *an amazingly powerful dramatic device – that made me realize how seriously ill Joe was when on the face of it he quite often seemed okay*.

Two are impressed by *The CPN's quick arrival*. One indicates 'he was able to pull strings' while another says it shows 'how the mechanics of the mental health system work; how parents are supported by the system'. Four consider *EastEnders* accurate, one is unsure.

Liverpool A theme of schizophrenia *Affecting Family and Young People* is read through an objective frame. One respondent says: mental illness isn't easy to diagnose, the effect of mental illness on others especially the family. Opinions are diverse, some saying the soap helps show how Joe's behaviour is irrational. Another says it helps show mental illness as a part of everyday life. Two reflect the CPN does a good job. One views it a: convincing portrayal in a modern real-life setting. Three consider *EastEnders* accurate, one is undecided and three others think it inaccurate.

Group C – Mental Healthcare

Cornwall/Devon Through a professional frame seven read schizophrenia as having an *Adverse Effect* upon Joe's well-being. Ten note *EastEnders* is useful and four consider it *Well Researched* with schizophrenia's transformative nature given a good overview indicating its story references group knowledge about the condition well. One observes: *the programme gives you a better understanding about mental health*. Another explains it: *shows well the change in Joe's behaviour as a result of his deteriorating mental health*. Having a handsome young man playing this role reduces stigma. By making visible the different elements of schizophrenia, i.e., a set of scrambled emotions, belief systems and inserted thoughts, *EastEnders* meaning-making challenges stigma, making for a more effective portrayal; knowledge content in the soap accords with professional perspectives.

In general, opinions reflect *EastEnders* is an improved representation and good for public viewing, 24 respondents viewing it as accurate. Two view it as inaccurate, one is undecided and another does not respond. Five illuminate *Anyone Could Get the Condition* and another five applaud themes about the impact of the condition on *The Family*. Four criticize the lighting though opinion is mixed between its useful and adverse impacts. Three are critical of the *CPN Portrayal* saying: *they don't prescribe drugs*.

Hampshire Respondents read *Suffering Affects Families/CPN/Changing State of Condition* through a professional frame. Joe's schizophrenia is evaluated as a difficult problem for his family. One views that: *the portrayal reflects well the distress and confusion that Joe's behaviour causes in his parents. This suggests that individual mental health problems cannot be seen in violation but that they can affect others with whom the sufferer has contact.*

Therefore, the genre is regarded as useful for getting mental health into the public arena but words such as '*mad*' and '*nutter*' and the element of darkness do not help, they convey despondency. Favourable reviews about identity portrayal include the use of *Empathetic Language*, this, identified by eight, four of which indicate it '*provoked empathy*'. However, the CPN's portrayal is misleading: *their immediate reliance on medication, medical assessment and talk of MHA sections did not adequately reflect the depth of mental health nursing practice.* Nine indicate mental health in *EastEnders* is accurate and two are undecided.

Liverpool Read through a professional frame, respondents note themes of *Joe's Portrayed Well/Stress for the Family/Disruptive Illness/The Quick CPN?* Four view Joe's portrayal as favourable: it is an accurate portrayal – appearance, smoking, demeanour etc. of someone going through such distress. One notes: Joe's portrayal was very good, issues of paranoia – poisoning – radiation – not being able to trust the person closest to you. Dramatic action is applauded, several participants reading codes of his appearance, verbal and non-verbal language, as helping to understand *The Processual Nature of Schizophrenia*. Plot development helps mental health understanding: 'It developed in layers with more detail being gradually added, not as a fait accompli. This made it more realistic'. It shows a process of 'gradual breakdown' and 'not a snap shot' by way of an evolving *realism* that conveys the subjective nature of the condition. That his identity is portrayed 'in the family' is also useful as over time, it makes his behaviour less scary. Five note *It Can Happen to Anyone* but the condition is an 'added stress' for the family. Twelve respondents find *EastEnders*: *An Accurate Process of Schizophrenia, The Family and Language* while four do not commit a decision instead viewing the representation as having some accuracy/inaccuracy.

EastEnders – *Group Summaries*

Group A read *EastEnders* through personal frames, evaluating it via their experience to find it a more accessible representation. Unlike other relationships between responses and genres, this fictional form opens up a wider view through its depictions of schizophrenia. The character of responses present no mention of concerns over how the public might view it, indicating a change from previous mediations and remarks about stigma are largely absent. However, some problematic themes about dangerousness are apparent as are themes of accuracy over Joe's representation. His identity is seen to be portrayed well but lighting contributes to stereotyping when coded with darkness. However, there is no shift in disposition of the group. Also, CPNs do not arrive punctually. While this example is broadly accepted as a more useful representation, a significant shift in opinions does not occur. Some 40% record it as accurate, 26.7% say it is not and 33.3% are unsure, indicating tensions about representational components like lighting.

Group B reads the 'family is affected by mental illness' as a strong theme but surface meanings mostly prevail. That Joe's condition is a complex problem and also irrational, is indicative of how knowledge and views are aligned with 'objectivity' in their professional practice. In this generic form, groups view informational content as helpful though only one participant (from Cornwall/ Devon) found the fictional form contentious as a way of presenting information about an important issue. Most respondents consider the programme accurate but views about the CPN's practice and healthcare system as effective are in stark contrast with other group opinions. 60% view *EastEnders* as accurate with 25% indicating inaccuracy and 15% not responding or divided.

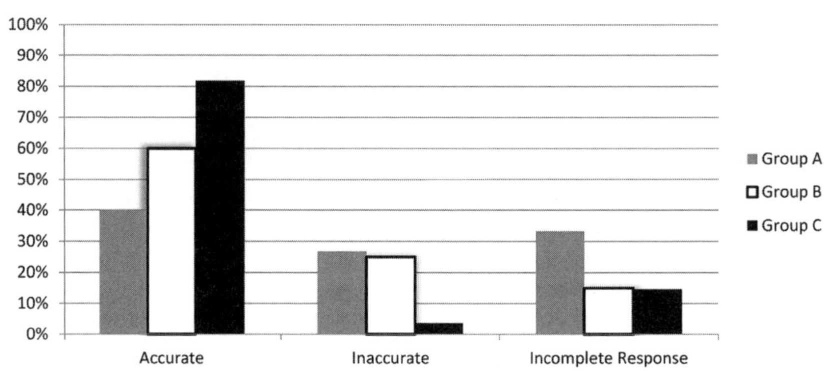

Figure 7.5 Soap Opera Genre–Group Comparison

Some 81.8% of Group C find the condition of schizophrenia accurately portrayed. Research for the programme also reveals the impact on the family and the processual nature of Joe's condition. Dramatic properties also help by way of using a handsome young man as a device to interest the audience; it makes the character accessible as does language used and is helpful toward reducing stigma. The story contains useful and factual information about the condition and helpfully references its transformative qualities. However, professionals question the accuracy portrayal of CPN practice. Allowing exploration of the condition, Group C views programme reduces stigma as the condition is effectively represented. 3.6% view the soap as an inaccurate with 14.6% divided over accuracy.

Conclusions

Group A view their identity in the television news example as criminalized, from meanings about dangerousness inferred in imagery from cop and western genre forms and adopt a position resistive to its content. The group consider this factual form as constituted of fictionalizing elements which are a concern as the mediation lacks reference to mental health facts. Knowledge content in framing identity is *very* important and so too are tonal variations in the delivery of language, it matters to this group how the public perceive them as unwell people. Misrepresentation of identity matters enormously as some meanings contain stigma that can lead to social exclusion and this is emphasized by the strong rejection of the tabloid news form. Direct references to horror films produce affective properties via problematic language and imagery, and are singled out for strong criticism because of its misinformation for the public. Again, fictionalization in non-fictional forms is criticized with group distrust generated from news misrepresentation *marking* their identity.

In the radio documentary, historical references in formal elements of folk music and language play an influential role as Group A object strongly to meanings conveying ideas from the past. Re-enactments contain potently affective information about the changing ways in which madness is seen across history and are viewed as unhelpful. Again, how the public view the group is a major concern. While personal testimonies work well this mediation entrenches dispositions making respondents very resistive. *EastEnders* does not produce any major shift of opinion though mention of stigma is largely absent, as is concern over how the public view their identity. Criticisms identify health service portrayals and representational processes like the use of darkness which convey stereotypical identity but this form is more accessible.

While all of Group B do not read dangerousness themes in the television news exemplar, they largely accept knowledge content with two out of three groups mentioning stereotypes but not stigma; themes of confinement are viewed as controversial but mention of imagery about the car is not. The Liverpool journalists accept knowledge content read in the form as fact but with the next mediation they question themes of dangerousness and are critical of headlines and language. Stereotypes are recognized by Group B but stigma is not, though a tension exists over tabloid content in that 'facts-are-right' with wrong impressions conveyed. In contrast to A, this group find the documentary useful in helping topic understanding and re-enactments like *King Lear* are praised in what is a well constructed programme that informs. Group B read that the condition of schizophrenia in *EastEnders* impacts the family unit and view the health service as working. They also see schizophrenia as a complex and irrational condition but no major shift occurs in group disposition.

Group C are concerned about the impact of themes referencing dangerousness in people with unwell mental health and a lack of mental health information in the news. The car imagery is not identified but, as with Group B, prison bars are; opinions note that no useful mental health knowledge is forthcoming. There is also concern over how people with unwell mental health will read the tabloid's stigma. Respondents are again critical about the documentary because historical data is simply not a useful source of information about mental health because it contains stigma. Accessed voice also works well to convey useful information about mental health. Group C view the representation of schizophrenia in the soap as well researched with the use of a handsome young man, a smart move. The processual and episodic nature of the condition is well portrayed and research is praised for its thoroughness and application.

Chapter 8

Phase Two, Part 2: The Community Project: Production Study Exploring Change: Approach, Alternative Images and Practices

Introduction

The second part of the community project aims to provide clues towards alternative practice concerning stigma by exploring the transformations in new mediations actioned by Group A, people with mental health conditions. The study is located broadly within the 'active audience' tradition, part of an interpretative approach, but is distinctive through its use of Community Theatre practices which seek a way forward in a practical eliciting of cultural readings. Using an approach developed from the works of Augusto Boal (1979 and 1990) and Paulo Freire (1970), the study is grounded in critical reflections from concrete stimuli. The reception phase serves as a foundation for actions or praxis for Group A with the intention to facilitate critical production processes in which they produce their own mediations; once completed these transformations present data from which to make evaluations.

Approach and Study Design: Theatre and Media for Development

In the production study, people question media artefacts through their critical encountering of them in performance processes. Using the processes of drama as a tool for understanding, people produce meanings via a process of *conscientização*, what Freire calls *conscientization* in a modified approach of Augusto Boal's *Forum Theatre*. This part of the Community Project was conducted for Group A over a period of five days (see Table 8.1). Participants worked in spaces where the reception and production projects could be achieved. The reception study involved spaces with audio-visual facilities and the production project used TV studios in two higher education institutions and a classroom in another.

Table 8.1 Media Production Project: Monday–Friday for Group A

	Monday	Tuesday	Wednesday	Thursday	Friday
Morning Activities	Reception Study Reading mental health mediations from television, radio and a newspaper.	Production Study Drama workshop.	Production cont'd Getting-to-know production facilities.	Production: Drama processes for alternative mediations.	Production: Drama processes for alternative mediations. Concluding previous day's work.
Afternoon Activities	Reception Study As above but for media and mental healthcare professional groups.	Production Study cont'd Drama workshop.	As above but most likely more rehearsing undertaken.	Production: Mediation processes for alternative mediations.	Production: Processes for alternative mediations. Concluding previous day's work.
Space Type	Spaces quiet for examining TV, listening to radio. Desks and chairs for reading printed media.	Floor space for drama.	TV studio/ radio production facilities and editing rooms. A space for drama.	TV studio/ radio production facilities and editing rooms.	TV studio or room. Final discussion of details about the study. Interviews.

Central to this study's objectives are Boal's 'poetics of the oppressed':

> In order to understand this *poetics of the oppressed* one must keep in mind its main objective: to change the people – 'spectators,' passive beings in the theatrical phenomenon – into subjects, into actors, transformers of dramatic action. I hope that the differences remain clear. Aristotle proposes a poetics in which the spectator delegates power to the dramatic character so that the latter may act and think for him. Brecht proposes a poetics in which the spectator delegates power to the character who thus acts in his place but the spectator reserves the right to think for himself, often in opposition to characters. In the first case, a 'catharsis' occurs; in the second, an awakening of critical consciousness. But the *poetics of the oppressed* focuses upon action itself: the spectator delegates no power to the character (or actor) either to act or to think in his place; on the contrary, he himself assumes the protagonic role, changes the dramatic action, tries out solutions, discusses plans for change – in short, trains himself for real action. In this case, perhaps theater is not revolutionary in itself,

> but it is surely a rehearsal for the revolution. The liberated spectator, as a whole person, launches into action. No matter that the action is fictional; what matters is that it is action! (Boal 1979: 122)[1]

In this phase, the focus is 'dramatic action' by social actors performing as protagonists; a process through which a spectator changes into an actor. For clarity's sake, *Forum Theater*'s four stages are introduced to outline Boal's approach. The First stage is: *Knowing the Body*; the Second is: *Making the Body Expressive*; and the Third stage: *Theater as Language* includes three levels. These are:

> First degree: *Simultaneous dramaturgy*: the spectators 'write' simultaneously with the acting of the actors;
>
> Second degree: *Image theater*: the spectators intervene directly, 'speaking' through images made with the actors' bodies;
>
> Third degree: *Forum theater*: the spectators intervene directly in the dramatic action and act. (Boal 1979: 126)

These lead to a fourth stage, *The Theater as Discourse*. However, in this study's approach the first and second stages are combined and Boal's *Cop in the Head* process is adopted in place of the third and fourth stage. The study now turns to an examination of how these stages function to facilitate development of participant's positions to a point where a transformation from spectator to actor can occur.

First Stage: Knowing the Body and Making the Body Expressive

The first stage celebrates the participants' cultural identity by overcoming participant ideas about theatre as being beneath a proscenium arch and before a seated arena; it does this by nurturing a body poetics. *Knowing the Body* establishes theatre as something people own, rather than a physical structure imposing particular values about how it operates. Consequently, the project takes place in a hall type space with a flat floor, rather than a stage-auditorium structure. Following a small number of physical and vocal warm-up exercises, participants, in groups of two, are requested to project an image of their 'self' showing an everyday cultural practice which celebrates their identity; this, reflecting their work or activities they undertake daily. This is a still image supported by a 'one word title'. Initiating *Making the Body Expressive*, the aim is to encourage expressiveness through use of the body. Our culture, as Boal points out, is one 'used to expressing everything through words, leaving the enormous expressive capabilities of the body in an

1 The term 'spectator' Boal uses is not understood, in the context of this study, to indicate passivity.

underdeveloped state' (Boal 1979: 130). Completing this first still image, the second process is then assisted by 'moving' the image, this time accompanied by spoken language; building significant detail into developing fictional world but in slow motion, exaggerating cultural practices. Through an atmosphere supportive of creativity the group watch, reading each image, making their meanings from it with the help of new language. This is a useful way of presenting identity and helpful in constituting a foundation for the next level. At all stages of the process, comfort in undertaking the work was afforded group participants with the proviso that if they wanted to stop or rest in the process, this was okay.

The Second Stage: The Cop in the Head Hypotheses: Mediated Identities and Osmosis

Reflecting upon mediations from the reception phase, this stage re-examines those representations and acknowledges how problems of identity posed by stigmatic values in cultural and media discourses constrain participants from everyday 'mental health' discussion.

> All the moral and political values of a given society along with its structures of power and domination, as well as its corresponding mechanisms of oppression are contained in the smallest cells of the social organization (the couple, the family, the neighbourhood, the school, the office, the factory, etc.) and even in the smallest events of social life (an accident at the end of a street, the ID control in the subway, a doctor's visit, etc.). (Boal 1990: 36)

In media however, pejorative values in mental health meanings are amplified as the reception study showed giving rise to essentialist identities. Across time, what Freire terms, 'generative themes' (1970: 86) promote difference in images about mental health identity, 'spoiling' it to use Goffman's (1963) term, as a diseased stereotype located outside social boundaries of normality. Media discourses produce certain implications for subjectivity, producing discomfort about a condition, marshalling a form of self-policing about sharing knowledge of the condition. This stage addresses the internalized oppressions which Boal describes as, the *Cop in the Head.*

> There are many people who dare not participate in a strike or other political actions. Why? Because they have cops in their heads. They have internalized their oppressions. The cops are in their heads but the headquarters of these cops are in the external reality. It is necessary to locate both the cops and their headquarters. (Boal 1990: 35)

Augusto Boal's three hypotheses are applied here and consequently the study design incorporates two principles underpinning *Theatre of the Oppressed* processes: '1) To help the spectator become a protagonist of the dramatic action so that s/he can 2) apply those actions s/he has practised in the theatre of real life' (Boal 1990: 36). Consequently, this stage, entitled Osmosis, leads to discussion about mediated identity against that of the experienced 'celebrated' identity; producing tensions that lead to the next stage, that of Metaxis.

The Third Stage: Exploring Mediated Oppressions: Metaxis

Oppressed people are 'infinitely rich, full of psychological and intellectual possibilities' (Boal 1990: 40) and this stage moves the focus to making media and alternative images about mental health. Small groups of two or three work with each other helping to produce artistic images of oppressions bringing about a process of 'aesthetic transubstantiation':

> When the oppressed-artist creates the images of her oppressed reality, she belongs to both the real and aesthetic world in an active rather than vicarious way. In this instance, we have the *metaxis* phenomenon; the total and simultaneous adherence to two different and autonomous worlds. The aesthetic transubstantiation belongs to the two autonomous worlds: reality and the image of reality that has been created by this process. (Boal 1990: 38)

In the Metaxis process, the oppressed person produces his/her own world of art through the creation of images from his/her real life oppressions. Produced is a key difference with conventional theatre holding special significance for this part of the study design. Boal's discussion about the *spectator/character* relationship in traditional theatrical performance highlights the contrasting processes of *empathy/sympathy* in theatre of the oppressed. As in the osmosis stage (above), Metaxis involves encounters with mediated meanings about identity. This stage requests participants to present one image they consider typical of ways in which media represent them pejoratively on the subject of mental health identities. They write out their oppressed situation for reading by the group who, if the image is autonomous, will be *sympathetically* received (as *sym* means 'with', indicating that people in the group are no longer led by another's action), they are now actioning subjects. Still images and a title are later organized for a more developed, but short-moving image sequence with original dialogue.

Once accomplished, these images of how participants view media seeing them are set in a creative dialogue and new ideas are introduced and practised. New images are rehearsed and titles produced via critical engagement with the dramatic processes to produce limit acts. They act out interpretations that produce potentiality for new characters and news presenters, with new language and dramatic components in dialogue.

> *The oppressed must be helped so that she can reflect upon her own actions, i.e., regarding possible alternatives shown to her by other participants based on*

> *their particular circumstances.* The protagonist must be able to see herself both as protagonist and as object. (Boal 1990: 42)

The Fourth Stage: Analogical Induction

In this final stage, the *Cop in the Head* approach allows the telling of individual narratives as well as whole group oppressions, and to this end:

> If an individual's farewell image or scene prompts other analogous images or scenes from colleagues in the session, and if one builds a model detached from the particular circumstances of each individual case using these images, such a model will contain the general mechanisms through which oppression is produced. This revelation of the general mechanism of oppression will enable us to study the different possibilities for breaking the oppression *sym*-pathetically. (Boal 1990: 41)

This process provides the opportunity for a *Forum* examining different perspectives as to why participants have chosen to take their action; its function, the provision of a Gestalt analytical process. Protagonists present different perspectives and from this, discussions are promoted about what sort of texts might be offered as alternatives to the originals. At this point, participants move forward toward making their new meanings about mental health in the production project and which leads to a finished and recorded piece.

Lib Spry (see Schutzman and Cohen-Cruz 1994: 171–84) raises useful questions about limitations in the *Forum Theater* process, pointing out issues concerning protagonist and antagonist structure. Relationships of 'us and them' are organized to produce useful ways of understanding hierarchies of power, but negative potentials always remain bi-polarizing characters and issues. This can maintain the very conflict inherent in 'power-over' relationships which the approach attempts to change; people with a mental health condition in a dialogue rather than oppositional situations. Thus, this project seeks ways forward of working together with media professionals. What Freire terms 'true revolution' is taken with a less directly political emphasis to mean 'change' and it is indicative that what must take place is a 'courageous dialogue with the people. Its very legitimacy lies in that dialogue' (Freire 1970: 109). At the conclusion of this production process, there is an exit interview for the group about the nature of the aims and intentions of their meaning-makings, the 'fictions' that can be taken back and applied to life.

Post-Production Processes and Arrangements

Mediated images about mental health made in group work were presented to the groups at other locations for review (i.e., triangulation of results). As facilitator the author requested participants interpret each other's work through discussion.

Broadly, all groups in all locations found a degree of unity and harmony in carrying out their work, both individually and together.

The production process differed slightly at each place. At Falmouth, there was a newly built studio with a crew keen to participate and at Winchester, there was a television studio supported by technicians. At Liverpool, the entire production project was undertaken by the author in a seminar room. Of interest here is the fact some technicians revealed their own mental health experiences and this proved reassuring to groups where they had doubts about their own ability to perform with others present.

Alternative Images, Narratives and Practices

This section describes and analyses alternative images and practices from the projects in Falmouth, Winchester and Liverpool. Broadly, the study categorizes them into 'identity narratives' and 'alternative images' but in view of the number of mediations made, the study is selective in its report about them. Beginning with the Falmouth project five alternative mediations are examined including a group video project about narrative identities. This is examined first.

Falmouth Group

Identity Narrative 1 Produced for a general audience, the portrayal is divided up into two parts. Both involve 'talking heads', mid-shots of group members presenting personal testimonies about their lives; giving account of positive personal attributes, social practices and achievements. After group members offer their ontological narrative,[2] the second section introduces each person again, this time continuing where they left off in their narrative but informing the audience of the conditions they experience and which inform their identity. This form is arranged as a way of allowing audience to know their personal qualities first and then to move forward to 'mental health' expositions.

Petra starts first explaining about her life, that she is a mature student studying among other things, the cultural representation of political images, of icons of individuals in marginalized groups. Her story continues, informing us that she is someone who travels a lot, visiting a range of countries including Spain, Cuba, Vietnam, Malaysia and Morocco, mostly in connection with research for her degree. Having worked as a tour manager and a merchant navy bosun, she has also won a gold disc for backing vocals on a number one single, as well as

---

2 Ontological narratives are 'the stories that social actors use to make sense of – indeed, in order to act in – their lives. Ontological narratives are used to define who we are; this in turn is a precondition for knowing what to do. This "doing" will in turn produce new narratives and hence new actions; the relationship between narrative and ontology is processual and mutually constitutive' (Somers and Gibson in Calhoun 1994: 61).

successfully undertaking a range of other jobs. Petra is followed by Anne who says she is a mother to one lively boy, she likes *Ally McBeal* on television and films, with a particular favourite star, John Cage. Julie introduces herself as someone who is a wife and a Christian studying for the ministry. William says that he is a campaigner, a flirt, enjoys bell ringing and likes his pint. Robin says he is a father and grandfather, and does relief work for a number of organizations that provide aid to countries such as Albania, Indonesia and Kenya.

A longer fade between this and the next talking head, signals a turning point. Anne is visualized: *Hello, Anne again. I am happy being me. I enjoy all these things, enjoy life and I am recovering from mild depression.* Next follows Robin:

> *Hello Robin again. I enjoy doing all the things I recently told you about but I actually suffer from severe depression, severe anxiety, I have panic attacks. I am being treated for post traumatic stress disorder. And just for a bit of luck I have got SAD in the winter as well. Thank you.*

Then Julie relates, *I am Julie and I suffer from some form of mental condition.* Next William concisely offers, *Hello, I am William. I live with depression.* In concluding, Petra finishes the piece, saying:

> *Hi! And I am Petra and as I have said, I am studying Visual Culture which includes analysis theory and criticism of all visual representation. And I believe that mental health conditions are misrepresented both by and within the health service and through all forms of popular media. I believe it is time those representations changed I think we ought to see the person and not just the disorder. I am Petra and I live with brain injury and a post traumatic stress disorder.*

Other Group A Reflections This selection of personal testimonies was very popular with both the Liverpool and Winchester groups. Each proposed it as good way of presenting people and getting a message over that they were just like everyone else in some ways, and yet distinctive in others. Daniel said that he liked the way William simply said, *I live with depression*, this according with his own view of experiencing the condition. In general, this portrayal was verified as a very good mental health representation.

The focus of Petra's message was to know 'the person' first and to see 'the condition' second. Presenting cultural identities and practices in their social world, these ontological narratives or holistic attributes were emphasized before members' conceptualizations of their mental health. Communicating about their identity in the 'relational setting',[3] they performed with an agency they wouldn't

---

3 This term is employed rather than 'society' which can be an all encompassing and denying of explicitness in social relationships. According to Somers and Gibson (in Calhoun 1994: 70), 'A relational setting is a pattern of relationships among institutions,

normally enjoy – facilitated through the confidentiality offered in the project. The encouragement to project their own mediated identity was central as this form of communication enables expression of who they are in terms of what they do, followed by the statement about their mental well-being. Through exposure of ontological narrative and identity, these mediations were 'limit acts' facilitated through confidentiality in the project, establishing trust and allowing a direct expression of identity. This alternative image allowed the audience an exploration of people first and conditions second; a freedom for identity unusual at a mediated level.

Barking Mad Productions: Mad Bob From In There (or One Who Flew Into The Cuckoo's Nest) This representation was intended as a radio comedy form, meant to be part of a series of programmes for a general audience. This episode, entitled 'The Chair', was also videoed. As this alternative depiction begins, an old time music hall tune is heard conveying themes similar to Dick Barton's[4] opening music and titles. A narrator gives the programme's title as, *Mad Bob From In There (or One Who Flew Into The Cuckoo's Nest)* and then, Bob is heard saying – '*Decisions, decisions, decisions*'. Every time this character speaks, it is usually only to say one word repeated several times; signifying, (comically) that Bob is like a simpleton. Based on satire the comedy reveals 'the decision' is: should Bob get up from '*his* nice' chair? The question is then posed as to whether or not, the chair would be sat in by '*luscious Lucy, the severely depressed*'. The comedic tension is raised by this person, framed as a threat to Bob's ownership of the chair. The absurd extended further by his reasoning that maybe he should sharpen his eighteen inch machete as a response to this intended danger – the sound of metal sharpening on metal is heard.

Continuing in the ridiculous vein, Che Guevara 'the multi-personality' is introduced as someone who could guard the chair but the question follows, 'Who is he today?' This is resolved by the narrator saying, 'To Bob's relief, he was *the FBI man*' and a relieved Bob is heard saying, 'Phew, yes'. The narrator then says there is a good reason needed by Bob to get Che to guard the chair and, 'Think, think, think, think', before the narrator informs, 'the idea hit him like a thunderbolt', and a thunderbolt sound is heard, followed by an 'ouch'. We are told Bob was keeping the seat warm for the President, and the 'Star Spangled Banner' is then heard hummed by the actors. This theme is continued as another women's voice is heard saying 'Morning all' in an American accent. 'Oh s***', is voiced by Bob with the narrator then stating, 'It was mincing Mary the fairy queen'. Another new character, Margaret the mathematician, who is usually known as 'the bar code

---

public narratives, and social practices. As such it is a relational matrix, similar to a social network. Identity formation takes shape within these relational settings of contested but patterned relations among narratives, people, and institutions'.

4 *Dick Barton – Special Agent* was a popular British detective radio genre in the 1940s and 1950s with a quick tempo musical introduction.

lady', is introduced, saying 'Good morning, 856930049' adding to the sense of the bizarre. The narrator asks 'Would Bob just have to go berserk instead of just crazy?' The narrator states that Bob has said, 'S***' but questions if this was Bob expressing his discontent. Bob is heard saying 'No … s***', implying something more literal and here toilet humour is introduced as feet are heard exiting the room and another voice saying, 'I've always wanted to sit in this chair'.

Other Group A Reflections In verification sessions, Daniel in the Liverpool group was critical of this piece saying that mental health was a serious issue and this example was flippant. But Don disagreed saying, '*They were trying to get a bit of fun out of the project*'. Daniel persisted with his view, that for him, it didn't work. There were also criticisms from within Robin's own group which were sensitive to similar points raised by Daniel and further emphasized the sensitivity around the subjective and how the social group viewed such portrayals. In contrast, one person in the Winchester group said it was quite creative making fun of things rather than taking mental illness seriously, but of all the representations produced in the study, this was the only one which drew criticism. Broadly, criticisms reflected fears that it might exacerbate problematic themes about mental illness already present in the social setting, perpetuating myths about mental illness.

Underpinning Robin's idea was that people experiencing a mental health condition are largely portrayed as 'sad' and 'depressed'. The intention to send up mediations about their imagined practices is reminiscent of other social groups inverting dominant discourses about cultural identity. Here, the producer is poking fun at the 'mad stereotype'; wanting to undermine it through a comedic trajectory. Despite audience views (above), Robin's intention to create irony around the identities of *Mad Bob*, *Che Guevara* and the *Bar Code Lady* etc., reveals a sophisticated double play on mad mediated realities. The idea of propelling a wide variety of dangerous characterizations intent on terrible deeds exposes a strong political decision to produce 'a play' on how such identities are viewed in mediations. To not only accept these essentialist identities, but also embrace their pejorative qualities and transform them into a comedic mediation is not so much a resistive discourse as an actively political one. Taking his and the other users' identities to make inverted meanings in an alternative media discourse is to turn upside down media meaning-making, producing the carnivalesque out of their portrayals. Here was an idea, not something just resistive but which moved beyond these boundaries, it was an active struggle for identity, considered with a degree of balance in an idea with depth that embraced itself and dominant culture with it; an identity that was, in many ways already mobilized to action.

Extra! Extra! Read All About It

This video targeted tabloid newspaper editors, employing dramatic imagery by the use of a silhouetted figure standing poised with a machete, set against a light background. As if about to undertake a downward strike upon something or someone, the image of the arm is still, the reading left open to the imagination as a voice-over announces in the call of street corner newspaper seller, *Extra Extra Read All About It, Psycho Killer, Mad Axe Murderer, System Fails*. Next, a mid-shot of a woman follows with her upheld palm facing the camera. She utters *Stop* followed by:

> *Dear Editors, I would like you to consider this. What would you think this man is doing?* (The silhouetted figure is returned to). *Is your first impression of him – this?* (The newspaper employed in reception study is visualized). *Chances are, you'd be wrong.* (A mid-shot of Anne is returned to). *This is just the type of stereotypical image that people in the media portray of a person with a mental health problem'. You totally misunderstand and misrepresent them. It's the kind of awful sensationalism you use to sell your newspapers. I think it is time for a change. Look at the bigger picture.*

The silhouetted figure is returned to once more, but this time moving. The man, who in real life is a gardener, is seen with the machete and wooden stake, sharpening it on a bench. Increasing lighting slowly illuminates the man and his actions, exposing for the audience the actual context of his situation.

The opening scene is dramatic not solely because of its image but through its idea of momentarily *setting* audience perception to register the violent stereotype and then, speedily, re-orienting it, disorganizing audience perception, re-*setting* parameters to raise questions about who the person is and what he is doing. It has a similarity with past television advertisements for the *Guardian* in which the menacing face of a skinhead is captured, as he runs threateningly along a street towards an old lady. The portrayal initially displays potential for violence but actually concludes in the young man saving her from being hit by falling debris from building.

For Anne, these identity constructions were highly questionable, her self-identity made fragile by dominant media content writing into the social world, an imagined cultural practice of her as a killer; media imagery associated her with a wide spectrum of violent behaviours including murder, a destabilizing influence for her ontological security. That her 'being' might be associated with violent themes created an anxiety/conflict about perceived relationships between her and the social world. Exploring the relationship between self-identity and the social world, Giddens (1991: 35–69) argues that ontological insecurity is in need of continual reassurance. However, here, this dimension becomes destabilized creating stimuli for her critical image aimed at tabloid newspaper editors. And here, her message was clear: misidentifications in this news form *are* a concern and there is urgent need for *change*.

Other Group A Reflections The Liverpool group unanimously agreed that they liked this portrayal; they considered it '*spot on*'. The Winchester members agreed it was '*well done*', the use of the hatchet portrayed a typical mediated mental health perspective, '*that we all go out and kill each other*', one participant concluded, another saying it was '*frank and honest*'. The entire Cornwall/Devon group favoured this image too, one member saying of such newspaper reports, they were '*the triumph of propaganda over common sense*'.

The conceptualizations in this representation gave important public and policy advice – to take a look at the bigger picture about their social identity. Offering to the public domain 'misunderstanding through misrepresentation', essentialist attributions of violence and dangerousness, far from contributing to useful knowledge about a health matter offer a misleading and inaccurate set of 'ideas' about mental health personhood. In actuality, generated stigma produces withdrawal and silence, the person with a condition consigned either to seek assistance or maintain an oppressed subjectivity; an identity therefore unable to form full relationships within his/her social setting.

Plea to Media Producers and William's Address

Julie's idea was to make a direct but general plea to media, appealing for a new ways forward in which new ideas could be produced to 'plant new seeds' of information in the minds of the public. William felt his contribution was best offered through a closing address, thanking people for watching.

Winchester Group

In the Winchester group one new mediation is examined with two described broadly. Two group members decided to examine an interview in news magazine form as a way of critiquing how presenters explore mental health topics. Within these forms power relationships about who says what, when, and how long they can speak for are always in play and regulated by the questioner. Aware of the different ways in which each position operates, these two actors wanted to perform their own view of how such an interview might go.

News Tonight – Parody on the Interview Genre Form The programme begins with the presenter explaining that mental health affects one in four of the population, though things soon change. Deliberately, the head of the interviewee is positioned to the side of the frame, interrupting the viewer's line of vision to the presenter. His introduction commences with this positioning intended as a play on the 'odd' stereotype. Across the programme, the interviewer's discourse is intended as authoritative but as the conversation continues, so too does the steady transference of power in the relationship. The interviewer himself pejoratively stereotyped as a mis-informer, wildly states inaccuracies and clichéd ideas about mental health. Initially, he poses the question, 'Have you always been schizophrenic'? The purpose here is to illuminate how schizophrenia often seems to be the *only* mental health topic discussed in such genres. Everyone with a mental health condition is, it appears, 'a schizophrenic'. The young woman begins assertively to address the interviewer, reining in his questions, providing information intended to add 'balance' to the knowledge produced in the interview.

Present in the interviewer's vocalization is a duality in tone, an ostentatious benevolence. For the mentally unwell person, this is a patronizing discourse that they are well used to hearing. The opening moments play on this idea. Carol states that she suffers from 'an anxiety state' and objects to his misinformation. She then informs him of her qualifications, interests and ambitions, talking of her usefulness to the social world. Taking control of the meeting and despite the interviewer's call, 'we're running out of time', Carol restarts the programme, re-introducing herself and him. Emphasizing his initials, GBH (grievous bodily harm), she challenges his information and his own state of mental health, suggesting that he has a 'personality disorder'. The interviewer, taken aback by this, is seen to steadily deteriorate as his control steadily slips away; power relationships inverted, interviewer becoming the interviewee. Carol states her concerns for him in the context of bigoted attitudes and advises a community psychiatric nurse, perhaps the Samaritans and the continuation of the pills he is seen taking. Finally noting that people can get better she concludes the interview.

Other Group A Reflections This interview genre was intended to be partly serious, partly comedy. Whilst addressing the matter of 'mental health' sincerely, it draws upon the stereotype through the initials GBH as a reference not so much to physical violence but, the violence of journalistic language. But the stereotype here is inverted in the sense that the person with a mental health condition is stereotyping the person from the dominant culture. Certainly in this playful inversion of power relationships there is a sense of 'the revengeful' taking place. Group members from other areas spoke of the 'irony' with Petra saying, *I would like to see this happen in reality*. Robin said, *I liked the way she turned it round but media are being very much more aware these days*. Its humour was appreciated by the Liverpool group raising laughs. Don voiced, *Brilliantly portrayed. Journalists can be just as sick themselves. It was to the point*. Daniel thought they were, *hamming up a bit, it was a bit over the top*. William and Anne both said, as soon as the presenter was accused of being mentally ill, it was interesting to see how he didn't like it. Generally, participants considered the inversion of power and control to be amusing.

However, for Malcolm and Carol, there was certainly a problem with the facts communicated in these forms. The presenter, as the holder of knowledge about mental health was their prime focus. Thus, the nature of 'change' in conceptualizations about mental health produced ideas that these programmes never communicate about people 'getting better'. Also, the communication of schizophrenia as synonymous with mental illness was indicative of how media obsessively focus on this condition and ignore many other different mental health conditions.

Consequently, this project sought to communicate that far too little information about mental health was produced by current affairs media; schizophrenia seemed to be the only one condition portrayed, with anxiety disorders ignored. By employing the interview form and undertaking to parody it, this play on the genre sought to enhance their point of view as interviewer positions became inverted and cultural power was transferred to user identity. It was a political project making clear how journalism is viewed by a particular social group and what they consider about the programme form. The play on form said as much about the genre as did the content they put into it with significant messages for presenters which correlate with findings in the reception study about patronizing discourses in news.

Julie's Poem In her portrayal, Julie wanted to recite a poem entitled, *Mental Health and Me*. This told of how, whilst experiencing her condition, she still wanted to be a part of the social setting in which she saw others enjoying themselves so much but this was a setting from which she felt socially and medically marginalized. What the poem essentially alludes to is social inclusion.

Roger's Life Narrative During this narrative, Roger's life is presented along with his achievements. These include his school work as well as working life, which show he was a highly capable person reaching positions of responsibility. However, highly stressful factors came into play, they caused a condition bringing considerable distress and concern.

Liverpool Group

Identity Narrative 2: Mark and James This representation was produced by two people from the same day centre in Liverpool; Mark who had suffered his health condition as a result of taking street drugs and James, who suffered from schizophrenia. Each wanted to tell about their life-narrative, their conditions and feelings about mediations. The piece opens with a mid-shot of each person sitting side by side, followed by a close-up of each member telling of their social realities.

James develops his narrative, telling of the social practices that constitute his existence as someone who suffers from schizophrenia. He says that at this moment, he is stable, trying to keep busy but not too busy, that not maintaining a 'balance' may have an adverse effect on his health, as he has found out in the past. He has to see his GP every two weeks and his psychiatrist once every three months. With an interest in martial arts, he has also played the guitar and was now undertaking a dance course which was restoring his confidence. James also noted he had been in hospital every year for five years because of self-harm, sectioned several times for his own protection because of bad hallucinations.

Mark also comments that he has been in hospital because of taking street drugs which stopped his self development; his 'addictive personality' encouraging the taking of the drugs, hindering him from being who he wanted to be. Both members discuss how drug taking hindered their development, determining that in the end the sensible thing was to give them up completely but also saw mediations as generally impeding personal development. From Mark's point of view, a wider range of portrayals are needed to counter the axe-murders and serial killer portrayals, as these are not accurate descriptions of mentally ill people. James made complaints about mediations of 'psychopaths', saying that more attention to what people have to do to get better would be welcome. In their narratives each reveal that when not in hospital, they are social actors fulfilling relationships in the society in which they live. They have friends, enjoy socializing and undertake creative cultural practices. They felt misunderstood by the media, the 'public narratives' that were produced hindered them in being who they wanted to be, constraining their social agency.

Among other things, these are narratives constituting myths of *dangerousness* about mental distress. Influencing his decision to take part in the project was one narrative in particular. In discussions, after filming his portrayal, James talked to me concerning the case of Paul Fahy who rode up to Princess Diana on a bicycle when she visited Liverpool and gave her a kiss. The *Daily Star* along with other tabloids ran scare stories about him with headlines *'HE'S A RAVING NUTTER'* (*Daily Star*, 9 November 1995), the details given about his mental health, were according to James, completely untrue. With such exposure, Paul felt victimized and had to leave Liverpool and since then, hadn't been seen in the city. This public narrative produced a politically difficult situation for Paul to which James could relate. To be identified publicly as 'mentally unwell' is to court not just ostracization but fear of violent threat because your self-identity would be seen as violent. Although the case of Fahy was an extreme example, it was typical of how those with experience of a mental health condition were unable to defend themselves against tabloid marginalization.

Daniel's 'Correct' News about Mental Health This alternative depiction was developed by Daniel, a mental health activist in the Liverpool community who was advancing a range of issues. He wanted to make a point about television news and its portrayal of mental health issues – and so employed the form, using the presenter's position from which to present his personal news testimony, revisiting factual points. Daniel's performance was achieved in a highly competent way (without a prompter). After a fade up from black, he begins his discourse:

> *Good evening. Here is the correct news about health. For many years now the media has been reporting and portraying mental health problems in a very poor light. They have never used the facts and figures at their disposal. Fact 1: A quarter of the population or 12 million people suffer from one form of mental distress in their lives. Of the 12 million, 7 million get G.P. assistance and five million are living their lives with no assistance at all. The majority of the people who suffer mental distress suffer anxiety and depression. Fact 2: Five thousand people a year commit suicide. Of these, four thousand are associated with depression. Fact 3: Approximately 600 murders are committed in this country every year, of those, approximately twelve to twenty murders are committed by people with a mental illness. When you consider these facts, the next time you speak to somebody you have a twenty five percent chance that they are suffering*

> *from a mental illness of some sort. But on the other hand these people are far less likely to harm you and more likely to harm themselves. If the media want to be seen as fair and open minded, they should stop using sometimes vulnerable and sensitive people and stop this ridiculous witch hunt. These facts are freely available and if used would present a clearer and accurate picture and help people feel less oppressed and discriminated against. I have suffered mental distress and I am disgusted. Is this a good way to treat the sick and infirm?*

The knowledge produced is centred upon 'facts', but with an emphasis upon the journalism accessing data within a value system sensitive to this group's health needs rather than values exploiting the 'dramatic'. His facts point to problems of 'representativeness', facts emphasizing suicide rather than murder, social inclusion rather than exclusion. That 'objectivity' is an integral element of news journalism is partly the focus here but also that it has significant implications in the way it is used for rendering issues of the 'subjective' (also identified in the reception study). Interviewed at the end of this project, Daniel indicated that the only changes he would make to his portrayal would be to include aspects of respect, dignity and love.

Other Group A Reflections In the Cornwall/Devon group, Julie said, *It was really well done, trying to get it right ... to do with news.* Petra said, *It was powerful, the public can relate to those statistics, those murders of 600 people being killed but only 12–20 by people with a mental health condition was important.* Robin said he would like to see Trevor MacDonald's *Tonight* programme take something like this issue and broadcast it to the public. Petra continued, saying, *The news gets away with communicating facts but without qualification.* Anne considered the facts about suicide to be useful, and that she had never heard them before. The Winchester group were impressed by this piece and one member said, he felt that the Liverpool group had got it right here, indicating people *were more likely to harm their self than hurt anyone so if the general public knew this ...* (it would be very helpful).

Alan's Narrative Alan's narrative was a short proud exposition of how he had worked for a shipping company in Liverpool before becoming a truck driver, and later owning his own rig. However, after his load had been wrongly secured, he had a major crash in Plymouth, this caused his ensuing mental health condition. Telling of his situation, he voiced concerns about mediation impact about mental health upon him when he was still coming to terms with his new situation.

Kim's Story – 'Questions' Kim (not her real name) was part of a project undertaken at Mary Seacole House, a drop-in centre mainly for people encountering racism and discrimination in Liverpool. This project component occurred after the other area visits had concluded (as a result of a mental healthcare worker's invitation, in the reception project). Kim represented a significant success in the project because the reception study, whilst prepared in precisely the same way as the other projects, proved problematic. Despite meetings with interested people beforehand, suspicion remained about the project's intentions. Where gaining participant confidence in the process usually took one and a half days, here two and half days resulted in the project's delay. This was despite taking a participant from the other Liverpool project (see reception study in Chapter 7) who wanted to reassure the centre's members. From this process, it was learnt that perhaps a two week period with a more relaxed approach might have been a good way forward – this group wanting to pace themselves, understandably, to their needs rather than the study's. Most significant was the prejudice they all felt about mediations in general. This was quite telling in that Kim was the only one from a group of five who said she would like to do something. However, television was to be avoided – her portrayal *had to be on radio*, the question of trust, still very much an issue. The idea of being seen was for most, dangerous; they wanted to retain their anonymity.

Subjected to abuse as a child, Kim had later rebelled. Her mother was confronted with the information but disbelieving of the stepfather's involvement, told him which culminated in Kim's punishment. An outcome of such violence was that Kim self-harmed and later ran away due to lack of recognition and help. She felt no-one was listening even after going through the courts and telling everyone about her situation. Many years later, watching a television programme about child abuse and recalling how she felt no-one was hearing her, she wrote *Questions*. It was, she said, something she wanted to present to the study, so anyone who would listen, could – because so many don't. I was asked to 'keep it as it is'. Her final words concerned media images produced by people with experience of a mental health condition was – *Show it as it is, it's more powerful*.

Will you listen to me when I tell my tale?
Of the tears, the pain and the terrible shame
Will you listen to me when I tell my tale?
No, I thought not

Can you see the tears and the marks of pain?
Only to be repeated again and again
Can you see them?
No I thought not

Can you hear my cries in the dark of night?
When they locked me in the shed 'til light
Can you hear?
No, I thought not

Will you tell about the tears?
The pain, the bruises and marks that still remain
Will you stretch out your hand and hold me tight?
'Til the dark of night and tell me things will be all right?
No, I thought not

Stigma: Controllability and Visibility

The power of stigma was apparent in all groups. However, in this group it was greater. They all felt that although they wanted to participate, they couldn't; the risk was too great, even though confidentiality forms were available ensuring their anonymity. While they stated trust for the researcher and the work, *trust* was still a major issue and the remotest chance of becoming visible in their community to the local public was a chance they could not take. The idea of becoming visible meant a lack of control and as such, they would not countenance losing their own grip on this very valuable but rare choice.

After being sent to a neurologist whom she felt was again not hearing her, Kim experienced another mental health condition. Referred from psychiatrist to psychiatrist, hospital to hospital, she now receives counselling for the abuse which occurred in her childhood and things seem to be working better. She knows that she was misdiagnosed and is not a schizophrenic but feels media misrepresentation about this condition complicates her subjectivity. She now *knows* that it is depression which has evolved from her early experiences. However, she is also aware that the UK media have a propensity for making anyone who is black with a mental health condition feel infinitely more ostracized from the community than any other marginalized group.

More than any of the previous examples, this one serves to strengthen the danger of stigma in mediations for people with experience of a mental health condition. Communications about mental health identities can be marked with meanings of diseased-ness. This project illuminates how trust, normally taken for granted in most everyday ontologies, if distorted by stigma, can lead to ontological insecurity. A 'being' in the world, if consistently pathologized by pejoratives, will be downgraded and derided, which undermines that subject's position in the social setting. The identity narrative above unfortunately provides example of a person experiencing stigma at its worst, where it constrains and socially contains the person.

The Confluence: People with Conditions, Media and Mental Healthcare Professionals

Throughout the process, the idea of involving media in any way was rejected. In a very real sense, people took part in the project because of the confidentiality offered to them through the research process. However, the production study as an incrementally developing component was a maturing project in which each group would develop their work, with the opportunity of doing something such as a Confluence with media and mental healthcare workers always a possibility.

The Cornwall/Devon group was approached first and duly accepted the Confluence with media and mental healthcare workers taking place in Plymouth. The primary objective of the Confluence was to reach new understanding about mental health and media portrayals of people with mental health conditions. Notably, the group from Winchester felt they did not want to show their images beyond the two groups from other areas in the verification and validation process; a recent negative portrayal of a friend and service-user by a local print media institution was still fresh in their memory and they could not see any hope in undertaking a Confluence. The Liverpool group agreed but one member was reticent about taking part. Out of respect for him and his condition other group members and the researcher agreed, the group would not participate in a Liverpool Confluence.

In the Cornwall/Devon Confluence, group members were approached by a Carlton Westcountry Television producer commissioned to make a campaign programme about mental health issues called *Mind Your Head.* A negotiated use of some of the new mediation footage was agreed by four members and in August of 2001, some of the material produced by respondents was broadcast across the Southwest region. This was a major achievement. The group's evolution from a significantly cautious group of people ready to reject the slightest notion of media involvement culminated in their agreement to have their identities broadcast across a sizeable area in which they were known. Of note here is that immediately after the programme's broadcast, one participant called to inform me about an extraordinary experience the next day. Petra said, 'I went to the newsagent the next day after *Mind Your Head* had been broadcast and the person behind the counter said, "You were on television last night, weren't you?"' Petra informed me she went rigid with fear. She said she only managed to respond with 'Yes'. The person behind the counter then emphatically said, 'You were brilliant!' Apparently, Petra left the shop elated.

Conclusion

The transformations made by Group A provide two types of new mediations with useful clues towards alternative practice for reducing stigma. *News Tonight, Daniel's Correct News about Mental Health* and *Extra, Extra, Read All About It* are distinct from *Identity Narratives* which express stories about mental health self-identity not usually found in media; the former mostly reference the non-fictional forms of news critiquing themes about dangerousness, language and imagery.

Participant decisions to critique non-formal forms correlate with criticisms about news genres in the reception study; their concern is that these mediations have previously not represented mental health identity at all well. Subsequently, participants choose to replay dramatic stark imagery (e.g., the machete) in '*Extra, Extra*'; there are strong objections to such visualizations by tabloids which produce misleading dangerousness themes. Facts that offer a balanced view and which better depict the unwell are sought in *Daniel's Correct News*. Power relations also surface as an issue in *News Tonight* because such broadcast discourses stigmatize people. Indicators from these forms and *Identity Narratives* are that:

a. Misleading themes about dangerousness require elimination from all forms.
b. In non-fictional forms, references to horror genres are wildly misrepresentative about identity and necessitate exclusion as they produce negative associations.
c. The population of people with mental health issues is considerable but so too is the diversity of conditions that exist. These need to be informatively examined giving a supportive impression, context and wider representation – there are other conditions beyond schizophrenia.
d. Non-fictional forms contain not just wayward information but patronizing discourses that carry the negative impact through stigma and should be avoided.
e. Broadcast talk about people with conditions should encourage ideas of equality, similarity and inclusivity within society.
f. Journalistic language must reflect far more useful information about mental health.
g. Combined language and imagery should show the bigger picture – about the person not just their condition.
h. Simplistic use of dark imagery, i.e., to show something like depression and light to represent 'normal' needs avoiding.
i. The direct expression/voice of people from a wide range of conditions is encouraged. This allows freedom to express their situation and the cultural power contained within their own self-identity necessary to facilitate change.
j. Great care is required in the representation of race and mental distress because the impact of stigma is doubled upon identity.

Validated and verified by the other groups in the triangulated post-production meetings, the above indications point to ways forward in helping to avoid stigmatizing mental health identity and subjectivity. Producers of non-fictional forms need to take note of the complex consequences of stigma for the person with a mental health condition, with Petra's 'bigger picture' about the person providing not only useful indicators for ways forward but also rationale as to why these mediations have been previously been a problem. One useful way would be to change imagery to recognize the person. But more than this, there are issues about 'trust' which emerge with Daniel's 'disgust' at news and his questioning of how such mediations mistreat.

Identity Narratives also present strong indicators for portrayals which show actual *changes* in a person's life – that precipitate conditions. These ontological narratives expose uncommon, new information about a person's situation showing *how* a person became unwell and *what* their lives were like beforehand. Personal in their tale these accord with what Arthur W. Frank (1994) calls 'orphan genres'. Similar to the notion of an orphan disease, where the frequency in diseases are too low for their development to be registered as a profitable research concern, people producing narratives about their conditions are also rare. When presented, these orphan genres are usually parts of processes seeking to reclaim a new life from that of being unwell and also represent the right to tell in a personal voice of a health experience over that of the medical. Most narratives about an illness are produced by physicians who have no health problem but distinctively, these narratives represent desires for recognition of identity, after experiencing a mental health condition.

Alluding to the complex nature of illness narratives, Frank points out that in these genres, it is 'their truth, but not the undeconstructed truth of reportorial accuracy' (1994: 2) which require explanation. Reflecting upon a period described as the 'not yet postmodern' (1994: 1), he also questions 'why those (*in the present*, [my italics]) who study literature and medicine (*and it is added, media, culture and society*) should attend to a non-fiction first person accounts of illness' (ibid.). Astutely, he makes the point, 'because what is told really happened' (ibid.) and argues that this answer still holds today but that its meaning has changed. He goes on to say: 'do you want good fiction or do you want to know what actually happens in the world of the ill?' (ibid.) noting how academic disciplines *preserve* boundaries in their claims to speak about the world in specific ways. Realist distinctions between fiction and non-fiction are naïve, formulating their own realities due to disciplinary boundaries and their way of speaking about the world in a singular manner. Academic genres maintain boundaries with *the ill* and *their voice*, the patient are continually objectified, their contribution secondary to the academic. With the narrative conditions usually avoided despite their value and integrity, these *identity narratives* forcefully support this argument for privileging personal experience and listening to this voice. Indeed, the benefits from listening shine through in the Confluence. A dialogue with media *does* take place and with extraordinary outcomes; the Cornwall/Devon group are viewed in a subsequent television 'mental health' mediation not just advocating change but also showing it is possible.

Chapter 9
Conclusion

The final chapter summarizes the main points of the study. It draws from features in Phase One's Genre Analysis and the Community Project's Reception and Production Studies in Phase Two. Indicators for mediation improvement are then discussed examining elements useful to policy makers and professional practice for the community. Finally, issues concerning research, influence and effect are reviewed.

Phase One – Genre Analysis

Phase One set out to analyse fictional and non-fictional forms referring to mental health. Fictional mediations included a comic strip as well as horror, drama and melodramatic comedy-drama forms from television and cinema. Non-fictional mediations included news and documentary forms from radio and television.

Mental Health Meaning-making in Popular Culture

In Genre Studies 1, meaning-makings about madness from history are significant because of the creative ways in which they are transferred into fictional films from previous texts. Prior to the nineteenth century, meanings made in art, literature and theatre introduced imaginative pleasures about madness which were popular with audiences. Consisting of meanings with only slight mental health reference, these ideas later multiplied in the development of horror forms and its sub-genres. Imaginative realisms in thematic and formal components produced by film directors were innovative with institutions exploiting notions about dramatic *transformations* of a person's identity from framed states of *normal* to others viewed as *fearful* and *strange*. While entertaining for spectators, horror forms conveyed an excess of mysterious, ambiguous meanings that were in contrast to the few films which referenced issues of mental health. Today, concepts about madness in horror film still dominate, blurring the processes of mental health *knowing*. When mental health films reference conditions by drawing on available social and psychological knowledge they allow, among other things, an imaginative and realist empathy with unwell identities and states.

Carefully researched and constructed film representations produce curiosity about mental health. In *Rain Man*'s film form, the repeated juxtaposition of dramatic moments with humorous situations produce informative meanings to help factualize the problems of autism. Director Levinson makes meanings high in levels of referentiality about autism and, through the film's inquiry, exposes not only the condition but also the person's experience of it. Through this film's significant impact, popular culture and popular knowledge are drawn closer to knowing the 'truths' of the condition. The films *Angel Baby* and *Family Life* also represent mental health through careful portrayal of characters and employ formal components to qualitatively reflect conditions and society. Be it through Loach's naturalism or realisms created by Rymer, the relationships between people with unwell health, their healthcare professionals, and relevant institutions are also portrayed with strong referentiality. The indicators from analyses are that selected forms allow for the development of an aesthetic, dramatic mental health discourse that creates non-threatening spectator relationships with unwell identities. This makes for more accessible representations which introduce helpful information to understanding a range of conditions.

Genre Studies 3 analysed fictional forms showing that in television drama, when a director's approach was informed by personal experience combined with research, informative and pleasurable meanings about conditions and identities could be portrayed. Psychological parameters were exposed through more holistic representations by way of dramatic and comedic moments facilitating movement between character circumstances and condition. Television (and film) dramas fostered *telling* mental health moments through the convention of the therapy session, a device revealing significant factors in living with a condition. These factors were sometimes physiological, hereditary, and sometimes familial or social; the result of broken marriages or difficult personal circumstances. These hybrid forms also show how the fixed meanings and points of value (cited by Thornham and Purvis (2005) in Chapter 6) from an earlier phase of modernity have shifted to produce more fluid notions formulated in new identities. In late modernity, such mediations show increasing popularity with a cultural appreciation of portrayed meanings to contemporary life issues reflected in the success of these forms. The comic strip's critique of psychiatry, media and society also raised the pertinent point that past societies have alienated people with unwell mental health rather than seeking to improve knowledge about conditions. In this form and those of the selected television dramas, the indicators are that the incongruities resulting from the clash of socially constructed and incompatible discourses are productive both of information and of representational pleasure.

Meanings Made about Mental Health for Public Knowledge

Genre Studies 2 shows how different dramatic styles of discursive practice in each news form's direct mode of address play significant roles in making different meanings about schizophrenia for public knowledge. Each presenter's ordered discourse, together with that of the reporter's, adds dramatic weight to a story's tone through the direct mode of address. Perceptual parameters for audience are *set* through words used, as well as in levels of gravitas established. Patterns of imagery and narrative organization operate as influential dramatic components that sometimes construct useful information but at other times foster stereotypical themes. Mental health is made accessible when its meanings are marshalled with proportionality to a reality properly representative of schizophrenia, as attributed in *Channel 4 News* and *The Today Programme*. Through these forms referencing facts, presenters/reporters tell stories which expose the situation of the family and patient with sensitivity. In the documentary video-diary form, observational pieces allow a strongly naturalist drama, showing people with schizophrenia in direct and indirect modes of 'letting it happen' before the audience, offering a fresh view of mental health identities.

From the genres analysed, the typology produced a wide variety of identities and conditions. In popular culture, fictional film forms record: monsters for identities and illnesses coupled with dangerousness; a vulnerable identity with special gifts; a condition exacerbated by institutional influences resulting in an objectified medical identity and; schizophrenia as a set of confusing mental experiences disorienting to the person. In other fictional forms, one television comedy-drama shows various unwell identities that are explained by psychological histories, and another similarly shows several conditions needing therapy with appropriate therapeutic detail. The comic strip form characterized not just the state of schizophrenia as the 'unwell' but also, society itself as equally unwell.

Non-fictional forms in news frequently organize the sense of a dangerous 'schizophrenic' condition and a murderous identity. Two mediations focus upon the policy of Care in the Community, one 'typing' schizophrenia as a complex condition confusing to a young person's sense of who they are, supported by real-world situations and academic data. The other similarly records schizophrenic identity as requiring care because of a complex condition connected with self-harm. The documentary form provides first person accounts of struggles for identity as localized and personal conditions inhibit ways forward in life.

Drama, Representation and Knowledge Tensions about Mental Health across Forms

Drama is clearly a tool with a wide aesthetic and discursive range for media producers engaging with mental health themes as knowledge tensions[1] about mental health exist in different values across all forms. In the crafting of communicative performance, dramatic components receive both spontaneous and considered attention in the *forming* of a mediation. However, while drama is inherent in varying ways across fictional forms, its emergence in non-fictional forms associated with public knowledge is less straightforward and more controversial.

1 Corner 2009: 141. This section borrows from that article adapting Corner's 'good' and 'bad' knowing in public knowledge and popular culture projects but here with regard to mental health.

The analyses of film forms in Genre Studies 1 showed how the horror form has dominated popular culture for a prolonged period, its dramatic pleasures about transformations securing regular economic return; this in contrast to few mental health genres providing entertainment of a thoughtful kind. This box office imbalance not just in money but in values about mental health meaning looks unlikely to change. However, evidence suggests some movement with more recent films showing similar representational prowess to the selected films. *Good Will Hunting* (1997), *American Beauty* (1999), *Girl Interrupted* (1999) and *Mystic River* (2003) tell stories attracting spectators to good knowing and offer subtle insight through a range of signs/meanings portraying mental health conditions and identities; they also draw significant economic returns. Such films may increase but need to be sustained as fluctuations will occur with films like *Shutter Island* (2010) and its dramatic violent content destabilizing this precarious balance with further themes of violence.

The values configured in television dramas in Genre Studies 3 also prove to be 'good' for mental health knowing and reflect a growing trend of genres representing condition with more detail and information. As noted above, audiences recognize mental health issues as part of their lifestyles which is why cultural forms like *The Sopranos* and *Takin' Over the Asylum* are popular, as they are seeing these reflected in such shows. Thus, these popular forms look set to continue, one example being the award winning comedy drama *United States of Tara* (created by Diablo Cody), which explores Disassociated Identity Disorder. The view proposed by Thornham and Purvis prevails, that 'dramas inscribe and incite audiences. On the basis of narratives, the truths of television dramas are affirmed, questioned or rejected by the range of identities who constitute the "audience"' (2005: 181).

However, in Genre Studies 2, the first analysed news genre represents schizophrenia using codes which connect it with dramatic properties reminiscent of the horror form, constructing the person as 'strange'. If problematic meanings about schizophrenia are unwittingly produced as public knowledge through these elements, then alternative dramatic components in the *Channel 4 News* and *Today* news forms shape informative 'knowing' about schizophrenia. These enable audience to empathize with parents, producing compassionate readings about each story's subject in thoughtfully structured narratives. Between Chapter 5's first and subsequent news forms, knowledge tensions over what schizophrenia *is* are evident. This tension is further highlighted in the documentary through drama of a different kind, qualitatively representing the cultural reality exposing two people struggling to resolve situations relevant to their conditions. Thus, when representational processes in non-fictional forms like news includes problematic choices of dramatic elements, different kinds of 'good' and 'bad' mental health *knowing* result. Of note here is that this theme recurs in non-fictions in the phases of the Reception Study.

Phase Two – The Community Project, Part 1: Reception Indicators

In Phase Two, the Community Project's two parts, the Reception and Production studies, continued the generic focus. Commencing first with the Reception Study, three special groups in three different regions examined four mediations from radio, television and printed media; three non-fiction forms included two news forms and documentary while one fictional form was a soap opera. Responses indicate what each group makes from each form's mental health meanings.

In non-fictional forms, Group A view news forms as criminalizing their identity through story content centred upon cases concerning unlawful activity; facts are limited and convey mistaken values. These responses are mostly received through personal frames with this group indicating their identity as targeted through dramatic imagery and language. This targeting leads to distrust, a sense of social exclusion and the attachment of stigma. From Group A's point of view (that of mental healthcare professionals), news forms do not offer useful knowledge to public culture but instead present stories which are an obstacle to the productive formation of identity in relation to mental health issues. This felt discrimination is voiced through presented views that the public are unable to recognize them as people with qualities similar to everyone else. Responses to the radio documentary indicate meanings from history carry stigma in pronounced ways that socially exclude. The soap form is accepted as an improved representation but responses here are marked more by a lack of criticisms than according of direct commendations.

The professional practice of Group B focuses strictly upon 'fact' in the examination of judicial proceedings but exclude condition details. The indicators are that journalistic news knowledge about mental health is mostly limited to a legal discourse. Indeed, the radio documentary proves useful to journalists as dramatic components actually help to inform them about aspects of mental health. Appreciative of this production's qualities, some media personnel show awareness about stereotypes and potential insensitivities in other portrayals but none mention stigma. Respondent readings show awareness about problematic practices in tabloids referencing associations with horror film and a discourse and vocabulary that promote dangerousness themes.

From Group C, concerns focus critically upon what themes of violence might mean for people with health conditions. Language and imagery generate stigmatizing components in news forms and are rejected in favour of fully researched topics that engage in an informed way with issues relevant to mental health. Tabloids are viewed as undermining identity through pronouncements made through pejorative words in large headlines referencing horror forms. Thus, two important indicators from this group of respondents are, first of all, that there is a limited knowledge about mental health and, secondly, that people with mental health conditions need to be recognized in a holistic way that conveys the full complexity and contexts of their individual and social identity.

The reception phase indicators as interpreted by each group point to the issue of mental health mediation as part of a wider cultural knowledge problem. Much of the mental health knowledge base from which media professionals draw is limited in quantity and quality. With news values attracted to stories about homicide, many less 'dramatically' valuable stories are not told. Factors referencing language limit the exposure of other mental health identities with the non-fictional form of news singled out for criticism by Groups A and C. Group A do not recognize themselves when self-recognition is crucial to processes facilitating personal development and civic inclusion. The study's triangulated responses show uniformity across Group A in critical remarks about influences from negative historical discourses carried over into contemporary media language and imagery.

Phase Two – The Community Project, Part 2: Production Indicators

The Production Study indicates that non-fictional forms present significant issues for people with conditions. Participant decisions to creatively address the news form point to where change is most needed as Group A want to see the person first and the condition second, with researched information illuminating more about mental health. New language that references the whole person as opposed to just the condition is proposed as are facts about conditions for improving public knowledge. The avoidance of patronizing discourses is also sought. Group A want to see their identity reflected with proportionality, more about who they are, not just what condition they may have. Fictional forms like *Mad Bob* indicate that people with conditions seek a hand up, not a hand out, but what people with conditions mostly want is information relayed that having a condition does not preclude personhood; mediations should portray conditions as just one facet of a person's larger and positive being. Also, the language of mental health requires review because representational inequities culminate in inequalities when naming mental health conditions and identities.

Identities as they are portrayed do not reveal any dramatic transformations that involve being OK one moment and then deranged the next. Rather, conditions are precipitated by extraordinary social, biological and other pressures. Thus, depression happens after traumatic events and anxiety can occur when substantive life transitions take place. Participants offered stories of *before* they became unwell, detailing accomplishments in busy lifestyles. Something occurred out of the blue changing their life and this was frequently cited as a defining life moment. These narratives reflect Frank's (1994) notions of orphan genres which are constitutive of the chaos in a life *changing* event of a person and a following desire to *restore* health. These voices and the others examining non-fictional forms are indicative of a quest for change in these mediations.

Potential Ways Forward

Where, then, do these indicators lead us? In defining 'policy' as a set of general plans and principles intended to address problems and guide decision-making made by policy makers we can ask the following questions: what can the community of mental healthcare professionals draw from the study? What can media professionals learn from the Community Project? What will the community of people with mental health conditions take from the project? Even more, how can the community at large prosper from improved mental health mediations? Organizations like NAMI, Mental Health America, The Samaritans and MIND have planned campaigns around improving information with media concerns central to their projects. The Royal College of Psychiatrists and the Institute of Psychiatry have also addressed this issue in various ways.[2] In the UK, the government Department for Work and Pensions has produced booklets and films[3] that pointedly address the acceptance of disability in the community. Indeed, all of these informational spaces retain potential to propose new ways forward. Yet, impediments to de-stigmatizing mental health in the USA and UK remain real with different contexts playing influential roles. This cultural knowledge problem requires attention on several fronts including language development, greater regulation (self or legally imposed) and activism by people with conditions.

The Mental Healthcare Community and Language

From this study healthcare professionals view mental health language as central to the problem of mediations (as do Group A) in the reception study. This language is informed however, not just by the history of cultural artefacts (as viewed in Chapter 3) but also by psychiatric classification systems which contain terms sometimes hundreds of years old. Roger and Pilgrim (2001) cite the DSM-IV (produced by the American Psychiatric Association) and the ICD10 (preferred by the World Health Organization) as the main medical models.

Unfortunately, these serve as complex linguistic templates from which producers appropriate language into mediations, often ones showing healthcare professions recycling complex descriptions. One fictional form employing

---

2 The Royal College of Psychiatrists has signalled its campaign intent in various ways, one of which was a short film entitled *1 in 4* as part of a Changing Minds campaign (2000) to increase awareness. The Institute of Psychiatry has offered practical advice to media organizations concerning representation issues.

3 The DWP has produced useful work in its public health films and booklet work. One film positions audience as a hospital employer and asks them if they would employ a person with the right qualifications but having a mental health condition. If they would not, the voice-over challenges the decision, indicating the selection has just turned down Florence Nightingale. See http://webarchive.nationalarchives.gov.uk/20100308133329/http://campaigns.dwp.gov.uk/employability/resources.asp.

this complex language is *Law and Order: Special Victims Unit*. FBI forensic psychiatrist Dr George Huang, (played by B.D. Wong) regularly explains conditions for fellow officers and vicariously for viewers. However, such explanatory discourses remain as a set of recycled psychiatric descriptions in which few with conditions recognize their subjectivity; the description thus serving to confuse rather than clarify condition understanding. Additionally, dated language occurs in the mental healthcare profession and beyond. In the United States the 'r' word persists not only in everyday discourse but also in many states which still have departments of 'Mental Retardation'. With such language permeating many levels of healthcare, it is clear why the politics of identity for people with conditions is complicated by the fact they cannot recognize themselves in its dominant discourse. Language misuse is also prevalent with publishers often preferring the nebulous and dramatic term 'madness' in book titles to attract attention and boost sales.

Knowing that societies are confronted by an increasing range and frequency of conditions (Lopez et al. 2006) with probably more unchecked stigma, language about mental health and well-being requires development at the expense of these other terms; some, like schizophrenia,[4] need replacement. People with conditions need a 'user-friendly' language for the public to know about conditions and media professionals need new language guidance to make this topic more accessible; the gap between perceivers and targets (Heatherton et al. 2000) needs to be reduced. Simon Cross, writing about past and present cultures of madness, agrees we 'need to better understand their terms and our definitions' (2010: 180), and rightly points out that 'we', who view ourselves as the 'normal' (i.e., perceivers), are also often, if only potentially, 'them' (i.e., the targets). However, not to tackle derogatory language directly would be a mistake, which reception study participants clearly saw as stigmatizing and in need of change. Consequently, development should not be a matter of separate professional projects but collective and unified approaches with integrated philosophies, be they psychiatry, psychology, or from promotion or prevention movements. Also, central to this process would be the inclusion of people with conditions in a way that enables self-recognition in new terms. New language can help to demythologize and liberate from, if not by itself entirely reduce, stigma as well as resituate ideas of 'mental health' in society. Seedhouse's ideas (see Chapter 2) provide starting points. In this way, the community at large would benefit from clearer concepts and improved knowledge.

Another discussion point for mental healthcare professionals is for those requested to participate in media accounts. Being aware of stigma and the way in which a well intended message may be framed by media producers requires perspicacity and a clear and critical orientation towards media producers before an

4 Academics especially are prone to using the term 'schizophrenic' to represent 'fragmentation' but this quickly becomes an abused word employed in a range of other discourses with little understanding of its complex meaning or stigmatic qualities.

interview. Indeed, promoting 'good' mental health stories about effective research is a key part of improving people's lives.

The Community of Media Professionals

Media professionals may learn from the Community Project that current language adversely impacts people with conditions, none more so than in the non-fictional form of news. However, carefully chosen words and thoughtfully structured stories can, by contrast, have beneficial repercussions. Critical responses from Group A in the reception study indicate refocusing upon a wider set of topics to redress the balance of 'trust'. Institutional policies must take note that people with conditions need to be able to recognize themselves in improved mediations. A qualitative change can occur if addressed, but boards of governors, institution owners, shareholders and editors also need to agree improved journalistic practices that support professional value systems and work to reduce, if not eradicate, stigma. Clearly, the organizations mentioned (like NAMI and MIND) provide useful information about what to say and what not to say. There are useful guidelines for journalists representing mental health (in the UK) such as those cited at: http://shift.org.uk/mediahandbook/. By targeting early professional practice in schools or colleges of journalism and/or communications, awareness can be raised particularly when led by professionals[5] and people with conditions. All must be more involved in informing about mental health for public well-being. However, news media professionals should have one first objective: to replace mediation themes referencing violence with ones presenting more comprehensive mental health data and linking this data, where appropriate, to physical health.

It also requires noting that different contexts exist for journalists working in the UK from those in the USA. UK media history is constituted through successive changes of established public service broadcasting and independent sectors subject to a degree of audit and regulation, in which communications are governed by internal producer guidelines but also by external bodies responding to complaint. Internal self-regulation has evolved to produce self-regulation that seems to work albeit broadly for minorities, notwithstanding the call for improvements here. In contrast, the American context operates within a frame of strong economic influences operating around much smaller Public Broadcasting Service and National Public Radio institutions. While these latter two institutions rely in part upon public and government donations, each US commercial network's survival is driven by the acquisition of high audience ratings within a predominantly consumer focus.

When mental health issues arise in other media sectors like talk radio, freedom of speech to say anything, even if inflammatory, often prevails at the expense

5 An information booklet from the Samaritans provides an example and very useful information for journalists about suicide and self-harm and the risks involved in supporting writing about mental health stories. The *Introduction* by Jeremy Paxman also lends weight to the issue. See: http://www.samaritans.org/pdf/SamaritansMediaGuidelines-UK2008.pdf.

of thoughtful contributions; even issues about race are still not fully immune to the play of outdated values. There are examples of successful opposition to this practice of discrimination, sometimes leading to advertisers withdrawing support for a programme and the firing of offending broadcast staff. Problematic mental health mediations require similar responses from the community. However, whether the potency of such outcries for mental health can equal those concerning race and gender remains to be seen.

While many major news networks in the United States are mostly responsible in presenting cautious and careful mental health portrayals, greater self-regulation is required to avoid relapses. The case of Jared Lee Loughner, who took the lives of six people and shot US Representative Gabrielle Giffords on 8 January 2011 is one example. Many US news networks boarded the moral panic bandwagon addressing the issue without informed knowledge. CNN's *State of the Union* programme (a political interview genre broadcast 16 January 2011) attempted a significant research process and endeavoured to portray this topic with sensitivity, by securing people with personal and professional relationship to schizophrenia. However, lower third graphics served to frame the entire mediation as being about the mentally unwell as dangerous while self-harm as the predominant condition characteristic was not addressed. The following week, audience feedback strongly featured users of services and family members making for a more representative commentary on the condition and the identification of a deficient mental healthcare system.

The Community of People with Conditions

More recently, developments in cultural movements and technology present societies with new hope through an effective mode of criticism. As formal components about transformations in horror films have emerged in film comedies like *Me, Myself & Irene* (2000) and *Tropic Thunder* (2008), disability advocacy groups have begun with increased energy and focus to contest meanings that exploit mental health conditions. Organizations like NAMI[6] and Mad Pride[7] now challenge media organizations to seek improved representations. Pressure groups will effectively direct new information to institutional representatives through increased electronic and web-based, messaging (see Dahlgren 2009). It is these developments that are likely to prove important in the future, placing the electronic targeting of specific issues and organizations at the centre of calculated cultural and political projects seeking change. Certainly, the local will not be ignored as national/federal projects for change make their presence known

6 In the United States the National Alliance on Mental Illness has organized groups to censure problematic representation: http://www.nami.org/template.cfm?section=fight_stigma.

7 Mad Pride originated in Toronto, Canada and has grown into a global project across Europe, Africa and Australia and New Zealand.

through disability rights movements and ultimately, through global forums. These possibilities raise questions not just about cultural power in the future but also about critical review of the past, especially in relation to projects of scholarly and professional research.

Research Reflections

Chapter 2 showed that previous research findings were broad but found no data offering changes to the circumstances of people with conditions. This situation led to three different approaches examining the problem of mental health mediation in genre study, reception and production. In the analysis of genre, analytical frameworks were outlined while the Community Project's reception study utilized a quantitative method employing a coded system for interpreting responses. The production study applied practices from Theatre and Media for Development using the work of Augusto Boal. Emerging from these approaches, indicators also point to how the variety of methods employed to address problematic mediations connected with more general complexities of media research, especially those around influence and effect.

The history of media research into influence and effects is highly contested and this study may add to debates (see Corner 2000 for a concise history of this field). In the Reception Study, indicators revealed that Group A identified communicative properties as strongly influential, from television news forms to the tabloid and the radio documentary. Meanings from history in words, music, and these combined elements in re-enactments were highly persuasive. These created tensions in felt freedoms to respond to problem mediations because of the presence of stigma and also restrictions at the level of civic equality/inclusion. While the population of this study is small, its indicators determined from triangulated outcomes suggest that influence and effect is more complicated than previously apparent with history playing a significant role and producing powerful consequences in mediations. The trend of analysed meanings showing direct meaning-drift from horror to news forms is a frequent mediation feature and, as we have seen, this, in terms of its consequences for persons with a condition, proves a denial and a restriction. The idea that either influence or effect might not be a sole media factor needs to be reconsidered; what a cultural group brings to the consequences of mediation also bears further consideration. Findings suggest that new ways of thinking about 'effects' as a media research idea distinct from Gauntlett's views (1998 and 2005) are needed as are new approaches to studying identity and audience as in this work and Gauntlett (2007).

Identity in this study is about subjectivity and the elements that constitute a person's self-knowledge and self-identity. However, when mediations containing problematic themes challenge a person with a condition, they do so personally as well as publicly. In this study, the historical continuity of prejudice is also a factor in how language carries meanings, for instance in the lyrics of folk music. Thus, the personal, the social and the historical levels all become mutually implicated. As Ruddock argues in his discussions about scholarship, concerning the relationships between audiences and media, in this situation of multi-dimensional factors, multiple methods of addressing the same topic are a useful way forward (Ruddock 2001: 181). Indeed, multiple approaches in a triangulated format enable a more comprehensive set of values from which to make critical judgements. With approaches like Theatre and Media for Development, engagement with a wider range of perspectives can also enable alternative views about a research problem.

Theatre and Media for Development is an example of how applied theatre enables not only a space for change[8] with regard to meaning-making about identity, but also liberation from the constraints of neo-liberal influences. *Personal* narratives, more than academic, master, or meta-narratives, did the more powerful speaking in Chapter 8's new cultural forms, forms that looked at the sources of problems through processes that 'distanced' people from their situation. Thus, the contradictions within which dominant mediations referencing mental health were manufactured could be critiqued in the production study to generate these new perspectives. As Prentki notes:

> a version of Brecht's *Verfremdungseffekt* becomes a key prerequisite for applied theatre processes. Until participants are supported in efforts to make the familiar world of neoliberalism strange through finding different ways of looking at that world, it is unlikely that they can embark on a journey towards a new self-definition that is not bound up by a dominant discourse. (Prentki and Preston 2009: 365)

Through processes of self-empowerment Group A showed how active they are in their contributions, but these processes simultaneously illuminate how other more restrictive types of research processes can limit information gathering. Cross's (2010: 179) respectful criticism of the Glasgow Media Group's 'empirical template' idea is repeated here, in that this study accepts that useful information is acquired in such studies. However, some methods examining dominant media representations are also bound by research histories and traditions which can constrain the potential for development of a topic. Applied theatre however, offers fresh ways forward, one similar example to the work in Chapter 8, Lissele Terret's *Who's Got the Power*, exploring self-advocacy for people with learning disabilities (see Prentki and Preston 2009: chapter 48).

Concluding Comments

With regard to the future, mental health research can discover more about stigma's impact from looking at mediations concerning different groups of people,

8 See Prentki and Preston (2009) for further examples of these approaches.

producing, so to speak, a demographic profile of the situation. A regularized, quantitative study can function as a barometer on how mediations might or might not be improving. Clearly, the work of MIND and NAMI celebrate examples of good practice but these require greater coverage at national or federal levels perhaps correlating with connected studies in other countries, to inform greater awareness. This type of good practice has led to the construction of relationships between mental healthcare and media institutions monitoring the qualities of media representation. While Cross (2010) and Harper (2009) view a brighter future with regard to media representation about mental distress, this author remains more cautiously optimistic. Dismantling prejudice takes time though it will be education, more creative media processes and activism that will hasten the process of stigma reduction.

Finally, the problem of mental health mediation should not be viewed as a problem solely caused by a lack of media knowledge. Certainly, there are deficiencies in messages amplified en route to culture and society, but there too is a profound need for improved general knowledge in all public and professional spheres as well as in media practice. Despite how difficult some conditions may be to understand, no person with one deserves to have their identity or condition defined in a stigmatizing way. Equally, everyone deserves information to help them 'know' as fully as possible about mental health and not to have to depend upon a narrow set of discourses. The next challenge specifically concerning mediation should be *how* to produce new, stigma-free, clear and diverse information about mental health for as many people as possible.

Bibliography

Adorno, T. and Horkheimer, M. 1979. The culture industry: enlightenment as mass deception, in *Dialectic of Enlightenment*, edited by T. Adorno and M. Horkheimer. London: Verso.

Albertazzi, D. and Cobley, P. 2010. *The Media: An Introduction*. London: Pearson Education.

American Psychiatric Association. 2000. *Diagnostic and Statistical Manual of Mental Disorders*. 4th edition. Washington, DC: American Psychiatric Association.

Ang, I. 1996. *Living Room Wars*. London and New York: Routledge.

Appleby, L. and Wessely, S. 1988. Public attitudes to mental illness: the influence of the Hungerford massacre. *Medicine, Science and the Law* 28(4), 291–5.

Argyle, M. 1988. *Bodily Communication*. 2nd edition. New York: Routledge.

Atkinson, J.M. and Coia, D.A. 1995. Families coping with schizophrenia: a model of group work for family support, in *Families Coping with Schizophrenia*, edited by J. Willey. Chichester: Wiley.

Bakhtin, M. 1981. *The Dialogic Imagination*, edited by M. Holquist. Austin: University of Texas Press.

Bakhtin, M. 1986. *Speech Genres and Other Late Essays*, translated by V.W. McGee, edited by C. Emerson and M. Holquist. Austin, TX: University of Texas Press.

Barham, P. and Hayward, R. 1991. *From Mental Patient to the Person*. London: Routledge.

Barthes, R. 1968. *Elements of Semiology*, translated by A. Lavers and C. Smith. New York: Hill and Wang.

Barthes, R. 1972. *Mythologies*. London: Cape.

Beers, C.W. 1908. *A Mind that Found Itself*. London: Longmans, Green.

Belson, W. 1967. *The Impact of Television: Methods and Findings in Program Research*. London: Crosby Lockwood.

Benson, S. 1997. The body, health and eating disorders, in *Identity and Difference*, edited by K. Woodward. London: Sage.

Berardinelli, J. 1997. *Angel Baby* [Film review.] [Previously available online at http://movie-reviews.colossus.net/movies/a/angel_baby.html] (accessed 8th January 2001).

Berger, A. 1992. *Popular Culture Genres*. Thousand Oaks, CA: Sage.

Birch, J. 1991. Towards the restoration of traditional values in the psychiatry of schizophrenia, in *Context* 8, 21–26.

Birch, M. 1995. *The Representation of Mental Health in Televisual Media: An Audience Reception Study*. Aldershot: Ashgate.

Birch, M. 1996. Takin' over the asylum: promoting meanings of mental health? in *Promotion of Mental Health*, vol. 6. Avebury.

Birch, M. 1998. Promoting mental health in media: in search of an effective methodology. *Promotion of Mental Health*, vol. 8. Avebury.

Bird, L. 1993. *The Fundamental Facts: All the Latest Facts and Figures on Mental Illness*. London: Mental Health Foundation.

Bird, L. 1999. *The Fundamental Facts: All the Latest Facts and Figures on Mental Illness*. London: Mental Health Foundation.

Bjerke, Ø.S. 1995. *Edvard Munch and Harald Sohlberg: Landscapes of the Mind.* London: University Press of New England.

Boal, A. 1979. *Theater of the Oppressed.* London: Pluto.

Boal, A. 1990. The cop in the head: three hypotheses. *Drama Review* 34(3) (T127), 35–42.

Boal, A. 1992. *Games for Actors and Non-Actors.* London and New York: Routledge.

Bordwell, D. and Thompson, K. 1993. *Film Art: An Introduction.* 4th edition. New York: McGraw-Hill.

Boyd, W.D. 1994. *A Preliminary Report on Suicide: Confidential Inquiry into Homicides and Suicides by Mentally Ill People.* Henry Ling.

Boyd, W.D. 1996. *Report of the Confidential Inquiry into Homicides and Suicides by Mentally Ill People*. London: Royal College of Psychiatrists.

Branigan, E. 1992. *Narrative Comprehension and Film*. London and New York: Routledge.

Bristol, M.D. 1985. *Carnival and Theater: Plebeian Culture and the Structure of Authority in Renaissance England.* New York and London: Routledge.

Broadcasting Standards Council. 1994. *A Code of Practice*. 2nd edition. London: Broadcasting Standards Council.

Brockington, I. et al. 1993. The community's tolerance of the mentally ill. *British Journal of Psychiatry* 162, 93–9.

Brook, A. and Griffiths, C. 2003. Trends in the mortality of young adults in England and Wales, 1961 to 2001. *Health Statistics Quarterly* 19.

Brown, Chester. 1998. *The Little Man: Short Strips 1980–1995*. Montreal: Drawn and Quarterly.

Budd, M. 1985. *Music and the Emotions: The Philosophical Theories*. London and New York: Routledge.

Burrows, A. and Schumacher, I. 1990. *Portraits of the Insane: The Case of Dr Diamond.* New York: Quartet Books.

Buscombe, E. (ed.) 2000. *British Television: A Reader*. Oxford and New York: Oxford University Press.

Burstow, B. and Weitz, D. 1988. *Shrink Resistant: The Struggle Against Psychiatry in Canada*. Vancouver: New Star Books.

Butler, I. 1970. *Horror in the Cinema*. London: Zwemmer.

Byrne, P. 1998. Fall and rise of the movie 'psycho-killer'. *Psychiatric Bulletin* 22(3), 174–6.

Calhoun, C. (ed.) 1994. *Social Theory and the Politics of Identity*. Cambridge, MA: Blackwell.

Caplan, P.J. and Cosgrove, L. (eds) 2004. *Bias in Psychiatric Diagnosis*. Lanham, MD: Oxford Jason Aronson.

Caprani, H. 2009. Get me Sporty Spice. *New Statesman*, 23 March.

Carlson, M. 1996. *Performance: A Critical Introduction*. London and New York: Routledge.

Carroll, C. and King, P. (eds) 2003. *Ireland and Postcolonial Theory*. Cork: Cork University Press.

Cascardi, A.J. 1992. *The Subject of Modernity*. New York: Cambridge University Press.

Castells, M. 1989. *The Informational City: Information Technology, Economic Restructuring, and the Urban Regional Process*. Oxford and Cambridge, MA: Basil Blackwell.

Chesler, P. 1972. *Women and Madness*. New York: Doubleday.

Clarens, C. 1968. *Horror Movies: An Illustrated Survey*. London: Secker and Warburg.

Clarke, B. 1975. *Mental Disorder in Earlier Britain: Exploratory Studies*. Cardiff: University of Wales Press.

Clarke, K.B. and Clark, M.P. 1939. Skin color as a factor in racial identification of negro preschool children. *Journal of Social Psychology* 11, 159–69.

Clayman, S.E. 1991, in *Broadcast Talk*, edited by P. Scannell. London: Sage.

Cockerbaum, William C. 2004. *Sociology of Mental Disorder*. 7th edition. New Jersey: Pearson Education.

Collins Pocket Dictionary of the English Language. 1989. London: Collins.

Cook, P. 1985. *The Cinema Book*. London: British Film Institute.

Cook, P. and Bernink, M. (eds) 1999. *The Cinema Book*. 2nd edition. London: British Film Institute.

Cordess, C. (ed.) 2001. *Confidentiality and Mental Health*. London: Jessica Kingsley Publishers.

Corner, J. 1980. Codes and cultural analysis. *Media, Culture and Society* 2(January), 73–86.

Corner, J. (ed.) 1986. *Documentary and the Mass Media*. New York: Edward Arnold.

Corner, J. 1991. Meaning, genre and context: the problematics of 'public knowledge' in the new audience studies, in *Mass Media and Society*, edited by J. Curran and M. Gurevitch. London: Edward Arnold.

Corner, J. 1992. Presumption as theory: 'realism' in television studies. *Screen* 33(1).

Corner, J. 1995. *Television Form and Public Address*. London: Edward Arnold.

Corner, J. 1996. *The Art of Record: A Critical Introduction to Documentary*. Manchester: Manchester University Press.

Corner, J. 1998. *Studying Media: Problems of Theory and Method*. Edinburgh University Press.

Corner, J. 1999. *Critical Ideas in Television Studies*. Oxford and New York: Clarendon Press.

Corner, J. 2000. 'Influence': the contested core of media research, in *Mass Media and Society*. 3rd edition, edited by J. Curran and M. Gurevitch. London: Edward Arnold, 376–97.

Corner, J. 2009. Public knowledge and popular culture: spaces and tensions. *Media, Culture and Society* 31, 141.

Corner, J., Richardson, K. and Fenton, N. 1990. *Nuclear Reactions: Form and Response in Public Issue Television*. London: John Libbey.

Corner, J. and Hawthorn, J. (eds) 1994. *Communication Studies: An Introductory Reader*. 4th edition. London: Edward Arnold.

Creeber, Glen (ed.) 2001. *The Television Genre Book*. London: British Film Institute.

Creeber, Glen (ed.) 2006. *Tele-Visions: An Introduction to Studying Television*. London: British Film Institute.

Crisell, A. 1994. *Understanding Radio*. London and New York: Routledge.

Crocker, J., Major, B. and Steele, C. 1998. Social stigma and the self: meanings, situations and self, in *Handbook of Social Psychology*. 4th edition, edited by D.T. Gilbert, S.T. Fiske and G. Lindzey. Boston: McGraw-Hill, vol. 2, 504–33.

Cross, Simon. 2010. *Mediating Madness: Mental Distress and Cultural Representation*. Basingstoke: Palgrave Macmillan.

Cullen, Mary (ed.) 1998. *1798: 200 Years of Resonance: Essays and Contributions on the History and Relevance of the United Irishmen and the 1798 Revolution*. Dublin: Irish Reporter.

Curran, J. and Gurevitch, M. (eds) 1991. *Mass Media and Society*. London: Edward Arnold.

Curran, J. and Gurevitch, M. (eds) 2000. *Mass Media and Society*. 3rd edition. London: Edward Arnold.

Dahlgren, P. 1994. *The Media, The Public Sphere and the Horizon of Civil Society*. Paper submitted to Turbulent Europe: Conflict, Identity and Culture EFTSC.

Dahlgren, P. 1995. *Television and the Public Sphere*. London: Sage.

Dahlgren, P. 2009. *Media and Political Engagement: Citizens, Communication, and Democracy*. Cambridge: Cambridge University Press.

Davies, T. and Craig, T.K.J. (eds) 1998. *ABC of Mental Health*. London: BMJ Books.

Day, D. and Page, S. 1986. Portrayal of mental illness in Canadian newspapers. *Canadian Journal of Psychiatry* (December), 813–17.

Deaux, K. and Major, B. 1987. Putting gender in context: an integrative model of gender-related behaviour. *Psychological Review* 94, 369–89.

Dekker, Thomas. 1979. *The Shoemaker's Holiday*, edited by D.J. Palmer. London: Black.

Denzin, N. 1989. *Interpretative Biography*. New York: Sage.

Department of Health. 1993. *Attitudes to Mental Illness*. London: Department of Health.

Derry, C. 1977. *Dark Dreams: A Psychological History of the Modern Horror Film*. New Jersey: Barnes.

Deutsch, A. 1948. *The Shame of the States*. New York: Harcourt, Brace.

Deutsch, A. 1949. *The Mentally Ill in America: A History of their Care and Treatment*. 2nd edition. New York: Columbia University Press.

Diagnostic and Statistical Manual of Mental Disorders: DSM-IV-TR. 2000. 4th edition. Washington, DC: American Psychiatric Association.

Domino, G. 1983. Impact of the film *One Flew Over The Cuckoo's Nest* on attitudes to mental illness. *Psychological Reports* 53, 179–82.

Douglas, M. 1966. *Purity and Danger: An Analysis of the Concepts of Pollution and Taboo*. London: Routledge.

Dovey, J. 2000. *Freakshow*. Pluto Press.

Dovidio, J.F., Major, B. and Crocker, J. in Heatherton, T. et al. (eds) 2000. *The Social Psychology of Stigma*. New York and London: Guilford Press.

Downie, R.S., Fyfe, C. and Tannahill, A. 1990. *Health Promotion: Models and Values*. Oxford: Oxford University Press.

Dunn, S. 1999. *Creating Accepting Communities: Report of the Mind Inquiry into Social Exclusions and Mental Health Problems*. London: Mind Publications.

Eisner, W. 2008. *Comics and Sequential Art: Principles and Practices from the Legendary Cartoonist*. New York: W.W. Norton.

Elam, K. 1980. *Semiotics of Theatre and Drama*. London: Methuen.

Elias, N. 1978/1939. *The Civilising Process, Volume 1: The History of Manners*. New York: Pantheon Books.

Elias, N. 1982/1939. *The Civilising Process, Volume 2: State Formation and Civilization*. Oxford: Basil Blackwell.

Elias, N. 1983. *The Court Society*. Oxford: Basil Blackwell.

Ellis, G.A. 1874. *A Memoir of Mrs. Anna Laetitia Barbauld, with Many of Her Letters*. Boston, MA: Osgood.

Elmes, S. 2007. Meet the disembodied friends of BBC Radio 4. *Daily Telegraph*, 29 September.

Elsaesser, T. and Barker, A. 1990. *Early Cinema: Space-Frame-Narrative*. London: British Film Institute.

Fairclough, N. 1989. *Language and Power*. Harlow: Longman.

Fairclough, N. 1992. *Discourse and Social Change*. Oxford: Polity.

Fairclough, N. 1994. Conversationalisation of public discourse and the authority of the consumer, in *The Authority of the Consumer*, edited by R. Keat, N. Whitely and N. Abercrombie. London: Routledge.

Fairclough, N. 1995a. *Critical Discourse Analysis*. Harlow: Longman.

Fairclough, N. 1995b. *Media Discourse*. London: Edward Arnold.

Fairclough, N. 1996. Border crossings: discourse and social change in contemporary societies, in *Change and Language*, edited by H. Coleman and L. Cameron. British Association for Applied Linguistics/Multilingual Matters Ltd.

Fairclough, N. 2000. *New Labour, New Language?* London: Routledge.

Ferriter, M. and Butwell, M. 2001. Confidentiality and research in mental health, in *Confidentiality and Mental Health*, edited by C. Cordess. London: Jessica Kingsley Publishers.

Fiske, S.T. and Neuberg, S.L. 1990. A continuum model of impression formation: motivation and attention, in *Advances in Experimental Social Psychology*, edited by M.P. Zanna. San Diego: Academic Press, vol. 23, 1–74.

Fiske, S.T. and Taylor, S.E. 1991. *Social Cognition*. New York: McGraw-Hill.

Fleming, M. and Manvell, R. 1985. *Images of Madness: The Portrayal of Insanity in the Feature Film*. Cranbury, NJ: Associated University Press.

Foucault, M. 1961. *Madness and Civilisation: A History of Insanity in the Age of Reason*. London: Routledge.

Foucault, M. 1971. *Orders of Discourse*. Paris: Gallimard.

Foucault, M. 1972. *Archaeology of Knowledge*, translated by A.M. Sheridan Smith. London: Tavistock Publications.

Foucault, M. 1973. *The Birth of the Clinic: An Archaeology of Medical Perception*, translated by A.M. Sheridan Smith. London: Tavistock Publications.

Foucault, M. 1976. *The History of Sexuality, vol.1 An Introduction*. Harmondsworth: Penguin.

Foucault, M. 1977. *Discipline and Punish*. Harmondsworth: Penguin.

Foucault, M. 1980. *Power/Knowledge: Selected Interviews and Other Writings 1972–77*, edited by C. Gordon. Brighton: Harvester Press.

Frank, A.W. 1994. Reclaiming an orphan genre: the first-person narrative of illness. *Literature and Medicine* 13(1).

Freire, P. 1970. *Pedagogy of the Oppressed*. New York: Seabury Press.

A Future Vision for Mental Health. 2009. *Future Vision Coalition* [Available from www.commissioningsupport.org.uk].

Gabbard, K. and Gabbard, G.O. 1987. *Psychiatry and the Cinema*. Chicago and London: University of Chicago Press.

Gallagher, Bernard J. 2002. *The Sociology of Mental Illness*. 4th edition. Upple Saddle River, NJ and London: Prentice Hall.

Gauntlett, D. 1998. Ten things wrong with the 'effects model', in *Approaches to Audiences*, edited by R. Dickinson, R. Harindranath and O. Linne. London: Arnold.

Gauntlett, D. 2001. The worrying influence of 'media effects' studies, in *Ill Effects: The Media Violence Debate*, edited by M. Barker and J. Petley. 2nd edition. London and New York: Routledge.

Gauntlett, D. 2005. *Moving Experiences: Media Effects and Beyond*. 2nd edition. London: John Libbey.

Gauntlett, D. 2007. *Creative Explorations: New Approaches to Identities and Audiences*. London and New York: Routledge.

Giannetti, L.D. 1976. *Understanding Movies*. 2nd edition. Upper Saddle River, NJ: Prentice Hall.

Gibbons, L. 1998. Alternative enlightenments, in *1798: 200 Years of Resonance*, edited by Mary Cullen. Irish Reporter Publications.

Giddens, A. 1990. *The Consequences of Modernity*. Cambridge: Polity Press.
Giddens, A. 1991. *Modernity and Self-Identity: Self and Society in the Late Modern Age*. Cambridge: Polity Press.
Gilman, S.L. 1982. *Seeing the Insane*. New York: Wiley.
Gilman, S.L. 1985. *Difference and Pathology: Stereotypes of Race, Sexuality and Madness*. Ithaca, NY: Cornell University Press.
Gilman, S.L. 1988. *Disease and Representation: Images of Illness from Madness to Aids*. Ithaca: Cornell University Press.
Gilman, S.L. 1995. *Picturing Health and Illness: Images of Identity and Difference*. Baltimore and London: Johns Hopkins University Press.
Giraud, P. 1975. *Semiology*. London: Routledge.
Glozier, N. 1998. The workplace effects of the stigmatisation of depression. *Journal of Occupation and Environmental Medicine* 40, 783–800.
Godsi, E. 2004. *Violence and Society: Making Sense of Madness and Badness*. Ross-On-Wye: PCCS Books.
Goffman, E. 1959. *The Presentation of Self in Everyday Life*. New York: Anchor Books.
Goffman, E. 1963. *Stigma: Notes on the Management of Spoiled Identity*. Princeton, NJ: Prentice Hall.
Goffman, E. 1981. *Forms of Talk*. Oxford: Blackwell.
Goldberg, G.J.P. 'Angel Baby' [Film review] [Previously available online at: http://www.roughcut.com/reviews/movies/vault/angel_baby.html (accessed 28th September 1999).
Greatbatch, D. 1986. Some standard uses of supplementary questions in news interviews. *Belfast Working Papers in Language and Linguistics* 8, 86–123.
Greatbatch, D. 1988. A turn-taking system for British news interviews. *Language and Society* 17, 401–30.
Hall, E.T. 1966. *The Hidden Dimension*. New York: Doubleday.
Hall, P. et al. 1993. A comparison of responses to the mentally ill in two communities. *British Journal of Psychiatry* 162, 99–108.
Hall, S. 1980. Coding and encoding in the television discourse, in *Culture, Media, Language: Working Paper in Cultural Studies, 1972–79*, edited by S. Hall et al. London: Hutchinson, 197–208.
Hall, S. (ed.) 1997. *Representation: Cultural Representations and Signifying Practices*. London: Sage.
Halliwell, Leslie. 1990. *Halliwell's Film Guide*. 7th edition. London: Paladin.
Harris, L. 1995. *The Secret Heresy of Hieronymus Bosch*. Edinburgh: Floris Books.
Heatherton, T.F. et al. (eds) 2000. *The Social Psychology of Stigma*. New York and London: Guilford Press.
Heritage, J.C. 1980. *The Availability of Context*. Warwick: University of Warwick.
Hoijer, B. 1990. Studying viewers' reception of television programmes: theoretical and methodological considerations. *European Journal of Communication* 5(1), 29–56.
hooks, b. 1994. *Outlaw Culture: Resisting Representations*. New York: Routledge.

Horton, D. and Wohl, R.R. 1956. Mass communication and para-social interaction: observations on intimacy at a distance. *Psychiatry* 19, 215–29.
Howe, J. (ed.) 2001. *Edvard Munch: Psyche, Symbol and Expression*. Chicago and London: University of Chicago Press.
Huizinga, J. 1924. *The Waning of the Middle Ages*. London: Edward Arnold.
Huxley, P. 1993. Location and stigma: a survey of community attitudes to mental illness – Part 1. Enlightenment and stigma. *Journal of Mental Health* 2, 73–80.
Hyler, S. et al. 1991. Homicidal maniacs and narcissistic parasites: stigmatisation of mentally ill persons in the movies. *Hospital and Community Psychiatry* 42(10).
ITN Fact Book. 1990. London: Michael O'Mara Books.
Jacobson, E. 1964. *The Self and the Object World*. New York: International Universities Press.
Jary, D. and Jary, J. 1991. *Dictionary of Sociology*. London: Collins.
Jodelet, D. 1991. *Madness and Social Representations*. New York and London: Harvester Wheatsheaf.
Jones, E.E. et al. (eds) 1984. *Social Stigma: The Psychology of Marked Relationships*. New York: Freeman.
Jordan, W.K. 1960. *The Charities of London 1480–1660*. New York: Russell Sage.
Kafka, Franz. 1960. *Description of a Struggle and the Great Wall of China*, translated by Willa Edwin Muir and Tania and James Stern. London: Secker and Warburg.
Karpf, A. 1988. *Doctoring the Media: The Reporting of Health and Medicine*. London: Routledge.
Katz, I. 1981. *Stigma: A Social Psychological Analysis*. Lawrence Erlbaum Associates.
Kernberg, O. 1980. *Internal World and External Reality: Object Relations Theory Applied*. New York: Jason Aronson.
Kernberg, O. 1984. *Severe Personality Disorders: Psychotherapeutic Strategies*. London: Yale University Press.
Kierkegaard, S. 1980. *The Sickness unto Death: A Christian Psychological Exposition for Upbuilding and Awakening*. Princeton: Princeton University Press.
Kinser, S. 1990. *Rabelais's Carnival: Text, Context, Metatext*. Chicago and London: University of California Press.
Kleck, R.E. and Nuessle, W. 1968. Congruence between the indicative and communication functions of eye-contact in interpersonal relations. *British Journal of Social and Clinical Psychology* 7, 241–6.
Kohut, H. 1971. *The Analysis of the Self*. New York: International Universities Press.
Kress, G. and van Leeuwen, T. 1990. *Reading Images: The Grammar of Visual Design*. Geelong, Victoria: Deakin University Press.
Kristeva, J. 1986. *The Kristeva Reader*. Oxford: Basil Blackwell.

Laing, R.D. 1960. *The Divided Self: A Study of Sanity and Madness*. Chicago: Quadrangle Books.
Laing, R.D. and Esterson, A. 1964. *Sanity, Madness and the Family*. London: Tavistock Publications.
Lash, S. 1990. *A Sociology of Postmodernism*. London: Routledge.
Lash, S. and Urry, J. 1987. *The End of Organised Capitalism*. Cambridge: Polity.
Lash, S. and Urry, J. 1994. *Economies of Signs and Space*. London: Sage.
Le Roy Ladurie, E. 1979. *Carnival in Romans: A People's Uprising at Romans 1579–1580*, translated by M. Feeney. New York: G. Braziller.
Lewis, H.B. 1971. *Shame and Guilt in Neurosis*. New York: International University Press.
Lindlof, T.R. 1995. *Qualitative Communication Research Methods*. Thousand Oaks, CA: Sage.
Linfert, C. 1971. *Hieronymus Bosch*. New York: Abrams.
Link, B.G. et al. 1997. On stigma and its consequences: evidence from a longitudinal study of men with dual diagnosis of mental illness and substance abuse. *Journal of Health and Social Behaviour* 38, 177–90.
Livingston, S. and Lunt, P. 1994. *Talk on Television: Audience Participation and Public Debate*. London: Routledge.
Lopez, A.D. et al. (eds) 2006. *Global Burden of Disease and Risk Factors*. Washington, DC: World Bank; New York: Oxford University Press.
Lorde, A. 1984. *Sister Outsider*. Trumansburg, NY: Crossing Press.
Louw, E. 2001. *The Media and Cultural Production*. London: Sage.
Lyons, J. 1977. *Semantics*. Cambridge: Cambridge University Press.
McCarty, J. 1993. *Movie Psychos and Madmen: Film Psychopaths from Jekyll and Hyde to Hannibal Lecter*. Secaucus, NJ: Carol Publishing.
McCloud, S. 1993. *Understanding Comics: The Invisible Art*. New York: HarperCollins.
MacDonald, M. 1977. *Mystical Bedlam: Madness, Anxiety and Healing in Seventeenth Century England*. Cambridge: Cambridge University Press.
Macdonell, D. 1986. *Theories of Discourse: An Introduction*. Oxford: Basil Blackwell.
McKenna, Terence. 1991. *The Archaic Revival: Speculations on Psychedelic Mushrooms, the Amazon, Virtual Reality, UFOs, Evolution, Shamanism, the Rebirth of the Goddess, and the End of History*. San Francisco, CA: HarperSanFrancisco.
McKnight, G. (ed.) 1997. *Agent of Challenge and Defiance: The Films of Ken Loach*. Trowbridge: Flicks Books.
MacLean, U. 1969. Community attitudes to mental illness in Edinburgh. British *Journal of Preventive and Social Medicine* 23, 45–52.
McQuail, Denis. 1994. *Mass Communication Theory: An Introduction*. 3rd edition. London: Sage.
Martin, M. 1968. *Le Langage Cinématographique*. Paris: Editions du Cerf.

Mead, G.H. 1934. *Mind, Self, and Society*. Chicago: University of Chicago Press.

Merriman, V. Definition taken from 'Structures for Ownership' lecture from the campaign document Drama within the Arts as part of a full Educational Entitlement published by the National Association for the Teaching of Drama, 2 November 1990.

Merton, R.K. 1948. The self-fulfilling prophecy. *Antioch Review* 8, 193–210.

Mies, M. 1993. Towards a methodology for feminist research, in *Social Research: Philosophy, Politics and Practice*, edited by M. Hammersley. London: Sage, 64–82.

Miller, C. and King, E. 1999. *Managing for Social Cohesion*. London: Office for Public Management.

Miller, D. et al. 1998. *The Circuit of Mass Communication: Media Strategies, Representation and Audience Reception in the AIDS Crisis*. The Glasgow Media Group/Sage.

Mills, S. 1997. *Discourse*. London: Routledge.

Montgomery, M. 2007. *The Discourse of Broadcast News: A Linguistic Approach*. London and New York: Routledge.

MORI. 1979. *Public Attitudes to Mental Illness*. London: Market and Opinion Research International.

Morrison, D. 1992. In *Sex & Sexuality in Broadcasting*, edited by A. Millwood-Hargrave. London: John Libbey.

Murphy, B. 1972. Monster movies: they came from beneath the 50's. *Journal of Popular Film* 1(1).

Murray, C.J.L. and Lopez, A.D. (eds) 1996a. *Global Burden of Disease: A Comprehensive Assessment of Mortality and Disability from Diseases, Injuries, and Risk Factors in 1990 and Projected to 2020*. Harvard School of Public Health.

Murray, C.J.L. and Lopez, A.D. (eds) 1996b. *Global Health Statistics: A Compendium of Incidence, Prevalence and Mortality Estimates for Over 200 Conditions*. Harvard School of Public Health.

Neale, S. 1980. *Genre*. London: British Film Institute.

Neale, S. 1985. *Cinema and Technology: Image, Sound and Colour*. Basingstoke: Macmillan.

Neale, S. 1990. Questions of genre. *Screen* 31(1).

Neale, S. and Krutnik, F. 1990. *Popular Film and Television Comedy*. London and New York: Routledge.

Nelmes, J. 1996. *An Introduction to Film Studies*. London: Routledge.

Nunnally, J. 1957. The communication of mental health information: a comparison of the opinions of experts and the public with mass media communications. *Behavioural Science* 2, 222–30.

O'Donnell, W. and Todd, L. 1980. *Variety in Contemporary English*. London: George Allen & Unwin.

O'Sullivan, T. et al. 1994. *Key Concepts in Communication and Cultural Studies*. 2nd edition. London and New York: Routledge.

Palmer, D.J. (ed.) 1975. In *The Shoemakers' Holiday by Thomas Dekker*, edited by D.J. Palmer. London: Benn.

Pêcheux, M. 1982. *Language, Semantics and Ideology: Stating the Obvious*. London: Macmillan.

Philo, G. (ed.) 1996. *Media and Mental Distress*. London: Longman.

Philo, G. (ed.) 1999. *Message Received*. Harlow: Longman

Philo, G. and Miller, D. 2001. *Market Killing: What the Free Market Does and What Social Scientists Can Do About It*. London: Longman.

Pickering, M. 2001. *Stereotyping: The Politics of Representation*. Basingstoke: Palgrave.

Pilgrim, R. and Rogers, A. 1993. *A Sociology of Mental Health and Illness*. Buckingham: Open University Press.

Porter, R. 1987a. *A Social History of Madness: Stories of the Insane*. London: Weidenfeld and Nicolson.

Porter, R. 1987b. *Mind Forg'd Manacles: The History of Madness in England from the Restoration to the Regency*. London: Weidenfeld and Nicolson.

Porter, R. (ed.) 1991. *The Faber Book of Madness*. London: Faber and Faber.

Poster, M. 1990. *The Mode of Information: Poststructuralism and Social Context*. Cambridge: Polity.

Prentki, T. and Preston, S. (eds) 2009. *The Applied Theatre Reader*. London: Routledge.

Ray, E.B. and Donohew, L. 1990. *Communications and Health: Systems and Applications*. New Jersey: Lawrence Erlbaum Associates.

Roach, J. and Yamey, G. 2000. Two minutes to change minds. *British Medical Journal* 321, 21 October.

Rockett, W.H. 1982. *Perspectives. Popular Film and Television* 10(3).

Rogers, A., Pilgrim, R. and Lacey, R. 1993. *Experiencing Psychiatry: Users' Views of Services*. London: Macmillan and Mind Publications.

Rogers, A. and Pilgrim, R. 2001. *Mental Health Policy in Britain*. 2nd edition. London: Palgrave.

Rosenthal, A. and Corner, J. (eds) 2005. *New Challenges for Documentary*. Manchester: Manchester University Press.

Ross, T.J. 1972. *Focus on the Horror Film*. New Jersey: Prentice Hall.

Ruddock, A. 2001. *Understanding Audiences: Theory and Method*. London: Sage.

Said, E. 2003. Afterword: reflections on Ireland and postcolonialism, in *Ireland and Postcolonial Theory*, edited by Clare Carroll and Patricia King. Cork: Cork University Press.

Sapsford, R. and Jupp, V. (eds) 1996. *Data Collection and Analysis*. London: Sage.

Scannell, P. (ed.) 1991. *Broadcast Talk*. London: Sage.

Scannell, P. 2000. Public service broadcasting: the history of a concept, *British Television: A Reader*, edited by E. Buscombe. Oxford and New York: Oxford University Press.

Schlesinger, P. 1978. *Putting Reality Together: BBC News*. London: Constable.

Schlesinger P., Murdock, G. and Elliot, P. 1983. *Television 'Terrorism': Political Violence in Popular Culture*. Comedia.

Schutzman, M. and Cohen-Cruz, J. 1994. *Playing Boal: Theatre, Therapy, Activism*. London: Routledge.

Scull, A.T. 1975. From madness to mental illness: medical men as entrepreneurs. *European Journal of Sociology* 16, 219–61.

Scull, A.T. 1979. *Museums of Madness: The Social Organisation of Insanity in Nineteenth-Century England*. London: Allen Lane.

Secker, J. and Platt, S. 1996. Why media images matter, in *Media and Mental Distress*, edited by G. Philo. London: Longman.

Seedhouse, D. 1998. Mental health promotion: problems and possibilities. *International Journal of Mental Health Promotion Inaugural Issue*.

Seedhouse, D. 2002. *Total Health Promotion: Mental Health, Rational Fields and the Quest for Autonomy*. Chichester: Wiley.

Seiter, E. et al. (eds) 1989. *Remote Control: Television Audiences and Cultural Power.* London: Routledge.

Shakespeare, T. 1994. Cultural representations of disabled people. *Disability and Society* 9(3), 283–99.

Showalter, E. 1985. Representing Ophelia: women, madness and the responsibilities of feminist criticism, in *Shakespeare and the Question of Theory*, edited by P. Parker and G. Hartman. London: Routledge, 77–94.

Showalter, E. 1987. *The Female Malady: Women, Madness and English Culture, 1830–1980*. London: Virago.

Signorielli, N. 1989. The stigma of mental illness on television. *Journal of Broadcasting and Electronic Media* 33(3), 325–31.

Simon, B. 1978. *Mind and Madness in Ancient Greece: The Classical Roots of Modern Psychiatry*. Ithaca: Cornell University Press.

Solomon, A. 2002. *The Noonday Demon: An Atlas of Depression*. New York: Touchstone Simon and Schuster.

Steadman, H. and Cocozza, J. 1977. Selective reporting and the public's misconceptions of the criminally insane. *Public Opinion Quarterly* 41, 523–33.

Stevenson, R.L. 1886. *The Strange Case of Dr. Jekyll and Mr. Hyde*. London: Longmans, Green.

Stowe, H.B. 1852. *Uncle Tom's Cabin, or, Life among the Lowly*. Boston, PA: Jewett.

Styron, W. 1992. *Darkness Visible: A Memoir of Madness*. New York: Vintage Books.

Swann, W.B., Jr. 1987. Identity negotiation: where two roads meet. *Journal of Personality and Social Psychology* 53, 1038–51.

Szasz, T.S. 1972. *The Myth of Mental Illness: Foundations of a Theory of Personal Conduct*. London: Paladin.

Tajfel, H. and Turner, J.C. 1979. An integrative theory of intergroup conflict, in *The Social Psychology of Intergroup Relations*, edited by W.G. Austin and S. Worchel. Monterey, CA: Brooks/Cole, 33–48.

Taylor, A. et al. 1970. *Introducing Psychology: An Experimental Approach*. London: Penguin.
Thornham, S. and Purvis, T. 2005. *Television Drama: Theories and Identities*. Basingstoke: Palgrave Macmillan.
TNS. 2007. *Attitudes to Mental Illness 2007 Research Report*. London: Department of Health. [Online]. Available at: http://www.dh.gov.uk/prod_consum_dh/groups/dh_digitalassets/@dh/@en/documents/digitalasset/dh_076514.pdf (accessed 28th November 2010).
TNS. 2009. *Attitudes to Mental Illness 2009 Research Report*. London: Department of Health. [Online]. Available at: http://www.dh.gov.uk/prod_consum_dh/groups/dh_digitalassets/documents/digitalasset/dh_100651.pdf (accessed 5th March 2011).
Todorov, T. 1981. *Introduction to Poetics*. Brighton: Harvester.
Tolson, A. 1991. Televised chat and synthetic personality, in *Broadcast Talk*, edited by P. Scannell. London: Sage.
Tomkins, S.S. and McCarter, R. 1964. What and where are the primary affects? Some evidence for a theory. *Perceptual and Motor Skills* 18, 119–58.
Torgovnick, M. 1994. *Eloquent Obsessions: Writing Cultural Criticism*. London: Duke University Press.
Tudor, A. 1974. *Image and Influence: Studies in the Sociology of Film*. London: Allen & Unwin.
Tudor, A. 1989. *Monsters and Mad Scientists*. Oxford: Basil Blackwell.
Tulloch, J. 1999. *Performing Culture*. London: Sage.
Van Leeuwen, T. 1993. Genre and field in critical discourse analysis. *Discourse and Society* 4(2).
Volosinov, V.N. 1973. *Marxism and the Philosophy of Language*. New York: Seminar Press.
Vousden, M. 1989. Loony Lefties and Mad Mullahs. *Nursing Times* 85(28), 16–17.
Wahl, O. 1995. *Media Madness: Public Images of Mental Illness*. New Jersey: Rutgers University Press.
Wahl, O. 1999. *Telling is Risky Business: Mental Health Consumers Confront Stigma*. London: Rutgers University Press.
Wahl, O. and Leftowits, J. 1989. Impact of a television film on attitudes towards mental illness. *American Journal of Community Psychology* 17(4), 521–8.
Westerweyer, J. and Kroll, J. 1978. Violence and mental illness in a peasant society: characteristics of violent behaviours and 'folk' use of restraints. *British Journal of Psychiatry* 133, 529–41.
Williams, H.N. 1906. *Later Queens of the French Stage*. London: Harper.
Williams, K. and Hawton, K. 2001. The connection between media and suicidal behavior warrants serious attention. *Crisis: The Journal of Crisis Intervention and Suicide Prevention* 22(4).
Williams, R. 1952. *Drama from Ibsen to Brecht*. London: Penguin.
Williams, R. 1975. *Drama in a Dramatised Society: An Inaugural Lecture*. Cambridge: Cambridge University Press.

Williams, R. 1989. *Raymond Williams on Television: Selected Writings*, edited by A. O'Connor. London: Routledge.
Wilson, M. 1996. Asking questions, in *Data Collection and Analysis*, edited by R. Sapsford and V. Jupp. London: Sage.
Wober, J. 1989. *Healthy Minds on Healthy Airwaves: Effects of Channel 4's 1986 Mental Health Programme Campaign*. London: Independent Broadcasting Authority Research Department.
Wober, J. 1991. *Television and Mental Ill Health*. London: Independent Television Commission Research Department.
Wood, R. 1979. See Britton, Lippe, Williams, Williams and Woods (eds).
Woodward, K. (ed.) 1997. *Identity and Difference*. London: Sage.
Younger, D.P. 1991. *Multiple Views: Logan Grant Essays on Photography 1983–9*. Albuquerque: University of New Mexico Press.

Index